Daviborshch's Cart

DAVIBORSHCH'S CART

CART *Narrating the Holocaust in Australian War Crimes Trials*

DAVID FRASER

UNIVERSITY OF NEBRASKA PRESS

LINCOLN AND LONDON

Library of Congress
Cataloging-in-Publication Data
Fraser, David.
Daviborshch's cart: narrating
the Holocaust in Australian war
crimes trials / David Fraser.
p. cm. Includes bibliographical
references and index.
ISBN 978-0-8032-3412-3
(cloth: alkaline paper)
1. War crime trials—Australia.
2. Holocaust, Jewish (1939–
1945)—Ukraine. I. Title.
KU43.F73 2010
341.6'90268—dc22   2010015804

Set in Ehrhardt by Bob Reitz.
Designed by Nathan Putens.

A chronicler who recites events without distinguishing between major and minor ones acts in accordance with the following truth: nothing that has ever happened should be regarded as lost for history. To be sure, only a redeemed mankind receives the fullness of its past—which is to say, only for a redeemed mankind has its past become citable in all its moments. Each moment it has lived becomes a *citation à l'ordre du jour*—and that day is Judgment Day.

WALTER BENJAMIN

Contents

List of Illustrations *ix*

Acknowledgments *xi*

A Note on Language *xiii*

Introduction: The Long and Winding
Road from Ukraine to Australia *1*

1 History, War Crimes, and Law in Ukraine *15*

2 A Brief Political and Legal History
of Australia and Nazi War Criminals *50*

3 Law and History in Australian War
Crimes Trials: Ukrainian Foresters, the
Shoah, and the Polyukhovich Case *94*

4 Mikolay Berezowsky: The Case of
"The Witness Who Knew Too Much" *146*

5 The Story of Daviborshch's Cart:
Law, History, Truth, and the
Holocaust in Ukraine *192*

6 Translating Law, Translating History,
in Australian War Crimes Trials *242*

7 Telling Stories about the Shoah:
Perpetrators, Victims, and the Politics
of Australian Identity in *The Hand
That Signed the Paper* *263*

8 Law, Memory, and Justice:
The Australian Experience *297*

Notes *321*

Bibliography *347*

Index *363*

Illustrations

IMAGES

1 Ivan Polyukhovich and his wife
   outside court, Adelaide 95

2 ID card for Ivan Polyukhovich 96

3 Mikhail Berezowsky leaving
   the court, Adelaide 147

4 Example of Berezowsky
   SIU photo board 157

5 Heinrich Wagner and wife
   outside Adelaide court 205

6 Drawing by witness Velikiy depicting
   Wagner as policeman 232

7 Artificial leg from the Serniki
   pit excavation 303

8 The Stubla—Serniki, Ukraine,
   November 1991 306

TABLE

1 Ghetto liquidations around
   Serniki, autumn 1942 126–27

Acknowledgments

A project like this is impossible without the assistance and encouragement of others. The principal instigator and source of ongoing support for this book is the Honorable Justice Michael David of the Supreme Court of South Australia. Michael opened his archives, his chambers, and his home to allow me to carry out the lengthy process of accessing the legal materials that have served as the basis for this work. My gratitude for his generosity and that of his family cannot be rendered into an adequate written formula.

I am also grateful to Michael's chambers' staff, who welcomed me on my numerous trips to Adelaide with warmth and a willingness to help that far exceeded mere politeness. A particular thank-you is owed to Pam Gabell for all her assistance.

Several participants in, and observers of, the Australian war crimes process kindly gave their time and insights in the form of interviews. Mark Aarons, David Bevan, the Honorable Michael David, the Honorable Greg James, Professor Konrad Kwiet, Grant Niemann, Lindy Powell QC, and Ian Press all have my thanks. Mark Aarons also very kindly granted me access to his personal papers and Australian war crimes files deposited at the State Library of New South Wales. David Bevan trusted me with his precious file of photographs, for which I am in his debt.

My friend and colleague at the University of Adelaide, John Gava, provided a warm welcome and access to the materials of the law school's library, the staff of which also greeted my requests with a kindness beyond my expectations.

The State Libraries of New South Wales and South Australia, the Fischer Library at the University of Sydney, and the Freehill's Law Library of the University of New South Wales gave assistance with a smile. The Institute of Advanced Legal Studies, London, provided a home away from home during my time as Visiting Senior Research Fellow and gave me the opportunity for the first, tentative public renderings of my research. Professor Robert McCorquodale, then Head of School at the University of Nottingham, enabled research leave to finish the work.

The two anonymous referees read the manuscript with care and offered insightful comments that have improved the final version of this book.

The Harry Frank Guggenheim Foundation of New York provided generous and necessary funding for my travels to Australia. Without the foundation's support this project would not have seen the light of day. I offer them my thanks for funding this project.

As always, without Kathryn, none of this would be possible.

The usual caveat remains. I alone am responsible for what follows.

A Note on Language

In his moving account of the search for the stories of the fate of
the members of his family killed in the Shoah, Daniel Mendelsohn
offers a telling anecdote: "There is a joke that people from this part
of Eastern Europe like to tell, which suggests why the pronunciations
and spellings keep shifting; it's about a man who's born in Austria,
goes to school in Poland, gets married in Germany, has children in
the Soviet Union, and dies in Ukraine. *Through all that*, the joke
goes, *he never left his village!*"[1]

The tragic events recounted in the three legal proceedings that took
place in South Australia in the late 1980s and the early 1990s occurred
in German-occupied Ukraine between 1941 and 1944. Australian
attempts to prosecute the three individuals whose stories are the subject of this book—Ivan Polyukhovich, Heinrich Wagner, and Michael
Berezowsky—began at the time of the Cold War, continued into the
period of glasnost and perestroika, and then proceeded following the
breakup of the Soviet Union and the creation of an independent
Ukraine. As the joke recounted by Mendelsohn indicates, the ethnic
and linguistic nature of the area in which the relevant events hap-

pened is and was complex. Government structures fell consecutively under the Austro-Hungarian Empire, Poland, the Soviet Union, Nazi Germany (not to mention neighboring areas that were occupied by Romanian forces during World War II), the Soviet Union, and an independent Ukraine. The towns and villages where the killings of Jews occurred included a Jewish population, as well as Ukrainians, Poles, Russians, and ethnic Germans, the Volksdeutsche.

This ethnic, cultural, religious, political, and linguistic mix informs the historical events that are central to the accounts that follow. But the multiethnic nature of the area also raises a practical problem for the telling of the tale today.[2] Family names, given names, and nicknames of various individuals had and have different versions in Yiddish, German, Ukrainian, Polish, and Russian. Many of the eyewitnesses in the Australian cases give testimony alternatively in Ukrainian and Russian or a mixture of both. Some of the survivors who fled to Israel gave evidence in Hebrew. Similarly, place names changed according to the usage not just of the population but also of the official state language, which shifted according to geopolitical reality. These names were then translated into English for the purposes of Australian legal proceedings. Sometimes villages physically disappeared as the result of war. Jewish areas and their populations were eradicated as part of the Final Solution. Evidence of a historical Jewish presence was destroyed or allowed to disappear.[3] In other instances place names were changed as a new regime took over. In the renderings of these names of individuals and places, I have adopted the practice of repeating, whenever possible, the formulations used in English translations by Australian authorities throughout the criminal investigations, depositions, and committal hearings, unless common and accepted usage demands otherwise.

Unfortunately, even this official usage in the various legal proceedings was variable, as different translators were involved and as translations of names and places into English occurred from original documents and statements in German, Russian, and Ukrainian. There was never a formally agreed translation process in the three cases in Adelaide, and linguistic difficulties informed all efforts to prosecute and defend the accused. Where there are multiple spellings and renderings of place names, for example, deployed in a variety of official sources, I have attempted to adopt the most commonly used version of the usage likely to be most familiar to readers or to the relevant protagonists.

The accused in the Australian cases were not citizens of the German Reich. Technically, they were not Nazis. Nonetheless, common usage refers to the prosecutions as "Nazi war crimes trials," rather than the more cumbersome but more accurate "Nazi collaborationist war crimes trials." I use the phrases interchangeably, as appropriate.

I use the phrase and description *war crimes trials* in the discussion throughout the book. Yet in two of the three cases, those of Berezowsky and Wagner, formal legal proceedings stopped at the committal stage, though for different reasons. Only the case of Ivan Polyukhovich went before an Australian jury. Nonetheless, for the sake of both brevity and broader access and understanding, I use the more general *trial* to describe all proceedings involving the three individuals charged with offenses under the Australian War Crimes Act. In the more detailed discussion of each of the three cases, the more correct *committal* or *trial* is used when required to render an accurate account.

Finally, a few words about legal terminology are necessary. American readers familiar with criminal procedure will recognize the term *voir dire* in relation to the process of examining potential members of the jury to determine whether they are acceptable to both sides. In Australia the term is used to describe a process within a committal (preliminary hearing) or a trial to decide a legal question, such as the admissibility of a certain piece of evidence. The process sometimes takes place by way of oral argument by the lawyers for each side, while on other occasions a witness is examined and cross-examined to determine the nature and content of his or her potential testimony. In a voir dire during a trial the argument and/or examination takes place in the absence of the jury because it concerns only matters of law.

Daviborshch's Cart

Introduction

The Long and Winding Road
from Ukraine to Australia

Daviborshch's Cart

The lightning attack of Operation Barbarossa in late June and early July 1941 led to the rapid advance of German troops into Ukraine amid the retreat in disarray of the Red Army. Special extermination units of the ss, the Einsatzgruppen, accompanied the German advance, killing tens of thousands of Ukrainian Jews in the first wave of mass shootings.

One year after the arrival of German forces, as workers on the collective farms toiled in the fields throughout the region, the second wave of mass killings of Ukraine's Jewish population began. The remaining Jews in the village of Israylovka, later renamed Berezovatka, were rounded up by Ukrainian police, the Schutzmannschaft, in the final mass *Aktion*. As the Russian and Ukrainian inhabitants of Israylovka looked on from the doorsteps and windows of their houses, their neighbors, the Jews, were marched two kilometers to a ravine, which served as a killing pit, near the neighboring village of Kovalevka, where they were shot by Ukrainian forces.

The same day local police were given a list of names of so-called mixed-race (*Mischlinge*) children in Israylovka. They were the progeny of Jewish fathers and Ukrainian mothers. The fathers were for the most part absent, having joined the Red Army and retreated eastward before the German advance a year earlier. The Ukrainian policemen instructed the mothers to bring their children to the local administration building for registration.

On this bright, sunlit summer morning in 1942 a twenty-year-old Ukrainian man, Nikolay Nikitovich Daviborshch, was going about his usual business. Too frail to have been drafted into the local police, Daviborshch was employed on the local collective farm. He made deliveries of water on his cart, a two-wheeled gig pulled by a twin team of horses. This day started out much like any other for Daviborshch as he made his way to Israylovka with a cart filled with water barrels. Events would soon change his life forever. As he began his work in the village, he was accosted by two Ukrainian police officers, Zhilun and Gering, and told to bring his cart right away to the village administration building. After changing his team of horses, Daviborshch took his cart to the town hall. There he was confronted by a scene of heartbreak and hardship that would haunt him for the rest of his life.

The mothers of the *Mischlinge* and their children were brought from the town officials' offices, where they had come, as instructed by the police, for "registration." Amid screams and cries of horror the children were torn from their mothers' arms, grabbed, and thrown into the back of Daviborshch's cart. The women were beaten back by the police. Soon Daviborshch's cart, which measured three meters long by one meter wide, was filled with wailing children. They ranged in age from four months to eleven or twelve years old. Among the children of Israylovka for whom this would be the last summer day of their young lives were the four offspring of Nadezhda Lozhkina; the four young children of Nina Kigel; three children of Kharitina Rybkina; three more belonging to Dusya Flesher; the only child of Yarina Fel'shtayn; three youngsters of Klavdiya Gurevich; and Volodya and Tolya, the two children of Tat'yana Shul'kina.

Once the children had been loaded into the cart by the police, Daviborshch, who had sat silently throughout this part of the ordeal, accompanied by Zhilun, who sat behind him in the cart, and other police on horseback ordered the horses to begin the journey to the ravine near Kovalevka. Following directions from guards posted on the road near the site, Daviborshch drove his cart off the road to an area about five or six meters from the pit. Local police grabbed the children from the cart and dragged them to the edge of the pit. As they threw them in, they began shooting. Daviborshch was ordered to leave. Fifty years later, as he recounted the events of that summer day in 1942, he still trembled from the memories. "I was afraid of everybody. I was sitting on that cart and I thought I would be shot with the others."

In 1991 Heinrich Wagner, one of the local police identified as having been present at the pit that day, near a ravine on a road leading from Israylovka to Kovalevka, in the Ustinovka district of the Kirovograd region of Ukraine, was arrested by Australian police and charged in Adelaide, South Australia, with killing both the adult Jews and the *Mischlinge* children. It was alleged that he killed the youngest child by throwing her in the air and shooting as she fell into the pit. The information filed before the Supreme Court of South Australia in the case in the January Sessions of 1993 alleged that Wagner, some-time between 1 May and 31 July 1942, had committed a war crime that "involved the wilful killing of about (a) 104 persons and (b) 19 children aged between about 4 months and 11 years of age."[1]

Khokum's Shed

In September 1942 Dmitry Ivanovich Kostyukhovich was a nineteen-year-old member of the Ukrainian partisans. He had been sent to his native village of Serniki, in the Rovno district, together with his friend Sidor Alexeievich Polyukhovich, to gather information for his commanding officer. The fighters had recently received intelligence that the Jews of Serniki were to be killed. Kostyukhovich visited his aunt at her house on the outskirts of town near the Stubla River. His aunt's property bordered another farm (*khutor*) owned by a local Jew, Moishe Aaron. Just beyond these properties nearer the river was an outbuilding, a shed, on land belonging to another Serniki Jew, known as Khokum.

Kostyukhovich and his comrade spent a night and the following day sheltering in the farm building. On the second day, from his vantage point in Khokum's shed, he witnessed the *Aktion* in which German troops and local police rounded up the inhabitants of Serniki's recently established ghetto, about eight hundred Jews. Ukrainian police removed the Jews from their homes. The ghetto clearance was characterized by frenzied screaming and crying. The Ukrainians used their rifle barrels to marshal the reluctant and panicked Jews. The Germans waited nearby, while the local police gathered the Jews of Serniki into columns. While the Jewish population of the area was being marched to a spot in the forest outside Serniki, where they would be shot and killed in a large pit dug especially for the occasion, as in dozens of other Ukrainian towns, villages, and hamlets, Kostyukhovich and Sidor Polyukhovich watched the unfolding terror happening below them through the hole in the wall of Khokum's shed.[2]

While the procession began its march, two youngsters, probably aged fifteen, broke away from the group and ran toward the bridge and the river in an attempt to escape the fate that would soon befall their fathers, mothers, brothers, sisters, aunts, uncles, cousins, and neighbors. One of the men guarding the convoy turned and pointed his rifle at the running boys. He calmly shot one then the other. Neither one moved again. The shooter was identified by Kostyukhovich as Ivanechko, Ivan Timofeyevich Polyukhovich, a local man who worked as a forest ranger for the German occupation authorities. The column continued along the road to the forest. The boys' bodies were collected and loaded into a cart later that day by two members of the Ukrainian police. A few days later Kostyukhovich returned to the forest outside Serniki with several of his partisan comrades. They saw the freshly covered pit area. The ground on the surface was soaked with blood still seeping up from below.

On Australia Day (Australia's national holiday, the equivalent of the United States's Fourth of July), 26 January 1990, Ivan Timofeyevich

Polyukhovich was arrested in Adelaide and charged with participating in the pit shootings of about eight hundred of Serniki's Jews. The information charged that Polyukhovich, "between about the first day of September 1942 and about the thirtieth day of September 1942 near the village of Serniki in the Rovno District in the Ukraine, Europe, was knowingly concerned in the murder of about eight hundred and fifty persons, whose names are not known but who are described as the Jews from the Serniki Ghetto, such killings being wilful killings, and did thereby commit a war crime contrary to Section 9 of the War Crimes Act 1945."[3]

Schors Street, Gnivan, May 1942

In May 1942 Mikhail Abramovich Raykis was a twelve-year-old Jewish boy living with his mother, his three sisters, and younger brother in the village of Gnivan, in the Tyrov district of the Vinnitsa region, Ukraine. Around two hundred Jews remained in the village. Others, including Raykis's father, had disappeared during the first killing wave. One night a German soldier knocked on the family's door and ordered them all to get dressed and hurry outside. Mrs. Raykis, Sonja, and her three daughters, Betia, Liza, and Masia, complied. Mikhail's younger brother crept under his bed, but his whimpering brought the German soldier back to the house and his hiding place. He was dragged outside to join the female members of the Raykis family. Mikhail stood silently behind the bedroom door and escaped the notice of the Germans. He fled out the back of the house and hid in woods that bordered his family's home and the town. He stayed there all night, and through his young terrified eyes watched as the Jews of Gnivan stood or sat on the ground outside the local government office building, the former Soviet Council headquarters. Through the night German soldiers and members of the Schutzmannschaft, stood guard, heaping abuse on their terrified wards, swearing at them and yelling at the mothers to quiet their crying infants. Guard dogs barked, and bright lights shone until dawn on the terrified Jews of Gnivan.

At first light they were ordered into columns and marched along the road, which would be named Schors Street in the development of the village in the postwar era. The cobble road made a turn as it left the built-up area and led to the nearby forest. Among the local police who accompanied the Jews to their deaths in the forest on the outskirts of Gnivan was Mikolay Berezowsky, head of the local detachment. As the column of Jews was herded at gunpoint toward the pit, Berezowsky, walking back and forth from one side of the group to the other, hurled abuse at them, "Bloody Jews, parasites!" Young Mikhail followed all of this, hidden among the bushes and trees. The Jews came to a pit, where they were stripped and gunned down. Raykis remembered Berezowsky: "They feared him as if he were a spirit."

In August 1991 Mikolay Berezowsky was arrested at his home in Adelaide and charged by Australian police with the murders of the five members of the Raykis family who perished that night in Gnivan and with the killings of several other of his Jewish neighbors. The charges alleged that Berezowsky "was by his own acts, directly knowingly concerned in or party to the murder of one hundred and two Jewish people being described as the Jews of Gnivan, comprising mainly women and children and some elderly males, most of whose names cannot be ascertained but including the following: (i) Sonya Froymovna Raykis, aged about 40 years and her daughters Betya Abramakovich, aged about 21 years, Liza Abramovna Raykis, aged about 18 years, Manya Abramovna Raykis, aged about 16 years, and her son Filya Abramovich Raykis, aged about 5 years."[4]

HISTORY TRUTH LAW: THE SHOAH, UKRAINE,
AND AUSTRALIAN WAR CRIMES TRIALS

The chapters that follow track in greater detail some of the most important aspects of the long and complex path that led from the forests, marshes, villages, and shtetls of Ukraine, from Volhynia and Galicia, from Serniki, Israylovka, and Gnivan, in the harsh years of German occupation, to the quieter, more peaceful, sunny climes of Adelaide, South Australia, in the early 1990s.

In the sixty-odd years that have followed the trials of major German war criminals before the International Military Tribunal at Nuremberg to the establishment of the International Criminal Court, a vast academic literature has followed (and caused) the creation of "international criminal law" as a separate discipline and area of professional expertise. The prosecutions of Anthony Sawoniuk in the United Kingdom and Imre Finta in Canada have received significant attention in studies of national criminal justice responses to the presence of alleged Nazi war criminals in those two countries.[5] Sawoniuk was a member of a local police unit in Belarus and was convicted of murder under the operative provisions of the United Kingdom's War Crimes Act of 1991. Finta, a member of the Hungarian Gendarmerie, was charged under the provisions of Canada's Criminal Code for his participation in rounding up, confining, and deporting Hungarian Jews to Auschwitz but was acquitted following the decision of the Canadian Supreme Court on a technical legal question. Both of these cases are noteworthy and deserving of the attention they have received. Each involved the prosecution of Holocaust-related crimes fifty or more years after the event. Each followed a political decision by the elected representatives of these countries that new legislation was required to bring perpetrators who had escaped their homelands to justice in their adopted countries, where they had lived for many years free from trouble or worry about their pasts.

The three Australian cases deal with similar issues. All three accused men had worked under the occupying German forces in Ukraine and were alleged to have participated in mass atrocities against their Jewish neighbors. After intense political and legal debate, Australia, like Canada and the United Kingdom, passed new legislation in order to permit these prosecutions to go forward many years after the tragedy of the Shoah.[6] Yet for some reason, perhaps attributable to the tyranny of distance, the physical isolation with which Australians live every day, or the intellectual isolation and ignorance that arise from Australia's geography, even the most extensive, detailed recent literature dealing with various international and national efforts to prosecute Holocaust perpetrators remains silent about the Australian experience.[7] By examining the untold stories of Australia's attempts to create a system to try these war criminals, this book addresses that omission.

This book integrates three distinct yet overlapping areas of interest. First and foremost, it examines the law, tracing the little-known story of the way in which Australia's national Parliament came to introduce the legislation amending its existing war crimes legislation. Second, there are several interrelated tales of police and forensic investigation to identify perpetrators, to locate them in Australia, and to uncover the physical evidence and eyewitness testimonies in Ukraine and elsewhere that would serve as the bases for the three cases. Finally, there are the stories of the cases themselves—of the rules of evidence and the confrontation with facts more than a half-century old; of eyewitnesses who had never left their native villages in Ukraine flying to Australia, staying in a beachside hotel in an Adelaide suburb, and being confronted, through court interpreters, with the forensic skill of Australian lawyers; of the rules relating to "prior inconsistent statements" in South Australian criminal proceedings and the issue of the "protocols" of postwar Soviet investigations and trials of traitors to the Motherland; of the conflict in war crimes trials between legal consequences and goals, innocence or guilt, and the desire to "prove" something more: the reality of survivors' suffering, the enormity and horror of the Shoah, and the eternal truth of justice.

The second genre involved in the complex stories of these Australian war crimes trials, history, then comes to the fore as "the historical study and judicial investigation of the Holocaust have been inextricably intertwined, as historians and lawyers have used the fruits of one another's labors."[8] The tale of the efforts to bring Holocaust perpetrators who had found a safe haven in postwar Australia is largely a historical saga. In addition to the issues surrounding investigations into the flaws in immigration policy and practice that allowed these individuals to come to Australia in the first place, Australian prosecutors had to rely on historical expertise not only to establish the necessary technical elements of the war crimes offenses—that is, war, occupation, an extermination plan—but they also needed to establish the identity and culpability of the individuals accused. Konrad Kwiet and a team of historians undertook unprecedented and historically significant research efforts to determine these identities. Archives were identified and documents examined with the fine-tooth comb of professional historians' expertise. Most significantly perhaps, for the first time Western historians were granted virtually unfettered access to previously restricted Soviet archival holdings.

Other important issues about historical methodology and discursive practices also arose in the course of the Adelaide proceedings. At a basic level a historian who testified in these cases did so as an expert witness. As such, he or she did not "belong" to either the prosecution or the defense but instead acted as an expert for "the Court." Moreover, as the proceedings evolved, it became clear, especially in the Polyukhovich case, that there was a conflict between the perception of the facts and the broader demands of "truth" held, for example, by Kwiet, the chief historical expert at trial, and Justice Brian Cox (Cox J), the trial judge. In the end, after lengthy and heated evidentiary proceedings, Kwiet was asked to testify not about what happened in Serniki but about his expert opinion about what occurred and who was involved, a subtle but vital distinction in the circumstances.

An important subgenre of historical inquiry has emerged, post-Nuremberg, a subgenre in which historians now study war crimes trials as historical events in themselves. Two types of professional practice and focus are in play. The first is that these trials—the documents, witness testimonies, and statements that emerge from them, the forensic anthropological and medical evidence uncovered—serve as new sources of historical knowledge about the Shoah. The second potential result of these Holocaust trial studies is that the killing of European Jews by the Nazis and their local collaborators may take a back seat to the study of the trials as primary phenomena. In such cases the issues of memory and forgetting, truth and justice, which have heretofore been central to the positioning of war crimes trials within historiography and broader political and social practice, while not entirely forgotten, may be redefined and therefore constructed as the subjects of new types of understanding.[9]

The third genre that arises in the context of Australia's war crimes trials is, somewhat ironically perhaps, fiction. While they operate from different perspectives, with their distinct goals and methodologies, both law and history are to a certain extent concerned if not with "truth," then at least with facts. Fiction may well be concerned with explorations of various concepts of truth, but it usually does so without significant concern for fact as understood by lawyers and historians. Yet it was precisely a form of fiction that was presented as being grounded in fact, in relation to war crimes trials and the history of the Shoah in Ukraine, that arose in Australia at the same time as the cases of Berezowsky, Polyukhovich, and Wagner took place, affecting the wider Australian society significantly. The controversies surrounding Helen Demidenko's fictionalized account of her Ukrainian-Australian immigrant family, *The Hand That Signed the Paper* (1994), raised the same questions and public debates about law and justice, identity and belonging, memory and amnesia, that had surrounded the introduction of the War Crimes Act Amendment Bill in the Australian Parliament and the three cases in Adelaide.[10] An account of the Australian experience of Nazi collaborationist war crimes trials would be incomplete without taking into account the interactions between and among the professional practices of the judge, the historian, and the author.[11]

LAW AND HISTORY IN ADELAIDE

Noted Holocaust historian Michael Marrus has proposed a taxonomy of six types of legal/historical encounters with the Shoah—international trials, the most well-known of which is the International Military Tribunal at Nuremberg; trials held by the victors, from Soviet proceedings at Krasnodar and Kharkov to the "zonal trials" held in the four Allied occupation zones in Germany (and in Austria); successor trials, proceedings that took place before national tribunals in various countries of formerly occupied Europe; Holocaust-related trials of Jews by Jews for crimes of collaboration (ghetto police, e.g.); so-called third-party trials in countries not directly involved in Nazi atrocities against the Jews (Canada, Australia); and the final category of Holocaust denial proceedings.[12]

This book addresses the stories surrounding the Australian experience in these fifth category proceedings and tangentially the Soviet prosecutions of war criminals in the wartime period and its aftermath as well as subsequent prosecutions in Ukraine in the 1950s and beyond. The discussion will outline the historical background and political debates that led to the adoption by the Australian Parliament of legislation permitting the pursuit before Australian courts of those accused of Holocaust-related offenses committed during World War II. The chapters that follow will also examine issues of history, memory, and forgetting and of the conflicts between historical knowledge and legal processes as they manifested themselves in the concrete and forgotten context of Australia's war crimes trial program in the late 1980s and early to mid-1990s. These issues and the disciplinary intersections and disjunctions will be elucidated through a study of important aspects of the legal and historical record established throughout the brief but momentous history of Australia's war crimes trial program.

This book fills in the gap in the scholarly record, a gap that runs the risk of entrenching a historical and legal "forgetfulness—forgetfulness without memory."[13] Such a combined amnesia/amnesty characterizes scholarship about war crimes trials and the way in which international legal and historical experts have ignored the Adelaide cases and the Australian experience more broadly. This forgetfulness also typifies attempts to come to grips with the interdisciplinary gaps and overlaps that are embodied in the cases of Berezowsky, Polyukhovich, and Wagner.

The Belgian philosopher Paul Ricoeur, in dealing with the issues raised by the multiplicity of methodologies and disciplines that are confronted in relation to specific aspects of the Shoah, focuses on

the key concept of judgment. Each genre—law, history, and literature—deals with notions of memory, forgetting, and responsibility
through its particular frame of deploying "facts" in the process of
forming judgment.[14] More important, each genre's methodology and
capacity for judgment can be and is influenced by those of the other
disciplines. Law is compelled by the very nature of the criminal trial
to narrow its focus, to concentrate on issues of proof, admissibility of
evidence, and its ultimate and defining characteristic of determining
individual culpability. Moreover, the rules of the trial require a balance between prosecution and defense, under which all aspects of
each side's case must be treated with at least equal respect (putting
aside the important question of burden of proof) and from which
judgment must be withheld until the final stage. These inherent limits
within legal practice only become clearly understandable as limits
if one sheds light on the evidence, on the events under judgment
in a case, through the lens of historical analysis. Law then becomes
understandable in a wider frame only as history. Law is "fixed" by
the trial process, with its institutional focus on individual responsibility, whereas history itself must remain open to "new evidence"
and must address a plurality of sources that are subjected to different
rules of analysis.

At the same time, history must cope with the tensions and difficulties inherent not just in the facts and facticity of the Holocaust but
with the limits that arise in the process of imposing, or coming to,
moral judgment internal to all explanatory and even descriptive tax-
onomies in relation to the Shoah.[15] When faced with complex versions
and explanations of a particular pit killing in Ukraine, for example,
evidence must be sorted, versions compared, and a determination of
historical truth asserted. Omer Bartov argues, "The historian cannot
escape acting as judge in this context."[16]

The final relevant genre, literature, is also a complex yet limited
undertaking. Literary renderings of the Shoah, especially those that
deal with victims' suffering or perpetrator behavior and/or motivations, are subjected to limits and conflicts with historiographical

discursive and narrative practices. Each of these areas of overlap and disjuncture occurs most commonly in relation to the issue of "testimony"—legal, historical, and fictional—a key component of the chapters that follow.

Former perpetrators, Ukrainian police officers such as Zhilun, former victim/survivors such as Mikhail Abramovich Raykis, and bystanders such as Dmitry Ivanovich Kostyukhovich all have different testimonial standpoints and experiences, all of which, in combination with others, constitute the narrative of the Shoah in Ukraine that was distilled, however imperfectly, in the Adelaide war crimes cases. Each witness lived through and was trying to work through, in the psychoanalytic, ontological, and epistemological senses, different experiential realities, all of which tell a story about the killing of Ukraine's Jews under Nazi occupation.[17] The other participants in the criminal justice processes in Adelaide, the police and forensic scientists, the magistrates and judges, the solicitors and barristers, the historians, each received these facts, statements, and testimonies and in turn used them according to the demands of their own disciplinary knowledge and role in the system itself. Authors of fiction and literary critics further this process by rendering historical fact within the more open-ended conventions of their genre, allowing perhaps through this translation access to history and law to new and different readers.

The question that was raised throughout the Australian war crimes trials experience and which informs much of this book is one of "translation," not just in the technical sense but perhaps more significantly in its ethical manifestation. In all instances the foundational elements of the cases and debates surrounding the prosecution of alleged war criminals must all be (re)situated at the level of the ethical.[18] How can we translate these individual experiences, with the frailties of memory, the traumatic nature of the events in question, the passage of time, the foibles of individual psychology, the self-interest of the witness, and the rules of evidence—into an ethically, historically, and legally, sound and accurate and acceptable account of the fate of the Jews of Serniki, Gnivan, and Israylovka?

An Italian proverb offers a warning and a frame for reading all of the historical and legal record that informs the rest of this book: *Tradurre è tradire* — to translate is to betray.

ONE

History, War Crimes,
and Law in Ukraine

The odysseys that brought Ivan Polyukhovich, Heinrich Wagner, and
Mikhail Berezowsky from the hinterlands of Europe, from war-torn
Galicia and Volhynia, through a defeated and ruined Germany, to the
peaceful suburbs of Adelaide are complex biographical episodes that
are retold in the mass of court and investigative documents compiled
during the efforts to prosecute them. In addition to these biographies
of the three alleged war criminals, any complete accounting of the
cases would have to include a detailed history of what would become
present-day Ukraine. For it is in the intersections of the micro-histories
of the three men and the macro-history of Ukraine and World War II
in particular that the events that came to fall under the rubric "war
crimes" and "crimes against humanity" were and are located. These
events are situated in this complex mix of history and biography not
just because the stories of what happened in Adelaide in the 1990s are
directly related as a simple matter of fact to the Holocaust in Ukraine
but also because the very structure of the War Crimes Act under which
they were prosecuted required that the crimes of murder of which
the three men were accused be directly linked to the furtherance of

Nazi policies in occupied Ukrainian territory. The stories of Ivan Polyukhovich, Heinrich Wagner, and Mikhail Berezowsky are not simple crime stories; they are war crimes stories.

It is perhaps best at this early stage to offer a formal caveat and to indicate as clearly as possible what the book is not about. This is not a detailed and nuanced history of Ukraine, with its complex political and ethnic structures.[1] Neither is it a more focused study of World War II in Ukraine, the brutal occupation regime and its tragic consequences.[2] Nor indeed is it a history of the Holocaust in Ukraine.[3] Instead, it focuses on how and why, in the case of three identifiable individuals, these historical interethnic issues of national and cultural identity, which were unleashed in the horrific violence against the Jewish members of the communities, towns, and villages of Ukraine, came to be seen in Australia as war crimes or crimes against humanity, crimes of such transcendent terror that the government of a country far removed from the events and enmities themselves decided to deploy its criminal justice system in order to bring the perpetrators to justice more than fifty years after the fact.

This relatively limited focus does not mean that I intentionally fail to value the importance and subtlety of the longer-term history of Ukraine or of the complexities of the processes and governmental, military, and police structures that led to the mass extermination of Ukraine's Jews. Instead, I mean only to underline that this is not a book of Ukrainian history nor one that seeks to offer a complete description of the Shoah in that country. Each of these topics obviously informs the socio-legal history of the Australian war crimes trials, and account must be taken of them. But I do not pretend to the expertise, professional or linguistic, that would permit any idea that what follows is a history of the Holocaust in Ukraine or even a history of war crimes and crimes against humanity in that country. Rather, this chapter provides an overview that offers at least some historical and the historico-legal context to those events that would form the core of three sets of criminal charges before the South Australian courts in the late 1980s and early 1990s.

The borders of present-day Ukraine embody a complex and fascinating geohistory. Parts of the country have been at one time or another under the jurisdiction of Lithuania, Poland, the Hapsburg Empire, the Soviet Union, Romania, Hungary, and the Nazis.[4] Historically, a multinational, multilinguistic, and multireligious area, its more recent history has been informed by complex, mutually reinforcing, and mutually distrustful relationships between and among its principal ethnic groups. In the areas of most immediate concern to the subsequent history of Australian war crimes trials, Poles, Ukrainians, Russians, ethnic Germans, and Jews lived in uneasy proximity.[5]

The end of World War I saw the collapse of the preexisting social and political orders and the dismantling of the old Austro-Hungarian Empire, the creation of the Soviet Union, and more generally, the formalization at the level of international law and politics of the Wilsonian liberal vision of independent nation-states.

> The First World War and the collapse of Europe's old continental empires signaled the triumph not only of democracy but also—and more enduringly—of nationalism. With the extension of the principle of national self-determination from western to central and eastern Europe, the Paris peace treaties created a pattern of borders and territories which has lasted more or less up to the present. Yet the triumph of nationalism brought bloodshed, war and civil war in its train, since the spread of the nation-state to the ethnic patchwork of eastern Europe also meant the rise of the minority as a contemporary political problem. Where a state derived its sovereignty from the "people," and the "people" were defined as a specific nation, the presence of other ethnic groups inside its borders could not but seem a reproach, threat or challenge to those who believed in the principle of national self-determination.[6]

In Galicia and Volhynia Polish and Ukrainian (and Russian/Soviet) irredentist forces made national claims for the redrawing of postwar borders, and Jews, who had to some extent found an accommodation within the dominant ethnic/nationalist order under Austrian imperial rule, now found themselves caught in the middle of a battle to create a "new" Ukrainian (or Polish) nation.[7] At the same time, broader political and national forces were at play, leading to the Soviet-Polish war and the peace of 1921, with its division of territory between the Polish nation and the newly established Soviet Union. Ukrainian nationalist ambitions were at least temporarily rendered unrealizable as the geographic territory of Ukraine fell under Polish sovereignty or became part of the Ukrainian SSR.[8] The German-Soviet nonaggression pact of August 1939 and the secret protocol of the Ribbentrop-Molotov agreement led to the further "territorial and political rearrangement of the areas belonging to the Polish state," as Ukraine's traditional territories now fell to be divided between the Third Reich and the USSR.[9]

The invasion of the territory of the Soviet Union in late June and early July 1941 by German forces in Operation Barbarossa would not just change operative sovereignty in Galicia and Volhynia but would give rise to hopes for a new Ukrainian nation-state. The perfect storm of resurgent Ukrainian nationalism and National Socialist rule would not be good news for the large Jewish population of the newly conquered territories of Ukraine. Conditions of total war combined with Nazi antisemitism and Ukrainian nationalist Jew-hatred. The Ukrainian space now became not just nationalized, but more significantly, it became racialized in a violent fashion.

The Shoah in Ukraine

While it is impossible fully to contextualize the Shoah in Ukraine without an analysis of the military reality of the war in the Soviet Union and the key ideological connections between "total war" and the killing of Ukraine's Jews, a fuller exploration of these complex and interrelated historical phenomena is impossible here. Geoffrey Megargee's detailed work on the invasion of the USSR in its full military, historical, and ethical contexts offers the interested reader the most recent useful insights into the nexus between war and the

Shoah.[10] Omer Bartov's catalog has long offered important details and careful analyses of the ideology of Nazi racism and its role in the mass killings on the Eastern front.[11] Despite more recent controversies surrounding the exhibition on Wehrmacht atrocities by the Hamburg Institute for Social Research, there can be no doubt either about the close relationship between total war and the Shoah in Ukraine or about the key role played by the German army in the mass killings of Ukraine's Jews.[12] I return in a subsequent chapter to the ways in which this question was considered as part of an inquiry into the exact nature of German military involvement at the Serniki pit killings in the Polyukhovich case because there the issue was of real legal and historical significance.

Similarly, it is historically important to an understanding of the Holocaust in Ukraine to situate properly the role of Einsatzgruppen units in the killing of Ukraine's Jews, especially in the first wave of killings in the immediate aftermath of the invasion and military advances. These key questions, which might and do apply to a broader understanding of the Holocaust in Ukraine, are equally beyond my more limited concerns, as are important questions about the roles of broader Nazi security forces in "antipartisan" and other anti-Jewish actions.[13] Interest in the Order Police and their role in massacres of Jews has risen over the last two decades as a result first of Christopher Browning's pathbreaking work on Poland and the critical debate surrounding Daniel Goldhagen's differing view of the motivations of these ordinary killers.[14]

The nature and function of the German Order Police in the killing operations are also important to a fuller and more nuanced understanding of the dynamics of killing operations against the Jews in Ukraine. Jürgen Matthäus has demonstrated that "in Byelorussia and Ukraine in early spring 1942, following arrangements made at the highest level of the German occupation institutions, mass-executions began again, targeting especially the numerous scattered places of Jewish residence in the countryside. In this second killing wave the order police in general, and the Gendarmerie in particular, developed into an agency of prime importance for the successful implementation of the 'final solution.'"[15]

Among those "numerous scattered places" of Ukraine where the local Jewish population was targeted for extermination in 1942 were the villages of Serniki, Israylovka, and Gnivan, where Ivan Polyukhovich, a forester in the German-controlled administration, Heinrich Wagner, a Volksdeutsche liaison officer intimately involved with the Ukrainian and German police forces, and Mikhail Berezowsky, a member of the local Schutzmannschaft, were alleged to have been intimately implicated in such killing operations. While a complete historical account of the involvement of German police forces in the Shoah in Ukraine is not possible here, it is at the level of the involvement of local, indigenous Ukrainians and Volksdeutsche in this second wave of killings that we find a more direct connection with events that would unfold in Adelaide fifty years later.

What emerges from even a cursory examination of the history of Ukraine are the complex and interwoven factors that informed the occupation of Ukraine after 1941, most significantly the connection between the complex interethnic historical background of Nazi-occupied Ukraine and the involvement of members of the local, indigenous populations in the persecution and killing of the country's Jews.

Norman Naimark argues that preexisting ethnic enmity, on its own, is nothing more than a necessary, but never a sufficient, condition for the unleashing of large-scale violence in the form of pogroms, mass killings, crimes against humanity, or the more recently coined ethnic cleansing.[16] Timothy Snyder makes the point that in the Ukrainian context local Ukrainian participation as killers in the Holocaust always needs to be contextualized because "from 1941 collaboration in the Final Solution changed the collaborators, transformed Ukrainian boys in Volhynia from the kind of men they could never have become otherwise. Ukrainians who joined the German administration and the German police in 1941 were acting on several motives: to continue a career they knew, to have influence over their own affairs, to steal property, to kill Jews, to gain personal status, to prepare later political actions."[17]

In this respect Ukrainian perpetrators were and are little different from any other national collaborators who willingly participated in the Nazi Jew-killing machine. They acted for a complex variety of reasons, ranging from the strictly personal to the more broadly influential social and ideological factors operating in their local situation. In Ukraine long-held nationalist dreams and concomitant anti-Jewish sentiments clearly operated on a broad scale. Nationalist political and military formations sought to participate in an active fashion in police forces as a precursor to the creation of an independent Ukraine, with greater or lesser success, depending on local circumstances and the real will and long-term goals of the Nazi occupiers.[18] Nationalist aspirations were encouraged by certain influential factions of the Church in some parts of Ukraine.[19] More recent memories of the bitter and harsh Soviet occupation of the country also influenced nationalist collaboration with the German regime. The experience of mass hunger and starvation in Ukraine, the famine caused or ordered by Stalin, known as the *Holomodor*, also played a vital role.[20] This action was reinforced by mass executions of "traitors" by the Narodnyi komissariat vnutrennikh del (NKVD, later the KGB) as its agents retreated with the Red Army before the German onslaught. More specifically, the pernicious historical canard that drew a direct and uninterrupted semiotic link between Jews and Communists,[21] between the Soviet NKVD and "Jews," created a popular and populist mythology in Ukraine that saw these Jews as the direct agents of Ukrainian suffering and death. Additionally, in the former Polish territory a mythology developed according to which the Jewish members of the population had in fact welcomed the Soviet takeover following the Ribbentrop-Molotov Pact and had benefited disproportionately under the new Communist regime.[22] Thus, at an important level Jews were constructed as Communist enemies of the Ukrainian nation. This construction also signifies that a deeper contextualized study of the idea and practice of "collaboration" and its causes must be carried out in relation to geographical considerations. The *Holo-modor* would not have figured as prominently in the memories and historical consciousness of Ukrainians in former Polish territories, but more recent "Jewish collaboration" with the Soviets would and did constitute an important part of popular and populist discourse in that part of Ukraine. Vladimir Melamed argues that a distinction between the former Polish and former Soviet territories can be found even in the motivations of the most brutal collaborators, Ukrainians who directly participated in the killing of the region's Jews. "The macro-level of collaboration, i.e. service-rendered perpetration of the auxiliary Ukrainian police and the civil Ukrainian administration in the ethnic Ukrainian territories of the former Polish state, differed from that of the Soviet Ukraine. It could be argued that the Ukrainian police and local administration of eastern Volhynia were more politically motivated, seeing its alliance with the Nazi regime as a thorny but an inevitable way to build up Ukrainian armed forces, laying the foundations for an eventual independent Ukrainian state, and ad hoc preserving a Ukrainian nation."[23]

There can be little doubt that the Nazi occupation regime had its own particular agenda, both generally in relation to the future of Ukraine but more specifically in relation to the project of making Ukraine *Judenrein*. Conflicts between military and civilian administrative priorities, and between centralized orders and local government initiative on the "Jewish question,"[24] played important roles in the ways in which the Final Solution was carried out in occupied Ukraine.[25] The complexities of Ukrainian nationalism and its factionalized political and military organization also significantly informed some aspects of Nazi policy but never distracted from the primary goal of killing Jews.

One central, inescapable fact emerges and remains, however, no matter how multifactorial any explanatory schema about Ukrainian collaboration with the Nazis must always be. It is clear that whatever the reason, collaborating Ukrainian police and related paramilitaries killed Jews. The second wave of killings in 1942 Ukraine, which would be directly implicated in the Adelaide war crimes trials, involved Ukrainian units and individuals in the mass shootings of Jews. The most recent analyses of the Shoah in Ukraine count the number of Jews killed between 1941 and 1944 at 1.6 million, or approximately 60 percent of the country's prewar Jewish population.[26] The proportion of killings in western regions—Galicia, Volhynia, and Podolia—reached 80 percent of Jews.[27] A leading historian of the Holocaust in Ukraine, Dieter Pohl, analyzes the slaughter of Jews there as follows, "The massacres in Volhynia-Podlia [*sic*] between May and November 1942 were characterized by the systematic use of the Schutzmannschaft."[28]

In many isolated areas of rural Ukraine the Gendarmerie, the police units of the Wehrmacht, were the only real armed German presence. Regular army units were deployed in the main strategic centers or were required in the advance farther into Soviet territory (and then in the subsequent retreat). The Security Units of the Sicherheitspolizei und Sicherheitsdienst (SiPo/SD) were equally dispersed and few in real numbers. The intensive killing mechanism of pit shootings used throughout Ukraine required a manpower capacity that far exceeded what was available from purely German sources. Martin Dean describes the situation: "In particular, the direct participation of the Order Police and local collaborators in rounding up the Jews for execution was necessitated by the skeletal nature of the Security Police structure, which had only a handful of men to cover the vast territories of the occupied East."[29]

Local Ukrainian police units, the Schutzmannschaft, mostly occupied auxiliary roles in the shootings. They were typically charged with identifying Jews (in those areas where no ghettos had been established); rounding them up; escorting them from the village to the killing pit in a nearly forest or ravine; and establishing a cordon at the shooting site. While the Schutzmänner were sometimes armed, the question of providing rifles and ammunition to potential Ukrainian nationalist insurgents who could turn their weapons against the occupiers in the struggle for an independent Ukraine occupied the German mind. As a result, the local forces more often filled in as auxiliary forces, while Germans did the shooting, although this was not always the case. Ukrainian police forces did in other instances take a more active role in killing Jews, depending on local circumstances. In addition, as local forces, they were almost inevitably charged with the post-massacre mopping-up operations of hunting down and killing the few Jews who had escaped the roundup of the mass *Aktion* by hiding with neighbors or in the nearby woods or marshes.[30]

Any examination of the second-wave killings of Jews in Ukraine in 1942 underscores not just the central, active, and important role played by local Ukrainian collaborationist police forces in the German program of exterminating the Jewish population but also the fact that these killings, which involved the local police, were very public events. The second-wave killings in the Holocaust in Ukraine are not characterized by secrecy nor by industrialized killings by gas in specially constructed facilities. These shootings were open, public, and intimate. Jews were routinely rounded up, temporarily assembled in a public place, marched through the village in daylight and in full view of the local inhabitants. The killing pits were close enough that most villagers could hear the shooting, which sometimes continued for a long period of time. Children and others often directly witnessed the shootings from hiding places near the killing sites. Other villagers were more directly, if involuntarily, implicated. Musicians were sometimes drafted to come to the pit to entertain the killers; other villagers were instructed to use their carts and wagons to take those Jews unable to walk under their own power, the elderly and children, to the killing area; still others had to prepare and serve food and drink to the shooters as they took a well-earned rest or meal break as the killing continued around them; villagers sometimes had to gather clothing and valuables left by the victims at the edge of the pit and sort them; some local inhabitants, often the Volksdeutsche, were given the best of these now ownerless goods and/or took possession of newly vacated houses.[31] While the victims could never testify against their killers, the very nature of the Shoah in Ukraine meant that there were many eyewitnesses who could and did identify the perpetrators.

As Soviet Red Army forces reconquered Ukrainian territory, the issue arose about what mechanisms, if any, would be used both to accumulate evidence about the fate of Ukraine's Jews and to build a prosecution file to punish local collaborators. The liberation of Ukrainian territory also gave rise to a legal issue—would the information gathered be put to judicial use against collaborationist killers? Both questions and the answers thereto would play important roles in the Australian investigations and prosecutions many years later.

THE SHOAH IN UKRAINE AND THE SIGNIFICANCE OF SOVIET LEGAL PROCEEDINGS AGAINST WAR CRIMINALS

Dieter Pohl has recently written that "the NKVD conducted several thousand investigations into the activities of former Schutzmannschaft members and local administrators. In many cases, killing Jews lay at the heart of the legal proceedings. Draconian sentences were handed down for collaboration, especially for participating in killing operations."[32]

Pohl estimates that fifty-four thousand investigations into collaborationist crimes were conducted in Ukraine alone.[33] The system of investigations and trials of collaborationist war criminals established in the Soviet Union is important for the subsequent cases in Australia for several interrelated reasons. The historical and political importance of the Soviet investigations and trials is found in the fact that they can offer important insights into the historical (and legal) evolution of Soviet attitudes to the extermination of Soviet Jewry and to the changing ideological position of the Shoah in Soviet political and legal discourse and practice.[34] How, or indeed whether, Soviet investigators sought to elicit information from witnesses about the killing of Jews as an inquiry distinct and separate from the killing of "innocent Soviet civilians" reveals a great deal about the complexities and shifts within Soviet nationalities policy and about the construction of the broad taxonomy of collaboration, as does the choice of whether or when participation in killing Jews figured in trials against Ukrainian perpetrators.

Another set of factors, more closely related to the evolution and practice of Australian war crimes prosecutions, also emerges. The existence of the widespread Soviet war crimes trial system and the record of severe punishment meted out to Ukrainian collaborators in the killing of their Jewish neighbors, and the fact that many members of the Schutzmannschaft and other collaborationist police and (para)military units had retreated with the withdrawing Nazi forces and had found refuge in the West in the postwar period, led to the creation of a sense of resentment and injustice. These tropes of "justice delayed" and "war criminals among us" would become powerful social and political rhetorical weapons in debates in Canada, the United Kingdom, the United States, and Australia in the 1970s and 1980s. The idea that the country had become a refuge for those who had escaped the well-deserved fate of their comrades who had been captured and tried by the Soviets would be an important one in the eventual adoption of the War Crimes Act in Australia, under which Berezowsky, Polyukhovich, and Wagner, would be brought to the bar of Australian justice.

On the other hand, the very fact that these proceedings were "Soviet" and had been the intimate concern of the NKVD, and various military intelligence branches, served to create intriguing political, social, and legal counter-narratives in those Western countries faced with the dilemma of how, or indeed whether, to deal with these alleged war criminals on their soil. For opponents of trials the general fact of Cold War reality carried the day and put the matter beyond dispute. These investigations and trials of "collaborators" were Soviet proceedings, and that fact by itself, irredeemably and forever, placed the proceedings into the category "show trials." At the level of individual accused, this would mean that all evidence against them—whether historical (i.e., from these postwar Soviet proceedings) or present-day (e.g., from Soviet source documents or by way of testimony from Soviet-based eyewitnesses)—was by definition untrustworthy and not up to the admissibility standards of the Anglo-American criminal justice tradition.

Ironically perhaps, the Soviet question further meant that three of the jurisdictions most concerned with the issue of war crimes trials in the 1970s and 1980s—the United Kingdom, Canada, and Australia—all decided that the American option of denaturalization and deportation of alleged Nazi collaborators was unacceptable because the country of destination in any deportation or even extradition cases would likely be the USSR.[35] The consequence at an important level for the development of both domestic and international criminal law was that each of these three common-law countries asserted some form of claim of universal jurisdiction over crimes against humanity and war crimes. The Soviet war crimes trials program compelled these jurisdictions to create their own domestic legal response to the crimes of the Holocaust.

For history generally and for the Adelaide war crimes trials in particular, the system of investigation and trial developed in the USSR also serves, with the appropriate reservations, as a key and important source of documentary and eyewitness evidence about the Holocaust in the Soviet Union and, in the cases addressed here, in Ukraine. It offers a great deal of emerging knowledge about the day-to-day practice and reality of the Shoah at the local level. Indeed, one important lesson that can be gleaned from the Soviet procedures and practices is that of proximity in the Holocaust in Ukraine. The killers, victims, and eyewitnesses were neighbors. This has important consequences for both history and law. For the historian it provides clear insights into the mechanisms of the killing apparatus and into the identity of the killers. For the lawyer it offers, at some level at least, a degree of reliability that might counter the "Soviet = unreliable" equation asserted by opponents of trials and by defense lawyers in some war crimes litigation. These killings took place where the perpetrators and victims lived. The eyewitnesses whose testimony was gathered by the Soviet investigators, tribunals, and courts had a close physical and existential relationship to the events they recounted. As a matter of the law of evidence, their identification of participants and victims might be given more weight both because the identification was contemporaneous, or as close in time as possible in wartime conditions, and because they knew the perpetrators and victims in circumstances that predated the shootings. In many cases the perpetrators identified by eyewitnesses to the shootings were not strangers, seen only once, in traumatic circumstances that could lend themselves to discrediting such evidence as unreliable. They were their neighbors, people they had seen since childhood on surrounding farms or on the streets and in the shops of the local town or village.

Of course, even if such arguments can be, and indeed were, made, it is also important to underline that the search for reliable historical evidence that might fill in gaps, nuance, and make more complete, historical knowledge about the mechanics of the killing of Ukraine's Jews, and the question of the reliability and admissibility, of such evidence, and the weight to be afforded to it, in a criminal trial, in which the accused is presumed innocent and the prosecution bears the burden of proof beyond a reasonable doubt, are ultimately exercises in the search for different kinds of facts and distinct types of truth. This difference between history and law would define the core conflicts and many of the central issues in the Adelaide proceedings.

Finally, the investigations and trials of war criminals and collaborators in the Soviet Union are important for a fuller understanding of the evolution of international criminal law.[36] The two most well-known proceedings conducted during the war, the trials at Krasnodar and Kharkov, were the first real public, concrete manifestations of the declared Allied policy of bringing war criminals to the bar of justice.[37] While the weight of legal history appears to credit or blame Justice Robert Jackson, the chief U.S. prosecutor at Nuremberg, with the jurisprudential construction of the Nazi state as a hierarchical conspiracy to commit war crimes, it is quite clear from the indictments and proceedings at Krasnodar and Kharkov, and from other important declarations of the official view, that the Soviet positions on command responsibility and the ultimate directing role of the Nazi elite in the conduct of the war were strikingly in agreement with the main position adopted at Nuremberg.[38] In combination the trials as Krasnodar and Kharkov demonstrated that both German military men and local collaborators would be held legally responsible for their acts and that the principles of public international law could and would be given concrete force by national tribunals. The Soviet system that established a juridical mechanism for the prosecution of wartime collaborators would serve as an example of how Berezowsky, Polyukhovich, and Wagner had escaped justice and had at some level established an awkward and embarrassing point of comparison with postwar Australian attitudes to perpetrators of the Holocaust in Ukraine.

THE SOVIET POSITION ON NAZI WAR CRIMES
AND INTERNATIONAL LAW AND POLITICS

The Allied powers expressed their concern over Nazi war crimes and atrocities committed against civilian populations at a relatively early stage in the war. Indeed, on 25 October 1941, before the entry of the United States into the conflict, U.S. president Franklin Roosevelt and British prime minister Winston Churchill each issued statements condemning Nazi actions. Roosevelt's intervention was limited to the German policy of executing civilian hostages as reprisals against attacks on their troops, but his statement was also addressed to "those who would 'collaborate' with Hitler."[39] Churchill issued his statement in solidarity with the sentiments expressed by the American president, but he completed his remarks with an important declaration about future policy. "Retribution for these crimes must hence-forward take its place among the major purposes of the war."[40]

While Churchill speaks of "retribution" rather than justice and invokes it as a reason for prosecuting the war rather than as a post-war goal of the Allies, the two statements served as the first important American-British indication that Nazi war crimes would figure prominently on the Allied agenda. As students of history and international law will know, these sentiments became more focused as the war progressed and as knowledge and awareness of the scope and scale of the Nazi killing machine increased. The St. James's Palace

Declaration of 1942 put the first meat on the skeleton of an emerging international criminal law norm. While the USSR was represented at the meeting, it was not a signatory to the declaration. Nonetheless, the other assembled parties agreed to begin the formalization of a set of international criminal law principles and stated that they would "place among their principle war aims the punishment, through the channel of organised justice, of those guilty of or responsible for these crimes, whether they have ordered them, perpetrated them or participated in them, (and) resolve to see to it in a spirit of international solidarity that (a) those guilty or responsible, whatever their nationality, are sought out, handed over to justice and judged, (b), that the sentences pronounced are carried out."[41]

The Allies saw the issue of Nazi criminality as one that transcended narrow national interests, a theme that Soviet declarations on the question of Nazi collaborators would continue to highlight for the next fifty years. The Allies also sought to establish that as a matter of first principle, what they saw as endemic Nazi criminality would be dealt with, however harshly, within the strict limits and the civilizing frame of the rule of law. Moreover, the bitter experience of the failures of action against German war criminals in the aftermath of World War I required a serious commitment by all parties that the goals of pursuing Nazi war criminals would be concretely achieved within the competent national jurisdiction. Mere lip service to the interests of international law and justice outweighed in practice by an overwhelming duty to perceived national self-interest would have no role in the new postwar international legal order.[42]

The Moscow Declaration of October 1943 further elaborated the evolving rules of the international regime and brought the Soviet Union into play as an active participant. The declaration established the operative principle of national jurisdiction for offenses committed on the soil of the country concerned. Alleged offenders "will be sent back to the countries in which their abominable deeds were done in order that they may be judged and punished according to the laws of these liberated countries and of free governments which will be erected therein."[43]

The three powers—the United States, the United Kingdom, and the Union of Soviet Socialist Republics—agreed to pursue the criminals "to the utmost ends of the earth" in order to deliver them to their accusers. The declaration also explicitly enunciated the idea that Nazi leaders "whose offenses have no particular geographical localization" would be subjected to special joint action.[44] They agreed to compile lists containing all possible details on war criminals in occupied Europe.[45] This undertaking would lead to the creation of the United Nations War Crimes Commission (UNWCC), which was tasked with the international investigation of Nazi atrocities and their perpetrators.[46] Despite its original agreement to participate, the USSR, as a result of its insistence that each Soviet Socialist Republic in which war crimes had been committed should have a separate membership and ongoing political disagreements with the other powers, never did join the commission, despite numerous entreaties to do so.[47] Although it did not formally become a member of the commission, the Soviet Union was nonetheless one of the four prosecuting powers at the International Military Tribunal (IMT) at Nuremberg. It also continued to insist that international cooperation was vital to hunting down and prosecuting Nazi and collaborationist war criminals and that all countries should comply with the provisions of the Moscow Declaration as well as subsequent international legal norms asserting national jurisdiction over war criminals and creating a concomitant duty to hand over alleged perpetrators.[48]

The Soviet role in the pursuit of Nazi and collaborationist war criminals was not limited to the issuance of formal international declarations. From the beginning of the period of Nazi occupation, Soviet diplomatic efforts had maintained a steady flow of information in the international and multilateral domains concerning atrocities being committed on Soviet soil. On 25 November 1941 Viacheslav Molotov, people's commissar of foreign affairs, issued a formal note that was sent to all governments with which the USSR had diplomatic relations. The note, titled "Appalling Atrocities Committed by the German Authorities against Soviet Prisoners of War," documented

Nazi actions and made the information about this form of Nazi war crime available on the world stage.[49] On 6 January 1942 Molotov issued a similar note, this one titled "Wholesale Robbery, Despoliation of Population and Monstrous Atrocities Committed by Authorities in the Invaded Territories," which contained a specific reference to the massacre of the Jews of Lvov.[50] The note also referred to the "horrible slaughter and pogroms" in Kiev (Babi Yar), where "German bandits killed and tortured 52,000 men, women, old men and children, mercilessly dealing with all Ukrainians, Russians and Jews who in any manner displayed their loyalty to the Soviet Government."[51] The next paragraph describes in some detail the process of the pit shooting of the capital's Jews.

The next note from Molotov, dated 27 April 1942, concerned "the monstrous crimes, atrocities and acts of violence perpetrated by the German Fascist invaders in the occupied Soviet areas and the responsibility of the German government and military command for these crimes."[52] This diplomatic missive offers more details about the accumulated Soviet evidence in relation to Nazi criminality and establishes the juridical foundations of the future claim against the Nazi state and military hierarchy that would feature at Nuremberg. As the front shifted back and forth with consecutive German and Red Army advances and retreats, Soviet military intelligence officials seized key enemy documents. According to Molotov, these German papers showed that "it is clear that the bloodthirsty crimes and atrocities of the German fascist army are being perpetrated in accordance with carefully drawn up and thoroughly worked out plans of the German Government and at the orders of the German Military Command."[53]

The April 1942 note identified several subthemes in relation to Nazi war crimes that would constitute the taxonomy of most subsequent Soviet statements on the question. The invaders were accused of (1) general looting of the country; (2) razing cities; (3) seizure of land; (4) slave and serf labor; (5) the abduction of Soviet citizens for labor in Germany; (6) the destruction of Russian culture and other national cultures in occupied territories; and (7) mass murder of Soviet civilian and POW populations.[54] Each of the crimes is then detailed extensively with documentary and eyewitness evidence. One subtle but important shift that occurs in this document from that of 6 January is the virtual absence of any mention of crimes committed against Jews as specific targets of the Nazi killing apparatus. Instead, atrocities against "peaceful Soviet citizens" or against the "peaceful Soviet population" are described in some detail. When the specific origin of victims is mentioned, the list includes Russians, Byelorussians, Ukrainians, Moldavians, Latvians, Estonians, Crimean Tatars, and Karelo-Finnish citizens.[55] When the situation in Ukraine is specified, the list of victims includes "Ukrainians, Russians, Jews, Moldavians and peaceful citizens of other nationalities."[56]

Without diminishing the suffering of many ethnic groups and "national minorities" during the Great Patriotic War of 1941–45, it is clear that in many of the instances mentioned—for example, in the Baltic states—the massacres in question were carried out in large part against Jews. But at this stage of its international campaign the USSR was reluctant to identify Jewish victimhood as a specific outcome of "Hitlerite criminality." Instead, the focus was on the overall destruction of the Soviet Union and its people. This ideological ambivalence toward the Holocaust as a specificity would continue to characterize Soviet actions and reactions both during and after the war. This did not mean, however, that the fate of the Jews was irrelevant to the Soviets or that the Shoah was subjected to a prolonged and uniform silence. On 19 December 1942, for example, the Information Bureau of the People's Commissariat for Foreign Affairs released a statement that dealt specifically with the "execution by Hitlerite authorities of the plan to exterminate the Jewish population in the occupied territory of Europe."[57] In addition to expressing its solidarity with statements of governments of other Nazi-occupied territories on the fate of the Jews of Europe, the People's Commissariat documented, thanks to eyewitness survivor testimony and statements from German POWs, that "brutal massacres of Jews" had also occurred in the various Socialist Republics occupied by the Germans. "Data are available which testify to the fact that in this atmosphere of insane orgies of terror the Hitlerites are also applying their plan of wholesale extermination to Soviet citizens of Jewish nationality. Thus the intensification of terror against the Ukrainian population in the summer and autumn of this year was marked by Jewish pogroms in a number of populated places of the Ukrainian Soviet Socialist Republic."[58]

The second wave of killings was then public knowledge throughout the hierarchies of the Soviet Union as well as at the local level in Ukraine. The international community was also now made aware of the fate of Ukraine's Jews through Soviet propaganda efforts. While the invocation of Nazi atrocities against Jews was not consistent, Soviet documents nonetheless continued to provide examples of such targeted violence throughout the course of the war.[59]

One other related feature of these public declarations about the Shoah in the Soviet Union and Ukraine is that anti-Jewish violence (and other atrocities) is always attributed to the Germans. There is little, if any, discussion of nationalist forces and their collaboration with the occupiers until a later period. Although this situation would not obtain for long, it is nonetheless interesting to note the phenomenon that may well be attributable in part at least to an ongoing confusion about how to define, let alone deal with, collaboration on such a large scale and often by individuals who had previously been Party officials or Red Army soldiers.[60] But whatever the ideological and political forces at work, both in relation to the specificity of Jewish suffering and as far as constructing a workable model of collaboration was concerned, the Soviet legal apparatus for documenting and punishing war crimes was formidable.

THE EXTRAORDINARY STATE COMMISSION:
THE CREATION OF HISTORICAL AND LEGAL
KNOWLEDGE IN THE GREAT PATRIOTIC WAR

By decree on 2 November 1942 the Supreme Soviet of the USSR established the "Extraordinary State Commission [ESC] for ascertaining and investigating crimes perpetrated by the German-Fascist invaders and their accomplices, and the damage inflicted by them on citizens, collective farms, social organizations, State enterprises and institutions of the U.S.S.R."[61] The chair was the head of the Soviet Trade Unions, and members included several academicians and the Metropolitan of Kiev and Galitsk. The ESC was created with several interrelated missions. It was designed to gather and archive complete records of various Nazi crimes committed on Soviet soil; to coordinate the investigations carried out by all state organizations, including those that had already commenced from the earliest days of the invasion;[62] and to identify wherever possible the perpetrators of the various offenses it investigated "so that they may be handed over to court for severe punishment."[63] The ESC was empowered to delegate investigative functions to appropriate organs of the state apparatus and to involve local organizations in its procedures. The commission's mandate was finally confirmed on 16 March 1943.[64]

Local commissions were formed in republics and administrative districts, or oblasts, that had been subject to German occupation. By early 1944 one hundred such commissions were at work establishing evidence of Nazi atrocities. According to George Ginsburgs, over seven million people participated in the ESC's activities, mostly by providing statements of evidence.[65] The central ESC read more than 54,000 statements and more than 250,000 protocols of witness interrogations and declarations in relation to Nazi crimes.[66] A key aspect of the commission's mandate was that it was tasked with investigating not just Nazi or German criminals but their "accomplices," Soviet collaborators, as well.

The operation of the investigative apparatus and the evidence amassed by the ESC embody one of the most important aspects of Soviet investigations and prosecutions of collaborators, the element of proximity. This was true both in the geographic and in the temporal sense. Local officials, civic and trade union organizations, and individuals from the communities affected by Nazi criminality were intimately involved at all stages of the investigations. The summary provided by Ginsburgs establishes the centrality of this proximity to the commission's activities:

> The pertinent facts had to be recorded in protocols drawn up on the basis of statements made by Soviet citizens, interrogation of witnesses, forensic evidence and examination of the scene of the crime. Particular attention here was paid to determining the identity of guilty parties—organizers, inciters, executors, performers, accomplices, their names, the designation of the army units, institutions, organizations. The dossiers had to contain the most complete description possible of the crimes committed, the full name and place of residence of the individuals furnishing the evidence, all the relevant documents—minutes of interrogations, statements by citizens, the conclusions of medical experts, films, letters from Soviet citizens carted off to Germany, German documents, etc. The documents had to be drawn up at the scene of the crime within one month following the locality's liberation.[67]

Kiril Feferman's more recent study indicates that interrogators and investigators often asked a series of specific questions about the fate of Jews. Therefore, ESC records, which have long remained closed, could offer important new insights into the Holocaust in the Soviet Union. Yet he adds important caveats. First, whether the fate of the local Jewish population was a subject of the commission's inquiry appears to have been a matter that depended exclusively on the interrogator's questions.[68] Feferman also finds evidence, similar to that in other Soviet documents, that emphasis on crimes against Soviet Jewry was prominent in the early stages of the ESC's work but that the Holocaust later disappeared as a matter of reporting.[69] Again, this is consistent with the evolutionary changes in Soviet attitudes and policies on the issue of the specificity of Jewish suffering, changes that are probably most evocatively embodied in the now well-known story of the attempt by the Jewish Anti-Fascist Committee (JAFC) to be directly involved in the work of the ESC. When that effort was rejected, the JAFC tried to conduct its own investigations in order to document the specific nature and extent of crimes committed on Soviet soil against Jews. Cooperation by ESC officials was limited and sporadic. The resulting *Black Book*, prepared by Ilya Ehrenberg and Vasily Grossman, appeared only in expurgated form and then passed into a censored silence for several decades.[70]

Marina Sorokina offers an even more nuanced, or negative, reading of the work of the ESC and of its utility than does Feferman. While the formal structure of the ESC was deliberately broad-based and representative of "civil society," its actual operations were less open. The work of the commission, according to Sorokina, beyond its clear propaganda function, and despite the fact that much of its evidence found its way into collaborator trials in the Soviet Union and into the Soviet case at Nuremberg, was always shrouded in secrecy.[71] Moreover, as she highlights, one of the principal investigations carried out by the commission was of the massacre at Katyn. This infamous event figured prominently in the Soviet case at Nuremberg and is a permanent stain on the IMT, which accepted the contrived Soviet case that the murder of Polish officers had been carried out by the Germans.[72] The "Chekist" origins of the commission, its intimate links to Soviet military and intelligence branches, will always make it an object of suspicion, a suspicion confirmed by the Soviet insistence on publicizing the ESC's "findings" on Katyn in its English-language publications. At the same time, however, it must be noted that many of the commission's investigations were based, in large part at least, on captured German documents. The reports also rely heavily on statements made by eyewitnesses, accounts that carry a ring of consistency and credibility. This might be either the product of skillful manipulation by interrogators or of the fact that most nonparticipant eyewitnesses were local inhabitants who gave their statements at a time and in a place where the facts of what happened and who had participated in the massacres were still reasonably fresh in their minds.

Doubts about the ESC as a source of knowledge of the Shoah in Ukraine bring us back to the broader question of the reliability of

Soviet source evidence that would arise consistently in Australian (and American, Canadian, and British) debates about Nazi war criminals and their fate. For some the taint of the Soviet era is such that all evidence of this sort is simply irredeemable. For others the documents compiled, the investigations and interrogations conducted in close temporal and physical proximity to the scene of the crime, the statements given by the neighbors of both victims and perpetrators, must be taken seriously as possible sources of knowledge. They can and should be tested, using other evidence, other sources of knowledge, or as was sometimes the case in Adelaide, tested by the thrust of the rules of evidence, the art of examination and cross-examination, ideas of reliability, and the common sense of a jury. Of course, these discrepancies mean that some ESC evidence might be deemed reliable by professional historians using the criteria of their discipline, while it might be found to be unreliable by the processes and criteria of a criminal trial. Neither genre can offer a definitive judgment about the truth of a particular witness statement nor of the facts related therein in a metaphysical sense. But neither genre, despite the pretensions of some tragically misled natural law enthusiasts, deals in metaphysical truth.

THE SOVIET WAR CRIMES TRIALS

Whatever its flaws, whether real or perceived, or a combination of the two, the work of the ESC served as the basis for an extensive war crimes trials program in the Soviet Union, both during and after the war. The Soviet system was the first and most active not only in the pursuit of German offenders but also in trying and punishing native collaborators. The pursuit of Germans would have a direct influence on the emerging system of international criminal law, which would reach its temporary apotheosis at the IMT in Nuremberg, in the Tokyo trial of Japanese war criminals, and in various national proceedings against Nazi war criminals in liberated Europe.[73] The trial of native collaborators would also find domestic equivalents in several European jurisdictions and would have both direct and indirect impacts on the subsequent proceedings against the three alleged Ukrainian collaborators in Adelaide.

According to Ginsburgs, approximately 2.5 million collaborators were convicted of "counter-revolutionary crimes," such as treason, "military crimes," and common crimes, before Soviet military tribunals during the war.[74] Dieter Pohl enumerates 54,000 investigations into collaborationist crimes in Ukraine alone.[75] For her part Tanya Penter quotes Russian sources that indicate that between 1943 and 1945 more than 320,000 Soviet citizens were charged with collaborating with the occupying German forces.[76] Martin Dean places postwar arrests for collaboration offenses at over 300,000.[77] It seems clear from this astonishing array of figures that the Soviet pursuit of those citizens who had collaborated with the Germans was both widespread and fierce.[78]

The most well-known of Soviet wartime trials took place in relation to atrocities in Krasnodar and Kharkov.[79] They served both as early precedents in the development of international law on war crimes and as a clear indication that law would be used against Nazi criminals. On 19 April 1943 the Presidium of the Supreme Soviet issued an edict, which has never been published, that introduced the penalty of death by hanging, rather than by shooting, for "fascist occupiers and their collaborators."[80] The edict would be enforced for the first time against the defendants in the Krasnodar case.[81] More significantly, the eleven defendants in the case were Soviet citizens accused of collaborating with the occupying German forces in a series of atrocities against the Soviet people. The trial took place under the provisions of the Soviet Criminal Code, articles 58-1(a) and 51-1(b), dealing with treason. The indictment dealt with several specific offenses, the particulars of which all identified the German military and Gestapo officials under whose command the crimes had taken place. The accused were charged with assisting the Gestapo in various actions against the local population, including the torture and murder by burning of prisoners in the cellar at Gestapo headquarters. They were also charged with assisting in the operation of "murder vans," large trucks in which "Soviet citizens," including 320 clinic patients and sick children from the children's hospital, were gassed. The final number of murder van victims was put at seven thousand. All eleven accused pleaded guilty.[82] Eight of the defendants were sentenced to death, and three, "being the least active of the accomplices," were given terms of twenty years of penal servitude in exile.[83] Those sentenced to death were hanged on 18 July 1943 in the central square before fifty thousand onlookers.[84]

While the trial was limited to Soviet defendants and took place under the treason provisions of the Criminal Code and therefore did not directly involve German perpetrators, the indictment and the evidence presented as a result of ESC investigations, clearly identified the individual Germans in charge of the criminal operations in which the accused took part. The evidence also established the Soviet view that ultimate responsibility for the offenses in question would eventually and ultimately be attributed to the Military High Command and the German political elite.

Allied officials followed the Krasnodar and the subsequent Kharkov trials with great attention. The Kharkov trial in particular caused consternation and objection in certain circles because it directly placed German soldiers in the dock. Some Allied officials were afraid that Germany would carry through on threats to put Allied military personnel held as POWs on trial before German courts in retaliation. The Kharkov case also depended heavily on evidence adduced during the ESC proceedings. The accused included a German police corporal, a military counterintelligence officer, an assistant commander of an SS Sonderkommando, and "their accomplice the traitor to the motherland, Bulanov, who served as a chauffeur with the Kharkov *S.D. Sonderkommando*."[85]

The case dealt almost exclusively with the deployment of murder vans and once more carefully constructed an attack on the Nazi political and military hierarchies as those ultimately responsible. In order to establish the actual basis of the criminal liability of the accused, particularly the German defendants to whom Soviet treason provisions could never apply, the prosecutor invoked the terms of the

Hague Convention of 1907 governing armed occupation and the 1929 Geneva Convention as well as "the universally accepted provisions of international law."[86] The accused were convicted and sentenced to death by hanging. The sentence was carried out at 11 a.m. on 19 December 1943 in the City Square in Kharkov. Over forty thousand people attended. "The reading and execution of the sentence was received with great satisfaction and stormy and prolonged applause by the working people of Kharkov and the collective farmers of the districts of Kharkov region who were present."[87]

Although the Krasnodar case dealt directly with local collaboration in Nazi atrocities and the Kharkov trial with the use of murder vans, neither case contains a specific reference to the murder of Jews. While the available evidence of a specific Nazi program aimed at the extermination of European Jewry was overwhelming, and the Soviet government had publicly acknowledged this reality, and despite the fact that the ESC had gathered equally overwhelming evidence on the practice of mass killings of Jews on Soviet soil, the first two major trials of collaborators and their Nazi masters in the USSR did not specifically deal with the subject.

The situation continued in many cases that followed. When memory of the Holocaust was not completely suppressed, Jewish specificity was neutralized under the generalized formula "innocent Soviet citizens." This construction was, as Tanya Penter argues, part of the broader Soviet discourse that constructed the war and the suffering of the citizens as part of the struggle of the Soviet motherland against the forces of fascism. A necessary component of this effort was that specifically Jewish victimization was encompassed under the more acceptable and ideologically consistent notion of the suffering of the entire population at the hands of the foreign fascist invaders. The same ideological strategy carried over into the description and construction of the local perpetrators. Many of the trials took place under the provisions of the Criminal Code dealing with treason. The actions of Ukrainian police, members of the Schutzmannschaft, were therefore portrayed within the frame of Soviet law and justice not in relation to their immediate victims, the Jews killed in pit shootings, but rather, in terms of their betrayal of the USSR. Penter argues that "in the understanding of the Soviet authorities, it was worse to be a Ukrainian nationalist than to participate in the murder of hundreds of Jews."[88]

Nonetheless, particularly in postwar trials, the Holocaust did figure more prominently in a number of cases, especially those involving collaborators in areas with significant Jewish populations. According to Alexander Victor Prusin, this was a consequence both of local circumstances and developments in international law after Nuremberg:

> In contrast to the Krasnodar and Khar'kov cases, the postwar trials introduced Holocaust-related crimes as one of the principal charges against the defendants. The Soviet government took into account the Nuremberg proceedings, in which a great deal of attention was paid to the genocide of Jews. More important, however, the scope of the Holocaust and the involvement of the ss, the regular armed forces, and the civil administration in its implementation provided the tribunals with the ultimate opportunity to convict the majority of defendants.[89]

While one might dispute Prusin's reading of the prominence of the Holocaust before the IMT, it does seem clear that in many postwar cases collaborators stood accused of crimes involving their participation in anti-Jewish actions. The question that remains is that of the potential impact of these trials for more recent events, especially those that occurred in Australia in the late 1980s and early to mid-1990s.

Many would claim that these Soviet Ukrainian trials can be of little or no relevance in Western democratic societies because they are fundamentally tainted. For the most part they took place before military, rather than civilian, jurisdictions. In addition, they were heavily influenced by NKVD and then KGB involvement. "Confessions" and interrogation protocols are therefore worthless. Soviet rules of evidence and procedure did not offer the same guarantees of due process that the Anglo-American system establishes as a cornerstone of criminal justice.

A vociferous critic of Soviet criminal legality, F. J. M. Feldbrugge, argues that Western criticism of Soviet prosecutions of collaborationist war criminals did a disservice not just to the victims of Nazi atrocities but also to Soviet citizens more worthy of attention. "The defendants in the trials were Soviet citizens and most or all of them were presumably guilty of the most dreadful atrocities. During the same period there were other Soviet citizens who were immeasurably more deserving of moral and legal support from abroad."[90]

Feldbrugge touches here on an issue that goes to the heart of many of the debates and questions that arise not just in relation to the Soviet war crimes trials system but to debates about Soviet source evidence in Nazi war crimes trials in Western jurisdictions. Most of the Soviet proceedings did in fact identify those who were guilty of the worst crimes. Prusin argues that even by internal Soviet standards of criminal justice the proceedings against alleged collaborators did not operate outside the norms of Soviet legality. He explains that the use of "confession," for example, needs to be understood within the context of European criminal justice practice generally and Soviet practice more particularly. The idea of a criminal accused invoking a right to silence and never offering an explanation is simply foreign to many European, including the Soviet, systems of criminal law. Interrogations and witness statements occur in a context in which the accused is expected to explain him- or herself.[91] The accused is asked to reply to the declarations of a witness in the case with whom he or she is confronted, a procedure that at some level at least complies with an understanding that criminal defendants are entitled to be informed of the case against them and to confront their accusers. Prusin therefore concludes that, even if one takes into account the political and ideological nature and characteristics of collaborator trials, they in fact occurred within a broader Soviet procedural norm and cannot and should not be dismissed out of hand.

Penter invokes the term *show trial*, which would reoccur consistently in Australian debates as shorthand for all the perfidies of Soviet "law," to describe the Krasnodar proceedings and several of the trials of

Organization of Ukrainian Nationalists (OUN) members in Western Ukraine.[92] Such a description in the circumstances of the Krasnodar trial is misplaced. There can be no doubt that the trial and execution of the convicted prisoners served ideological and propagandistic purposes, but so do many high-profile criminal prosecutions in every Western jurisdiction. Indeed, the idea of war crimes trials as pedagogic events, as spectacular occasions in which the trial is used to offer a political history lesson, is fairly commonplace in Western discussions of such proceedings.[93] The term *show trial* as it relates to the Stalinist Soviet Union and Soviet satellite countries would, and should, I believe, more accurately carry with it an essential and core idea that the accused, who often did "confess," was in fact innocent. This was not the case at Krasnodar.

Penter goes on to point out that, even if she insists on this characterization of the Krasnodar process, collaborator trials for the most part could not fall under this description. They were in fact most often held in secret and therefore had no propaganda value. She concludes that "these trials often convicted real war criminals and fulfilled political functions at the same time, which is probably also true for most of the war crimes trials in the west."[94] As a result, she argues that a study of Soviet collaborator trials can serve important functions, relevant for the Australian war crimes proceedings. Records of Soviet cases can give detailed accounts of the Holocaust at the local level. They can offer insights into biographical profiles and motives of collaborators who became Holocaust perpetrators.[95] The utility of all such detail must be placed in its full context. Moreover, it needs to be situated in the frame of the professional inquiry that is most relevant. Thus, Martin Dean correctly concludes that "the postwar public discourse on collaboration in eastern Europe remains incomplete and unsatisfactory. Examining collaboration, however, also requires the identification of the collaborators and the deconstruction of the more comfortable personal histories they have preferred to live with—a painful process indeed, which perhaps can only be successfully undertaken when they are unable to argue back. But that time is now fast approaching."[96]

This is an accurate and important summary of the vital necessity of studying and understanding the phenomenon of collaboration. In the more specific context of the Shoah in Ukraine, identification of collaborators and the unveiling of their real motivations are essential. As Penter and Prusin demonstrate, war crimes trials can and should serve as potential sources of such information and knowledge. But the agenda of historians and political scientists is not the agenda of lawyers, police, and judges. Identification and motive are to be established according to a set of criteria that begins with historical sources and knowledge and then goes beyond or least in another direction, with another aim in mind. The goal of law in these circumstances is to require the collaborators to answer back, or at least to answer for, their acts but only within a highly constrained set of discursive rules. Law and history have different aims, different methodologies, and different fates in mind for their subjects. At times the goals intersect, and at times they diverge radically. But in their interest in Soviet war crimes trials of Holocaust perpetrators they appear to have a strong set of common interests.

SOVIET WAR CRIMES TRIALS AND THE COLD WAR

Several factors came to the fore as the USSR continued its pursuit of collaborationist war criminals. Changes were made in both substantive and procedural law that resulted in a legal imbroglio surrounding both the applicability of the death penalty and the question of whether a limitation provision had in fact allowed suspected war criminals to benefit from the simple passage of time.[97] In March 1965 the Presidium of the Supreme Soviet decreed that "the Nazi criminals guilty of the gravest crimes against peace and humanity and war crimes shall be brought to court and punished irrespective of the time that has passed since the crimes were committed."[98]

As the Cold War intensified, and as émigré groups militated against the Soviet Union, the Soviets replied with accusations that many leaders and activists in these anti-Soviet agitations were in fact war criminals and mass murderers who had escaped with the retreating

Germans and had found refuge in Western countries. It is also necessary to underscore that émigré politics were more complex than either pro-Western or pro-Soviet propaganda would have us believe. Some Ukrainian groups were distinctly pro-Soviet and contributed to a flow of literature attacking "fascist elements" among their fellow citizens. Still other longer-term Ukrainian immigrants, especially in Canada, had little truck with either their ultranationalist, collaborationist, or pro-Soviet fellow citizens.[99] Nonetheless, the Soviets asserted, not without justification, that the Western countries were ignoring their international legal obligations and the principles of a universal duty to hunt down war criminals and hand over perpetrators for trial. A typical Soviet argument was that, "despite international agreements on the inevitable punishment of war criminals, some people in disregard of the general human standards of morality and humanism, and the principles of international law, have persisted in concealing the nazi criminals. Breaking international laws and their own commitments, aggressive forces, notably in the United States, are hypocritically trying to prove that the problem of war criminals no longer exists."[100]

In addition to making a series of requests to various countries—including the United States, Canada, the United Kingdom, and Australia—for the extradition of identified collaborationist war criminals, the Soviet authorities continued to agitate at the international and diplomatic levels more generally. At the international conference held in Moscow in 1963 on the history of resistance to Nazi occupation in Europe, for example, the USSR reproduced a series of captured German documents, many well-known since Nuremberg, with the aim of bringing the history of the suffering of "peaceful Soviet citizens" once again to the world's consciousness and to bring pressure to bear on Western democratic regimes.

Two elements of the Soviet strategy are worth noting. First, the documents of Nazi crimes are produced according to a thematic that is virtually identical to the collections produced for Allied consumption during World War II—the Nazi occupation regime; the mass extermination of the Soviet population; criminal mistreatment of

Soviet POWs; slave labor and mass deportations; and the pillaging, theft, and destruction of Soviet property. The second element is the virtual absence of any mention at this stage of the Holocaust or the specificity of the Nazi extermination policy aimed at Jews. Only one document, from the ESC archives, contains an eyewitness account of the mass roundup of Jews at Babi Yar.[101] The title of the document, however, refers to the execution of "Soviet citizens."

Throughout this period the USSR continued to try and to convict "nationalist traitors" for offenses committed during the Great Patriotic War. These cases frequently focused on Holocaust-related crimes. From 1960 onward, after the correction of limitation issues and after the release of many prisoners in a series of amnesties, trials occurred on a somewhat sporadic basis, but when they did take place, they received extensive domestic press coverage.[102] In 1980 in Volyn three Ukrainian defendants were convicted of collaborating with the Nazi occupiers, including participation in pit shootings of "Soviet citizens of Jewish nationality."[103] All three were sentenced to death by shooting. In 1982 a similar trial was held in Ternopil, where the charges also involved mass shootings of Jews. Both defendants also received the death penalty.[104]

During the 1970s and 1980s, as agitation in relation to the presence of alleged war criminals and Holocaust perpetrators grew in several Western jurisdictions, the Soviet Union kept up its calls for action by these governments. It continued to insist that, in compliance with the Moscow Declaration and subsequent confirming international agreements, the accused be sent to stand trial in the country where they had allegedly committed the offenses.[105] The Soviet government also handed over evidence in the form of documents, witness statements, investigative protocols, and trial records to assist Western prosecutors in cases against collaborators. This effort met with mixed success insofar as German prosecutions were concerned, but Soviet cooperation first with the United States authorities and then more formally and substantively with the Australian investigators and officials led to the opening of archives that have since served as valuable sources of historical and legal information.[106]

The historical, political, linguistic, ethnic, and military complexities of life in Ukraine must be considered as part of the necessary broad context in which events that would be subjected to political, historical, and legal scrutiny in Australia. At the same time, each of these elements formed part of the lived reality of the direct participants—the accused and the eyewitnesses—who would constitute one important section of the key actors in the Adelaide proceedings. The translation of the complexities and subtleties of this reality at the level of the capacity of the other parties to the process—historians, police, prosecutors, defense lawyers, and magistrates and judges, not to mention a South Australian jury—would prove vital to the way in which the Australian attempt to prosecute alleged Holocaust perpetrators ended. A further level of necessary complexity was added to the mix as a result of the way in which the Australian legislation constructed and defined the "war crime" offense, transforming difficult concepts of collaboration and the pursuit of Nazi ideological and political goals into core elements of the offense, thereby requiring the jury in the case of Polyukhovich, for example, to grasp not just political, historical, ethnic, and religious contexts but to transform that into difficult legal categories of the intention to commit a crime, the *mens rea*, and essential physical elements of the offense, the *actus reus*.

The evolving and historically contingent concepts of war crimes and crimes against humanity are not only in and of themselves difficult and multifaceted, but they played a more concrete role in the political and legal debates that surrounded Australian attempts to deal with the presence of war criminals and Holocaust perpetrators on Australian soil. The Moscow and St. James's Palace declarations, the establishment of the United Nations War Crimes Commission, and the IMT, all created apparently clear and morally justifiable bases for the unrelenting lawful pursuit of Holocaust perpetrators and the handing over of these individuals for trial. But Cold War ideology, émigré political influence, and the relative amnesia about the Holocaust appeared to have trumped the imperative for justice for the unrepresented victims of Nazi extermination policies. Soviet demands for the handing over of perpetrators instead became part of the great game of Cold War diplomacy.

The deeply embedded prejudices of the Cold War, of anticommunism, then had to confront the jurisprudential and historical reality of the Soviet war crimes program. The ESC and the various military and civilian tribunals and courts that had dealt with collaborators and their crimes, including their crimes against Jews, had compiled mountains of evidence, depositions, interrogations, witness confrontations, and court records that at first blush could serve greatly to assist the belated Australian search for justice. Potential perpetrators living in Australia had been identified. Many hurdles would have to be overcome—continuing anti-Communist sentiment, doubts about the reliability of Soviet source evidence, the passage of time, among others. Most or all of these difficulties could be dealt with if and when unfettered access to records and to witnesses could be negotiated with the Soviet authorities. But two seemingly intractable questions would always inform the Australian project—first, how to translate history into law, archives into proof; and second, how to translate law into justice. The following chapters will illustrate these dilemmas and the Australian attempt to bring a hint of justice to the memory of Hitler's victims.

TWO

A Brief Political and Legal History of Australia and Nazi War Criminals

The first, legal part of the story of the war crimes trials program that unfolded in the three proceedings in Adelaide begins with Australia's membership in the United Nations War Crimes Commission (UNWCC).[1] As a party to the UNWCC, Australia positioned itself at the level of diplomacy and international law as a country dedicated to the pursuit and punishment of Nazi war criminals. Yet as was the case with most other participants in the UNWCC, other priorities, both domestic and international, soon came to the fore. In 1947 Australia readily agreed that the UNWCC's job was done. As Prime Minister Ben Chifley wrote to the UK secretary of state for commonwealth relations in October of that year, "Its major tasks have been completed and the principles of law for war crimes have been adequately developed."[2]

Fourteen years later in a statement to Parliament, Chifley reiterated the Labor Party's position that the time to finish with the pursuit of Nazi war criminals had come. At a time when information was still coming to the attention of Australian authorities concerning the presence of Nazi collaborators and war criminals among newly arrived European migrants, Chifley, having returned to the opposition benches, told Parliament:

> I could not see much purpose in continuing investigations aimed at tracing war criminals. That sort of thing could go on for the next twenty years, and new criminals could be located almost daily . . . The situation has stirred up considerable public feeling, and has caused some criticism, not only of the former Government, but also of this Government. Many people ask how long these trials and investigations are to continue, Church representatives have criticized the long drawn-out trials at Nuremberg.[3]

While Australia accepted the common view that the UNWCC should be wound up, at the level of both ideology and international law, the government nonetheless concurred with a position that it never formally retracted. It continued to express the view that international law condemned Nazi and collaborationist crimes and that the prohibition of crimes against humanity now formed part of the international legal regime to which Australia, as a civilized country, adhered. The concrete content of Australia's commitment to these aspects of international law, and the apparent contradiction between the country's legal position and its political practice, would come to the fore forty years later during debates about the presence of Nazi war criminals on Australian soil.

The next part of the story of Australia's war crimes trials in the late 1980s and early 1990s begins in postwar Europe. Millions of refugees, displaced persons (DPs)—"reffos," as they would come to be known in Australian slang—were found throughout Allied-occupied Europe. For those who had fled the Soviet bloc, captured as POWs, or who had been deported for labor purposes by the Nazis, a new home had to be found. Return to the clutches of the new enemy of the emerging Cold War was not possible. A complex screening process was established by the Allied powers, including Commonwealth countries such as Canada and Australia, which acted largely under the aegis of the United Kingdom authorities. The purpose was to weed out undesirable

"Nazi" elements and to permit others to migrate to a new life. The screening process was singularly unsuccessful. Many war criminals from what was becoming the Soviet bloc—Yugoslavia, the Baltic states, Hungary, Poland, and Ukraine—"slipped through the net," often with the assistance of Allied intelligence agencies. Among the tens of thousands of legitimate DPs who made new lives in Australia were hundreds of war criminals and Holocaust perpetrators.[4]

Yet the failures of Australian immigration screening were not some hidden aspect of the country's past discovered only in the 1980s. From the earliest arrivals of these new European migrants, revelations about a Nazi presence in DP camps in Australia quickly emerged.[5] In the years immediately following the entry of the DP population into Australian society, it also became clear that many "ethnic" social clubs and political groups harbored notorious antisemites and former collaborators.[6] In 1949 and 1950 Australian newspapers carried reports identifying "alleged Nazi collaborators."[7] The information was passed on to Australian police and security officials, but no further action was taken by the government, a government that continued to adhere to the international legal regime, including the new UN Genocide Convention in 1949.[8]

In 1950 the issue again surfaced in public political debate when then immigration minister and future prime minister, Harold Holt, revealed plans to recruit migrants to Australia not just among "Germans" but among Volksdeutsche populations.[9] In reply to accusations that if German migration was in and of itself problematic at the time, the proposed influx of Volksdeutschen would almost certainly mean the arrival of war criminals into the country, Holt stated: "I, for my part, have never said . . . that no Volksdeutsche were at any stage Nazis. To do so would be folly. It would be just as foolish to say that no Australian is a communist. But it would be equally as wrong to generalize and say that *all* Volksdeutsche were Nazis because *some* were as to generalize and say that *all* Australians are communists because *some* are."[10]

Holt's response, which is reflective of Australian postwar immigration policy and politics more generally, incorporates the tropes and rhetorical devices that would inform ongoing debates about the presence of Nazi war criminals in Australia well into the 1990s. There is first the problematic equivalence made between the twin totalitarian evils of Nazism and Communism. More profoundly, there is the ineffable trace of anticommunism, which would inform all war crimes debates in Australia. It is not possible to begin to understand or to situate the politics and law of Australian war crimes legislation and trials unless the centrality of anti-Communist fears and rhetoric that informed the post–World War II era in the country's politics is given its due. Australia would live through the drama of the Petrov affair, which revealed an existing Soviet espionage ring in the country;[11] a Royal Commission that would "uncover" not just the details of this Soviet spy operation but specific details of attempts by the USSR to infiltrate and discredit émigré organizations;[12] the passage of a law to outlaw the Communist Party;[13] a national referendum on the ban and a High Court decision overturning the statute on constitutional grounds;[14] and a long-term split in the Labor Party over the issue of Communist influence.[15]

Attempts to identify and deal with Nazi war criminals whose presence in Australia had been known from the very beginning of the postwar migration naturally and not surprisingly soon fell under the broader rhetorical structures and political realities of Australian anticommunism. Yugoslav requests for the extradition of alleged collaborators were met not just by a refusal but by intelligence agency assurances to the government that the individuals in question provided invaluable, if limited, assistance to the general campaign against Communism. In the early 1950s the Executive Council of Australian Jewry (ECAJ) on several occasions intervened and provided the federal government with information about, and lists of, Nazi collaborators and war criminals who were living in Australia.[16] No action was forthcoming.

The government attitude and failure to act can clearly only be understood in the broader frame of Australian and international anticommunism. The Holocaust was not in the early 1950s what it would become as a sociological, political, historical, and legal phenomenon following the Eichmann trial in Jerusalem and the emergence of new historiographical knowledge. At this point Nazism, militarily defeated and judicially erased at Nuremberg, had largely been forgotten and replaced by the currently real specter of Communism. In the Australian context as it relates more directly to allegations about the presence of Nazi collaborators, this took on a particular shading because of the primary source of these allegations, the organization known as the "Jewish Council to Combat Fascism and Anti-Semitism." The council was originally founded and based in Melbourne, but the Jewish Unity Committee, later the Jewish Unity Association, operated a similar presence in the Sydney Jewish community. It later became the Sydney Jewish Council to Combat Fascism and Anti-Semitism.[17] While the groups' relationships with the powerful Jewish Board of Deputies were somewhat more amicable in Sydney than in Melbourne, in both of Australia's largest Jewish communities interactions were fraught largely because of the public left-wing affiliations of all the leading members of the Jewish Council to Combat Fascism and Anti-Semitism.[18] If the position of the council was problematic and difficult within the evolving internal dynamics of organized Australian Jewry, because of its leftist orientation, its persuasive powers and potential influence at the level of secular governmental authorities were essentially nullified.

Reports from the council and the information that it handed on to the government and police agencies were publicized in the media but were given short shrift by those with power to act. Harold Holt might well have insisted to Parliament that his government took such allegations seriously and that, should they be proven, the government had "ample powers" to deport undesirable immigrants, but the reality was that complaints about the presence of Nazi collaborators were always dismissed as Communist disinformation.[19]

An internal report in the Attorney-General's Department reveals the worldview operating in Australian government and security circles at this time. The government was cognizant of the fact that anti-Nazi agitation still had a certain powerful resonance among the population. Investigations were carried out in response to the story published in the *Truth* about the presence of twelve identified Nazi collaborators in Australia.[20] But the main focus by government officials was not on the veracity of the story or on actions to be contemplated against war criminals in Australia but on the source of the leak to the press.

> Although the Investigation Service has not completed its enquiry, the report suggests some significance in the fact that the letter received by [Jacob] Segal was handed to one Judah Waten, Manager of the Jewish Council to Combat Fascism and Anti-Semitism. It is thought that there is a distinct possibility that this Council furnished the information which forms the substance of article in Truth. According to the report from the Investigation Service, Judah Waten is a well-known Communist, and the Jewish Council to Combat Fascism and Anti-Semitism is considered to be under Communist domination.[21]

A secret intelligence file also revealed that Waten had been expelled from the Party in July 1945 but that "he was still regarded as a Communist at heart."[22]

A note prepared for the minister in relation to the *Truth* article also identifies another element that characterizes the history of Australia's treatment of the questions surrounding the presence of Nazi war criminals on its soil. Besides being dominated by Communists and Communist sympathizers, "the Council naturally is weighted to Jewish members who have always been very anti–displaced person."[23]

It is no doubt true that organized Australian Jewry was vocal in its opposition to the mass influx of displaced persons in the postwar period. In this respect they were not alone. Their opposition, however, was in fact not aimed at DPs in particular. It was, instead, twofold in its focus. First, there was understandable and justified concern that among these European migrant groups were to be found notorious antisemites, collaborators, and war criminals. Second, Australian immigration policy, both before and after the Shoah, was distinctly and identifiably tainted by a blatant antisemitic bias.[24] Opposition to the influx of European migrants from Australia's Jewish communities and their representative bodies was for the most part aimed at the exclusionary policies implemented by the government against European Jewish migrants.

Notwithstanding the government's refusal to act, and within the atmosphere of anticommunism and antisemitism, the Jewish Council to Combat Fascism and Anti-Semitism continued to agitate and organize against the threat posed by the presence of Nazi war criminals on Australian soil. In addition to earlier protests against proposed German migration, the council acted to "Keep Australia Free from Nazis" and on the theme "Do You Want Nazi Allies" in 1952 and against known members of the Hungarian Arrow Cross and the Slovak Hlinka Guard in Sydney a year later.[25] The struggle continued with "The Tenth Anniversary of the Surrender of Nazi Germany" in 1955, "Krupp Comes to Australia!" on 20 February 1958, and "Citizens' Protest Meeting against the Revival of Nazism and Anti-Semitism" in January 1960.[26]

But the Australian Liberal government of Robert Menzies stuck to its anti-Communist guns. In early 1961 the USSR sent an extradition request to Australian officials. The subject of the request was Ervin Viks, an Estonian immigrant who was accused of murdering twelve thousand Jews and Roma in the Tartu concentration camp. The Australian position unfolded on two fronts, one formally legal and the other political. On the one hand, the Australian attorney general (and later chief justice) Sir Garfield Barwick highlighted the absence of a formal extradition treaty between the two states as a solid legal reason to reject the Soviet request. At the same time, however, Barwick realized that this legal roadblock was merely formal in nature because, even absent a bilateral extradition agreement, the prerogative executive power to order the removal of a suspected war criminal was still vested in the Menzies government. The refusal to extradite Viks then had to be grounded in the rhetoric and practice of politics and ideology. Barwick's speech on the matter to the House of Representatives is (in)famous:

> Two deep-seated human interests, however, may well here come into conflict. On the one hand, there is the utter abhorrence felt by Australians for those offences against humanity to which we give the generic name war crimes. On the other hand, there is the right of this nation, by receiving people into this country to enable men to turn their backs on past bitternesses and to make a new life for themselves and for their families in a happier community. This has formed a precious part of the heritage of the West, in which Australia has an honourable share.
>
> In a given case the choice between these two human interests may present a government with a difficult decision. In the present instance, however, the Government came to the clear conclusion that, all questions of legal obligations apart, if such a choice had been necessary to resolve the matter, its right of asylum must have prevailed. Australia has established a thorough, though of course not infallible system for shifting and screening the hundreds of thousands of migrants who have enriched our national life since the World War. In default of a binding obligation requiring Australia at this point of time to do otherwise, those, who have been allowed to make their homes here, must be able to live, in security, new lives under the rule of law.[27]

In his unforgettable phrase Barwick concluded that "the time has come to close the chapter."[28] In doing so, of course, Barwick did little more than echo the remarks made from the Labor Parliamentary benches, by Ben Chifley, several years earlier about the passing relevance and importance of the ongoing pursuit of war criminals. He first begins his statement by drawing an absolute moral balance between Nazi atrocities and upholding Australia's right to govern its own immigration and refugee policy, however fallible. He then asserts that the comparison demands that Australia give precedence to its narrowly defined domestic interests, thereby implying that

Nazi mass murder is in fact less important than living a quiet life in Australia, under the rule of law.

Ironically, if unintentionally, Barwick establishes the principled argument that Australian rule of law norms almost demand that the Shoah be forgotten. Ervin Viks, the mass murderer of Jews and Roma in the Nazi concentration camp at Tartu, must be allowed to continue to contribute to Australian society. He can live in a "happier community" because Australia permits him to leave behind "past bitternesses." The unanswered question is exactly what Barwick means by these past bitternesses and what relationship, if any, they might have to the "utter abhorrence" Australians feel about Nazi crimes.

Viks's bitternesses are clear—he was a murderous antisemite. How do the utter abhorrence for Nazi crimes against humanity and the insistence that Australia lives under one of Western culture's signal achievements, the rule of law, fit into the refusal to recognize the overwhelming evidence of Viks's culpability? Only a transcendent dedication to anticommunism as a dominant informing norm can possibly inform Barwick's (and Australia's) morally bankrupt performance. Viks was tried and sentenced to death in absentia in the Soviet Union. He died peacefully under the rule of law in Australia.[29]

AUSTRALIA'S WAR CRIMES LEGISLATION:
TO THE MENZIES INQUIRY

Mark Aarons summarizes subsequent developments in the struggle to bring Nazi collaborationist perpetrators to justice in Australia in familiar geopolitical and historical terms:

> Following the refusal of the extradition requests for Ervin Viks, Ain Mere and Karl Linnas, the Soviets turned the whole issue over to the KGB's propaganda section. From 1963 onwards, Soviet intelligence turned out a tidal wave of propaganda detailing with considerable precision and basic accuracy the names, war crimes and locations in Western countries of hundreds of Nazi mass killers

from Latvia, Lithuania, Estonia, Ukraine, Byelorussia and other parts of the communist empire. The main aim of this propaganda was to embarrass the West over its protection of mass killers.[30]

The continuing Soviet propaganda campaign occurred in an evolving international political, historical, and legal context. The Cold War lost if not its rhetorical bases, at least some of the material reality in which it had been grounded as West German Ostpolitik and other forms of engagement with the Communist enemy evolved concomitantly with the ever-decreasing power of the USSR. The political and historical reality of the Holocaust underwent significant transformation as well. The Eichmann trial in Jerusalem and the first publication of Raul Hilberg's monumental study gave rise to a renewed (or simply new) professional engagement with the Shoah as a subject for academic historical study. "It is well to remember how recent is the beginning of professional study of the Holocaust and how short a period of time the enterprise has had to establish itself. Up to the time of the Eichmann trial in Jerusalem in 1961, there was relatively little discussion of the massacre of European Jewry."[31]

As international awareness of the crimes of the Holocaust grew, so too did an understanding that many perpetrators had escaped justice in the immediate and chaotic aftermath of the war. At some level the ongoing Soviet propaganda campaign also coincided with a moral shift in many Western countries as a renewed interest in the question of justice for the victims and punishment of the guilty came to the fore in a way that had been absent from many stunted political debates such as those that occurred in Australia in the 1940s, 1950s, and 1960s. The entire history of the escalating pursuit of perpetrators is beyond the scope of this chapter, but at a certain moment in time, a conjuncture of events on the international scene was translated into the domestic political reality of Australia.

As a by-product of his inquiries into CIA involvement in Australian politics during the time of the Whitlam Labor government, Australian Broadcasting Corporation (ABC) journalist Mark Aarons came upon sources who indicated that another story of CIA involvement in Australia was also waiting to be told — the tale of intelligence agency cooperation in secreting Nazi collaborators out of Europe after the end of World War II. This revelation led naturally to investigations into those collaborators and war criminals still living in Australia.[32] In 1979 Aarons presented an ABC radio program highlighting the story of Ljenko Urbancic, a high-ranking and powerful official in the ethnic political circles of the New South Wales (NSW) Liberal Party. Urbancic, known as "Ljubljana's 'Little Goebbels,'" had been a high-ranking collaborationist official in occupied Slovenia, a notorious antisemite and Nazi propagandist. The story of a Nazi in NSW Liberal Party ranks created a storm within and outside the party, culminating in the ultimate victory of an entrenched and powerful right-wing element, encompassing émigré groups and ultraconservatives in the Liberal Party.[33]

Aarons followed up on his research and in 1986 produced several radio broadcasts for ABC Radio's *Background Briefing* program as well as an episode on ABC TV's leading current affairs program, *Four Corners*, in 1986. These programs offered convincing evidence, based in extensive archival research in Europe, including Eastern bloc countries, not just of Australian officials' complicity in allowing the entry into the country of known war criminals in the immediate postwar period but also of the continuing presence of Nazi mass murderers on Australia soil. The evidence uncovered by Aarons and subsequently confirmed by the *Menzies Report* and investigations undertaken by the Special Investigations Unit (SIU) indicated "that between 150 and 200 exNazis illegally entered Australia under our postwar immigration schemes."[34] This time reaction would not remain within the confines of bitter factional rivalry inside the New South Wales Liberal Party.

Events other than Aarons's reporting offered happy synergies in relation to attempts to bring Nazi war criminals to justice in Australia. At around the same time, a Royal Commission of Inquiry into similar questions was taking place in Canada, under Justice Jules Deschênes of Québec.[35] An official United Kingdom inquiry reached the same conclusions about postwar immigration policy and the presence of war criminals among migrant groups.[36] The Honorable R. J. L. "Bob" Hawke had been elected as Labor prime minister in 1983. Hawke had particularly close relations both with Australian Jewry and with Israel from his previous time as a high-ranking trade union official engaged in international activities and in the creation of strong bilateral ties with Israeli unions. In 1986 an international conference organized by the World Jewish Congress, commemorating the fortieth anniversary of the Nuremberg Trials, had taken place in Israel. Representatives of Australian Jewry were in attendance. Among the topics addressed was the ongoing attempt to track down Nazi war criminals and bring them to justice.

In the immediate aftermath of the conference the Executive Council of Australian Jewry (ECAJ) unanimously decided that it, and in particular its president, Leslie Caplan, would take the lead in the Australian push to deal with the Nazi war criminals issue. It set lobbying the federal government as an immediate and urgent priority.[37] Caplan met with Bob Hawke on 18 February 1986. Caplan and Aarons spoke with the influential Labor caucus subcommittee on immigration and ethnic affairs a few weeks later, and the subcommittee urged the government to act on the war crimes question.[38] The international and domestic political stars were aligned. There was renewed interest in the question of "hidden" war criminals; a Canadian inquiry was already under way and served as an example to guide possible Australian action; and the ECAJ had the ear of the Labor prime minister, and together with the influential members of the immigration and ethnic affairs subcommittee, Hawke could drive the party where he wished.[39] Aarons's radio and television revelations reverberated through the Australian public and political consciousness. The Australian press had largely ignored the issue of Nazi war criminals in Australia since the *Truth* and *Argus* stories had appeared decades earlier.[40] Now Jeremy Jones could report to the ECAJ that "the experience so far has shown tremendous media understanding of the Holocaust, and sympathy to our view that the problem is moral, effecting the entire community, and agreement that it is a matter for government, which has been the dual thrust of the E.C.A.J. calls."[41]

The strategy adopted by the ECAJ and other proponents of Australian war crimes legislation sought to turn Garfield Barwick's rhetorical narrative on its head. The Holocaust was portrayed not as a "Jewish" issue or an "ethnic" issue of concern only to European migrant communities but as one of general significance — it was a crime against humanity. The moral issue that was posited as central to the politics of war crimes legislation was no longer Barwick's desire that immigrants leave past bitternesses behind or that they be able to live peaceful lives under the rule of law. In the new discourse about law and the Shoah in Australia in 1986, a different vision of morality took center stage. The question of legal intervention was henceforth driven by a moral imperative to seek justice against the perpetrators and for the victims.

While there was a clear attempt at this moment to frame the question in terms of a universal moral condemnation of war crimes and war criminals, the real politics of a multicultural Australian society soon came to the fore. The Ukrainian community in particular had been following the Canadian Deschênes Royal Commission closely and with increasing concern. Because of the importance of a large and long-established Ukrainian community in Canada, that inquiry focused significant time and resources on the issue of the presence of potential war criminals among postwar Ukrainian migrants. Canada had welcomed several waves of earlier immigrants of Ukrainian origin. The most recent influx of Ukrainians after the war had been greeted by a politically powerful and "assimilated" Ukrainian-Canadian community. The Ukrainian community in Australia was much smaller than that in Canada and much less well established. The group in Australia consisted mainly of arrivals from the immediate postwar period. Both intragroup dynamics and relations with the broader community were thus significantly different in each country. Nonetheless, the Australian-Ukrainians looked upon the Canadian experience with trepidation.[42]

The Australian Ukrainian community adopted the view that the Royal Commission in Canada, because it was "judicial" in nature, had taken on an adversarial atmosphere that pitted the Ukrainian and Jewish Canadian communities against one another.[43] Its leaders were anxious to avoid a similar situation in Australia and therefore sought both to ensure that the federal government would not adopt the Royal Commission mechanism and that, more generally, all ethnic groups would work together on the issue. On these points they were joined by representatives of the various Baltic communities and of the Australian Croatian community. All these groups consulted with the ECAJ in the search for common ground.

At the meetings it was clear that all communities were anxious to avoid the bitterness that had been caused by the Deschênes commission. With little difficulty, agreement was reached that if there were in Australia war criminals from either side of the political spectrum, for whom there was proper evidence of guilt, then they should be brought to justice. Guilt was understood to require evidence beyond any reasonable doubt, being the standard of Australian criminal law. It was acknowledged by all parties that there were particular difficulties in using Soviet-supplied evidence.[44]

These meetings in fact set the official interethnic agenda. They established both the ideological and juridical frameworks for what would become the Australian Nazi war crimes trial program. Any proceedings would occur according to the standards and rules of the ordinary Australian criminal justice system, and the vexed question of Soviet source evidence would always be high on the political, as well as the legal, agenda. The ECAJ and the representatives of some of Australia's most important immigrant communities set a framework of criminal justice that would mean that, as subsequent events unfolded, there would always be a tension between the level of moral discourse and the practice of criminal law in war crimes trials. While what was at stake, historically and morally, was a universally agreed upon search for justice, what was to occur at the practical legal level was the search for a more limited goal within the frame of justice as practiced before the courts.

In this legal context what would be in play was the simple question of the guilt or innocence of a named individual in relation to a particular criminal offense. The discourse would not be one of morality and universal condemnation in relation to the Shoah. Instead, the entire process was transformed into one aimed at the more limited and limiting goal of establishing the essential elements of a criminal offense beyond a reasonable doubt. Of course, this does not mean that broader issues would not be canvassed or that this narrow inquiry into guilt/innocence is the only story that unfolds in any ordinary criminal trial, let alone a Holocaust-related trial. Broader historical narratives are invoked, as is the language of pedagogy in war crimes trials as a matter of course.[45] Moral discourse undergirds and informs debate and discussion of the trial process itself. Nonetheless, this tension between and among law, justice, history, and memory was present from the very beginning of the political and cultural debates around the question of what to do about the presence of Nazi collaborators and war criminals in Australia.

These developments also occurred within the social and cultural context of Australia's "ethnic politics." While a series of meetings did take place between the ECAJ and the representatives of major immigrant communities, and agreement at the level of principle was apparently reached, other familiar recurrent elements of the narratives of the Holocaust and the law also resurfaced, not the least of which was antisemitism. From the beginning the ECAJ was on its guard because, in its eyes, "the representatives of the eastern European communities brought to these meetings a resonance of centuries of anti-Semitism that had climaxed in the Holocaust."[46]

Antisemitism would continue to inform a significant part of the broader political and social debate throughout 1986 and 1987 as the level of government interest and involvement in the war crimes issue grew.[47] Although intergroup relations remained tense, the meetings produced an official truce in which the publicly stated position of all concerned groups was that they joined in a universal moral condemnation of the Holocaust and in a joint belief that perpetrators should be brought before the bar of Australian justice if sufficient evidence of their culpability existed.

The debate this time entered Parliament as various elected representatives demanded a government response to the proof unearthed by Aarons's broadcasts and other emerging evidence that Australia had indeed welcomed war criminals to its shores in the postwar period. The question of the ABC broadcasts was raised in the Senate on 14 April 1986, the day after the first radio program, and in the lower House two days later.[48] After all the broadcasts had aired, the acting minister for immigration and ethnic affairs informed the House that the government had asked his department to "conduct a review of relevant files to see what the basis was for testing immigrants at that time."[49] At this stage the government was limiting itself to an internal historical investigation into immigration practices in the postwar period in order to determine if there could even be a factual basis for an assertion that war criminals had managed to enter the country. Given the history of revelations of the presence of alleged war criminals in Australia since the earliest arrivals of DPs from Europe and repeated Soviet claims concerning clearly identified individuals, which had never been denied by Australian officials and had been investigated by Australian intelligence services, it was clear at this stage that the Labor government was playing for time.

Labor Party leaders continued to come under pressure to do more than instigate an internal departmental inquiry that could have no other result than to confirm long-standing evidence that Nazi collaborators and war criminals had entered the country. The leader of the opposition Australian Democrats at the time, Don Chipp, kept at the government in the Senate, demanding a royal commission. But Chipp's intervention was carefully gauged in terms of establishing an official inquiry in order to verify the allegations contained in the ABC programs not solely to investigate the issue of Australian government and security and intelligence agency involvement but also to "protect innocent people who may have been maligned."[50]

Government and bureaucratic officials continued to insist that they could uncover no evidence of systematic involvement by officials or agencies in bringing alleged war criminals to the country.[51] At the same time, however, Labor members of the lower chamber insisted that the matter be debated as a matter of public importance. That debate began on 5 May 1986.[52]

At this stage the concern expressed by the ECAJ that the question of war criminals in Australia be treated as a matter of great moral significance, and as one of importance to the general Australian public, took a backseat to the demands of partisan politics. Instead of analyzing the historical evidence and insisting that the government and nation were ethically compelled to correct what was clearly a moral and legal error, the debate originated on the left of the Labor Party benches. Members persisted in placing their discourse at the level of party politics by attacking the Liberal Party, particularly the New South Wales branch, concerning revelations about the presence on the right wing of the Liberal establishment of an entrenched ethnic power base at the core of which were Nazi collaborators such as Ljenko Urbancic. In other words, they revisited the issue of war criminals in Australia from the perspective of Aarons's original 1979 broadcast. "The Liberal party could not throw him [Urbancic] out because of the grip these people have on the Party."[53]

The Liberals responded in kind, pointing out that Ben Chifley's Labor government had been in power when DP migration began. They further asserted that the entire war crimes debate was a political ploy by and creation of the left of the Labor Party and their "communist colleagues," ably assisted by the known left-wing biases of the ABC.[54] Other Liberal members attempted to attack the Labor intervention on the question by asserting a more general moral frame. The member for Wentworth, for example, argued that "war crimes, which involved the slaughter of innocent people on a vast or even on a small scale, remain a crime whether committed yesterday or 40 years ago.

At the same time, we should have no truck with any attempt to libel individuals or whole ethnic groups under parliamentary privilege or with the debasing of the issue for crude political advantage."[55]

In the Senate Sir John Carrick, had an intimate involvement in events in the NSW Liberal Party. He had been at the forefront of the unsuccessful attempts to purge the party's ranks of notorious antisemites and fascist sympathizers. He also attacked the left-wing partisan bias, which he argued had informed the debate to that moment. At the same time he articulated the same moral and legal position as his colleagues in the lower House when he stated: "I want to make it clear that members of the opposition—the Liberal Party and the National Party—are firm in their minds that we have an absolute abhorrence of the holocaust. We are determined that the world shall never forget it, that is must never occur again and that anyone who is clearly identified and proven to be a nazi war criminal should be brought to justice no matter how long it is since the end of the war."[56]

The opposition had staked out significant moral and legal ground on the issue of the alleged presence of war criminals in Australia. They were clear that the Holocaust was an abhorrent historical phenomenon and that all efforts should be engaged in the pursuit of perpetrators. Perhaps more significantly in light of subsequent debates, they asserted that the passage of time since the commission of the crimes was of absolutely no principled importance. Justice must be done.

The earlier Labor Party vision articulated by Chifley's assertion that too much time had passed to continue the pursuit of alleged war criminals had also been abandoned by his party. Barwick's position, articulated in 1961, that years had passed since the commission of the offenses and people should now be allowed to live in peace under the rule of law was completely and utterly rejected by members of the Liberal Party in 1986. The absolute moral abhorrence with which civilized people regarded the Shoah and its perpetrators demanded that they be brought to justice. The simple passage of time could be no bar to criminal proceedings against war criminals. To be sure, the necessary safeguards of the criminal justice system would have to be maintained, admissible evidence would be required to convict, and liability had to be determined in accordance with these principles in a court of law, against identified individuals. Group defamation and any assertion or insinuation of collective guilt were to be rejected on the same bases as prosecutions were to occur—that is, in accordance with principles of fairness and the rule of law.

As the opposition, no doubt in part for its own partisan political purposes, reestablished the public political narrative for the debate about war criminals in Australia, the government sought at one and the same time to control the agenda and to establish a mechanism that would give the appearance of an objective inquiry into the issue. Faced with opposition from various ethnic community groups to either a public inquiry or the royal commission mechanism, grounded in the perception of the negative and ethnically charged political environment surrounding the Canadian Deschênes Royal Commission, the Hawke Labor government followed up on the original recommendation of the caucus subcommittee on immigration and ethnic affairs and established an independent inquiry under the auspices of a former senior civil servant, Andrew Menzies QC. The Menzies inquiry was born.

It is not my intention here to offer a complete reading, review, or critique of the Menzies inquiry. This discussion will simply highlight matters and concerns that arose during Menzies's investigations and/or as a result of his report that have an important and substantive link with the subsequent proceedings before the courts in Adelaide. Thus, I will not concentrate on the primary question of postwar immigration policy and practice or on the issues relating to government and intelligence agency implication in the introduction of alleged war criminals into Australia. I could not hope to add anything to Mark Aarons's studies of these questions. The terms of reference given by the special minister of state to Menzies included a study of "(a) . . . whether war criminals are now or have been resident, in Australia . . . and (d) whether further investigations are required; and (e) any other consideration relevant to (d)."[57]

Menzies identified the background events and questions that gave rise to his inquiry and clearly set out the moral and legal framework that had come to inform the war crimes question in Australia. After recognizing that a new generational approach to the issue now dominated Australian interest in the subject, he specifically rejected the Barwick vision of the question: "Allegations have been recorded by the Review . . . that persons guilty of serious war crimes, indeed crimes involving the murder of many persons, in some cases hundreds of persons, have entered Australia. In the case of such crimes, the argument that the culprits, by coming to this country, have turned their back on such events, has, in my view, no validity."[58]

The chapter closed by Barwick had now been reopened. The argument that the passage of a significant period of time was in principle a bar to prosecution was again rejected. Menzies echoed the important idea of an amalgamation of morality and criminal justice: "Some of the offences the subject of allegations recorded by the Review are of such seriousness that, if the allegations are confirmed by a full investigation, justice, however long delayed, should be, and be seen to be, administered. In this way, the Australian community would express its determination that the offences should not re-occur and its deep felt abhorrence of the crimes."[59]

The resonances with other narrative interventions about war crimes, war criminals, and war crimes trials are clear. The offenses are so serious that by their very nature they call for both moral condemnation and legal punishment. Justice in such cases knows no period of limitation. The process of prosecution of such crimes and criminals necessarily involves a message of general deterrence and one of moral condemnation. Justice must also be seen to be done, but it must be seen to be done within the normal rules of domestic criminal law.

Again, a tension may be said to exist even though it is not more specifically articulated. The nature of the crimes alleged makes them special, so special that previous policy and practice must be rejected, overturned, and replaced with a new vision, informed by a combined moral condemnation and ordinary criminal justice practice. At the same time, groups such as the Australian Federation of Ukrainian Organisations staked out their opposition to the use of Soviet source materials in any Australian proceedings.[60] The war crimes trial is awkwardly positioned as at one and the same time a normal and an extraordinary process. The pedagogical and ethical functions of the criminal justice system and the trial process are openly articulated as particularly important in such instances, while at the same time assertions are made that such trials can never comply with our standards because they are inevitably tainted by the influence of Communist regimes on much of the evidence. All of the easily recognizable narratives about the Shoah in Eastern Europe coexist in a dubious and problematic balance with assertions about the purity of the rule of law in Australia.

Menzies consulted with Canadian, United States, German, and United Kingdom officials and received submissions from ethnic community groups and from interested individuals. In addition to his focus of postwar immigration practice, he received evidence about alleged identified war criminals. Among the reported criminal activities were examples of "participation in police or so-called 'security' units which had the task of deporting, ill-treating or murdering persons on racial or political grounds; in some cases these people worked under German orders, in other cases they operated largely independently."[61]

Having concluded that it was likely that war criminals had indeed entered Australia, Menzies recommended that the government establish a small investigative unit similar to the American Office of Special Investigations to deal with the necessary further inquiries into allegations against individuals that were beyond his limited purview.[62] Most important, he recommended that "the Government make a clear and positive statement to the effect that, as regards serious war crimes, it does not regard the Chapter as closed (contrary to the Barwick statement in 1961) and that it will take appropriate action under the law to bring to justice persons who have committed serious war crimes found in Australia."[63]

Once again, he added the vital caveat that any such legal mechanisms would need to incorporate the basic safeguards of Australian criminal law and criminal justice and that guilt would be established according to the same principles and only against individuals, not against any ethnic group.

The stage was therefore set for the creation of an Australian war crimes trial mechanism. All interested parties, from community groups to members of the House of Representatives and senators from all parts of the political spectrum, were in agreement on all matters of fact and of principle. There was convincing evidence that Holocaust perpetrators had indeed been permitted to establish themselves in Australia after World War II. The Shoah was morally abhorrent, and its perpetrators could not escape justice simply because they had found a home in Australia or because of the passage of time. Australian law would operate according to its ordinary practices, and justice, in the narrow and broad meanings of the term, would both be done and be seen to be done. The dual claims that mass killers had found sanctuary in Australia and that the Australian state and Australian society more broadly had a moral duty to bring them justice had now been accepted as the normative bases for future debate. For more than forty years these arguments had been dismissed under the countervailing twin rubric that it would be better for the country to "close the chapter" and live peacefully under the rule of law, on the one hand, and that allegations of the presence of atrocity killers were the product of the Soviet KGB propaganda machine meant to discredit and sow disharmony among immigrant communities, on the other. Now the principles of the Moscow Declaration were to be embodied in Australian criminal law.

Everyone agreed, or not.

THE WAR CRIMES ACT: PRINCIPLE, POLITICS, AND LAW

In February 1987 the Hawke government announced its intention to implement the main recommendations of the *Menzies Report*. Lionel Bowen, the attorney general, assured the House that the normal standards of Australian law would apply to any future prosecutions, and the principle of individual, not collective, responsibility would be the founding norm of the government's legislation. No slur would be attached to any ethnic group in Australia. Instead, individual guilt would be determined according to the application of normal and accepted practices of the Australian criminal justice system.[64] The Liberal opposition announced its agreement in principle with the government's agenda. Again, the spokesman for the party, Syd Spender, confirmed its support for the pursuit of war criminals despite the passage of time: "The nature and immensity of the war crimes committed by the nazi regime and its supporters in World War II are such that the interests of civilisation and justice require that those responsible be brought to book, however late in the day it might be."[65] At this stage there was agreement on all sides of politics that moral imperatives and the rule of law demanded that Australia act against any Holocaust perpetrator who might still be in the country. The only question that remained related to the exact technical nature of the legislative provisions that could bring these principles into a concrete legal form.

The Australian War Crimes Act 1945 had been passed by the country's Parliament on 4 October 1945. In the period immediately following the end of hostilities in the Pacific theater, Australian authorities had tried over 900 mostly Japanese war criminals in almost 300 trials; among those convicted 148 were hanged. The mechanism established by the original War Crimes Act was trial by military tribunal. The act also obviously contained a death penalty provision. Neither aspect of the existing legislative regime in relation to war crimes was acceptable to the Parliament or to the public in 1987 Australia. In addition, the Australian legislation would have to be extended to cover hostilities in Europe if it were to deal with the problem of the pursuit of Nazi war criminals. Thus, when the amendments to the War Crimes Act 1945 were introduced for first and second reading in the House of Representatives on 28 October 1987, Attorney General Bowen explained that "the scheme, therefore, involves the hypothetical transfer of the act alleged to constitute the offence from outside Australia to some part of Australia."[66]

Bowen elaborated in a statement that took a step back from his earlier recognition that the bill involved aspects of retrospectivity:[67] "The Bill therefore extends to Australian courts jurisdiction to try to punish crimes recognised at international law as war crimes. The Bill does not create offences retrospectively. The offences described in the Bill have existed for many years and many of them are cognisable by military courts under the War Crimes Act as it presently stands."[68]

Bowen's introductory speech sets out the basic frame for the government's position at both the political and moral levels and on the more technical legal issues. The legislation is necessary to bring perpetrators to justice. The scheme ensures the application of normal standards of criminal law and procedure, with the guarantees for the defendant that entails. Substantively, the offenses set out in the act are existing crimes recognized under Australian law as common-law offenses such as murder and, under international law, deportation and enslavement, for example. If offenders are charged under Australian law, they will be pursued for acts that were criminal at the time and place they were committed. There is no substantive retroactive creation of a "new" crime.

As significant as the rule of law argument about the substance of the offenses under the proposed amendments to the War Crimes Act 1945 is the limited nature of the jurisdictional retrospectivity. Jurisdiction is transferred to Australian courts to try defendants resident in Australia for acts that they committed against, in the cases studied here, local Jewish populations in Ukraine under Nazi occupation. The victims were not Australian citizens. The claim to jurisdiction set forth by the Australian government is twofold. First, the accused is a resident or citizen of Australia. The Australian government and the Australian judicial system therefore have a simple physical, corporeal jurisdictional claim over the prospective defendants. But the substantive legal assertion of jurisdiction over the offenses is much broader. It is grounded in the morally based ideal of the Moscow Declaration and other subsequent international criminal law instruments that the nature of the offenses themselves is a crime against humanity, a crime against civilization, and the rules of international society. Australia's jurisdictional claim in the pursuit of Nazi war criminals was the embodiment within a national setting of a principle of normative universality.

Of course, the claim to universal jurisdiction was ironically a limited one in the Australian case. The amendments to the War Crimes Act 1945 were ultimately restricted both geographically and temporally to cover crimes committed in Nazi-occupied Europe between 1939 and 1945. No other war crime, crime against humanity, or act of genocide was brought under the act. The act in its practical application would only cover Holocaust-related crimes. And it would cover these offenses only in the context of the application of Australian criminal law to acts committed by those physically present in Australia at the time charges might be laid.

The *Menzies Report* had canvassed the possibility of extraditing war criminals to the country where the offenses had been committed, according to the basic principle of national *actus reus* jurisdiction over such offenses set out in the Moscow Declaration. The Hawke government rejected this possibility in favor of an Australian limited universal jurisdiction approach.[69] The opposition spokesman, Peter Reith, who gave his party's acceptance in principle to the Hawke government's plan, voiced what was the commonly accepted view on the deportation option: "Clearly, having regard to concerns about the Soviet system of justice and the lack of confidence that any person extradited to the Soviet Union or its satellites could receive a fair trial by our standards, we should oppose extradition to those countries."[70]

While accusations about war criminality in areas of the Soviet Union occupied by the Nazis had been accepted as broadly plausible, Australian politicians could not accept what a few American courts had done in deporting war crimes suspects to the USSR. Anticommunism could no longer serve to trump the accepted broad moral claim, asserted by Reith in voicing the opposition's support in principle, that "the starting point must be that time should not be a bar to the prosecution of such atrocious crimes against mankind."[71]

Indeed, support for the legislative regime proposed by Labor was so deeply embedded in principles held by the Liberal Party and its MPs that Reith was able and willing to reject any concern over the question of the retroactivity of some of the bill's provisions. He did not accept Bowen's revised jurisprudential claim that the changes to Australian law were not substantively retrospective. Instead, he asserted that moral calculations about the substance of the alleged offenses could overcome any idea that an absolute abhorrence of retroactivity in criminal law was essential to maintaining the rule of law: "In the end, retrospectivity is a policy issue. In this case, there are competing policy interests, but there is no doubt in my mind and in the mind of members of the Opposition that the policy that criminals must be brought to justice must predominate."[72]

Nonetheless, the opposition did attempt to impose some extreme limits on the operation of the act. First, it sought a sunset provision for the war crimes process. Reith proposed first that the government be compelled to introduce indictments against any accused within three years and that the Special Investigations Unit that had already begun to operate within the Attorney-General's Department, following the recommendation of the *Menzies Report*, be wound up within two years.[73] Moreover, the opposition spokesman continued to voice serious concerns not just about the Soviet disrespect for the rule of law but especially about the vexed question of Soviet source evidence. As it stood in November 1987, the Hawke government seemed to be well on the way to implementing a legislative regime that would permit the substantive and detailed investigation of allegations about war crimes committed by persons now resident in Australia during the Nazi occupation of Europe. Community groups and political parties of all persuasions agreed in principle that moral condemnation of the Holocaust needed to be concretized within the criminal law. They were also in agreement with the idea that a criminal justice solution that granted jurisdiction to Australian courts and would include trials following Australian standards and rules was the only acceptable mechanism for dealing with alleged Nazi war criminals. The chapter of Nazi war criminals in Australia was no longer closed, but if the opposition were to have its way, it would not be open for long.

Substantive debate in the lower House proceeded along predictable and familiar lines. Speaker after speaker condemned the horrors of the Holocaust and echoed the idea that common human morality demanded justice. Liberal Party interveners nonetheless sought to highlight the left-wing bias that had informed the ABC broadcasts that had originally brought the matter to public awareness. They referred consistently to atrocities committed by Pol Pot in Cambodia and the situation in Afghanistan at that time as proof of the perfidy of Communist regimes. Doubts were expressed on both sides of the House about the reliability of Soviet evidence, but an overall faith in the capacity of Australian justice to deal with such issues was also expressed. The positive contributions to Australian society of various immigrant groups were highlighted, and calls were made for intergroup harmony as Australian society put its faith in the rule of law.[74]

At the same time, the opposition hammered away at the issue of Soviet evidence and arrangements being negotiated by Australian authorities to gain access to Soviet archives and witnesses. Liberal Member Phillip Ruddock expressed his party's views: "I regard it as a serious matter that we are addressing this Bill before there has been clarification about the nature of any agreement reached with the Soviet Union. I would hate to think our Prime Minster is going off to the Soviet Union to conclude, in some formal way, an agreement of which we have no knowledge or notice of here."[75]

Throughout the debate concern was raised about the possibility of prosecutors going to the Soviet Union, interviewing witnesses on commission, and having such evidence admitted into evidence at trial in Australia. In addition to the question of the coercive nature of the totalitarian Soviet state and the reliability of such evidence, issues were raised both about the ability of the defense to cross-examine such witnesses and about the jury's eventual capacity to judge the demeanor of the witness and the veracity of the testimony if the evidence were submitted without the witness being present in

Australia. Additional allegations that Soviet documents could be, and indeed had been, forged were also made.[76] All of these objections and queries about the investigative and trial mechanism were met with assurances from the government that war crimes prosecutions would take place within the system of Australian justice—Australian investigators would assess the evidence, wherever it came from, according to Australian standards; Australian lawyers, judges, and juries would weigh the evidence presented to them.[77]

One further aspect of the echoing presence of Australian anti-communism found its way into the debate and ultimately into the law itself. Liberal Party members demanded that the definition of the time of "occupation" that circumscribed the temporal and geographical ambit of the proposed legislation be amended to include the Soviet "invasion and occupation" of the Baltic states following the secret Ribbentrop-Molotov protocol.[78] Again, the element of irony can inform our own retrospective reading of events. There was no mention in these debates of the division and occupation of Poland and "Ukrainian" territories under the same agreement. At the time of the debate in Parliament, and as events would unfold, many of the allegations of war criminality that were being made and were being investigated related to Latvian, Lithuanian, and Estonian DPs who had entered Australia. Various representative bodies acting on behalf of these Baltic communities were active in lobbying government, opposition, and public opinion on the war crimes issue. The Liberal amendment was therefore perfectly understandable both in contemporaneous political terms and in terms of a broader and more pernicious anti-Communist rhetoric and historical narrative, which portrayed and deployed Soviet crimes as the practical, ideological, and moral equivalent of Nazi acts, including the Shoah. While the Labor government was reluctant to include such an amendment, realpolitik required them to do so.

The opposition kept up the anti-Communist orientation by attempting unsuccessfully to insert an amendment that would have legislated a prohibition on extradition to the Eastern bloc.[79] The bill then went to the Senate, where it received a first reading on 26 November 1987.[80] After a relatively short debate, the Senate agreed to an opposition motion that the bill be put on hold while certain relevant matters were referred to the Standing Committee on Legal and Constitutional Affairs.[81] The terms of reference for the committee precluded a substantive review of the law but did require the members to investigate some of the issues that had always been at the forefront of the narrative agenda about Australian war crimes law and politics, particularly in relation to Soviet evidence and related matters. The terms of reference required the standing committee to inquire and to report at the first sitting of 1988, Australia's bicentennial year of British "discovery," on the following related matters:

> (a) whether the general nature of the evidence and related material believed to be available in foreign states, in particular the Soviet Union and eastern European countries, is likely to be of sufficient evidentiary value to warrant the institution of any prosecutions (in inquiring into this matter the Committee shall not encompass the facts of particular identified cases); (b) if so, what procedures should apply to the collection of evidence in foreign states; (c) the most appropriate procedures for presentation of that evidence in an Australian trial; and (d) the most appropriate procedures for instituting and conducting war crimes trials, having regard to the need to ensure that there is no diminution of the normal standards of justice applicable in Australia.[82]

The committee invited submissions from interested parties and held public hearings on the questions in Canberra on 1 and 2 February 1988.[83] Once again, the themes are recognizable, as is the identity of those directly involved as witnesses and submitters to the committee. On the first day of hearings representations were heard from the ECAJ; the Baltic Council of Australia; Mark Aarons; S. Paul Zumbakis, an attorney from the United States who had represented several clients alleged to have committed war crimes in denaturalization and deportation hearings and author of *Soviet Evidence in North American*

Courts;[84] representatives from the federal Attorney-General's Department; and Robert Greenwood QC, who was in charge of the Special Investigations Unit.

The committee, and especially members from the opposition parties, were particularly active in getting from the government and SIU representatives the key details on the question raised in Parliament by Phillip Ruddock about the nature and content of negotiations being conducted by Greenwood with Eastern bloc countries on access to witness and archival evidence. Government representatives insisted on the general application of Australian rules and procedures to any investigation and/or case under the proposed legislation. They flagged to the committee what they saw as the key distinction between evidence that was available in the Soviet Union and evidence that was admissible before an Australian court. Only the latter would be ultimately relevant to a determination of guilt or innocence. They also emphasized the obvious fact that all evidence would be weighed by an Australian magistrate or judge at committal and trial and be subject to traditional practices of defense cross-examination and to the ultimate judgment by an Australian jury.[85]

The ECAJ equally placed its faith in the Australian legal system to operate under fundamentally fair rules and to arrive at a fair result.[86] Greenwood attempted to answer the committee's concerns but had to underline that no formal agreement existed at that time with any foreign government or prosecution authority. For him discussions or negotiations with foreign governments and officials were best conducted in relative privacy and not under instructions by a parliamentary committee.[87]

Members from all ethnic groups once again acknowledged the general principle of support for pursuing war criminals, subject to the formal guarantees of Australian criminal justice. But within this context they asserted that Soviet evidence, in the form of eyewitnesses and documents, was inherently unreliable and should be treated with great skepticism, if not excluded altogether as a matter of law. The Baltic Council, for example, argued in its submission that any agreement with the USSR would be useless because the Soviets would simply ignore any obligation that did not suit their purposes.[88] They asserted that all eyewitness statements and documents were likely to be the political product of Soviet interference or forgery and entered academic legal articles to support their contentions.[89] They also continued to highlight the position, already accepted by the government, that the defense be guaranteed equal access to Soviet witnesses and documentary evidence and that all proof be tested before an Australian court. The first conclusion of their submission established their priorities: "Soviet supplied evidence is unreliable."[90]

In their oral testimony before the committee they again asserted the basic principle that all evidence, especially that of eyewitnesses, be tested before an Australian court. "The obvious difficulty is how to distinguish the good evidence in these cases from the bad, keeping in mind the resources which the Soviet Union as a totalitarian state has at its disposal to falsify evidence should it choose to do so."[91]

The basic and most important questions that arise in the context of these submissions and testimony before the committee is whether the communities in question were in fact truly willing to admit to the presence of Nazi collaborators among their fellows in the first place and, second, if they really believed in bringing them to justice. For all their protests about an overarching commitment to the morally compelling pursuit of Holocaust perpetrators, the underlying theme of all the submissions from émigré groups is that all of this talk of war criminals was really no more than the continuation of a Soviet plot to embarrass and destabilize ethnic immigrant communities. The KGB manufactures documents and falsifies eyewitness statements either through intimidation or by other means. Allegations against individuals originate from Soviet authorities, and all evidence against them comes from the USSR. On top of all this, the focus on Nazi crimes ignores the real criminals in the KGB who committed equivalent crimes against national minorities and anti-Communists in the USSR.

These themes were repeated when representatives of the Croatian and Ukrainian communities appeared before the committee on its second day of hearings.[92] The Australian Federation of Ukrainian Organisations came succinctly to the point:

> We submit, that serious doubt already exists in Soviet supplied evidence and witnesses, and therefore should not be admitted. We further submit, that the Soviet Union has a special interest in providing any information to ensure that the "Nazi War Crimes" issue remains in the public eye, not for the purpose of obtaining justice but to divert attention from their own war (and other) crimes, and to create friction between ethnic communities in western democracies. The interests of justice cannot be served by the morass of deception, forgery, subornation and character assassination practiced in the Soviet Union.[93]

A new, or at least explicitly articulated, discourse in relation to the pursuit of Nazi war criminals emerges. The Holocaust is now rendered in scare quotes as "Nazi War Crimes" and is deployed by the Ukrainian Federation as a kind of trope for all the fictions and dirty politics that in their experience characterize the USSR. The Ukrainian evidence before the committee echoed and referred specifically to the argument about Soviet source evidence submitted in Zumbakis's work.[94] They also relied heavily on submissions by the Ukrainian community to the Canadian Deschênes commission.[95] Like the Canadian submission, authored by a lawyer who would later become a justice of that country's Supreme Court, the Australian Ukrainian's argument was largely anchored in the twin deployment of anti-Soviet, anti-Communist discourse and in arguments aimed at "decriminalizing" Ukrainian collaboration in the Holocaust. The strategy is again to set up an alternative historical and legal framework and to establish a narrative, within law, in which Ukraine becomes a dual victim of Nazi aggression and Soviet oppression. The real crimes of war were committed against ethnic Ukrainians. According to the Ukrainian community view, the dominant discourse around war crimes ignores historical truth. The complexity of war is thus reduced to the alleged criminal activity of a few individuals and then generalized and re-projected over a whole community. Meanwhile, the proposed Australian statute ignores Ukrainian suffering at the hands of the Germans and the Soviets during World War II.[96]

It is not surprising that, given the specific and limited terms of reference of the standing committee, with its focus on the issues surrounding Soviet evidence, such heavy emphasis was placed by many of those who appeared before it on anti-Communist discourse. At the same time, however, it is perhaps more problematic that the weight of submissions and of the questions of the members of the committee should have ignored assertions of such a historical revisionist tenor as those to be found in many of the submissions.

When the ugly specter of antisemitism appeared in a public and unreconstructed fashion, the members of the committee allowed it to pass without comment. The Hungarian exile lawyer Anthony Endrey, an Australian QC and former high-ranking legal advisor to the Australian Senate, not only repeated the standard arguments about Soviet and Eastern bloc lip service to legality but added a directly antisemitic flavor when he wrote: "Local Jews played a prominent part in the setting up of Communist regimes and the operation of Communist regimes and the operations of the secret police and this fact is well documented . . . Many Jews in these countries therefore committed serious inhumanities during the period covered by the Bill which would constitute war crimes under the provisions discussed above. A number of these Jews are now in Australia."[97]

The well-known canard that "the Jews" were the real criminals because the KGB and related Communist bloc secret police and security organizations were in fact run mainly by Jews is one that would find another resonance in Australian public discourse about history, multiculturalism, and Australian war crimes trials in a different but related context during the Demidenko affair. What is remarkable is that the Senate committee allowed this comment to enter into the public record of its proceedings without challenge or contradiction.

Likewise, the committee in its public hearings never properly explored evidence of Canadian and American practices in dealing with allegations about Nazi war criminals from Soviet sources. The Deschênes commission report and the experience of American prosecutors and courts was much more complex in relation to the issue of Soviet evidence than the submissions that formed the majority of the committee's public record would lead one to believe. Such evidence had been admitted before United Sates courts and subjected to cross-examination by defense attorneys without any substantive proof of a miscarriage of justice in any individual case.

In Canada the question had been well traversed before the Deschênes commission. Justice Deschênes had devised a succinct set of rules that he believed the commission would follow should it be called upon to gather or to consider such evidence. He concluded after extensive consultation, much of which was repeated to the Australian Senate standing committee, that "there is no reason in fact why evidence should not be sought and heard, even in Eastern Bloc countries. There is no reason of policy why this evidence should be automatically excluded. There is no support in jurisprudence why this effort should be stopped *à* [sic] *priori*. Thus the law, the facts and the jurisprudence point to the advisability of the Commission pursuing its efforts, even on foreign soil."[98]

The gathering of such evidence would be subject to rules and procedures that insured confidentiality to protect reputations, independent interpreters, access to original documents, and all previous statements by witnesses, unhindered examination of witnesses, the applicability of Canadian rules of evidence, and the videotaping of all witness examinations.[99] The United Kingdom war crimes inquiry, basing itself on the West German, Australian, Canadian, and American experiences and on its own meetings with Soviet authorities, would reach a similar position. The UK investigators concluded that Soviet evidence had been proven to be authentic and reliable and that it could be best tested by an English court according to ordinary rules and standards of evidence.[100]

At the time of the submissions by various parties about the inherent unreliability of Soviet evidence, German and United States courts had already relied on such materials within judicial systems that would be regarded as complying with shared rule of law values. The eminent jurist in charge of the Canadian Royal Commission had decided that, following appropriate domestic rules and procedures, such evidence could be reliably gathered and considered. Yet throughout this part of the Australian experience, from the submissions and testimony before the standing committee and subsequent parliamentary debates, the issue of Soviet evidence continued to be invoked in an effort to stymie the implementation of an Australian war crimes trial system.

The narratives, occurring within the narrow delegated power of the committee's terms of reference, which the committee permitted to stand largely unchallenged, presented a warped and ideologically biased tale of the perfidy of Communism and the KGB and ignored the substantive history of the Holocaust. Similarly, debates in both houses of Parliament had focused largely on ensuring that issues of the collective guilt of various immigrant communities be dismissed as inappropriate and on defining the exact nature of any possible agreement with Soviet and other Eastern bloc authorities under the general concern over Soviet evidence. While there had been comments from all sides of politics in Parliament about the moral abhorrence with which Australian society regarded the Holocaust and about the ethical demand for justice, and for the judgment of perpetrators, these morally infused discourses were soon replaced with a frame of narration that over and over again gave voice to doubts about the reliability and veracity of Soviet statements and documents. When taken in the narrow context of anxiety over justice and the integrity of the Australian judicial system, such concerns can be understood as being consistent with these principled domestic issues. If one were arguing that justice demanded war crimes prosecutions, then a morally and jurisprudentially consistent approach would also require that the norms and practices of Australian justice be followed.

Once again, however, two levels of difficulty—for law, morality, and history itself—present themselves within this framework. First, the inevitable tension between the specificity and horror of the Shoah and its placement within normal and standard discourses and practices becomes evident. The Holocaust is special, and the crimes associated with it demand justice even after the passage of decades. For some, such as Peter Reith, even retrospective legal changes are permissible as a matter of policy when confronted with the unique horrors of the Nazi killing of European Jewry. But normal rules of evidence and procedure, standards and burdens of proof, and so forth must all be deployed in order to ensure that criminal liability is imposed only within a recognizably ordinary criminal law system.

Second, the problem of Soviet source evidence then complicates matters both for the criminal justice system that must incorporate these "facts" into its ordinary operation and also for political and historical practice. The existence of a complex, massive, and contemporaneous Soviet system of criminal sanctions of Holocaust perpetrators, under the ESC system and subsequent perpetrator trials, offered a wealth of historical and legal evidentiary material. But the Soviet nature of these proceedings taints—from a variety perspectives, for different reasons, and to differing effect—the material evidentiary basis both for history and law. Inevitably in all of this, the specificity of the Shoah and the reality of the mass killings of Jews in the Nazi-occupied Soviet Union became submerged in more technical and focused debates on the admissibility and reliability of evidence in purely legal terms as well as within the broader, still powerful anti-Communist discourses of Australian politics.

In its formal report the Senate Standing Committee on Legal and Constitutional Affairs simply ignored all of these complexities and the substantive content of most of the submissions it had received. It opted for a simple solution, making recommendations, among other things, on technical amendments in relation to the availability of legal aid for accused persons. On the bigger question it simply confirmed the principle of "ordinariness" that had informed the debates on the war crimes trials issues in political circles from the very beginning. It recommended that "if the Bill is enacted and prosecutions brought for alleged war crimes, the normal rules of evidence and procedure be applied in any such trials."[101]

All other issues would be matters to be considered by the House and Senate when the government returned the bill to Parliament. As the siu continued its work, gathering evidence against alleged war criminals, the Hawke government hesitated to interrupt Australia's Bicentennial celebrations with public parliamentary debate about the Shoah. More than a year after the bill had been presented from the House to the Senate, on 15 December 1988, in the last few days of the parliamentary session before the long Australian summer break, the Upper House began its substantive consideration of Australia's war crimes legislation at the second reading stage.[102]

Anyone looking for the Senate debate to offer moral elucidation about the crimes of the Shoah and to give voice to Australia's overarching ethical duty to bring Holocaust perpetrators to justice would be disappointed. The unanimity of condemnation that had characterized the original debates in the House gave way to ugly partisan debate and the public elaboration of bad history. Opponents of war crimes trials have extensively studied the strengths and especially the weaknesses of war crimes trials both in terms of substantive justice and in the broader claims made by proponents to pedagogical status for the war crimes trial as "event." Whatever the merits of such analyses, what emerges from even this necessarily brief review of Australian parliamentary interventions in the field of Nazi war crimes and war crimes trials is the bankruptcy of that country's elected officials in staking out a normatively acceptable public, political position on the issues. Instead, we find public and permanently recorded narratives of antisemitism and politically motivated (in the worst sense of the term) revisionist histories. In this respect the Australian experience closely mirrors the most egregious parliamentary interventions in the Mother Parliament in London.[103]

Government members of the Senate attempted to argue for the bill in terms of justice and of the pedagogical effects such an enactment would have on a younger generation of Australians who had not lived through war.[104] But the opposition Liberal and National parties senators insisted on their own agenda, an agenda that did not adhere to their own parties' declarations of principle in the House a year earlier. Senators re-canvassed the issue of Soviet evidence and consistently deployed the well-known arguments about Soviet perfidy, falsification, forgery, and intimidation. The Liberal senator from South Australia set the tone early. He insisted on beginning his intervention by referring specifically to "Communist atrocities after the Second World War."[105] This statement was followed by assertions in relation to the Dresden bombings and an attack on the left-wing bias of the Australian Broadcasting Corporation. Other senators raised the obvious scare tactic that the legislation would be used to arrest and try Australian former soldiers for war crimes they may have committed. In doing so, they ignored the temporal and geographic limitations to the European theater of war and the substantive legal definition of the relevant offenses that required that acts that constituted punishable war crimes be carried out in pursuance of Nazi occupation policy. In raising this argument, senators echoed the ill-founded campaign waged by the Returned Services League (RSL, the Australian equivalent of the American Legion or the Veterans of Foreign Wars [VFW]) against the legislation.[106] But the rhetorical and potential political influence of references to maligned and endangered Australian "diggers" was too much to resist. The facts of the legislation were displaced by a narrow and absurd jingoist narrative that managed to find some purchase on talk radio and in the popular press.

A more general debate on adopting universal war crimes legislation would have had to deal with all these issues, but the Australian approach adopted by the Hawke government was much more limited and targeted very particular offenses. Any objection to such legislation on the grounds that it could cover Australian service personnel is in and of itself, without further elaboration, morally offensive. There can be no acceptable argument that Australians are by definition incapable of committing atrocities in time of war. Nor can any argument that they should be exempted because they were "our boys" be countenanced. But in the real context of the War Crimes Act proposal before the Senate at the time, any such arguments were factually irrelevant.

The limited scope of the legislation, however, did not stop opposition senators from making equally problematic assertions. Liberal Party senator from Victoria David Hamer continued to blast away at the "disgraceful" ABC broadcasts and to insist that advocates of the law "have an agenda which does not include the interests of Australia."[107] Hamer then went on to insist that Australian Jewry had forgotten about other victims of the Holocaust—Gypsies, homosexuals, and Communists.[108] Others invoked the case of the Cossacks murdered by Stalin when they were returned to Soviet jurisdiction, other Stalinist "genocides" and Japanese war crimes that remained unpunished. Still others resorted to more familiar narratives by invoking arguments about contingency and context. For them it was simply impossible for us to judge the complex realities that faced, for example, the people of Lithuania, Latvia, and Estonia because "we discover that many of the people from the Baltic states were caught in the middle of political turmoil in the course of events preceding and including World War II."[109]

Those Balts who served as police officers and who participated in the extermination of local Jewish populations are now portrayed in a radical parliamentary attempt to engage in the rewriting of the historical record, the same rewriting of the Holocaust in these countries perpetrated by various exile and émigré groups since the end of the war. Local police and paramilitary auxiliaries are presented as innocent victims and nationalist heroes, caught between the twin evils of Nazism and Communism. This continuous narrative thread of Communist oppression of the so-called Captive Nations was consistently used to hide the more significant truth of voluntary, willing, and often enthusiastic local participation in mass shootings of Jews.

Senator Hamer also brought barely concealed antisemitic tropes into the parliamentary narrative on Nazi war crimes. He argued that the instigators of the bill did not even originate in Australia. The Liberal senator from Queensland, David MacGibbon, for example, would refer to the bill as the product of Bob Hawke's payment of a debt to his supporters "who see it in an ideological way."[110] Senator David Brownhill from New South Wales adopted a Christian point of view and argued that forgiveness rather than retribution should be the Australian way.[111] Another opposition senator, Noel Crichton-Browne, simply accused the prime minister of having "locked himself into a group in the community."[112] When challenged to be more explicit, the senator did not hesitate to voice the sentiments that had implicitly underscored many interventions against the war crimes trial program from parts of the opposition benches: "By and large this legislation is intended to appease sections of the Jewish community."[113]

The ECAJ's earlier hope and its strategy of portraying the Holocaust and the war crimes issue in a way that would situate the question of legislative action at a high moral level of justice as the concern for the entire Australian community were confronted over and over again with blatant and barely concealed antisemitism. This was combined with a Cold War historiography that largely wrote the Shoah out of existence in favor of accounts that highlighted Captive Nations's suffering at the hands of Nazi and Soviet occupiers. Notwithstanding these pervasive discursive elements, the bill proceeded through the Senate and House.[114] The attention of Australia's legislators shifted to the actual operation of administrative elements of the war crimes investigation and prosecution system. An annual reporting requirement was placed on the SIU.[115] In late December 1988 Australia had a formalized legislative system for the investigation and trial of the alleged Nazi war criminals whose presence in the country had been signaled to government agencies forty years earlier.

THE WAR CRIMES ACT

It is important to highlight some of the provisions of the Australian statute that would have a substantive impact on the actual practice of investigating, charging, and trying the Berezowsky, Polyukhovich, and Wagner cases. The War Crimes Act's preamble offers a succinct summary of the outcome of the debates about pursuing alleged war criminals in Australia. It stated:

WHEREAS: (a) concern has arisen that a significant number of persons who committed serious war crimes in Europe during World War II may since have entered Australia and became Australian citizens or residents; (b) it is appropriate that persons accused of such war crimes be brought to trial in the ordinary criminal courts in Australia; and (c) it is also essential in the interests of justice that persons so accused be given a fair trial with all the safeguards for accused persons in trials in those courts, having particular regard to matters such as the gravity of the allegations and the lapse of time since the alleged crimes.

The general framework both ideologically and politically is again one that situates war crimes proceedings within ordinary Australian criminal justice practices while at the same time recognizing that important and fundamental moral and rule of law concerns inform the legislative scheme. Substantively, the act allows for the prosecution of "serious war crimes" that are defined in section 6 as "an act if it was done in a part of Australia and was, under the law then in force in that part, an offence" such as murder or manslaughter. A serious crime becomes a prosecutable war crime under the provisions of section 7 if it was committed either "(a) in the course of hostilities" or "(b) in the course of an occupation" and, according to subsections c and d, was directly connected to the conduct of war or occupation on behalf of a power conducting the war or occupation. Subsection 2 further imposes the requirement of a direct, rather than coincidental, connection with war or occupation. Subsection 3 imposes the "crimes against humanity," or genocide, element of international law that the act be done "(i) in the course of political, racial or religious persecution; or (ii) with intent to destroy in whole or in part a national, ethnic, racial or religious group, as such." Occupation is defined in section 5 to include in part "(a) an occupation of territory in Latvia,

Lithuania or Estonia as a direct or indirect result of: (i) the agreement of 23 August 1939 between Germany and the Union of Soviet Socialist Republics; or (ii) any protocol to that agreement."

The substantive provisions of the act embody the consequences of the political debates that gave birth to the legislation. Specific reference is found to the Ribbentrop-Molotov agreement, although in practice this provision would have no impact. More significantly, the act embodies the specific "Australianization" of the criminal offenses that would be investigated and pursued. The substantive offenses of murder and relevant ancillary offenses of aiding and abetting or being knowingly concerned in murder are defined as crimes that would have been subject to sanction under Australian law at the time they were committed, thereby avoiding any valid claim of substantive retroactivity. The offense that would be the focus of the three Australian cases would be murder and directly related offenses. The crimes of war that would be pursued would be "ordinary" offenses with which Australian judges, lawyers, and juries would be familiar.

The next stage of the formal legal structure is the one that incorporates the level of "specialness" of the crime. Simple murder, even of eight hundred people, is not enough. The murder must have occurred as a war crime —that is, as an act committed at a specific and legislatively limited time, in a geographically circumscribed space, and under particular circumstances. In other words, the murder must have occurred during war or occupation and in conditions in which the act was committed "in the course of political, racial or religious persecution; or with intent to destroy in whole or in part a national, ethnic, racial or religious group, as such." This aspect of the essential elements of a war crimes case under the act placed specific and onerous burdens on the prosecution.

In addition to establishing the circumstances surrounding a particular massacre that occurred in Ukraine more than forty years previously and proving beyond a reasonable doubt the defendant's participation therein, the prosecution also had to establish the facts of war and occupation as essential elements of the alleged crimes. It had to be proved that the killings took place in circumstances that related to the special elements—that is, in the course of persecution and/or with the intent to destroy an identified group. In the context of the Australian cases that went to court, this would mean introducing historical evidence of local collaboration in the execution of Nazi extermination policies aimed at Jewish populations. It would not be enough to prove that an accused person had killed a Jew or Jews. The killings had to be specifically linked to formal involvement in execution of the Final Solution, and each of these elements had to be established beyond a reasonable doubt by the prosecution. The existence of these "extra" essential elements highlights the special nature of war crimes and war crimes prosecutions. This is more than murder; it is murder under particular historical circumstances and for particular ideological, racial, or political purposes.

Prosecutors involved in such cases openly and willingly recognize that it is perfectly reasonable and in accord with our understandings of criminal justice and the rule of law that such additional elements be part of these special crimes and that the prosecution be compelled to establish each of the elements of an offense beyond a reasonable doubt.[116] Indeed, the attitude of those lawyers acting for the government is broadly reflective of the entire framework of the Australian war crimes cases. They were both special and ordinary. That the special character of the alleged offenses required extra police work, specialized expert testimony, and complicated legal argument was seen by the prosecutors and other members of the SIU team as perfectly natural and in accordance with normal criminal law practice.

It must be recognized that these special conditions clearly mean, in other words, that in writing about the three Adelaide cases, we are never narrating, studying, or explaining trials that are fundamentally "ordinary." The intellectual contradiction inherent in war crimes trials—between the special nature of war crimes, crimes against humanity, and the ordinary crime of murder, for example—makes itself apparent. Additionally, it is clear that such a burden puts the prosecution at a potentially crucial disadvantage in a jury trial. Besides establishing the ordinary elements of murder, prosecutors would in the three Adelaide cases also lead often quite technical explanations in evidence of the history of World War II, of the occupation of Ukraine, of the existence of a plan to exterminate Jews, and of the intentional participation therein of local auxiliaries.

Not only does such evidence challenge the attention and knowledge level of ordinary Australian jurors (not to mention trial judges or magistrates), but there is also a fine historical, jurisprudential, and legal line to be walked in leading such evidence. The danger is that some of the relevant evidence of historians on such matters as war, occupation, and collaboration that would go to this part of the prosecution's burden of proving elements of the offense might have an adverse impact on the other more traditional elements of the criminal justice system. For example, historically accurate and necessary evidence of the participation of Ukrainian foresters in Nazi occupation practices generally, and in the hunting down and killing of Jews in so-called antipartisan or antibandit operations more particularly, might seep unconsciously into the jurors' consideration of the actual culpability of a particular defendant such as "Ivanechko," Ivan Polyukhovich. Such a particular inference drawn from general testimony is deeply problematic within the rules of evidence and concepts of fairness that underpin the criminal justice system.

The Australian experience in the trials of Polyukhovich, Berezowsky, and Wagner would test all of these historical and legal assumptions that formed key parts of the political debate surrounding the adoption of Australia's War Crimes Act.

THREE

Law and History in Australian War Crimes Trials

Ukrainian Foresters, the Shoah,
and the Polyukhovich Case

Following the successful passage of the War Crimes Act amendments, which left little of the 1945 statute intact, the Special Investigations Unit (SIU) continued its inquiries. The files that were felt to contain the strongest evidence were sent to a leading Sydney criminal lawyer, Greg James QC, who reviewed the information and evidence and advised the Commonwealth's director of public prosecutions (DPP) on those cases that in his opinion could be pursued through the courts. The practice that was adopted conformed with the underlying ethos of the prosecution scheme that had informed the Australian war crimes process from its beginnings. The director of public prosecutions was careful to maintain investigative and prosecutorial integrity by calling upon an outside lawyer to act as an independent filter. The process was seen as one in which the normal standards of criminal justice would be applied, and only those cases with sufficient merit were to be pursued.[1]

In January 1990 Ivan Polyukhovich was arrested and became the first man to be charged under the new legislation.[2] Adelaide journalist David Bevan has recorded the entire history of the Polyukhovich

94

1. Ivan Polyukhovich and his wife outside court, Adelaide. © Newspix.

proceedings. Bevan witnessed the process from beginning to end and was present for virtually all of the court proceedings.[3] I shall not repeat his efforts here. Nor shall I detail the ultimately unsuccessful efforts of Polyukhovich's first set of legal representatives to challenge the constitutional validity of the act before Australia's High Court.[4] Polyukhovich was charged with having participated, as an armed for-ester (*heger*) employed by the German-controlled Ukrainian Forestry Administration, in the mass shooting of Jews during the liquidation of the ghetto in Serniki.

The area around Serniki, on the edge of the Pripet Marshes, had been Polish territory before 1939 and was incorporated into the Soviet Union following the Ribbentrop-Molotov agreement. In June 1941 the land fell to the Nazi onslaught of Operation Barbarossa. At the time, approximately 1,173 Jews lived in Serniki.[5] In the earliest days of the invasion, as in other parts of Ukraine, spontaneous pogroms broke

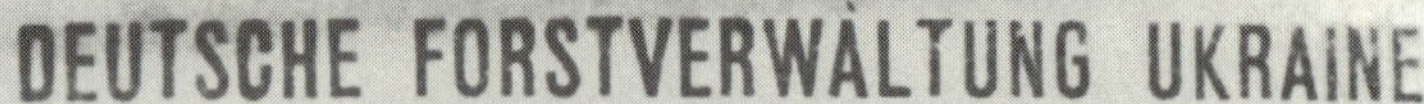

DEUTSCHE FORSTVERWALTUNG UKRAINE

FORSTDIREKTION LUCK — AUSSENSTELLE PINSK

NIEMIECKI

Zarząd Lasów Ukraina

Dyrekcja Łuck- Oddz. Pińsk

ГЕРМАНСКОЕ

Лесное Управление Украина

Дирекция Луцк - Отд. в Пинске

DIENSTAUSWEIS

LEGITYMACJA-УДОСТОВЕРЕНИЕ

Persoenliche Unterschrift — Własnoręczny podpis

Собственноручная подпись

2. ID card for Ivan Polyukhovich, Deutsche Forstverwaltung Ukraine (German Forestry Service Ukraine). Crown copyright. Used by permission of the Attorney-General, South Australia.

out. Members of the local ethnic Ukrainian population targeted and destroyed Jewish property and engaged in acts of physical violence, including murder, against their Jewish neighbors.[6]

In the first wave of German organized mass killings against Ukraine's Jews, from June to the end of August 1941, approximately 150 Jewish men from Serniki were shot. The Jewish population of many towns and villages in Ukraine, including Serniki, were later placed in ghettos, and in the summer and fall of 1942 these ghettos were "liquidated." At the time of the liquidation, in September 1942, approximately 500 of Serniki's Jews attempted to escape into the surrounding woods and marshes. Only 279, mostly young men and women, managed to find shelter in the forest. Another 102 of them died, including 10 to 12 Jews who were killed in combat as partisans.[7] The remaining Jews of Serniki were rounded up, shot, and buried in a pit on the edge of the village.

Ivan Polyukhovich was born in the village of Serniki in 1916. He lived for most of his life in Alexandrove, approximately five to seven kilometers from Serniki. He was employed as a forest warden and remained in that position under the occupation regime, in the service of the Deutsche Forstverwaltung Ukraine.[8] His principal functions consisted of patrolling the forests of the region to guard against poaching and the destruction and theft of wood. Polyukhovich's position is described alternatively as "gamekeeper," "forester," and "forest warden" in various siu files and in the transcripts of proceedings against him. During both the committal and trial hearings Professor Konrad Kwiet discussed the correct appellation for Polyukhovich's function at length. In German it is rendered as *heger*.

The prosecution would also allege that as an armed Ukrainian in the employ of the Germans, he participated in the hunting down, capture, and killing of Jews who had sought refuge in the forest as part of "antipartisan," or "antibandit," activities. The principal allegation against Polyukhovich was that he was the forester identified by eyewitnesses as "Ivanechko," who had taken part as an auxiliary in the mass shooting of the Serniki Jews during the ghetto clearance operation in the fall of 1942.

Like tens of thousands of other Ukrainian collaborators, Polyukhovich escaped with retreating German forces as the tide of the war turned. Together with his second "wife," Maria Andreyevna Polyukhovich, and her two children, Anna and Luba, he fled to Germany, where he worked as a farm laborer until after the war.[9] Like many of his counterparts, he, with Maria and the girls, became one of the mass of European DPs who emigrated to Australia in 1949.[10] In fact, Polyukhovich never married Maria. He had lived with his first and only wife for a short time in Ukraine before leaving her and taking up with Maria, with whom he remained for the rest of his life. The couple obtained a "Testimony of Marriage" document in May 1949 at a DP camp in Germany, shortly before leaving for Australia, but the information that they had married in Ukraine in 1935 was false.[11]

The narrative of Ivan Polyukhovich's life is in its most important aspects quite typical of the stories of any number of Ukrainian perpetrators. He continued his work as forest warden when the Germans took over in occupied Ukraine. He participated in the mass killings of his neighbors, escaped unscathed with the retreating German forces, and found a safe haven and peaceful life in Australia. The chapter of his participation in the Shoah, like that of so many others, seemed to have been closed—until Polyukhovich's two stepdaughters, Anna and Luba, returned to Ukraine to visit relatives in the early 1980s. The fact that he was living a peaceful existence in a quiet Adelaide suburb then became common knowledge in Serniki. The year 1986 was the fortieth anniversary of the Nuremberg Trials, and the authorities throughout the USSR ramped up their propaganda machine, once again highlighting the West's failure to live up to its international legal and moral commitments, recognized since the Moscow Declaration, to hunt down and punish Nazi war criminals.

The narrative of Ivan Polyukhovich's life becomes typical of the stories of any number of Ukrainian perpetrators. In December 1986 a public meeting of over five hundred people took place in the Culture House of the Zarechye district, the area around Serniki, in the Rovno region of the Ukraine SSR. Representatives composed a letter that was sent to the appropriate Australian authorities, demanding that action be taken against the Australian resident, Polyukhovich. The style and content of the letter were typical of Soviet propaganda discourse of the period in relation to collaborationist war criminals being protected in the West. They wrote:

> During the past war, this monster in human form turned traitor to his own people and became most actively involved in punitive missions against Soviet partisans and in beastly reprisals over civilian residents. He took part in the extermination of perfectly innocent people. Testimony rendered by numerous eyewitnesses show that the hands of this ruthless hangman are washed in the blood of some 50 humans which he personally tortured and butchered. One of Poliukhovych's most heinous atrocities is his participation in the shooting of 725 citizens of Jewish nationality at the village of Sernyky.[12]

Soviet authorities identified Polyukhovich as a Holocaust perpetrator who had found safety and peace on Australian soil. They kept up their campaign. A telex containing the allegations against Polyukhovich, with the names of identifiable witnesses, was sent to the local newspaper, the *Adelaide Advertiser*.[13] The paper then ran a series of stories repeating the allegations emanating from Ukraine.[14] At around the same time, Australian Broadcasting Corporation (ABC) journalist Mark Aarons was conducting a series of interviews, often in sub-zero conditions in the middle of the Ukrainian countryside, with potential eyewitnesses to Polyukhovich's crimes.[15] Those statements and other relevant materials were handed over by Aarons to the SIU.[16]

One broad issue that would figure in more refined forms at the core of the Australian proceedings against Polyukhovich was related directly to the Soviet practice of holding public meetings to denounce war criminals being sheltered by Western governments. Doubts would be raised, especially during the course of defense cross-examination of a number of prosecution witnesses, about the source of the witnesses' knowledge about Ivanechko, about Ivan Polyukhovich, and about Polyukhovich's identity not just as Ivanechko but as the Ivanechko who was seen at the ghetto liquidation. The defense established with some success that much of the knowledge claimed by various witnesses came from their attendance at the public meeting, where they heard the stories of the policeman Polyukhovich and his crimes. Others gleaned their knowledge from conversations that flowed naturally from public life and daily social intercourse in Serniki. The conflicts that might arise in terms of law, history, and testimony are clear. The public process of identifying and decrying the crimes of Polyukhovich, when reiterated within the interpretive domain of Australian criminal law, might be seen as having tainted in a real way the evidence of a number of witnesses. Moreover, the public spectacle of such meetings and the flourish in the language contained in the Soviet denunciation could easily find a place in the discourses of anti-Soviet groups, which would dismiss all accusations as machinations of the KGB.

Finally, the source of knowledge of facts in the cultural milieu of rural Ukrainian villages was understood differently by Australian law and by the witnesses who would travel from Serniki to Adelaide to testify at the committal and the trial of Ivan Polyukhovich. For these Ukrainians certain facts were known because everyone in the village knew them to be true. For them the question of how they came to know these facts was culturally irrelevant; they were simply common knowledge. In a criminal trial, on the other hand, the source of a fact being recounted by a witness is the most relevant question. Amid technical legal rules about knowledge and identity and in the confusion created during public attempts to resituate the debate in terms of Soviet perfidy, the truth about the fate of the Jews from the Serniki ghetto risked being forgotten.

It is not my intention to offer a full account of the Polyukhovich case, which involved extensive investigations in the USSR, Ukraine, and the Federal Republic of Germany, among others, a full committal hearing before a magistrate, and then a full jury trial in the Supreme Court of South Australia before Justice Brian Cox. Instead, I want to trace the more specific issues surrounding the intersections between the genres of law and history as they manifested themselves in the Polyukhovich proceedings. In doing so, I will highlight the apparent conflicts as well as the synergies between the two discourses and professional practices. The purpose of this particular examination is to offer the Australian experience as a case study of the difficulties and the strengths and weaknesses of the war crimes trial mechanism as either a pedagogical tool for teaching broad and accessible public lessons about the Holocaust or, more narrowly, of even achieving its stated political aim of bringing perpetrators to justice.

In the trials of Holocaust perpetrators these tensions, similarities, and differences are underscored because of the competing and yet complementary roles played by law and history in such processes. Additional complexity comes from the nature of the issues at stake for law, justice, and a fair verdict, the pedagogical function of such events, the place and role of the historian as expert witness, among other things. For Patricia Heberer and Jürgen Matthäus "the borderline between rendering justice based on specific charges and providing a forum for the public perception of monstrous crimes remains elusive."[17]

French historian Henry Rousso famously refused to testify as an expert witness in the Holocaust trial of the Vichy functionary, Maurice Papon. He asserted that the historical and judicial functions are inimical particularly because the latter must and should focus on issues of individual guilt or innocence, while the historian must normally refrain from issuing judgments on such issues. Rousso adds that because history is also always subject to revision, modification, and argument as new sources come to light, or new readings of old sources are offered, it would be too dangerous and inappropriate to offer or to accept the evidence of a historian as in any way offering the degree of certainty required for proof in a criminal trial.[18]

Others echo Rousso's concerns and highlight the distinctly different tasks of the prosecution lawyer, who starts from the provisions of the Criminal Code or the common-law definition of murder in such cases and argues the facts to fit that definition, or the defense attorney who seeks to exclude the client from the operation of such definitions. The historian brings an entirely different set of professional practices, background information, and context to the study of similar questions.[19] Another historian, Donald Bloxham, argues that a legal process such as a trial has by necessity a more limited focus on that which can or need be proved. Thus, it matters little to a prosecutor, in the technical scheme of things, if thousands were killed, if he or she can establish beyond a reasonable doubt that the accused is liable for a hundred victims.[20]

But two other interventions into the complex debates over the interactions between law and history offer potentially more interesting and perhaps more relevant perspectives on the context that emerged in the three Australian cases of Polyukhovich, Berezowsky, and Wagner. In his discussion of the prosecution of England's only successful war crimes case against Anthony Sawoniuk, Marouf A. Hasian Jr., a critic of such trials, underlines how the narrative structure of the unfolding proceedings offered important and contradictory stories about the events surrounding the accused's participation in the Holocaust.[21] This became particularly evident with the defense's decision to follow a strategy that included presenting an argument that portrayed the accused as a freedom fighter and led to Sawoniuk being put on the stand.

In his complex work on law, history, and the Shoah, Lawrence Douglas places a particular emphasis on debates surrounding the assertion that perpetrator trials (and prosecutions of Holocaust deniers) can and do have a positive pedagogic function and result.[22] Douglas argues that it may not be accurate to make blanket assertions, pro or con, about law, history, and the Holocaust. The International Military Tribunal (IMT) proceedings at Nuremberg, for example, created the legal concept of "crimes against humanity" that has entered the practice of international criminal law and popular understanding. The documentary record established as a result of the process at Nuremberg still informs both historical and legal scholarship. The trial of Adolf Eichmann in Jerusalem, some fifteen years after Nuremberg and following the creation of the state of Israel, served different pedagogical functions from the IMT proceedings, as did the later Israeli trial of John Demjanjuk.[23]

It is necessary, I believe, to see the Australian war crimes investigations and trials of the late 1980s and early 1990s through the prism of these two complementary insights from Hasian and Douglas. Different narratives are available and can be constructed according to the relevant circumstances. The pedagogic potential (if not the reality) of the trials of perpetrators can and does differ from time to time and from place to place. The Australian proceedings occurred in a time and place far different from the proceedings studied in Douglas's impressive work. Australia in the 1980s and 1990s was not conquered and occupied Germany, nor was it the State of Israel, with its own reasons for creating a public spectacle and discursive pedagogy about the Shoah and its perpetrators. The Australian intersection between law and the Holocaust, and historical narratives about each, had been informed by practiced deception in relation to the immigration policies of successive governments on both sides of politics; the chapter had been declared closed by Garfield Barwick; and the presence of Holocaust killers in Australia had been either declared irrelevant to the nation's understandings of the rule of law or been dismissed as Soviet propaganda. Public discourse had to a large extent been misappropriated by Captive Nations's anticommunism. History had been replaced by partisan sniping between Labor and Liberals about "Nazis" in one political party and counterarguments about atrocities committed by regimes on the left. The Australian Jewish community was eager to highlight the realities of the Holocaust while at the same time desperate to ensure that any action against perpetrators be undertaken because the issue was of direct moral, political, historical, and legal import to the country as a whole.

Whether any of these factors ultimately played a role in Australia's war crimes prosecution program or whether the cases of Polyukhovich, Berezowsky, and Wagner had any significant impact on the country's historical understanding of the Shoah, or its citizens' understandings of the connections between rule of law discourse and the Holocaust, are sociological, historical, empirical questions of some significance. But the underlying point, at this stage at least, is of at least equal importance. The Australian trials must be placed within their specific political, social, and legal historical contexts if we are to begin to understand them. Blanket and decontextualized assertions about the incompatibility of law and history are simply not ever likely to aid in our understanding of what happened in the Adelaide cases or in any other circumstances.

Another equally significant factor must also be considered. Douglas rightly points out that the proceedings at Nuremberg and in the Eichmann and Demjanjuk cases were not of a character familiar to the daily practice of criminal law in Anglo-American jurisdictions. The mixed English and civil law European heritage of the Israeli legal system and the very nature of the proceedings in the Eichmann trial, while clearly recognizable as resulting in a criminal trial, are distinct from Anglo-American process. Douglas also underlines that these circumstances do not mean that fundamental principles of fairness or justice were sacrificed.[24] But the issue of real significance resides precisely in the fact that the Australian cases took place under Australian rules of procedural and substantive criminal law. From the very beginning of the debates that led to the introduction of the War Crimes Act, all parties to the debate—the Labor government, the Liberal/National Opposition, the ECAJ, and the various Captive Nations groups—consistently asserted the principle that if Australia were to pursue alleged war criminals, the best and only acceptable mechanism would be one that applied Australian criminal law. The DPP took extraordinary steps to ensure that these principles and practices were followed. This is precisely what occurred in Adelaide in the Polyukhovich, Berezowsky, and Wagner cases. And this is precisely the specific juridical context in which the broader debates about law, justice, and history in relation to the Australian Nazi war crimes cases must be situated.

Hasian highlights the decision by the defense team in Sawoniuk to portray their client in a particular historical narrative of "resistance," which constructed both Nazis and Soviets as oppressors within a well-trod discursive terrain. Their choice to put him on the stand had both important practical consequences in relation to his guilt or innocence as determined by the jury and to rhetorical resonance about the ways in which the Holocaust was deployed and understood within the courtroom and beyond in journalistic accounts of the trial in the United Kingdom.

Stephan Landsman has underscored and highlighted the ideological, political, legal, and practical consequences of the choice to adopt a different strategy by defense counsel, the execrable Douglas Christie, in Canada's only Nazi war crimes prosecution, the case of Hungarian *gendarme* Imre Finta.[25] In that case the defense strategy was characterized by a barely disguised antisemitism and an underlying scent of Holocaust denial. This blemish was further exacerbated by the substantive provisions of the Canadian Criminal Code, which imposed on the prosecution a double burden in relation to the mental element of the offense, the *mens rea*. In essence the prosecution not only had to establish that the accused possessed the relevant intention to commit the underlying offense but that he intended to commit a war crime or crime against humanity. Without entering into a detailed technical legal analysis of the Finta case, a task completed admirably by Landsman, it is sufficient to point out that the entire legal context in which a particular criminal prosecution of an alleged war criminal occurs can and does have an impact on the legal aspects of the trial. Additionally, it can influence the place of history within the frame of the proceedings and the rhetorical and narrative elements about the Shoah that are reflected in accounts of the case. These elements then constitute the base of information produced in court that might serve to create the broad social and public pedagogical elements of such proceedings.

In the Australian context these elements would play crucial roles and fulfill vital functions in each of the three Adelaide cases. Polyukhovich went through a complete committal hearing before a magistrate. A committal resembles a preliminary hearing in the United States but can often go into far more detail about the prosecution's case than is usual in the American equivalent. In *Polyukhovich* the prosecution decided to present detailed historical expert evidence from Professor Raul Hilberg about the background to the Holocaust and aspects of collaboration in occupied territories. In addition, they chose to present extensive eyewitness testimony on each of the charges in the original criminal information. The prosecution was put to its proof in relation to each of the counts alleged against Polyukhovich. When he was arrested and originally charged, in January 1990, Polyukhovich was accused of having participated in eight different war crimes. He was alleged to have killed three women, one of whom known only as "Sercha," and Sercha's two daughters and grandson near Alexandrove in August or September 1941; it was said that he killed two other women and a child between June and September of 1942; he was charged with shooting three members of the Yankiber family, one woman and two men, again near Alexandrove during the same period; in September 1942 he was alleged to have killed one woman and three young children, aged fourteen, nine, and one; he was accused of having shot and killed "the miller's daughter" in the same month, also in Serniki; in April 1943 he was alleged to have killed members of the Turuk and Delidon families, who were discovered in the forest near the village of Brodnista; he was charged with having shot another individual named Pyotr Stephanovich Krupko and a woman described as "Tsalykha's daughter" in April or May of that year. And of course, he was alleged to have actively participated in the ghetto liquidation in Serniki in which "about eight hundred and fifty persons, who are not known but who are described as the Jews from the Serniki ghetto," were killed.[26]

Eight months later, on 7 August 1990, following extensive investigations by the siu in Europe, a new information was issued alleging other offenses, including the shooting of the two boys witnessed by the two partisans from Khokum's shed.[27] This information also contained more detailed references to the other essential elements identified in the War Crimes Act—war, occupation, the geographic location in Europe—that the offenses were committed in pursuance of the German policy of exterminating Jews. After a lengthy committal proceeding Polyukhovich stood trial on two counts of war crimes, one in relation to the ghetto liquidation killings and the other for murdering the miller's daughter in the aftermath of the pit shooting.[28]

Berezowsky and Wagner each went through the committal stage. Berezowsky was found to have no case to answer. The prosecution had been unable to establish even prima facie proof of his guilt, and his case came to an end. Wagner too went through a committal, and while the prosecution was found to have sufficient evidence to proceed against him at a full trial, he was granted a permanent stay of prosecution by the federal director of public prosecutions, Michael Rozenes, a Jew who had lost relatives in the Holocaust, when medical evidence was brought forward by his defense team indicating that his heart was too weak for him to stand trial.

Each of the three cases followed a different legal trajectory. One went to a full trial after committal, one ended at the committal stage when the prosecution could not meet even its minimal burden, and the third was called to a halt by the intervention the DPP "in the interests of justice." Each case therefore offers different insights into relevant legal, social, and ideological issues surrounding broader and less contextually sensitive discussions about law, history, and war crimes trials. Historians and historical expert evidence played a different role not just in each case but in different parts of each case. The burdens and tasks of the prosecution and defense at the committal stage are, for example, legally and practically distinct. The prosecution need only establish, and not beyond a reasonable doubt, that the accused has "a case to answer"—that is, that there is evidence of the accused's guilt to be considered on its merits by a jury.[29] The defense may and indeed often does use the committal stage to get its first real look at the strengths and weaknesses of the prosecution's case. It can test and probe witnesses, with the knowledge that if the case goes to trial, it will have a second kick at the can. It can also seek to have parts of the prosecution case thrown out on various grounds and challenge the evidence, as was the case in *Polyukhovich* in relation to a significant number of the offenses alleged in the information.

This technical legal aspect of what a committal hearing is meant to achieve also has distinct potential impact on the pedagogical function of the war crimes prosecution. A case before a magistrate, in a committal, is judged according to a different standard than that of a jury trial. Often different evidence is provided at this stage than what is presented at trial. It is possible that the lesser legal burden may translate into a lesser pedagogical impact of the proceedings more broadly.[30] Of course, part of this argument will depend on several layers of analysis. One must first accept that these trials have a hoped-for pedagogical function and/or that they have an impact at this level. Additionally, and perhaps more significantly for the Australian experience and context, the idea that committal proceedings, if the prosecution ends there—either because the prosecution does not meet its burden, as in *Berezowsky*, or because further proceedings are impossible because of supervening events, as in *Wagner*—have a lesser impact than a jury trial may depend on other factors.

Such an analysis is, for example, contingent upon granting an almost superior epistemological nature to the trial over the committal. At some level this condition will also require that the analysis cede an ideological status to the jury verdict that it might not necessarily warrant. The reason for this advantage, of course, goes back to old debates within law as well as familiar interventions about the differences between law and history. The fact that a jury finds an accused person not guilty does not mean by definition and to the exclusion of all other possibilities that the accused did not commit the crimes of which he or she was accused. It means in many cases that the jury was not convinced that the prosecution proved beyond a reasonable doubt that the accused committed the offense. Conversely, a guilty verdict does not irrevocably, except in the crudest positivist analysis, prove that the defendant did, to a metaphysical certainty, commit the act.

The questions go to the heart of the law/history/memory nexus. First, do we place historical facticity at the mercy of the vagaries of the criminal justice system? Clearly, there is a difference not just at the level of the particular nature of the focus of the two disciplines, individual guilt and a broader historical veracity, but one that goes to how we understand the idea of pedagogical function in war crimes trials. One might argue that they serve as a venue for broader education on general issues—for example, the Shoah in Ukraine, the realities of pit shootings, the implication of local auxiliaries in the killing of their Jewish neighbors—that form part of the context of the legal proceedings and which may inform some elements of the offense as defined in the War Crimes Act but which are ultimately independent from the legal outcome of a particular case. At the same time, of course, it is important never to forget another internal, self-replicating pedagogical function of law and of criminal law in particular. Whatever the outcome in such cases, at the same broad pedagogical level of analysis it is always possible to argue that law worked, that it pursued its own goals of determining guilt or innocence according to its internal and socially accepted criteria and practices.

In terms of public pedagogy it might also be possible to create an opposing argument, depending on the context, and to assert that because the nature of the evidence and the strategy of the two sides may well differ between committal and trial, that broader, more informative expert evidence about history and events surrounding the accused's acts might enter into evidence at the committal stage. In such circumstances it can then be argued that a committal hearing has a stronger general pedagogical impact than a trial in which such evidence might be subject to a more vigorous challenge.

At this stage it is not necessary to offer a definitive answer to the dilemma. It is simply important to highlight once again that all of the questions relating to the conflicts and synergies between law and history in Nazi war crimes trials are no doubt better addressed in the particular context in which they arise. While one must always seek to apply principled understandings, both lawyers and historians each recognize in the daily practice of their professions that context is everything and that without facts there is no context. I would argue simply that for both the lawyer and the historian the three Adelaide cases provide important opportunities for study and insight that are available only if one does not foreclose analysis by adopting some a priori position about law versus history.

When we compare the Australian cases with the English prosecution of Anthony Sawoniuk, we can note that none of the three defendants, who were represented for most, if not all, of the important proceedings by the same defense team of solicitors and barristers, would give evidence. There was no pretense by the defense that Ukrainian foresters, Schutzmannschaft, or other police auxiliaries were agents of a nascent Ukrainian nation-state, resisting both their Soviet and Nazi oppressors. While Polyukhovich gave an interview to police investigators of the SIU when he was arrested on 25 January 1990, his statements by and large were not inculpatory, and most were subsequently declared inadmissible.[31] The other defendants did not speak on any point of significance. What this means is that an alternative historical discourse about Ukrainian national history and suffering at the hands of the Soviets and Nazis, about freedom and nationalism, which was present in the Sawoniuk case in England in relation to neighboring Belarus, was entirely absent from the Adelaide hearings. There were no competing metahistorical narratives, or what Hasian calls "rhetorical vectors."

Likewise, the team of lawyers who defended the three accused—led by Michael David QC and assisted by Lindy Powell and David Edwardson—specifically rejected any proposal or idea that they would run a defense along the Holocaust-denying lines espoused by the Canadian lawyer Douglas Christie during a visit to Australia. They viewed the idea as repugnant.[32] Instead, they made the clear and conscious decision to conduct all three cases as ordinary criminal proceedings.

This meant that for them each case turned on the same issues as might arise in any other trial in Adelaide. The focus in *Polyukhovich* would center on his identity as the Ivanechko named by many of the witnesses as the perpetrator. He was, to put it simply and pass over many other important issues that also arose, for the defense lawyers not the man identified by the witnesses as the killer of Serniki's Jews. Likewise, Berezowsky's case would turn to a large extent on alibi evidence. Even if he were the Michael Berezowsky who belonged to the local Ukrainian Schutzmannschaft unit in Gnivan, at the time the killings of Jews of which he stood accused took place, he was attending special military training far away from the place where the shootings occurred. Wagner's case would depend to a large extent on the credibility and reliability of the eyewitnesses who alleged that he was present at, and took an active role in, the shootings of the *Mischlinge* children of Israylovka. The actual historical facts of the Shoah generally and of the shooting of Israylovka's Jews were not challenged by the defense.

Each case was treated by the defense as one involving basic and familiar issues with which Australian criminal defense lawyers dealt on a daily basis—it was not the accused but someone else; eyewitnesses are unreliable and mistaken; the witness has made inconsistent statements that challenge his or her credibility; the defendant was elsewhere when the crime is alleged to have occurred. Like the prosecution, they placed the trials within the broader context of normal Australian criminal justice. These rhetorical vectors are not, contrary to Hasian, ones that implicate either history or memory as these terms are commonly deployed in debates about Holocaust perpetrator trials. They raise issues of fact, of the burden of proof, and of the essential elements of each offense, the same questions that arise in every committal hearing and trial in every common-law jurisdiction in the world.

The defense did not ask for judgment about the Holocaust. The prosecution lawyers, the magistrates, the judge, and the jurors who heard these cases were never faced by a defense attack on history.

Historians were not challenged about their unprofessional, subjective biases against National Socialism, as Douglas Christie might allege. Instead, historical evidence was treated as all other expert testimony. Questions were raised about its relevance or its admissibility under the hearsay rules or about the sometimes fine line between providing historical context and offering facts that might tend to demonstrate individual guilt. When historical evidence wandered over the line from general explanation about what a Ukrainian *heger* might have been called upon to do, into territory that would imply a propensity attributable to the defendant to act in a certain way, standard rules of admissibility were invoked. There is an undisputed historical fact that Schutzmannschaft units and Ukrainian foresters hunted down and killed Jews. But law requires proof beyond a reasonable doubt that an individual, Ivan Polyukhovich, who happened to be a Ukrainian forester, was present on a particular day, at a particular time, and did certain acts that constitute the essential elements of the crime charged.

This does not mean that the cases were not extraordinary in other ways. The Adelaide proceedings shared in the ongoing conflict and tension between the special nature of war crimes and crimes against humanity and the necessity of using normal rules applicable to all criminal trials under the rule of law. The role played by historical experts in these cases would bear little resemblance to the way in which a normal murder case would have unfolded before a magistrate at committal or in the Supreme Court of South Australia. The very nature of the Australian legislation directly raised the question of historical evidence because it referred to war, occupation, and the Nazi policy of racial extermination as essential elements of the war crime offense. The prosecution would be put to its proof by the defense. While they did not challenge the historical facticity of the Holocaust, or of Operation Barbarossa and the German occupation of Ukraine, the defense team did demand that the prosecution offer historical expert evidence on key elements of the three cases. In Polyukhovich's case, in particular, the two worlds of law and history collided in intriguing and informative ways.

As the committal hearings approached, the team in charge of the SIU case against Ivan Polyukhovich expressed concerns about possible defense tactics. In November and December 1991 the SIU team contacted its overseas counterparts in Canada, England, Israel, and the United States, as they worried that Polyukhovich's lawyers were planning to challenge all historical expert evidence and to attack the admissibility of any opinion by historians that would seek to establish "that the crimes committed by Polyukhovich were in any way linked to or were carried out pursuant to the Nazis [*sic*] Genocidal policy towards the Jews."[33]

The defense did in fact adopt an attacking strategy in some of its cross-examination of Professor Konrad Kwiet, who was called as the principal historian/expert witness by the prosecution. The defense strategy, however, was not a frontal assault on evidence in relation to the existence of the Final Solution or its implementation in Ukraine. Instead, they interrogated the historical record in relation to their client's actions as alleged in the information against him and as recounted by eyewitnesses.

Before Kwiet offered his testimony, the prosecution proceeded to introduce authenticated copies of original historical, archival documents that they believed were relevant to establishing their allegations against Polyukhovich. A number of archivists were called to place the relevant documents into evidence, including Dr. Josek Henke, of the Bundesarchiv, Koblenz; Bruen Meyer, senior archivist, from the German Military Archives in Freiburg; Suzanah Pivcova, archivist in the Prague Military Historical Archive; Viktor Nikolayevich Bondarev, historian/archivist, from the Central State Archive, Moscow; Vyacheslav Selemenev, historian/archivist at the Central State Archive of the Republic of Belarus, Minsk; Tatyana Nicolayevna Franz, historian/archivist at the Zhitomir State Regional Archive, Ukraine; and Anna Vasilyevna Terebun, historian/archivist at the State Archives of the Brest Region of the Republic of Belarus.[34]

While the cooperation and appearance of West German authorities and the production of historical documents held in that country were hardly surprising, the fact that "historian/archivists" from Belarus, Czechoslovakia (as it existed at the time), Ukraine, and the USSR appeared before an Australian court in a war crimes case, producing as part of their testimony documents held since the war in Communist hands, was extraordinary. The entire debate surrounding the question of Nazi war criminals in Australia had from the late 1940s to the 1990s been informed by the Captive Nations's rhetoric of anticommunism. Always prominent in the narrative presented by various ethnic communities in Australia was the idea, indeed for them the indisputable principle, of KGB perfidy. According to this account, witnesses would be intimidated, and in the immediate context of the appearance of the archival authorities, documents would be forged in an attempt to discredit émigré groups. Without objection from the defense lawyers or the court, Soviet documents were admitted in an Australian criminal law proceeding.

Much of the credit for this turn of events must go to the director of the SIU, the late Robert Greenwood QC, who was in charge of running the delicate negotiations with Soviet and other Eastern bloc authorities for Australian investigative and legal access to witnesses and archives. The Senate Standing Committee on Legal and Constitutional Affairs had conducted extensive hearings and produced a detailed report on the issue of Soviet source evidence in any future Australian war crimes proceedings.[35] During the hearings Greenwood had been subjected to careful and lengthy examination about the state of discussions with foreign governments and on the subject of the assurances that he was seeking to avoid the possibility of intelligence agency trickery and deception as well as the application of Australian standards in any interrogation of witnesses.[36] Greenwood had been as forthcoming and reassuring to the committee as possible, but he had also insisted on the ongoing and delicate nature of his discussions with diplomatic and legal authorities in the relevant countries. The Memorandum of Understanding between the Australian Attorney-

General's Department and the Soviet Procurator's Office, formally agreed to in 1991 but operating in fact before that time, stipulated that each party, in the interests of the mutual pursuit of war criminals, would "co-operate in identifying relevant archival resources and specific material which may be relevant to an investigation; . . . furnish one another materials, archival documents, names of suspects and relevant information relating to suspects; . . . take evidence, if so requested and to the extent feasible, in accordance with the requesting party's rules of evidence; and . . . facilitate the travel of witnesses, experts and specialists to Australia and the USSR."[37]

In fact, SIU researchers were granted virtually unfettered and unprecedented access to Russian, Ukrainian, and Belarusian archives. Investigators and lawyers from both sides were permitted to travel to the Soviet Union, and later to an independent Ukraine, to conduct inquiries and to question potential witnesses formally and informally. While travel conditions, food, and accommodation facilities were often problematic by Australian standards, no participant in the process ever complained about Soviet obstructionism, coercion, or fraud.[38]

At the Adelaide committal hearing in *Polyukhovich*, the defense did not challenge any of the archival documents as they were admitted. The prosecution then submitted the written report compiled by the leading historian of the Shoah, the late Professor Raul Hilberg, which placed the documents tendered by the historian/archivists into a narrative context about the Holocaust in Ukraine.[39] The prosecution then called upon Professor Kwiet to testify about the documents and Professor Hilberg's statements. The committal proceedings therefore involved historical archival documents and a written historical narrative provided by Hilberg, supplemented by Kwiet's testimony. This is the legal, evidentiary context in which law and history had their first significant encounter in an Australian war crimes trial situation.

The Australian legislation established history as a key component of the essential elements of the charged war crime. The substantial and ordinary offense, in *Polyukhovich*, murder, becomes a war crime if and when it can be shown to have occurred, in Europe, during an occupation and in the pursuit of the Nazi policy of racial (or other) persecution.[40] In *Polyukhovich*, at the committal stage, the prosecution sought to introduce evidence through the archival documents and Kwiet's testimonial narrative about the Shoah in Ukraine as part of the broader Nazi Final Solution; the circumstances surrounding the killing of the Jews of Serniki in 1941 and in the ghetto liquidation of 1942; the identity of the German units in charge of the killings; the nature and functioning of Ukrainian Schutzmannschaft units and their possible participation in ghetto clearances, shootings, and the pursuit of escaped Jews; and finally, the nature and role of foresters, since it was alleged that Polyukhovich had committed multiple counts of killing Jews alleged in the original information (9, separate murders) and the modified version (11, different killing incidents) while working for the Deutsche Forstverwaltung Ukraine. It is not my intention to detail here the entire examination and cross-examination of Kwiet at the committal hearing. Instead, I will focus on several elements of his testimony that highlight the synergies between the disciplines of law and history and which also illustrate the disjunctions between the two professional practices and discourses.

One of the key pieces of evidence introduced through archival documents was the account of the German trial of Johann Meiss-lein. Meisslein was a German employee of the Organization Todt (OT), a multifaceted enterprise involved in the construction of Nazi infrastructure projects throughout conquered Europe, often using slave and forced labor.[41] As an engineer responsible for slave work-ers, Meisslein ordered the Lithuanian auxiliary police assigned as guards to his work unit to shoot two Jewish women who were physi-cally unable to carry out their jobs. He was reported for his actions and convicted by a German Military Field Court for exceeding his authority. The court held that "carrying out the shooting of Jews is, however, exclusively a matter for the police and the ss."[42]

Kwiet explained in his testimony that "not only permission, but authorisation had to be given to execute, and this was normally given by the security police and the ss particularly the security police, and was

in charge of jurisdiction in all matters for solving the Jewish problem.
There was no license to kill for any German, or non-German to go
around and shoot Jews."[43] Michael David homed in on this point in
his cross-examination of the historian:

> Q. A killing of a Jew that didn't comply with this would not be
> part of policy, would it.
> A. No.
> Q. It would not be part of policy because it was indeed made an
> offense.
> A. That's correct . . .
> Q. Do you yourself know of any situation where a Ukrainian
> policeman by himself has killed somebody, a Jew, and there is
> a record of it having been authorised.
> A. No, I have no record of that.
> Q. And if I could make the position perfectly clear; a Ukrai-
> nian policeman, any Ukrainian policeman in 1942 if he, for
> whatever reason of his own, killed Jewish people without
> complying with this order—
> A. He would be punished.
> Q. He would be punished.
> A. Yes.
> Q. And that would not be implementation of a German policy.
> You agree with that.
> A. I agree with it.[44]

To place the point beyond any doubt, David asked Kwiet:

> Q. You might have a situation in villages in 1942, small villages
> under direct surveillance, for instance private killings would
> take place that have nothing to do with war.
> A. Yes, but that would be murder not war crimes.[45]

The defense strategy on this point at this preliminary stage is
clear. Even if one were to accept, which the defense did not, that
Polyukhovich had committed the killings of Jews not related to the

ghetto liquidation and pit shooting in September 1942, the killings of one or two or three Jews he found in the forests around Alexandrove and Serniki in his job as a forester, the prosecution's own historical evidence, both in the form of historical documents including court transcripts and German orders dealing with the proper procedures for killing Jews, and Kwiet's expert opinion based on these sources, established that any such killings would, absent a specific order, have been contrary to German policy. Therefore, shooting Jews scattered in the forests around Serniki could not, as a matter of law, fall under the definition of a war crime as found in the legislation. If Polyukhovich shot Jews he found in the forest, even if he shot them because he did not like Jews, these actions were not part of the policy of extermination under the command and control of the Nazi occupiers. In this hypothetical situation established as matter of historically accurate principle by the defense, Polyukhovich would have been an antisemitic murderer but not a war criminal as defined in the Australian legislation under which he was charged.

Another key element of the law/history nexus is also evident in this part of Kwiet's evidence. The source for historical knowledge about the hierarchy of command and control on the question of who had the power to kill Jews is a German Military Court record. Law informs history, which then informs law some fifty years later in Adelaide.

A similar line of attack on the state of historical knowledge was mounted in relation to the position and function of foresters in hunting down and killing Jews who had escaped to the woods in and around the Pripet Marshes in the Serniki area. The prosecution attempted to establish through Professor Kwiet's testimony that Ukrainian foresters had actively participated in various antipartisan and antibandit activities as part of the ongoing German policy of eradicating Ukraine's Jews. The defense sought again to demonstrate that while foresters were enlisted as scouts and guides for other forces because of their familiarity with the wooded terrain, and while they did report sightings of "bandits" encountered during their patrols, the actual killing of Jews was not part of their official functions.[46] Again, the defense questioning was aimed at laying the groundwork for an argument, should it become necessary, that if any such killings were proved, they could not constitute war crimes because they would have taken place in a context that exceeded the legal powers invested by the Germans in foresters, as established in the prosecution's own historical documents. According to this interpretation of the historical facts, a Ukrainian *heger* such as Polyukhovich was not authorized by the Nazi authorities to kill Jews on his own initiative. If the evidence established that he did kill Jews whom he found hiding in the forests, his actions were not part of Nazi policy and therefore not covered by the War Crimes Act.

This question of law and legal limits imposed on Ukrainian auxiliaries by their German hierarchical superiors as a historical fact was raised throughout Kwiet's testimony. Kwiet was more than willing to agree that the historical record established that a system of military and police hierarchy existed in occupied Ukraine and that jurisdiction and power over the Jewish question had been explicitly vested in the security police. Indeed, the prosecution had to lead such historically verifiable evidence because it had to meet the burden of establishing the mirror opposite of what David and his team were attempting to gain from Kwiet's testimony. The prosecution had to demonstrate the hierarchical and ordered nature of the Nazi military/police administrative mechanism in occupied Ukraine in order to prove both that a Nazi policy for exterminating Jews existed in that territory and that it was carried out in the manner alleged in the information, with the assistance of local forces. Only by proving all these elements of the history of the Shoah in occupied Ukraine would the prosecution be able to establish the essential elements of the war crimes offense under the act. But Kwiet the historian was distinctly uncomfortable with the idea that the Nazi system in Ukraine was a system of "law."

When Kwiet was being examined about the Meisslein case, for example, the magistrate intervened to inquire whether this was "the application of some sort of German law." "Yes," Kwiet replied, "if you call that law. Then it applied to this region, and anyone, German or non-German, who let's say of his own free will, decided to kill a Jew, was brought to trial if this particular action was reported. Those actions happened, yes. But the individual was then brought to court, if reported."[47]

Kwiet rejected any notion that the shootings of the Jews in Ukraine were in any sense understandable in Australia as a case of extrajudicial killings "if they were sanctioned and ordered by the security police, or if they were carried out with a certain action which was commanded by the ordinary police, or the commanding officers, then there was no action taken against those who participated in the killing. On the contrary, they followed the orders."[48]

The magistrate's desire to find a jurisprudential category with which he might be comfortable came into conflict with the historian's more contextualized and sensitive understanding of the relevant circumstances as involving not "law" versus "non-law" but an internal German issue over who had jurisdiction to order the killing of Jews. When the magistrate returned to the question of which law was administered by the German Gendarmerie in occupied Ukraine, Kwiet informed the court that they applied German military and civil regulations published by the relevant occupation government authorities. While German civil and penal law applied to Germans, the killing of Jews took place outside the narrow conceptualization of formal legality proposed by the magistrate.

> A. So, the German law, if you like, in the Ukraine, but this law did not make any reference to the killing or extermination of the Jews.
> Q. You understand my question in relation to the German civil code, don't you.
> A. Yes. If you like, the civil code applied of course, to the behaviour of German personnel. If they did something wrong, they were punished according to German law, but the killing of Jews if authorised and sanctioned, was not punished.[49]

Other aspects of Kwiet's testimony highlight the confrontation between historical inquiry, on the one hand, and standards of judicial proof, on the other. On many of the key questions surrounding events in Serniki, from which military and police units had jurisdiction over the village to the even more pertinent issue of which German unit conducted the ghetto liquidation in September 1942, the historical documentary record is silent. All historians of World War II will of course be aware of the destruction of many documents either deliberately in the panic of retreat and defeat or accidentally through other acts of war. The absence of a paper trail from the German administration concerning Serniki is therefore unsurprising and far from unusual. The village of Serniki was also a backwater during the occupation. It was largely bypassed during Operation Barbarossa because there was no significant Soviet military presence with which the Germans had to concern themselves.[50] In addition, the area around the Pripet Marshes was not suitable for mechanized armed vehicles. Cavalry units were called upon to patrol the area and to deal with "saboteurs," "looters," "bandits," and "partisans" (Jews) in the area.[51] But the historical record in terms of documents that refer to Serniki is itself minimal.

During his testimony Kwiet was often unable to provide definitive responses based in documentary evidence that could be presented to the court. As a result, he was compelled to testify about the local military command structure in uncertain terms: "Once the administration had been firmly established my guess is that the village of Serniki fell under the jurisdiction of the orstkommandantur in Sarny but I'm not absolutely sure about that."[52]

While Kwiet as a historian would have preferred specific and identifiable documentary references on which to base his expert opinion, he was nonetheless still acting as a historian in offering his analysis of the command and governance structures from which he could conclude with a reasonable degree of historical certainty that the case was as he described it. But as Michael David pointed out to Kwiet in his cross-examination:

Q. Historians and lawyers have different criteria. You might
have realised that.

A. I have realised that.[53]

This exchange between the lawyer and the historian occurred in a
particular context of Kwiet's testimony that brought the two professional discourses into stark contrast. At the same time, the precise
context of this part of Kwiet's evidence highlights, better than any
other, the important synergies between the two disciplinary narratives
of the Holocaust in Ukraine and the symbiotic relationship that has
developed between law and history in this context. Significant parts
of the SIU's case against Polyukhovich, concerning events in and
around Serniki, were themselves based in legal, judicial sources, in
addition to the crucial Field Court decision in relation to jurisdiction
over killing Jews. SIU historians, particularly Kwiet and Martin Dean,
had conducted research in West German police and judicial archives
dealing with that country's investigations of alleged war criminals
that had taken place especially during the 1960s and 1970s.[54] Some of
those proceedings and investigations involved mounted cavalry units
that had been active in anti-Jewish actions in the Pripet Marshes,
in and around Alexandrove and Serniki. Australian historians and
police investigators then used these German judicial files for two
interconnected purposes, each of which went to the construction of
a complex set of institutional practices and discourses that brought
together history and law.

The sources themselves were both legal and historical—that is, they
were created and uncovered in the course of West German legal efforts
to investigate and prosecute war criminals for offenses committed in
occupied Ukraine. This undertaking involved legal interrogations,
police investigation, and the establishment of a historical record.
The Australian process piggybacked on these efforts for similar and
related historical and legal purposes. Kwiet constructed a historical
narrative about the killing of Jews around Serniki that would ground
some of the essential elements of the war crimes offenses of which

Polyukhovich was accused as well as adding to historical knowledge about the Holocaust in part of occupied Ukraine. At the same time, this historico-legal record established by West German investigators and courts in the 1960s and 1970s would allow Australian historians and investigators to identify potential witnesses who might have been present at the ghetto liquidation in Serniki in September 1942. In this feedback loop of investigation, trial, investigation, and trial, history becomes law, which is then transformed, in part at least, into history, only to be retranslated, in another circumstance years later and thousands of kilometers away, into law again.

When the evidence was presented by Kwiet during his committal testimony, however, the disciplinary practices and boundaries, both internal and interdisciplinary, between law and history again presented themselves in the legal context and interpretive frame of a criminal proceeding under Australian law. What Kwiet could present to the court, for example, was not historical fact as demonstrated in a concrete document that stated clearly and unambiguously that a named unit, on a particular day, enlisted local Schutzmannschaft units and other local help and killed one hundred Jewish men from Serniki in 1941. Instead, what he could testify to was his professional reading of the German investigative and trial material, based in his intimate and long-term knowledge of the Holocaust, from which perspective he could draw conclusions based on the available evidence. Speaking of Cavalry Unit 2, Kwiet essentially offered an informed guess:

Q. And who commanded that particular Cavalry Regiment 2.

A. An ss leader called Magill, and in particular, or of particular significance are the mounted units. It is my opinion that there was a third squadron, and within that the third group entered the village of Serniki in early August of 1941. In expressing this opinion, I am not relying on any concrete historical evidence, but my opinion is based on the evaluation of investigative material.

Q. What investigative material is that.

A. In the early 60s the West German judiciary conducted a trial against Magill and others, and in the course of these investigations, as well as of the trial as such, reference was made to the route via Serniki. And there is one particular evidence given in this trial where the name Serniki appeared, where one member of the third squadron, third group recalled and remembered that his platoon went to this village of Serniki.[55]

Kwiet relied on similar evidence to establish the approximate chronology of the ghetto liquidation in Serniki in 1942, of which no written record exists, and to identify the Germans in charge of the mass killings. He testified that he and Martin Dean had spent three or four years examining every piece of juridical and investigative evidence relating to ghetto liquidations and that his conclusions were based on this research.[56] His conclusion about the numbers of Jews killed in the liquidation actions was based on similar evidence.[57]

In addition to exposing the absence of a documentary record relating to the killings of Jews in and around Serniki in 1941 and 1942, Kwiet's testimony also reveals a problematic lacuna that will exist in every attempt to engage in the process of translating and reinscribing legal evidence into a historical frame that must then be retranslated and re-reinscribed into legal discourse. Serniki was simply ignored by West German investigators and prosecutors in their pursuit of German war criminals. In all likelihood they did not possess sufficient historical and geographical knowledge to identify the liquidation of the ghetto, for example, as an event of significance. Because it was not a subject of legal inquiry, the historical record is as a direct consequence impoverished.

Likewise, the West German records begin a priori with the same difficulties that face every historian (and lawyer) involved in investigating war crimes cases and relying in part at least on testimony of the (alleged) participants. They will seek to minimize if not deny their involvement and to offer other varieties of self-serving evidence.[58] Most of the police interrogations of surviving members of the cavalry unit reveal that individuals appear to have spent an inordinate amount of time in Serniki feeding and grooming their horses and looking for food for themselves. Very little if any time was spent in antipartisan activity (hunting for Jews), and when the unit did engage in such activities, they arrived too late to do anything because by then all the partisan activity had ceased and the enemy had fled. Perpetrator witnesses may also attempt to shift responsibility for the actual killings to local Schutzmannschaft units. In *Polyukhovich* this question of local participation in mass shootings was of course a key issue as far as the defense was concerned. David pressed Kwiet on his method in relation to the German postwar investigative and judicial material, particularly given the fact that many of the cases never went to trial and were abandoned.[59] The issue of law versus history was brought to the fore.

Q. Would you, as an historian, say that the reading out of statements that were presented at those trials to obtain information for this chart is not a strict historical way of historians doing it.[60]

A. I would be in a better position if I could rely my judgment on strict evidence. Since the evidence is not available due to the loss of these reports—put it this way, I'm convinced that there have been reports produced from all the various units involved reporting about the result but this material is not available. In that sense I have to rely on other material which, strictly speaking, is of less significance than strictly historical evidence.[61]

On the specific question of the extent of the historical record on the involvement of local police units in anti-Jewish *Aktionen* and the related and important methodological issue of how he evaluated testimony on this question, Kwiet highlighted the context and subtleties of understanding that a good historian would be able to bring to any reading of the West German judicial material: "That depends how honest and open the answers were. As a result I say many Germans

TABLE I

Ghetto liquidations around Serniki, autumn 1942

○ **DROHOTSCHYN**
September
c. 1,500 dead

○ **JANOW**
September 24–25
c. 2,000 dead

○ **PINSK**
October 29–November 2
16,000–20,000 dead

○ **SERNIKI**

○ **LUBESHOV**
Early August
c. 1,600 dead

○ **WYSOCK**
September 10
1,600–1,700 dead

○ **KAMEN-KASCHIRSK**
about August
c. 2,000 dead

○ **RAFALOWKA**
August 29
c. 3,000 dead

○ **SARNY**
August 28
10,000–17,000 dead

○ **LACHWA/KOZANGRODEK**
September 3
1,500–1,600 dead

○ **MIKASZEVICHE**
September
1,200–1,300 dead

○ **LUNINIEC**
September 18
1,000–1,500 dead

○ **MORROW**
August
280–300 dead

○ **DAVID-GRODEK**
September 9
1,200–1,300 dead

○ **STOLIN**
September 12
c. 5,000 dead

Source: Based on a table prepared by Konrad Kwiet
outlining ghetto liquidations around Serniki.

denied any participation in the evidence and tried to blame the locals. Some were very honest on that. A few even made no fuss about their participation but there is, of course, the overall tendency in the statements of denying any actual participation."[62]

He added that testimony about local participation was credible historically because of the established facts that the Germans' manpower was limited and their capacity was too stretched to have permitted them to carry out the ghetto liquidation killings without local assistance.[63]

Finally, Kwiet highlighted an essential weakness in the West German record, emphasizing a potential difficulty in relying on such instances to create a complete historical or even an accurate legal account of responsibility. This difficulty goes back to the point made by many historical critics of war crimes trials more generally that the focus in such trials is on what can be proved against a particular defendant or particular defendants. Because West German prosecutors were concerned with the modalities of execution only at a level of generality and because their focus was on the participation of the Germans who had been accused, they simply did not pursue evidence about the identity of local participants in the killings of Ukrainian Jews.[64] The identity of such perpetrators was historically important but legally irrelevant in the cases being pursued before West German courts. As a result, the West German investigative and trial material could not provide the direct evidence required by the Australians. In the case of Polyukhovich the identity of local killers was both historically important and legally relevant. Context, as they say, is everything.

THE TRIAL: LAW, HISTORY, AND UKRAINIAN FORESTERS

The intersection of law and history at the trial of Ivan Polyukhovich was again determined by an amalgam of the demands of each discipline in the particular context of the trial itself. Because the trial took place before a jury, the prosecution made an early strategic decision to limit the number of historical documents it would introduce as part of its case.[65] It did not want to distract jurors' attention from the basic facts of the case against Polyukhovich by burying them under an avalanche of technical historical documents about the nature of the Nazi state and the bureaucratic civilian and military administration of the Holocaust. The prosecution team relied instead on the testimony of Raul Hilberg to set out both the larger context of the Nazi plans to implement the Final Solution and the broad strokes of the mechanics of the Shoah in Ukraine.[66] This background would then be supplemented by the written and oral testimony of Konrad Kwiet, whose evidence would focus on the operation of the forestry service in Ukraine, Polyukhovich's employment as a *heger*, and the involvement of the forestry service in the Final Solution in Ukraine. A significant portion of Kwiet's testimony was to be based on newly uncovered documents relating to the Forestry Administration in Ukraine, discovered in the Brest archives by local researchers in the course of giving assistance to Australian investigators. On this underexamined aspect of local participation in anti-Jewish actions in Ukraine, law had served as the motor behind the revelation of previously unstudied documentation on the ways in which this part of the German administrative structure in Ukraine fit into the Nazi plan for the economic exploitation of the natural resources of occupied Ukraine. In addition, of course, the records revealed the extent to which foresters, both Germans and indigenous Ukrainians, had played a key role in combating partisans and bandits in the wooded areas of Ukraine and in hunting down hundreds of Jews who had escaped the ghetto liquidation process and sought shelter in the forests and marshes.

Key to Hilberg's largely unproblematic testimony at trial was his description of the nature of the process of carrying out ghetto liquidations—digging pits; surrounding and cordoning off the area; arresting and amassing Jews; shooting them and stealing their property; covering up the pit.[67] In his written statement he declared: "Sometimes elements of police battalions stationed in an area were also available for shooting operations. If, however, police forces were still insufficient to carry out an assignment, a variety of volunteers could be drawn from the German staffs of the civil administration or form [*sic*] native employees, ranging from interpreters to foresters."[68]

At a level of historical generality Hilberg's evidence served to establish that indigenous personnel, from police (Schutzmannschaft) to foresters, could be and were called upon to participate in killing operations. The problem that faced the court, the prosecution, the counsel for the defense, and Konrad Kwiet, however, was how to translate the level of historical generality about local participation in the Holocaust in Ukraine into proof beyond a reasonable doubt that on a specific day in and around Serniki in September 1942, an identified forester, Ivan Polyukhovich, known locally as Ivanechko, was present at and participated in the pit killings of over eight hundred Serniki Jews and the mopping-up operation that involved the shooting of the miller's daughter and the two Jewish children on the same day. History had to be made, insofar as this was possible, to fit within the terms of the "Statement of Offense."

At the beginning of his testimony Kwiet went into some detail about the organizational structure of the Forestry Administration and the various documents identifying Polyukhovich as a *heger* employed by the administration.[69] The prosecution then sought to lead Kwiet through a series of discoveries he had made in the archival record documenting the participation of indigenous Ukrainian foresters in antipartisan, antibandit, and anti-Jewish actions in the forests of Ukraine. At this stage the confrontation between law and history came to the fore. Following a defense objection, the jury was withdrawn, and a lengthy voir dire argument and hearing took place concerning the nature and extent of the permissible historical expert evidence to be offered by Kwiet.[70] In addition to legal argument from both sides and lengthy interventions by the trial judge, Konrad Kwiet was called back to proffer his evidence and the documentary record in support of his historical opinion so that a determination on the subject of its admissibility could be made.

This proceeding within the trial, a voir dire hearing on the legal limits of admissibility in relation to the historian's evidence, takes up significantly more space in the trial transcript than does Kwiet's actual testimony in the presence of the jury. Before detailing the most important aspects of the legal/historical debate that took place in the Supreme Court of South Australia, it is perhaps worth underlining once again the importance of context in all discussions of war crimes trials, law, and history. Little of Kwiet's research into the operation of the Forestry Administration in Ukraine and the involvement of foresters in tracking down and assisting in the killing of Jews would be admitted into evidence that could be considered by the jury. The public record of the trial of Ivan Polyukhovich offers little in the way of expert historical analysis of one key and understudied aspect of the Shoah in Ukraine and the role of this subset of indigenous collaborators in hunting down Jews. But the transcripts of the voir dire hearing and the documents introduced as part of Kwiet's historical testimony do contain all of these elements.

While the trial did not reach the public pedagogical level many proponents of such procedures might have hoped for and while the absence of such historical detail may well have had an impact on the final jury verdict in the case, it is nonetheless true that the Polyukhovich trial in its broader sense opened up new avenues of historical inquiry and research into the Shoah in Ukraine. It brought to light never before studied documentation about the role and function of the Forestry Administration generally and about the hunting down of Jews hiding in Ukrainian forests. If one places the analysis of the history/law conflict in this context, away from the technically legal aspects of the rules of evidence and the positivist analysis of the outcome of the criminal justice process, then there was and is a clear positive benefit to history that could only have been derived from the existence of the SIU and the War Crimes Act processes in Australia. Only an overestimation of law, which at the same time would require its reduction to a narrow positivist definition, would allow one to assert that the Polyukhovich case was a negative experience in terms of Holocaust historiography. Where one might place *Polyukhovich* in a broader analysis of the broad public pedagogical role and effect of the criminal law process is quite another question.

If we return to the actual confrontation between law and history at the level of the voir dire hearing itself, a different, and perhaps more traditional, set of arguments was invoked. The defense interrupted Kwiet's testimony at the stage of the introduction of his analysis of the historical documents setting out the involvement of foresters in antipartisan operations in the areas that they patrolled.[71] The defense position did not attack the historical accuracy of the evidence per se. Instead, the team asserted that such evidence was in the case at hand irrelevant and/or more highly prejudicial than probative.

The offenses with which Polyukhovich was accused at trial related only to events on the day of the pit killings as the outcome of the ghetto liquidation. The numerous other charges that had figured in the original information, many of which related to isolated killing events involving Jews hiding in the forests, had been stayed or dismissed for a lack of probative evidence at an earlier stage of the proceedings. Therefore, the only evidence that was relevant for the defense was that which related to the presence of the accused at the pit killings outside Serniki in September 1942. Evidence led by a historical expert about the participation of foresters in hunting down and killing Jews in so-called antipartisan or antibandit operations could, they argued, only have the effect of creating in the minds of the jurors the idea that Ukrainian foresters had a propensity for killing Jews. That would then lead to the legally unfounded conclusion that someone with such a propensity, such as Polyukhovich, would have had a good reason to have been present at the mass shooting of Serniki's Jews.[72]

The prosecution attempted to counter these arguments by asserting that it was seeking to introduce this kind of historical evidence to demonstrate that there was a policy of exterminating Jews, as it was required to do under section 7 of the War Crimes Act, and that indigenous foresters had participated in this policy. In other words, the historical evidence offered by Professor Kwiet went directly to essential elements of the offense and to their burden of proof in such cases. Because it was directly relevant to legal and factual issues at the heart of the indictment, Kwiet's testimony was, according to the prosecution lawyers, obviously admissible. The prosecution was attempting to create a legal buttress around the historical evidence by claiming that it was bound by the very definition of the war crimes offense to offer such proof. In doing so, however, the prosecution ignored two key elements of the legal context in which the debate was occurring, two elements that themselves go to the synergy of law and history in the Australian war crimes trial context.

The *Polyukhovich* defense team eschewed the obscene full frontal attack of the historical facticity of the Shoah. South Australian criminal procedure and evidence law provided, among other things, that "a person may admit on his trial any fact alleged or sought to be proved against him, and such admission shall be sufficient proof of the fact without other evidence: Provided that the admission shall be made by the accused either personally or by his counsel or solicitor in his presence, or, in the case of a body corporate, by its counsel or solicitor."[73]

Pursuant to this provision, Polyukhovich had already agreed that many of the elements of the war crimes offense as defined in the act were true and would not be contested. The defense admitted and was legally bound by that admission on the existence of the German policy of the Final Solution and that "this policy was implemented throughout the Pinsk area in a systematic way by shootings."[74] The defense further acknowledged the historical, and legal, truth that a ghetto had been created in Serniki, pursuant to the German policy of the Final Solution, and that in September 1942, "in implementation of the German policy of extermination of the Jews of Europe and with the intent to destroy the Jews of Serniki, not less than 550 Jews of Serniki were murdered by a German execution squad and their bodies placed in a mass grave."[75]

As a result of these admitted facts, the prosecution claim that Kwiet's testimony was essential to establish the basic elements of the war crimes offense has to be given a highly restricted interpretation. In effect, the policy that the prosecution was attempting to prove through the evidence of Konrad Kwiet was more specifically the policy of Forestry Administration involvement in the mechanics of the Final Solution in Ukraine. The problem again is the potential conflict between whatever probative value such evidence has insofar as essential elements of the offense are concerned and the potentially damaging effect of allowing the jury to hear that Polyukhovich's employers had a policy of participating in killing Jews. The prosecution argued that Kwiet should be allowed to testify to the fact that historical documents proved that foresters went on Jew hunts in the woods and that they sometimes guarded Jewish slave laborers, because such Jew hunts and the use of Jewish slave labor were intimate elements of the overall plan for the Final Solution. The prosecution sought, in other words, to introduce evidence about Forestry Administration involvement in order to paint a broad picture of how foresters were involved in their ordinary activities in anti-Jewish persecution and in the Shoah. All of these claims were and are historically true. The trial judge, Justice Cox, recoiled at such sweeping assertions and widely construed historical evidence: "But that is not really what it is all about. It is all about a pit killing at which you say this individual, whatever his occupation might be, participated in a way that made him criminally responsible in two particular respects. Now, he happens to be a forester and, understandably, you deal with that. That fits in. But let's not lose sight of the fact that what it's all about is whether some identified individual assisted in that killing."[76]

Following a similar intervention by the judge during Kwiet's examination on voir dire, the prosecution changed tack slightly and attempted to make the broad historical evidence more specifically applicable to the accusation against Polyukhovich.[77] This argument again highlights the importance of context and the contested and contingent nature of any law/history nexus. The prosecution now placed Kwiet's evidence about the Forestry Administration and foresters' involvement in various aspects of the Final Solution not in terms of its original argument about its positive burden to establish all essential elements of the war crimes aspect of the offense but, instead, in terms of an evidentiary preemptive attack on a possible argument of the defense.

In this version of why expert historical evidence from Kwiet about foresters and the Final Solution was admissible, the prosecution addressed the core issue of the accused's presence at the pit killings. It did not do so in terms of any specific historical documentary evidence that Kwiet could introduce about Polyukhovich at the pit because no such document exists. Instead, lawyer for the prosecution Grant Niemann put the case in terms of what the defense might assert. He argued that Kwiet should be permitted to give evidence about foresters' involvement in aspects of the Final Solution because the defense might, in the absence of such proof, argue that, as a forester, Polyukhovich had no reason to be present at the pit killing.[78]

The defense had admitted that a massacre had occurred at Serniki in September 1942 and that it had, as had other events in the Pinsk area, taken the form of a pit shooting. But the defense admission is also carefully worded to insist that "not less than 550 Jews of Serniki were murdered by a German execution squad."[79] Hilberg's unchallenged evidence made specific reference to the use of police and Ukrainian auxiliaries if ss security units did not have sufficient manpower to carry out the liquidation operation. At the committal stage much of Kwiet's evidence had related to his attempts to identify, by means of deductive reasoning, the actual German unit in charge of the Serniki liquidation. Some of the eyewitnesses against Polyukhovich had identified him as a "policeman," while others insisted that he worked in the forest. The public meeting in Ukraine that resulted in the letter from the people of the USSR to the Australian government about Polyukhovich in December 1986 spoke of Polyukhovich as a member of the "German-Ukrainian police force" and as a "former policeman."[80]

Much of Michael David's cross-examination of Kwiet on voir dire would emphasize the German command structure in relation to responsibility for implementing the Final Solution.[81] The cross-examination focused on the fact that local participation was subordinated to the German security apparatus and that Ukrainian participation in mass killings was largely limited to local police, Schutzmannschaft, units. In other words, a key aspect of the defense position was that if Ukrainians were involved in the shootings, they would have been members of the police, not foresters. Much of the evidence from the eyewitnesses, however confusing and contradictory it might be, as well as statements at the public meeting, identified Ivanechko as a policeman. For the defense team the inference from all this evidence was clear. Ivan Polyukhovich was not that Ivanechko, the killer at the pit, because that Ivanechko was a policeman and Polyukhovich was a *heger*.

David then extracted an important historical fact that would determine to a large extent the nature of what Kwiet would be allowed to present to the jury:

> Q. In all of your research—and I realise and accept that you
>   can only produce some documents to the court, otherwise
>   it would be very difficult, but in all your research, have you
>   found, a document where an indigenous forester is involved
>   in a pit killing?
> A. No.[82]

In addition to establishing the historical fact that there is no recorded instance of a Ukrainian forester having been present at a pit killing, the cross-examination of Konrad Kwiet on voir dire is important for another reason. It demonstrates that history, and the narrative authority of an expert witness, can be used to equal effect by either side in a war crimes case. It is obvious that, given the nature of the definition of a war crime found in the Australian legislation, the prosecution had to rely on historical expertise and documents to establish many parts of the essential elements of the offense. David's cross-examination, both during the trial itself and on voir dire, uses Kwiet's testimony to undermine several interrelated aspects of the prosecution's case.

Kwiet's introduction of various official documents identifying Polyukhovich as a *heger* in the Forestry Administration casts doubt on the various eyewitnesses who had testified, often in contradictory fashion, about Polyukhovich having been a policeman; about him wearing, or not, a police uniform; and about him carrying a submachine gun. David carefully established through Kwiet and relevant German documents that foresters had very limited and extremely well-regulated access to firearms. They were authorized to be armed only in exceptional cases, and in most instances they were provided with a shotgun or, even more rarely, a hunting rifle. Kwiet's expert testimony about the historical record in relation to the Deutsche Forstverwaltung Ukraine and the German hesitancy about arming Ukrainians served as an effective way to cast doubt on much of the eyewitness testimony identifying the defendant as Ivanechko, the armed policeman, and statements placing him at the pit. In addition, by establishing that he was a forester and not a member of the Schutzmannschaft unit, Kwiet placed Polyukhovich in a professional occupation unlikely, or less likely than a policeman, to have been present at the killing pit. Finally, the admission by Kwiet that there was no recorded instance of a *heger* having been present at a pit killing greatly weakened the prosecution's case.

All of this testimony demonstrates what should be self-evident but is often missing from many important debates about the nature and role of Shoah-related war crimes trials and about the proper (if any) role of professional historical narratives in such proceedings. History, its defenders assert, knows neither guilt nor innocence. To employ the disciplinary narrative of history in such legal proceedings will only distort the criminal process and the goals of the professional historian. But in this case, on these facts, or at least in the very limited context of David's cross-examination of Kwiet, history, the historical record, and the methodology of the professional historian created a legal discourse both about a general truth on the subject of Ukrainian foresters and pit killings and potentially about the more specific truth of the shooting of Serniki's Jewish population.

Following the cross-examination of Kwiet, the judge heard submissions from the prosecution and the defense on the extent to which the historian's testimony should be heard by the jury. The defense again insisted that most of the evidence about foresters or the Forestry Administration using forced labor and/or engaging in antipartisan warfare was irrelevant in a case in which the accused was charged only with participation in a pit shooting and its immediate aftermath. The prosecution continued to assert that most of Kwiet's evidence was admissible because it was directly relevant to the issue of the Deutsche Forstverwaltung Ukraine's ongoing, regular, and active participation in killing Jews. Professor Hilberg's testimony, largely unchallenged by the defense on this point, had, they argued, established that the German practice was to draft indigenous assistance in ghetto liquidations.[83] Kwiet's evidence complemented that argument by providing more detail about the use of forestry employees and officials. Grant Niemann conceded that the antipartisan warfare issue per se was problematic given the specific charges against Polyukhovich and would not be pursued. But he maintained the position that the more general issue of "the involvement of foresters in the implementation of the policy vis-à-vis the Jews" was nevertheless central to Kwiet's testimony and to the prosecution case.[84]

Similar arguments and objections surrounded another aspect of Kwiet's potential evidence as well. Documents had been uncovered relating to Polyukhovich's move from Alexandrove to Pinsk with his second "wife" and children and their subsequent evacuation to Germany as the Wehrmacht retreated. The prosecution attempted to introduce this evidence in order to further establish Polyukhovich's identity and to trace his movements from Alexandrove to Adelaide. For the trial judge, however, much of this evidence smacked of "really oblique propensity evidence or bad character evidence." "You are likely to be of bad character aren't you," he posited, "if the Germans are treating you as a good friend. That is the whole point of your evidence isn't it?"[85]

The prosecution attempted to save this part of Kwiet's testimony by arguing that it was in essence biographical information and possible identity evidence. The lawyers argued that there were other reasons, such as fear of Communism, that might equally explain flight westward, but their assertions were in vain. Defense counsel hardly had to interject at all on this point as Justice Cox ruled that Kwiet would not be permitted to introduce this evidence in front of the jury.[86]

The real point of contention then came down to the specifics of what Kwiet could lawfully say about Ukrainian foresters in the presence of the jury. As an expert witness, he could express his opinion on matters within an accepted realm of his professional expertise, but even that was subject to strict limits. He was of the opinion that foresters would have been and probably were present at pit killings, despite the absence of any written account.[87] Other parts of his testimony as well as that of Hilberg had highlighted the large-scale destruction of German records during the war. Pit shootings in Ukraine in the second-wave killings were largely undocumented in part because of aspects of German policy that wanted the facts about the killings to be closely guarded and partly because of conditions on the ground, not the least of which was the particular mobility of the units involved in the liquidations of ghettos in the region around Serniki in late 1942.[88]

Even if a report of the killings at Serniki had existed, it would not necessarily or likely be so detailed as to record the presence and assistance given by a lone forester named Polyukhovich. Other historical records established that foresters participated regularly in anti-Jewish actions in the areas they patrolled. Therefore, because of this information from available historical records, Kwiet could easily have formed the professional opinion that Polyukhovich could have been present at the pit. But the prejudicial value of such informed, professional opinion was clear. It offered indirect but powerful evidence against the accused. It was evidence by deduction. For the trial judge the solution was beyond doubt: "I don't think it is going to be before the jury."[89]

But on the more general issue of local or indigenous assistance in ghetto liquidations, the court was inclined to the position that Hilberg's evidence permitted Kwiet to add some more detail on the point without getting down to the specifics of the pit killing at Serniki.[90] "I can't see, for the moment, any ground on which you could be stopped from showing that the Germans couldn't possibly have done this operation alone, or even that that is highly likely to be the case and, therefore, they would have needed local assistance, and I don't know whether you can exclude the possibility that local police assistance would have been adequate. That is the next step, I suppose."[91]

The debates about the extent and nature of permissible evidence to be offered by Konrad Kwiet highlight several facts about the broader concerns of the intersection of law and history in the conduct of the Australian war crimes trials. It is obvious that an overarching set of rules about the admissibility of evidence and burden of proof always establishes the broad limiting framework in which all such historical evidence can and must be seen in any war crimes trial in which law establishes the ultimate hermeneutic frame. A trial is, and must be, a legal proceeding. Second, it is also clear that these issues are never predetermined or absolute in nature. Legal argument is set out by both sides, and by the judge, and in this instance Professor Kwiet is called back to offer further clarification of the historical record and therefore of the available proof. As the facts evolve, the legal and historical narratives themselves change, both separately and in a synergistic fashion.

Indeed, assertions about the very nature of the role of expert evidence were challenged by the defense. When the prosecution stated that it was attempting to use Kwiet's testimony to elicit proof of the existence of a policy involving the Forest Administration in the implementation of the Final Solution, defense lawyer Michael David countered, somewhat problematically, that because Kwiet's evidence, like that of Hilberg, established that the German practice in organizing ghetto liquidations and the accompanying pit shootings involved a series of ad hoc decisions that depended on local context and circumstances, that historical evidence demonstrated the absence of a policy. As a result, there could be no general and accepted historical opinion about the process to which Kwiet could legitimately testify.[92] David qualified Kwiet's testimony as an amalgam of "anecdotal evidence" that was outside the normal area of historical expertise.[93] On the general methodological issue the trial judge was (correctly) unmoved. He found that it was indeed precisely within the nature of a historian's professional expertise to piece together disparate elements and draw deductions from them.[94]

To settle the substantive question raised by lawyers on both sides during argument about what the historical record actually could show about local participation in ghetto liquidations, the judge had Kwiet recalled to testify once again on voir dire.[95] The focus this time was on the participation of members of the indigenous population in addition to the Schutzmänner in such events. This questioning would determine the extent to which Kwiet could testify to the jury about the historical record relevant to this case on the issue of the presence of a forester at a pit killing in the absence of any specific reference to such a fact in any known historical document. Kwiet offered an extensive review of the archival record documenting the use of the local population, *der Bevolker*, largely in the form of local guard units (*Wachmannschaften*) or auxiliary police (*Polizei*) but not limited thereto.[96] After hearing Kwiet's extensive explanation of the historical record, Justice Cox set out the limits of evidence Kwiet would be able to offer the jury when it was called back: "My inclination in this most sensitive, debated area, is that the witness is entitled to say that, in carrying out their policy of exterminating Jews and partisans in occupied territories, the Germans sometimes had the assistance of local indigenous people from the villages, not just police. There are instances of forest wardens assisting in this way, but no record of any indigenous forest warden being involved in a pit killing."[97]

The formulation arrived at by combining the historical record with the law's rules of evidence was not demonstrably false in terms of a historical narrative of the Shoah in Ukraine. Neither was it demonstrably complete. Konrad Kwiet was distinctly uncomfortable with the rules of the legal game. His experience in *Polyukhovich* has convinced him that lawyers are not really interested in the truth.[98] Indeed, the exchanges that took place between the historian and the judge embody in this concrete context of an Australian war crimes trial the discomfort, not to say the outright objection, articulated by those historians who have spoken out against the admixture of the two disciplines.

> PROFESSOR KWIET: If I can't answer the question, is the prosecution then allowed to address these questions in a way I can answer "yes" and "no"?
>
> HIS HONOUR: Yes, they know what you may permissibly say and it may be it will all be done in a sort of agreement, a conspiracy, to enable you to put it in this way, we will see.
>
> If you are embarrassed by a question because you think you are under constraint and that stops you giving an honest answer, you can send a silent signal to Mr. Niemann and he will understand and we will get the jury out.
>
> PROFESSOR KWIET: This is the strict limits in which I have to answer?
>
> HIS HONOUR: Yes.
>
> PROFESSOR KWIET: Even if I would disagree.
>
> HIS HONOUR: Yes, you probably do disagree. You probably think the evidence shows more than that.
>
> PROFESSOR KWIET: That's correct.[99]

Justice Cox reformulated and refined the permissible scope of Kwiet's evidence by clarifying that he could only say that, as part of carrying out the policy of the Final Solution, the Germans sometimes called upon local assistance. More precisely, he could state, "There are recorded instances of indigenous forest wardens or guards, hegers, assisting in this way, but no record of any indigenous forest warden or guard being involved in a pit killing."[100]

Cox again warned Kwiet that he could not stray from the formulation even if he disagreed with it. The establishment of the limits of what could and could not be said in a court of law in front of the jury in a criminal trial was the job of the judge, and like everyone else in the courtroom Kwiet must take care to adhere to the ruling.[101] The trial recommenced in the presence of the jury, and the prosecution led Professor Kwiet through the historical record in order to establish that indigenous personnel had played a role in carrying out the Final Solution during the ghetto liquidations around Serniki.[102]

During cross-examination defense counsel highlighted the contingent and contextual nature of the evidence to be called in war crimes trials and the use to which expert opinion evidence could be put by all sides. Again, David sought to elicit information from Kwiet about who was in charge of the ghetto liquidation. More specifically, he attempted to glean evidence about which German unit controlled the killings. Kwiet offered not fact but his professional expert opinion, as in the reality of a limited legal framework he was entitled and called upon to do.

A. This is my opinion—and I can only express an opinion since there is no written record on the execution of the ghetto of Serniki.

Q. But this is your historical opinion, is it?

A. It's my historical opinion, is based on the knowledge of surrounding pit killings at the same time, and the time factor, as well as the geographic and logistic factors, must indicate that the units stationed in the environment of Serniki must have conducted the pit killing of Serniki.[103]

The exchanges between the defense lawyer and the historian in front of the jury in *Polyukhovich* embody and highlight at least two key lessons that emerge from this case. First, and most obviously, historical expert evidence has a role to play in such proceedings. Historical evidence is not just relevant in a broad or even a narrow sense of the charges to be proved or challenged. It can, within obvious limits such as those set after the voir dire, take place at a level acceptable to the professional self-understandings and narrative structures of history. The absence of a documentary record of the ghetto liquidation at Serniki did not and could not prevent Kwiet from applying the skills and methodologies of the professional historian to the available evidence. In doing so, he was able to deduce enough information and to construct a convincing narrative about the German unit most likely to have been in charge of the operation. This is, as Justice Cox himself stated, exactly what historians do. While Kwiet was prevented from doing everything he would have wanted to do as a historian at the trial, he was able to do what historians do in this small, more limited, and legally restricted context. Moreover, in the broader context of his historical inquiry not constrained by the laws of evidence, he could and did undertake a historical review of previously unstudied primary source material and was able to construct a historically relevant examination of the role of the Forestry Administration in the Final Solution in Ukraine.

The second important element for any analysis of the law/history nexus, or the dissonance between the two disciplines, that emerges from this cross-examination of Konrad Kwiet is that at some important level history can be successfully deployed by either side in an Anglo-American criminal proceeding relating to war crimes. The construction of a competing narrative was clearly at the center of the defense strategy in *Polyukhovich*. By placing the primary responsibility for pit killings generally on Germans, assisted by Schutzmannschaft, the defense was able to tell a historical story that placed primary liability for the pit killings at Serniki on people other than their client. There was no denial of the Holocaust, no obfuscation of the horrors of ghetto liquidations as real historical events. Instead, there was a combination of facts placed within law and history to tell a different story. This story was grounded in law and in history, in the credibility of eyewitness identification evidence, in the narrative of German and Schutzmannschaft participation.

It was again an intriguing and perhaps instructive combination of law and history within a broader narrative structure that always asserted that this was an ordinary criminal case. Could the prosecution put Polyukhovich at the pit on that horrible day in September 1942?

Was he Ivanechko, or were the witnesses confused about policemen and foresters, about the color of uniforms and the weapons carried by a *heger*? It would have been impossible to create this alternative argument without Konrad Kwiet's evidence about German reluctance to give firearms to Ukrainians or the Brest and other archival documents about Polyukhovich's employment as a *heger*. The defense team could not have adequately created doubt about their client's identity without being able to rely on the established record about the nature of Schutzmannschaft uniforms, which could then be contrasted with apparently contradictory eyewitness accounts of Ivanechko's appearance or without historical expert evidence of primary German and local police involvement in ghetto liquidations. Without history there was no case for either the prosecution or the defense.[104]

FOUR

Mikolay Berezowsky

The Case of "The Witness Who Knew Too Much"

Mikolay Berezowsky of Royal Park, South Australia, was arrested by police attached to the Special Investigations Unit SIU and charged under section 9 of the War Crimes Act. The case against him was in many ways reflective of the historical understanding of the practicalities of massacres in Ukraine. The indigenous police, the Schutzmannschaft, typically functioned in the preliminary stages of the *Aktion* by surrounding the village or ghetto and rounding up the local Jewish communities. The prosecution alleged that Berezowsky was a member of the Schutzmannschaft in the village of Gnivan in the Vinnitsa area and that he had participated in rounding up the village's Jews as part of the *Aktion*, in which 102 individuals were "liquidated."[1] Berezowsky was accused of having been "directly knowingly concerned in or party to the murder." The charge did not go specifically to his personal involvement in the pit killing but to his role in the arrest and confinement of the Jews of Gnivan leading up to the actual shootings.

As in the Polyukhovich case, the defense adopted a strictly legalistic strategy. The lawyers did not contest the historical facticity of the

3. Mikhail Berezowsky leaving the court, Adelaide. © Newspix.

Shoah generally, nor did they dispute the existence of the pit killing of the Jews of Gnivan. During the committal hearing they did not put the prosecution to its burden of demonstrating that the Gnivan killings were part of the broader Nazi plan to exterminate European Jewry to any real extent. The definitional elements of the war crimes offense under the operative Australian legislation never really came to the fore in the historical parts of the case. Instead, the defense once again sought to conduct the committal as an ordinary proceeding for the crime of murder in South Australia. They focused on two essential elements of any criminal prosecution, the identification and identity of the accused as the individual named by the witnesses against him and, more significantly, on the defense of alibi. The prosecution, on the other hand, sought to rely heavily on expert historical evidence, grounded primarily in captured German documents, in order to establish the timing of the *Aktion* in Gnivan and to identify the accused as a member of the local auxiliary police.

The information alleged that the mass shooting of the Jews of Gnivan occurred "between the 1st day of March 1942 and the 31st day of July 1942."[2] The defense team argued that at a significant time during this period their client could demonstrate that he was not in Gnivan. A key focus of the examination and cross-examination of the two historians who gave expert testimony in the case, Jonathan Steinberg, then of the University of Cambridge, and Martin Dean, then of the Special Investigations Unit (SIU), would be aimed at establishing with a greater degree of historical certainty—or perhaps more accurately, probability—the date at which the pit killing outside Gnivan took place. History in the trial of Mikolay Berezowsky would once again be invoked not at the macro level of the historiography of the Nazi regime and the broad strokes of the Final Solution as planned and implemented in Ukraine but at the more specific levels of the relationships between and among the German security forces, the local German police, the Gendarmerie, and the Ukrainian Schutz-mannschaft and of the determination of rank and authority within the indigenous police force.

In this aspect of the nexus between law and history the Berezowsky case is largely similar to the two other Australian cases, those of Ivan Polyukhovich and Heinrich Wagner. Because the defense chose to construct its arguments within the normative and pragmatic framework with which it, the magistrates, the judge, and the jury were most familiar, as an ordinary criminal case, the broader questions of Holocaust history that might have informed other perpetrator trials, from Nuremberg to Eichmann, and to Finta in Canada and Sawoniuk in England, were largely absent from the Australian proceedings. Instead, the focus on narrow and confined legal issues of identity, identification, and alibi would mean that historical evidence needed to concentrate equally on such issues. The Australian experience in the late 1980s and early 1990s demonstrates in each particular instance that the question of the use and misuse of history in war crimes trials must itself always be placed in its own specific context if we are ever truly to grasp the subtle and important details and differences of approach that characterize these issues in practice.

Historian Erich Haberer has argued that the most commonly deployed arguments about the necessary dissonance between the demands of law and those of historical research in relation to Nazi and collaborationist perpetrator trials should be rethought and configured in a different legal and historical narrative frame. He bases his argument on a careful analysis of the experience of the use of historical evidence in West German investigations and trials of Nazi perpetrators by the apparatus set up at Ludwigsburg.[3] For Haberer the West German experience establishes a more positive accounting of the law/history nexus in which "the creative tension between the requirements of law and those of history generated invaluable evidence and documentary resources."[4]

Because context is everything, it is important to underline that the West German experience of law and history in Nazi perpetrator trials is itself determined largely by its own historical and legal—as well as its political, social, and cultural—situation. The pursuit of Holocaust perpetrators in the Federal Republic of Germany must clearly be positioned historically, culturally, and politically within discussions about the rule of law, national identity—rupture and coming to terms with the Nazi past—and the use of trial mechanisms in the pedagogic arenas of post-Nazi German citizenship and national identity.

Substantive elements of German law also determined the nature of the historical inquiry that had to take place and the evidence to be presented to the courts in that country. Thus, as Haberer himself highlights, German criminal law had to cope with particularly complex notions and elaborations of the defense of superior orders, a defense specifically excluded under the Australian legislation.[5] In addition, the German penal code definitions of the mental element of murder had a clear and substantive effect on the nature of charges that could be brought and the type of proof required.[6] Finally, the West German proceedings are characterized by a collective approach. Trials involved all living members of a particular unit implicated in crimes against humanity and war crimes. As a result, historical evidence was required and developed according to the idea of a "cluster approach" to the systematic "murder complex" (*Tatkomplex*) in which the unit was involved.[7]

Experience in Australia, on the other hand, like that in Canada and the United Kingdom, involved trials of individuals. In part this approach was due to the nature of the historical circumstances of immigration to those countries, which did not usually involve the arrival of an entire Schutzmannschaft unit in 1949, although some claims relating to war crimes by Ukrainian members of the Galician Brigade did involve allegations of mass criminality and group migration to Canada and the United Kingdom.[8] More significantly perhaps, the idea of a cluster approach, especially to a charge of murder, is almost entirely foreign to Anglo-American common-law experience of the ways in which trials are conducted. While it is not unknown to have several defendants in criminal trials, the paradigm, and the standard under which the Australian proceedings took place, is that of a single defendant. On these and other related legal questions, then, the Australian and West German experiences differ quite dramatically.

Nonetheless, the more general point raised by Haberer that the differences between law and history often create a synergistic relationship that benefits both disciplines and that critics of historical perpetrator trials often misunderstand and mischaracterize this relationship is evidenced and confirmed in several aspects of the expert historical evidence offered in the Berezowsky committal proceedings. Indeed, it might be argued that *Berezowsky* shows that Haberer understates the case for reading law/history in Holocaust perpetrator trials as constructing comparable narratives. He asserts that law and history treat and understand context in radically different ways:

> For the judge, context is used to assess the circumstances of a particular crime that may or may not mitigate the culpability of the defendant. For the historian, context is the Holy Grail of historical research: it determines the credibility of his sources and ensures the truthfulness of his representation of the past. This understanding of context also means that he is free, and even expected, to fill in missing pieces of evidence, relying on his "historical imagination" to complete the picture of an historical event as accurately as possible.[9]

While Haberer is no doubt correct in his description of historical method and the historian's search for truthfulness rather than truth, his characterization of the nature and function of context in law is mistaken or at least incomplete. Circumstances, if construed as circumstantial evidence, can be turned into fact upon which a jury might find a defendant guilty or not guilty of an offense even in the absence of direct proof. More pertinently to the Berezowsky case, it is precisely in the role of a historical expert witness in applying historical imagination and method to missing facts that the law/history nexus was experienced in Australian war crimes trials. This imagination is bounded, of course, not just by accepted historical methodological and interpretive practice but also by the rules of evidence, which both delimit expert evidence per se and establish a framework in relation to such elements as relevance, hearsay, and prejudicial or probative value for the translation of a historical narrative about the pit killing at Gnivan into a legally acceptable story about the massacre of the Jews of that village in 1942 and the involvement of the defendant. Again, in the Berezowsky case the key historical facts that had to be established and translated into legally admissible evidence concerned the issues of the date of the massacre and the identity/identification of Mikolay Berezowsky as the member of the Schutzmannschaft unit that rounded up Gnivan's Jewish population.

The defense approach in *Berezowsky* posed some difficult questions about tactical and strategic choices, choices that would in turn be reflected in the nature of the evidence led by each side at the committal hearing. In war crimes trials as experienced in Australia, the interaction between law and history and the roles to be played out in a particular case by this interaction were determined to a large extent by the overarching legal narrative that each side sought to construct. In *Berezowsky* the defense embarked on telling a story that posed some inherent dangers. First, it would contest prosecution evidence that identified Berezowsky not just as a member of the Gnivan Schutzmannschaft but as the highest-ranking Ukrainian in the village's police structure. Next, it would seek to undermine all evidence identifying Berezowsky as having been present at, or in charge of, the rounding up of the Jews of Gnivan in the evening before the pit killing; as having terrorized and beaten Jews as they were kept under guard during the night at the Village Administrative Center, or town hall; and as having been prominent in marching the column of Jews toward the pit, abusing and beating them along the way.

The defense lawyers would further attempt to establish, largely by means of the testimony and written evidence of the two historians, Steinberg and Dean, an alibi for Berezowsky, proving that he was away from Gnivan on a compulsory training course set up by the Germans for members of the Schutzmannschaft. In other words, the defense strategy involved a basic admission that their client was a member of the Gnivan indigenous Ukrainian police force and subsequent assertions that he was in fact a lower-ranking policeman who had been on a training course when the massacre of the Jewish population had taken place. Eyewitness testimony that identified Berezowsky as head of the Schutzmannschaft unit in Gnivan was, they argued, a case of mistaken identity, as was any evidence that placed him at the roundup of Jews. Perhaps there was another Berezowsky, or perhaps the person who was identified as "Berezowsky" was in fact some other policeman, but in any event the accused was not there when the Jews were rounded up and shot.

Historical evidence would be introduced that went to both levels of the defense case. In order to identify Berezowsky as the individual described as the "head" of the Schutzmannschaft, in addition to eye-witness testimony making such a claim, the prosecution would lead evidence about the hierarchy of policing in Nazi-occupied Ukraine, about the chain of command from Vinnitsa to Gnivan and from the German Gendarmerie down to the Schutzmänner. They would intro-duce further historical evidence, based on German wartime docu-ments as interpreted by the two expert witnesses, about the nature of Schutzmannschaft units, their makeup in terms of manpower and the distribution of ranks, and finally about the role of indigenous police in the killing operations aimed at the extermination of the local Jewish population. Indeed, Jonathan Steinberg would insist that history both gave and took away important elements of the defense's twin-pronged attack. He admitted that the historical documentary record appeared to provide part of the alibi offered by Berezowsky's lawyers by identifying him as having attended the training course. On the other hand, he insisted that Berezowsky's presence at this first training course offered strong historical evidence that he was a, if not the, top-ranking Ukrainian policeman in Gnivan.

On each point of history and law the defense would seek to counter the evidence and deploy the narrative constructed by the historians and the prosecution to create support for its version of events. Mikolay Berezowsky identified by eyewitnesses could not be the defendant because he never held a superior rank. The accused, Mikolay Berezowsky, was away at a training camp when the massacre occurred. On the last point both the prosecution and the defense would seek to situate the shooting of the Jews of Gnivan at a time that destroyed or affirmed the alibi.

Each of these questions would arise as part of the professional narrative about the *Aktion* in Gnivan because of the evidence led by the prosecution in relation to the identity and identification of Berezowsky through both eyewitness testimony and documentary evidence. Some of the key evidence on several of the most important points against Berezowsky came from protocols and other evidence derived from Soviet Extraordinary State Commission investigations and from Soviet era investigations of alleged wartime collaborators. In the protocol of her 1948 statement to the Soviet Ministry of State Security (Ministerstvo Gosudarstvennoi Bezopasnosti [MGB]), Ol'ga Ivanovna Ulitena testified that she had been abused and severely beaten by Berezowsky, who is described as having been "the Head of the Gendarmerie."[10] The same year Grigoriy Kriven'kiy had also identified Berezowsky as "head of the gendarmerie."[11] Ivan Vasil'yevich Khuda, who would testify against Berezowsky in Adelaide many years later, gave evidence to Soviet authorities in 1950. During the course of his interrogation he admitted to having himself served as a member of the Gnivan Schutzmannschaft and identified a "Nikolay Berezowskiy" as "Head of the Police in Gnivan" and as "Chief of Police."[12] Aksentiy Kalinkovich Rybak gave a similar description at his interrogation on 1 May 1950.[13] Pyotyr Arsent'yevich Malashkevich described his arrest by the local police in late 1942 or early 1943. He claimed that he was not beaten by the ordinary policeman but "by the police commandant Berezovskiy."[14] Other similar Soviet era protocols contain statements identifying a Berezowsky as "Head of Police."

There was therefore an established judicial or police record that uniformly identified someone named Berezowsky as being in charge of the local police in Gnivan. There is a remaining difficulty in that some of the statements are translated as placing this individual named Berezowsky as the head of the Gendarmerie. This is of course problematic, if not a historical impossibility, because the Gendarmerie was a rural police force made up entirely of Germans. As a native Ukrainian, it would have been impossible for Berezowsky, the defendant, to have been placed in such a position. This well-established historical fact about the nature and composition of policing in occupied Ukraine then leads to several possible explanations.

First, the witnesses who testified to this effect were simply confused or ill informed about the nature of that policing structure and used *Gendarmerie* incorrectly as a generic term for police. Ulitena was a local Ukrainian woman who was perhaps unaware of the police hierarchy. Likewise, Kriven'kiy was a local man arrested for being a Communist Party member, and the most obvious explanation is again that he simply misused the term. The other witnesses who identified Berezowsky as head of the police were in many cases fellow members of the Schutzmannschaft, and none of them makes the mistake of identifying Berezowsky as a member of a German police unit.

None of the Soviet protocols dealt with the events relating to the killing of the Jews of Gnivan. Instead, they concentrated most heavily on the involvement of collaborators in antipartisan actions. The protocols provide some evidence of the identity of a Berezowsky as the head of the local police in Gnivan, although they all situate him in that position at a date, 1943, which is subsequent to the pit killing. While their probative value as evidence in an Australian criminal trial is insignificant in real terms, these Soviet protocols did allow SIU investigators to identify individuals who had been members of the Gnivan Schutzmannschaft and other potential witnesses against Berezowsky. In this context legal historical documents from the Soviet Union in the form of investigative protocols can at one and the same time be dismissed for a variety of reasons as failing to establish facts, or a truth recognizable in an Australian court, and indeed perhaps, by themselves, in a historical inquiry. At the same time these Extraordinary State Commission (ESC) and other Soviet protocols could and did serve as invaluable investigative sources and tools from which other important historical and admissible legal evidence can be derived.

As a result of this and other evidence uncovered in the course of SIU investigations, several witnesses testified against Berezowsky at his committal hearing and identified him as being in charge of the indigenous Ukrainian police force in Gnivan. Mikhail Raykis, who as a young boy had escaped police notice and observed the roundup and execution of the Jews of Gnivan by hiding in the bushes and woods around his home, testified:

> Q. How did you know that uniform was a police uniform.
> A. They constantly wore.
> Q. Who are "they."
> A. The policeman and he, the head of police.
> Q. How did you know he was head of police.
> A. How could I not know as I lived there.[15]

Much of the cross-examination of Raykis went to this issue of identification, not just of Berezowsky as head of police but more specifically regarding the reliability of Raykis's identification of a man named Berezowsky. In particular the defense sought to determine exactly how many times Raykis had seen Berezowsky before the night and day of the roundup and shooting and whether he had in fact seen him at the town hall or involved in the procession of Jews to the killing pit. In the end it emerged that Raykis had really not seen Berezowsky but had "recognized" him by his general build characteristics and by the nature and quality of his voice. It also came out of the careful cross-examination of this important eyewitness that he had in fact only seen Berezowsky one or two times and that he had tailored his testimony because he knew some of it could not be independently confirmed. He was convinced that Berezowsky had been involved in the murder of his family, and he was determined

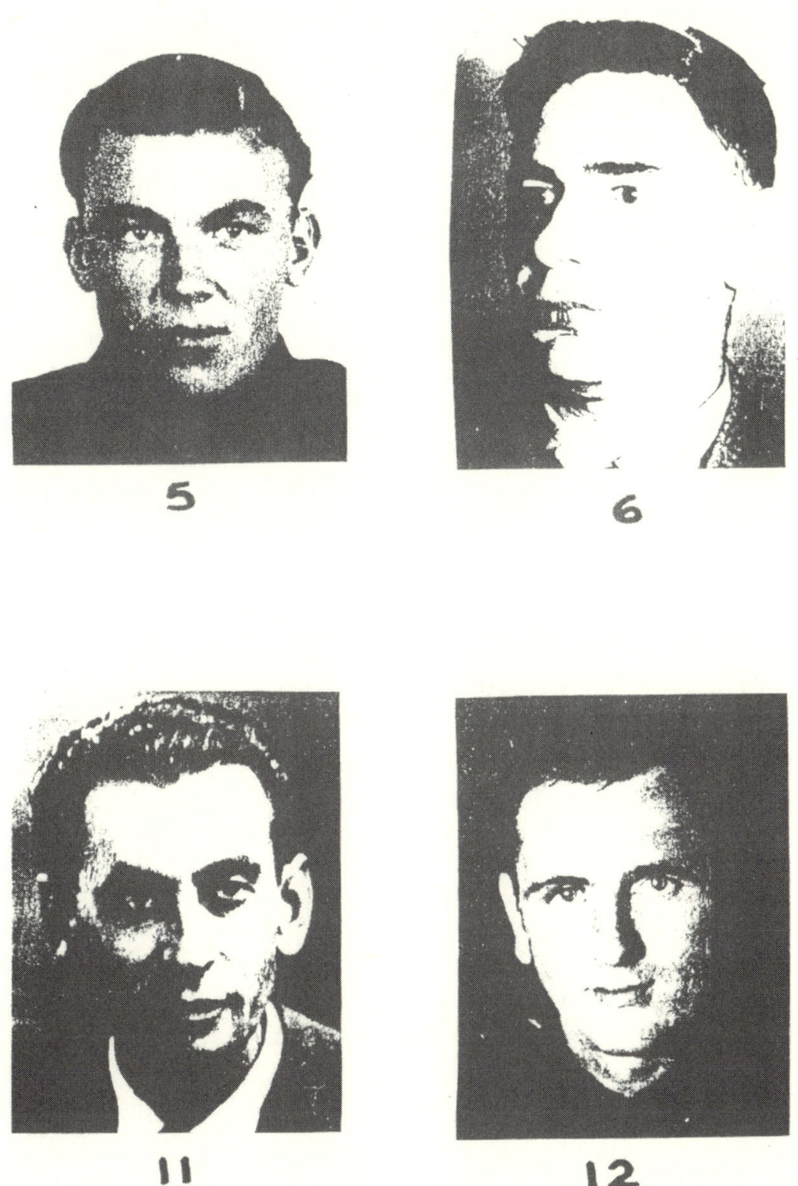

4. Example of Berezowsky SIU photo board — Berezowsky is number 6. Crown copyright. Used by permission of the Attorney-General, South Australia.

to see that his testimony helped convict the accused man, even if it involved testifying to facts that were not "facts" of which he had personal knowledge.

Nikolay Grigoryevich Vorona also offered identification/identity evidence against Berezowsky at the committal. He had joined the Gnivan Schutzmannschaft in 1943. He described Berezowsky as "the manager of the police"[16] and testified that Berezowsky had his own office in the police building.[17] He asserted that Berezowsky the "manager" was the only person of that name in the Gnivan police. He saw this Berezowsky every day and took orders from him on a regular basis.[18] Finally, it emerged from his evidence for the prosecution that when shown a photo board by Australian police, he was unable to identify Berezowsky among those pictured. On cross-examination by Lindy Powell for the defense, Vorona testified that when he saw him, Berezowsky always wore a green German Gendarmerie uniform.[19]

While Vorona identified someone named Berezowsky as the manager or head of the Gnivan police from 1943, he could not state that anyone whose face was presented to him in the police photo spread was the individual he knew as Berezowsky. Moreover, his testimony re-created the same institutional confusion around the proper identity of the person about whom he was giving evidence that had arisen in the earlier Soviet protocols. While he asserts that Berezowsky was the head, or "manager," of the Gnivan police, he also swears that the person he knew as Berezowsky wore the green Gendarmerie uniform. This is not the testimony of a member of the public who had a brief, if unpleasant, encounter with "Berezowsky" and who as a civilian might have been ignorant about matters of uniform, rank, and proper organizational nomenclature. Instead, Vorona had been a member of the Schutzmannschaft directly responsible to "Berezowsky." He had testified that when he joined the police in 1943, he had been given a white armband with *Schutzmann* written on it as his uniform.[20] This detail was consistent with what is known historically about the uniform of the Schutzmannschaft as it evolved from the earliest days of the Ukrainian militia, just after the German occupation of

Ukraine began. Historical evidence confirms the constant shortage of materials and the resultant makeshift nature of indigenous police uniforms and armament. On the other hand, evidence of a Ukrainian policeman wearing a German Gendarmerie uniform and commanding local police is not at all consistent with what is accepted as historically truthful accounts of the operational structures and daily workings of the Schutzmannschaft units.[21]

Ivan Khuda, who had identified Berezowsky as head of the police in Gnivan in his Soviet protocol in 1950, testified to similar effect at the committal hearing in Adelaide. He confirmed other evidence about the *Schutzmann* armband and insisted that Berezowsky conducted drill training for all ranks.[22] He also echoed Vorona's statement that Berezowsky enjoyed the use of his own office in the police building.[23] Afanasiy Andreyvich Nikolaychuck, another former member of the Gnivan Schutzmannschaft unit, from 1943, also testified that he had seen "Berezowsky" every day and that he was in charge of the local police.[24]

But Khuda's testimony about the command structure at Gnivan police headquarters was somewhat confusing. He testified that an individual identified as Mikhaylovskiy was Berezowsky's second-in-command and held the rank of "under officer."[25] After cross-examination in which he first appeared to have stated that Mikhaylovskiy held a higher rank than Berezowsky, he clarified his assertion by affirming that Berezowsky was the superior officer and that as such he held a rank higher than that of "under officer."[26] Khuda was later recalled to the stand by the prosecution and offered a positive identification of the defendant as "Berezowsky."[27] His former colleague Vorona was also recalled by the prosecution and asked to identify Berezowsky.

> Q. That man who was the manager of the police at the time that you were a Schutzmann there, do you see that man, in court here today. Do you see that man Berezowsky?
>
> A. No, I do not see. Where is he?
>
> Q. Do you see the man in court or not.

A. Is he here?

Q. Don't ask me, I'm asking you.

A. Is Berezowsky here? Where is Berezowsky? I would like to see him.[28]

Finally, yet another former policeman from Gnivan, Pyotor Mefod'yevich Mel'nik testified about "Berezowsky" as "head of the police" whom he had also seen everyday.[29] Mel'nik was asked to stand up and indicate if he saw Berezowsky in the courtroom. Over defense objections Mel'nik stood and put his glasses on. The transcript records the result: "WITNESS POINTS TO GENTLEMAN SITTING IN THE THIRD ROW ON THE NORTHERN SIDE OF THE COURTROOM AND ASKS 'IS THAT HIM?' WITNESS DOES NOT INDICATE THE DEFENDANT."[30]

After presenting its witnesses from Ukraine, the prosecution case was not particularly strong. While all the witnesses had identified "Berezowsky" as the head of the indigenous police force in Gnivan, the identification of the defendant as that Berezowsky was in some doubt. One witness had identified him, whereas one of his former colleagues had walked right past him on his way to and from the witness stand without a hint of recognition. The other former Gnivan policeman had pointed to a hapless and perfectly innocent American tourist, Robert Carswell, seated in the gallery and identified him as a Ukrainian war criminal.[31] After fifty years the frailty of eyewitness testimony and the difficulties encountered by a prosecution reliant on such evidence were obvious.

Other evidence from the former police offered confusing testimony about the nature of "Berezowsky's" uniform and rank, issues that were of vital importance to the prosecution case. The prosecutors' position was that Mikolay Berezowsky was indeed the former Gnivan Schutzmannschaft commander identified by colleagues and others as head of the police and leader of the roundup of the village's Jews just before the pit killing. Moreover, all of the evidence from former members of the police detachment in Gnivan related to "Berezowsky" as the head of the police when they were drafted into service after the beginning of 1943. Only some sketchy and problematic eyewitness identification, primarily from Mikhail Raykis, put "Berezowsky" as the head of police in 1942 and at the arrest of the Jewish inhabitants of Gnivan.

As a result of the weakness of many parts of the eyewitness case against Berezowsky, the prosecution would come to rely heavily on the evidence prepared, and the testimony given in court, by Jonathan Steinberg and Martin Dean. It was believed that German documents in particular would identify Berezowsky as a member of the Schutz-mannschaft in Gnivan and place the local police units at killing sites and/or as key operatives in the preliminary steps of surrounding ghettos or Jewish neighborhoods, arresting and collecting Jews, and marching them to the killing pits. It is not an exaggeration to say that Steinberg and Dean, with their German documents and historical expertise to guide the court, were central to the prosecution case. As it would turn out, a different narrative would emerge, one that placed history and historical expert testimony at the heart of the defense case.

JONATHAN STEINBERG: ALIBI, IDENTITY, AND GERMAN DOCUMENTS IN OCCUPIED UKRAINE

Many of the legal issues in the Berezowsky case came to be determined by and through the testimony of historians. In addition to the questions relating to identity and identification of the "Berezowsky" who had been named by several witnesses as head of the Ukrainian police in Gnivan, the key question that would be settled, insofar as that was both legally and historically possible, was the date on which the *Aktion* in Gnivan took place. The defense would assert that at the time the killings of the Jews occurred their client was attending a compulsory German training course run for members of the Schutzmannschaft. Historical evidence would be required to establish the presence of the defendant at the training course, the dates of the course, and the date of the shooting of Gnivan's Jewish population.

In his testimony Mikhail Raykis, a young boy at the time of the *Aktion*, had placed the date of the roundup and shooting at some time in the summer.[32] Another witness, Vanda Stanislavovna Lepsheyeva, a lifelong resident of Gnivan, remembered watching the column of Jews being led through the village to the killing site. When asked in what part of 1942 she saw the Jews being taken to their death, she replied: "You know, I can't remember whether it was April or May. Very early."[33]

Another important version of the killing at Gnivan emerged from historical research. A statement made to the ESC on 12 April 1945 by Moisey Srul'yevich Shnayder, a Jew from Gnivan who had survived, specifically and unambiguously identified Berezowsky, the "head of the gendarmerie," as having been in charge of the arrests of the Jewish population. Shnayder added, "On 6 June 1942, they surrounded the small town of Gnivan' and gathered together all the Jews."[34]

Shnayder's testimony had the added strengths both of local knowledge because he lived in Gnivan and of the relatively contemporaneous nature of his statement. This was not information gleaned in 1948 or 1950 during subsequent Soviet investigations of alleged collaborators and their crimes, nor was it a declaration made to a Soviet Ukrainian procurator or an Australian SIU investigator in the 1990s, more than fifty years after the events. Instead, Shnayder gave evidence in the first and immediate postwar, post-occupation wave of ESC investigations. Most significantly for subsequent developments in law and history in Adelaide, he fixed the date of the killings with precision. This was not a vague recollection of the event as having been early in the year or in an ill-defined "summer" of 1942. Instead, the closest eyewitness account of the massacre in Gnivan placed the events on a particular date, 6 June 1942.

Several difficulties would arise, however, in relation to the Shnayder document. There was still other evidence, including a subsequent collective ESC statement from various residents and officials in Gnivan to which Shnayder added his signature, which placed the time of the pit shooting at a somewhat later date in the summer. Thus, whatever value the 12 April 1945 protocol might have had on its own, it was contradicted by a subsequent statement that could also be attributed to Shnayder. This does not mean that the 12 April 1945 protocol was completely worthless either in historical or in legal terms. While in and of itself it could not be said to embody an absolute or unassailable truth for the historian or for the judge, it could still be introduced as part of a broader and deeper contextual analysis of the historical record. It was one element among many that might serve to situate the killing of the Jews of Gnivan into a historical and legal context that would, or could, assist in the crucial legal task of fixing a date for the killings. Without such a date no alibi defense could succeed.

But the protocol and other potential evidentiary materials in the case were the products of the Extraordinary State Commission procedures and investigations that for some would mean that they were almost by definition unreliable and of little, if any, evidential value. Indeed, even before Steinberg took the stand, Michael David for the defense raised two objections to the use of ESC protocols and conclusions in the case. These were not ideological or political objections to Soviet criminal justice procedures that sought to characterize the USSR legal system as inherently unjust, corrupt, or in violation of the norms of the rule of law. Such discursive elements can be found throughout political interventions about the situation of war crimes prosecutions in Australia but never figured in the Berezowsky proceedings in the Adelaide Magistrates' Court. They would, on the other hand, inform part of the court's position on historical evidence in the Wagner prosecution.

In *Berezowsky* the objections were raised in the simpler and more typical context of ordinary rules of evidence in criminal trials. David objected to the admission of the conclusions of the Soviet ESC, which named "N I Berezovsky" among those responsible for war crimes, mostly in relation to the killing of Soviet POWs and mistreatment of the civilian population, in the Tyvrov district.[35] The defense lawyer argued that because there was no indication of the procedures that had been followed and which informed this decision and others like it from the ESC, any evidence relating to the ESC was inadmissible in and of itself. Moreover, he argued, insofar as the findings of the ESC related to issues alive in the Berezowsky case, they were inadmissible before the magistrate, who had to reach conclusions on these matters solely according to proof presented to him and not to a Soviet ESC investigator fifty years ago. In addition, the defense lawyers objected to the admission of Shnayder's protocol on the traditional ground that because he was dead and unavailable for cross-examination, an extreme prejudice to the defendant would result from allowing it into evidence.

More significantly for the issue of the nexus between legal and historical discourses in this context, David objected to allowing either of the historians, Steinberg and Dean, to base their opinions as expert witnesses on these and similar documents. This, he argued, would be to bring in otherwise inadmissible evidence by "the back door," doing indirectly that which was forbidden directly.[36] The intersection between legal and historical proof, the nature of historical method and deductive reasoning, and the acceptable bases for this method and reasoning would be central to several of the fundamental legal issues at the core of the prosecution and defense cases. Intriguingly, the defense lawyers would thereafter tactically refrain from reasserting their objections in any real or substantive fashion on these points, especially in relation to the Shnayder statement. History, or one interpretation of the historical record, of which the ESC protocol was part, helped rather than hindered their case, so they remained silent about technical rules of admissibility, hearsay, and unfairness to the accused.

Jonathan Steinberg tendered his written statement and took the stand.[37] The defense again made it clear to the court that insofar as Steinberg's evidence went to issues about the historical facticity of the Shoah or on the point that Ukraine's Jews were targeted for extermination in the Final Solution, it would accept the historian's expert opinion without objection.[38] Steinberg, led by the prosecution, then proceeded to describe the nature of available archival sources, the destruction of many documents by retreating German forces that resulted in gaps in the historical record, and the general importance of placing all aspects of the record in proper context. He explained to the court that the historian engages in putting together a "jigsaw puzzle," often in cases in which both the number of pieces and the ultimate picture are unknown.[39] He then went on to explain why, to a great extent, the present case was a gift to historians: "The work which was done by the Special Investigations Unit was unusually thorough and they were able to gain access to archives which no western scholar had hitherto been able to use. They used archives in Kiev and Zhitomir and Vinnitsa and to places which western historian scholars have not been able to come across. The result is that they produce in some cases a very organisable set of documents."[40]

The set of materials available to Steinberg and to the lawyers in the Berezowsky case was historically significant and in Steinberg's opinion highly unusual. The benefits for future historical research are self-evident. As in the case against Polyukhovich, the work of the investigators, lawyers, and historians at the Australian SIU also served more generally to open up heretofore closed Soviet archives. There can be no doubt that at least one important aspect of the law/history nexus in the Berezowsky case worked to add important historical knowledge to our understanding of the Nazi regime in occupied Ukraine and of the practical implementation of the Shoah in Vinnitsa. But the historical knowledge and insight gained at the general level of professional practice still remained to be translated into the language of a criminal committal hearing in which Mikolay Berezowsky, formerly of Gnivan, was charged with being knowingly concerned in the shooting deaths of over one hundred Jews from his village. The precise questions of identity and identification and of alibi remained to be explored through historical evidence.

Steinberg proceeded, with reference to a mass of historical documents from German archives, to establish the organization and structure of the German occupation regime in Vinnitsa and to place the indigenous police force, the Schutzmannschaft, within the security apparatus.[41] He elaborated upon his written statement and confirmed that in Gnivan the indigenous police were always subordinate to the German police hierarchy, the Gendarmerie.[42]

He then came to the most important aspect of his testimony. According to his reading of the relevant documents provided by the siu and on the basis of which he wrote his opinion and gave his oral testimony, the German regional commander in Vinnitsa, Captain Dorge, was a stickler for proper performance and for rigorous training for the Schutzmannschaft. Senior ranks in the indigenous police force would normally only be held by those who had gone through one of three training courses that took place in the spring and summer of 1942. Noncommissioned officers (*Unterführer*) of the ranks of platoon commander (*Zugführer*), sergeant (*Feldwebel*), and below them *Unteroffizier* were subject to a review of their capabilities and their aptitude to continue to hold their rank. Passing the training course was a prerequisite to maintaining their position.[43]

The key document informing Steinberg's expert opinion was German Captaincy Order No. 18.42 of 25 July 1942.[44] Section 2 of the document is titled "Confirmation as Unterführer" and contains a list of eight names. The document states that "in so far as their qualification does not meet with the requirement of the rank of those concerned held up to now, they are as of 1.8.1942 to be recorded only as Unteroffizier."

Up to this point each of the eight had held the ranks of *Zugführer* or *Feldwebel*. In other words, the list was a demotion list. The document also contained another list that was one of "Confirmed 'Unterführer,'" among whom was "Unteroffizier Beresowski Nikolai of Gniwanj (Gnivan)." This document identifies an individual named Nikolai Beresowski as being a noncommissioned officer at the Gnivan Schutzmannschaft office. The issue of rank was central to the prosecution case, in which many witnesses had identified "Berezowsky" as the chief, or head or manager, of the indigenous police in Gnivan. It was equally important to the defense lawyers, who sought to establish that if their client were indeed the "Berezowsky" or "Beresowski" identified by witnesses and now named in this key German document, the document proved that he held the rank of *Unteroffizier*. He was not a platoon commander (*Zugführer*), nor was he a sergeant (*Feldwebel*). His rank was the lowest of the noncommissioned officer ranks available. Thus, the defense would argue, as holder of such a lowly rank, Berezowsky was unlikely to have been in charge of a large police station such as the one in Gnivan.

The second, and perhaps crucial, reason why this document figured so prominently in Stenberg's testimony is that it would serve as the basis for the defense attempt to establish an alibi for the time at which the pit killing took place. According to Steinberg, this document, together with others in the same series of "Captaincy Reports," demonstrated that members of the Schutzmannschaft were sent at Dorge's command to attend one of three training courses at Pogrebysche. Only those who had successfully completed the course would be confirmed in their rank.[45] Berezowsky from Gnivan had been confirmed in his rank. Concerning the training courses, Steinberg testified: "The last one started roughly 19 July and ended roughly four weeks later. The middle one started I think about the 13th of—no, the last one was 19 August, and then went into September. There was one from the middle of July until the middle of August, and there was one from the middle of May, roughly speaking, to the middle of June. In fact we do know the date the first course ended on 13 June."[46]

Steinberg explained his logic in relation to the list of confirmed noncommissioned officers. He asserted that the fact that this was a list of those who had been confirmed in their rank had to mean that they had successfully completed the training course. Dorge had clearly established in the documentary record of all the Captaincy Orders to which Steinberg referred that members of the Schutzmannschaft would maintain their rank only if they had completed the course in a satisfactory manner. Steinberg concluded that the list that confirmed Berezowsky's rank had to refer to the first month-long training course, which other documents showed had ended on 13 June, "because early in July Captain Dorge said 'I intend to confirm people who have completed the course.' He doesn't say the second course, we know that the second course was running at the time that this list was confirmed, the third course was much later. So I deduce this must be a list of people who satisfactorily completed the first course."[47]

Steinberg's analysis is based on his reading of a collection of German documents about the rank of various members of the Vinnitsa region Schutzmannschaft, Dorge's insistence that Ukrainian police undergo extensive and rigorous training, and the logical conclusion, which he calls "plausible,"[48] that the list of confirmed noncommissioned officers refers to those who successfully completed the first training course in Pogrebysche, a location sufficiently distant to have made a return to the village of Gnivan during the course impossible.[49] This is evidence about the time and place of the first training course and Berezowsky's presence that is the result of a historical analysis of a set of German documents, a piecing together of part of the larger jigsaw puzzle of the killing of the Jews of Gnivan. During his cross-examination Steinberg again insisted that what he was offering was not an absolute truth confirmed by direct documentary evidence. There was no single German document explicitly listing those who attended the first training course. "It's what I suppose one would have to call a chain of reasoning and the chain of reasoning is as strong as its weakest link . . . it took a lot of thinking to work out that it must be so. You've got to put together several piece [*sic*]."[50] Indeed, Steinberg seemed reluctant to offer a historical conclusion based on available sources because he was testifying in a criminal case.

> A. I can't doubt it but, as I say, outside a court of law I would not argue the point but one would have to say we do not have absolute confirmation. We could directly argue and I would accept your argument.
> Q. That would be your historical opinion.
> A. My historical opinion.[51]

The first part of the alibi proffered by Berezowsky's legal team was established as a matter of historical opinion. But it could only be a real and effective alibi if the timeframe coincided with the pit killing of Gnivan's Jews. The next part of the puzzle of the Shoah in Gnivan, as narrated in the Berezowsky committal by the prosecution, the defense, and the historians, would turn on the key question of the date of the pit killings.

The pit killings at Gnivan had been variously situated in time by eyewitness accounts as "early" in the year, April or May, or as vaguely in "the summer." The ESC Shnayder protocol from early 1945 had given the precise date of the roundup and shooting as 6 June 1942. If this is the correct date of the killings, then Berezowsky had been provided with a reasonably credible alibi created by the testimony of the expert witness, Jonathan Steinberg. If Steinberg's reading of the documents in question concerning training courses and the confirmation in rank of the successful attendees, of whom Berezowsky from Gnivan was one, then Berezowsky was in Pogrebysche, away from Gnivan, from mid-May until a week after the shootings. The eyewitnesses who had placed "Berezowsky" at the head of the police in charge of the roundup of Gnivan's Jews and present as they were marched to the killing pit were clearly mistaken. The question at this stage involved a debate between Soviet ESC protocol evidence in combination with historical interpretive method in the reading of a relatively complete set of German documents uncovered by SIU research, on the one hand, and eyewitness identification, on the other. But Berezowsky's alibi still depended on fixing the date of the shootings in Gnivan sometime between mid-May and mid-June 1942, at the time Steinberg had concluded the defendant was attending the training course.

In his written opinion tendered to the court, Steinberg had stated that "in the area around Vinnitsa we know that a wave of such mass killings took place in the early summer of 1942 at Illnizi some time before the 3rd June, when 434 Jews died (KO 13 A), at Rushin 606 Jews were murdered . . . at Gnivan probably on the 6th of June where roughly 100 Jews were murdered."[52]

When examined by the prosecution on the question of the probable date for the killings at Gnivan and the basis for this section of his professional historical opinion, Steinberg responded:

> [A.] I have two bases for that; one is that in the middle of May, the Special Investigations Unit sent me a paper on which they put down the dates on which they thought actions against Jews in this area took place.
>
> Q. And those actions are incorporated in this little section.
>
> A. They are indeed. In addition, testimony from a Soviet Extraordinary Tribunal after the war of a man called Schneider gave that date. More than that, I could not say.
>
> Q. So whatever the rights and wrongs of that guess, they're the sources, are they.
>
> A. Those are the exclusive sources I used.[53]

This brief exchange between the historian expert witness and the prosecution lawyer is an extraordinary moment in the history of history and law in Australian Nazi war crimes cases. When Steinberg's status as an expert witness was being put before the court, it had been clearly established that he was fluent in German and had extensive research experience and an impressive publication record in aspects of German and Italian military history, World War II, and the Holocaust. But it was also shown that he was not a Russian or Ukrainian speaker and that he had not personally been to any Soviet, Russian, or Ukrainian archive. Yet his expert opinion on the date at which the massacre of the Jews of Gnivan occurred is based in large part at least on the protocol of Shnayder's ESC testimony. In other words, this part of his expert testimony is based not just on evidence that was and is considered by many—politicians, lawyers, and historians alike—to be problematic per se, but it is based on archival sources that fall clearly outside his recognized area of expertise. In fact, Steinberg would subsequently admit that his reliance on the SIU-provided ESC protocol was contrary to his own conscious choice to limit himself in his expert testimony to German documents with which he was professionally comfortable.[54]

In addition, the second basis for his opinion that the killings in Gnivan "probably" took place on 6 June 1942 is information contained in a paper drafted by the SIU and sent to him to assist in the construction of his expert opinion and in the preparation of his testimony. It is grounded in a secondary source, not in direct access to archival materials or even in a translation of an ESC protocol. Steinberg's expert opinion about the date of the killing of the Jews of Gnivan, which relates directly to his expert opinion about the date of the first training course and Berezowsky's presence there, and thence to Berezowsky's alibi defense, is clearly and deeply problematic. It is not problematic in the sense that the 6 June 1942 date is entirely fanciful as a time when the killing of Gnivan's Jewish population may have occurred or in the sense that ESC protocols are inherently difficult historical and legal sources. What is questionable about Steinberg's written and oral assertions about the Shoah in the second wave of killings in the Vinnitsa region is that they are not based on any historical evidence in which he could be classified as having sufficient expertise to offer a valuable or even arguably a valid professional historical expert opinion.

What is also intriguing from the legal point of view about this entire part of Steinberg's expert evidence is the nature and character of the examination of the witness by the prosecutor in this case. There is a clear attempt to mitigate any damage that might have arisen from this testimony that confirmed the date and then by necessary implication and deduction gave weight to the alibi defense. He refers to Steinberg's statement about the 6 June 1942 date as a "guess." Nonetheless, the overall effect of the testimony in the absence of careful, critical, contextualized, and historically informed analyses is that the 6 June 1942 date remains on the record as the "probable" date of the killings at Gnivan as testified to by one of the two historical expert witnesses.

The date also remains on the record not as the result of detailed, forensic defense cross-examination of the expert but as part of the prosecution's case in chief. Indeed, it is worth recalling here that the defense opened the session of Steinberg's presence in the witness box by stating its objections to the admissibility of the ESC protocol of a dead witness because of the potential harm caused to the defendant when the witness who had made the statement could not be subjected to cross-examination. The defense objection also went to the use of the protocol by the expert witness in forming his historical opinion because that would be a "back door" admission of inadmissible evidence. The cross-examination of Steinberg did not return to the original objection. The defense let this sleeping historical dog lie.

Instead, Michael David focused on extracting stronger assertions about the date from the historian in order to supplement his expert opinion evidence about the mid-May to mid-June date for the first training course attended by Berezowsky. Steinberg was reluctant to offer a "definitive" opinion because of the lack of direct documentary evidence, but he did confirm his view that the best available historical evidence probably placed Berezowsky at the training course.[55]

On the 6 June 1942 issue Steinberg sought to retract or at least mitigate and contextualize the part of his written report that had fixed on this as the probable date and to revisit the question to complete or perhaps modify his oral testimony. When asked if it was his opinion that the massacre at Gnivan had occurred on 6 June, Steinberg recanted in part:

> A. No, that's not my opinion, it's based on a Soviet witness, and it was sent to me by the Special Investigations Unit in a table and with a piece of testimony from the Soviet Extraordinary Commission. It's impossible to form an historical opinion in the sense you were pushing me about before other than that . . .
>
> Q. In your statement presented to the court —
>
> A. Yes.
>
> Q. You put a date of 6 June.
>
> A. I did do that, that was the best information I then had at the time.[56]

David then pressed Steinberg on the point, insisting that if the dates previously given by him for the first training course were correct, and his assertion that Berezowsky was present at the first course was also accurate, then the date of 6 June 1942 as the day of the Gnivan killings provided Berezowsky with an unassailable alibi. While conceding the logic of the defense position, Steinberg now insisted that ESC reports and protocols were not "solid" historical sources.[57] The historian expert witness was now apparently conceding that his evidence, both in writing and in his sworn statement to the court during his examination in chief, was not, within the terms of his own professional discourse and practice as a historian, reliable.

David focused on Steinberg's previous statements about the destruction of German documentary evidence during the war, either by intentional act or as the consequence of combat. He extracted an admission that at some point in the war there would "almost certainly" have existed a German document setting out the precise date and other details of the *Aktion* at Gnivan.[58] As a matter of legal analysis, such expert testimony would perhaps go some way to establishing the basis for a potential subsequent argument that the accused could not receive a fair trial for reasons entirely beyond his control. Berezowsky asserted an alibi defense but was denied access to proof, through no fault of his own, that could establish that defense.[59] David then asked the historian to assume that before any historical, documentary research had been received by the defense in the case, Berezowsky had told his lawyer ("instructed his solicitor") that when the massacre of the Jews of Gnivan had taken place he had been away on a training course. He then asked Steinberg, given this assumed state of affairs, if the available documentary evidence "would totally and utterly support those instructions." Steinberg replied that "if that is the case it would certainly support those instructions."[60]

On the issues surrounding the law/history nexus, this exchange is again informative. First, the expert is asked to assume something not in evidence, a communication between Berezowsky and his lawyer. He is then asked to apply his expertise, which is the only basis on which his testimony could be admitted in the case, to this hypothetical, an intriguing manifestation of the ways in which legal practice and historical discourse are applied to a nonexistent "fact" to achieve both a historical opinion and a piece of evidence on which a legal narrative of alibi can be constructed. What David failed to emphasize in this part of his cross-examination, and what Steinberg appears to put to one side, is that the documents that he has classified by the application of accepted historical methodology and within his understanding of the limits of professional expertise, and to which he has applied his historical deductive reasoning and analysis, are the German Captaincy Orders. At this point Steinberg specifically rejected one of the essential premises of the David interrogation technique—that the date of the killings has been established.

Steinberg clearly rejected, at least at this point in his testimony, the ESC information. It was less than solid in the determination, historically speaking, of facts or of the truthfulness of a version of events. Even in response to David's hypothetical, Steinberg appears to have forgotten himself. The documents do not in fact, on their own, support the instruction given by Berezowsky to his legal representative. They support only the first part of the alibi defense by demonstrating, as Steinberg explained in both his examination by the prosecution and his cross-examination, that Berezowsky from the Gnivan Schutzmannschaft was indeed present at the first training course, which more than likely took place between mid-May and 13 June 1942. The documents do not support the second and necessary part of the alibi, the date of the pit shooting at Gnivan on 6 June 1942, because no German document giving the details of the Gnivan killings exists. The only document that gives that date is the Shnayder protocol from the ESC, and Steinberg has rejected it as unreliable. Steinberg again tried to reassert this position by stating that he could not find the date as being, in his professional opinion, a reliable one.[61]

David continued to hammer away, attempting to extract some greater degree of certainty about the date from Steinberg. The historian, on the other hand, sought to retrench and reaffirm his position. He highlighted the fact that his experience of the case had underlined for him that historical examination of the documentary record revealed more information the more he looked at the files. He did concede, if that is the appropriate characterization, that he had proffered an expert opinion that 6 June 1942 was the probable date of the massacre at Gnivan and that that date was based on the SIU information provided to him, including the Shnayder protocol. "My opinion was as strong as the Soviet Extraordinary Commission's testimony was strong,"[62] he explained.

In the middle of his cross-examination on the date/alibi issue, Steinberg added, somewhat gratuitously perhaps, that his examination of the files from which he had gleaned the idea that Berezowsky attended the first course also led him to another conclusion, which was that Berezowsky had been chosen to attend the course because he was "the senior person at that time in the Schutzmannschaft in Gnivan."[63] This opinion from Steinberg was not one that arose as the result of a direct question from either side. Instead, he threw it into the middle of a cross-examination about the alibi defense and more specifically during an interrogation on the date of the Gnivan massacre. The issue of Berezowsky's rank was of course of some importance given that several previous witnesses had described and identified him as the head of the police. Steinberg's assertion that Berezowsky's presence at the first training course was the result of his seniority was the consequence of his historical reasoning based in his interpretation of the series of Captaincy Orders. He argued that Dorge's emphasis on training meant "he wanted the first course, presumably, to be the top people, that's all I think I would add to that."[64]

Steinberg's seemingly spontaneous intervention on the question of rank had the clear effect of confirming from the historical expert's point of view the statements of the many eyewitnesses who had characterized Berezowsky as "head," "chief," or "manager" of the Gnivan Schutzmannschaft. If he had undermined the 6 June 1942 date by dismissing the ESC protocol as historically unreliable, and retracted in effect his written statement on this point, then Steinberg had now given more substance to the identification evidence of the other witnesses and had also, by subverting the alibi, given support to those such as Raykis who had named the chief of police Berezowsky as the person in charge of the mass arrest of Gnivan's Jews on the night before their execution. Ironically perhaps, although Steinberg does not refer to this point in his problematic historical analysis during his time on the witness stand, one of the first eyewitnesses to place the chief of police Berezowsky as the person in charge of rounding up the Jews was Moisey Srul'yevich Shnayder in his protocol in April 1945.

Michael David returned to the rank question and again raised the issue of the list of names found in the Captaincy Order and whose ranks had been "confirmed." David asked Steinberg if there were any specific reference in any of the available documents about the Gnivan and Vinnitsa region that stated that Berezowsky was head of the police in Gnivan. Steinberg admitted that no documentary evidence of that nature existed.[65] Nonetheless, Steinberg continued to insist that the presence of Berezowsky in the first course and his confirmation as *Unteroffizier* led him to conclude that it was "implausible" to maintain that he was not the person in charge at Gnivan.[66] David attacked this aspect of Steinberg's evidence by referring to German documents that set out the expected manpower and staffing requirements for each police post and which appeared to demand that a platoon commander (*Zugführer*) be in charge of each station.[67] Steinberg acknowledged that there was certainly no evidence that Berezowsky ever attained that higher rank. On the other hand, he insisted that the historical record in relation to the Schutzmannschaft within the policing structure in Ukraine established that the indigenous force suffered from constant recruiting and manpower shortages. While the leadership of a *Zugführer* was part of the ideal command structure, that ideal was seldom met in practice. Historically speaking, an *Unteroffizier* such as Berezowsky could easily have been the highest-ranking Schuma in a place like Gnivan.

This is the point at which historical expert evidence meets the demands of legal proof. Steinberg the historian insists that as far as his profession is concerned, the accepted state of expert knowledge meant that it was "plausible" that Berezowsky was in command.[68] His opinion on this point was based first on his awareness of the generalized personnel shortages from which the Ukrainian Schutzmannschaft suffered. It was then confirmed by his reading of the Captaincy Orders relating to Dorge's emphasis on training and what for him was the logical conclusion that the highest-ranking men would have been the first to undergo such training. David, on the other hand, had to focus on the particular in order to counter identification evidence from eyewitnesses in relation to Berezowsky's position. This was the purpose history had to serve for him, a translation from the general to the particular, with a special focus on recognizable documentary evidence. The defense lawyer sought in effect to weaken the impact of Steinberg's expert evidence by diminishing its impact on its own terms.

On further cross-examination Steinberg accepted that the documentary record did not establish that there was or that there was not a *Zugführer* posted to Gnivan.[69] While insisting that it was unlikely that there was someone of this rank at Gnivan, he did concede that the Captaincy Orders that confirmed Berezowsky as an *Unteroffizier* also contained a list of eight Ukrainian police who had been demoted, some from the rank of *Zugführer*.[70] While David sought the further concession that this might well mean that there was indeed a person of that rank at the Gnivan police station when Berezowsky attended the course, Steinberg merely admitted the theoretical possibility of such a circumstance. He continued to insist that his previous logic in reading the Captaincy Orders to place Berezowsky at the first training course also led him to conclude that he was present because of his senior status in Gnivan.[71]

The second historian to offer expert testimony in the Berezowsky committal was Martin Dean. Dean was in a different position in both the legal sense and the historical sense from that of Jonathan

Steinberg. Dean had worked for the SIU and as such was not professionally distant from the investigative process. This fact does not mean that his testimony as a historian was per se problematic because of his position or that he was debarred from serving as a historical expert witness. Konrad Kwiet, chief SIU historian, had testified in the Polyukhovich case. Nonetheless, in the context of an adversarial hearing, in which so much of the defense lawyers' key position on the issue of their client's alibi depended on expert historical evidence about the combined effect of the first training course and the correct date for the killing of Gnivan's Jews, it is hardly surprising that much was made, implicitly at least, about Dean's testimony on these points and the availability of objective historical evidence. This would take on a particular importance because of the second factor that distinguishes Dean's expertise from Steinberg's in relation to historical evidence in the Berezowsky case. ·

Unlike Steinberg, Dean read Russian as well as German. He had actually traveled to the various archives in Ukraine, Russia, and Germany and had seen the original documents on which the case now turned. Indeed, he had discovered the key set of Captaincy Orders and other vital documents in the Zhitomir and Moscow archives.[72] He was in a real sense the historian in the case, not just because of his personal involvement in the archival aspects of the research that underpinned both the prosecution and the defense cases but also because, unlike Steinberg, his expertise as a historian extended to Soviet archives and documents relating to ESC proceedings that figured prominently in fixing, or attempting to fix, with some precision, the date of the pit shootings at Gnivan. He confirmed Steinberg's evidence that no German document that might have permitted a more accurate pinpointing of the date of the Gnivan killings had been found.[73]

Instead, Dean's testimony would be based on three primary historical sources, each of which had intriguing and important links to legal processes. Much of the documentary record of the prosecution case against Berezowsky and of the defense's assertion that their client had an alibi came from legal sources. The law/history nexus that has been so important and controversial in many critical discussions of Nazi perpetrator trials took on a particular symbiotic character in the Berezowsky case. History formed part of the legal cases from which historical evidence was then drawn to provide proof in a subsequent legal proceeding. Law and history seemed to situate themselves in a relationship that circled upon itself in a way that was beneficial to both without distorting either. The integrity of both law and history was maintained because they were, in the context of the Australian war crimes prosecutions generally, and in *Berezowsky* in particular, in a relationship of mutual dependence. Erich Haberer describes the phenomenon in relation to the West German experience: "Both observed the rules and discourse of their respective professions and neither blurred the distinction between justice legally applied and truth historically defined. Although the temptation was there to use the courtroom as a forum for the presentation of history, the strict application of legal norms prevented this transgression of justice."[74]

The substance of Dean's testimony focused primarily on the question of the date of the pit shooting at Gnivan. His opinion, which would become problematic as the process of examination and cross-examination unfolded, was grounded in three principal historical sources—a series of ESC protocols and statements; German investigative materials relating to war crimes allegedly committed in the Vinnitsa region; and the series of ESC reports from Vinnitsa and surrounding areas reproduced in the book *Nazi Crimes in Ukraine, 1941–1944: Documents and Materials*, published by the Academy of Sciences of the Ukrainian SSR, Institute of State and Law.[75] Each of these sources, the ESC investigations and findings and the Ludwigsburg war crimes process, was deeply situated in the intersection between law and legal practice, on the one hand, and in historical research, on the other.[76]

After reviewing the Shnayder protocol that fixed the date with precision on 6 June 1942, Dean also discussed another ESC protocol/statement, signed by several local officials and by Shnayder, that this time set the date at 16 July 1942.[77] He then referred to many of the Ludwigsburg documents and investigative protocols that revealed a broad range of dates or times in the "summer or autumn" of 1942 for the killings of Jews in the region.[78] As a result of his careful rereading of all available sources, Dean testified that his opinion was that the likely timeframe for the Gnivan killings had to be expanded "to cover the period April to July."[79] In giving this timeframe, Dean modified in the course of his oral testimony the evidence that he had given to the court in his written statement. In that document he had written that "from available historical documentation it appears to me that the liquidation of the Jews of Gnivan took place in May or June 1942."[80]

This written evidence from Dean was obviously more consistent with the defense contention that their client had an alibi because the training course had taken place from mid–May to 13 June 1942. The expansion of the possible timeframe for the Gnivan liquidation to include longer periods before and after the training course potentially made such an alibi claim substantively weaker. It is hardly surprising that the cross-examination of Dean would focus extensively on this historical expert witness version of a prior inconsistent statement. Throughout his interrogation of Dean, Michael David sought to elucidate issues relating to the sources of Dean's opinion, the reasons behind his apparent change of mind about the crucial date in question, and the timing of his revised opinion.[81] In this series of questions and answers we encounter the clash of legal and historical narratives and the differing professional requirements of each discipline's way of reading, interpreting, and reasoning about a series of documents. For the lawyers the documents relating to the date of the pit shooting on the outskirts of Gnivan went to key legal issues of identity, identification, and alibi, while for the historian they went to establishing the acceptable basis for a historical truthfulness of what had happened to the Jews of Gnivan and more specifically when it had happened.

Dean began his response by setting out a historical explanation based in his discipline's method. He read a series of documents, none of which offered a specific reference to the liquidation of Gnivan's Jews, dealing with killings of Jews in the villages of the Vinnitsa region. From this information, which constituted the only documentary sources of historical knowledge, an approximation extending from April to July was the best timeframe possible.[82] When asked about Steinberg's statement that the probable date was 6 June 1942, Dean replied that while he understood the basis on which Steinberg had reached that opinion, it was not one he shared based on his reading of the complete available historical record.[83]

At first blush this is an example of the familiar trial phenomenon of battling expert opinions. One historian, Steinberg, says that in his professional opinion the massacre of Gnivan's Jews probably occurred on 6 June 1942, while the other, Dean, was only able to set a parameter of possible dates between April and July 1942. At the same time it is important to remember that the apparent debate between Steinberg and Dean is now taking place in the course of a cross-examination by a lawyer representing the defendant, who has an obvious stake in the 6 June 1942 date that establishes an alibi through expert opinion. What David, for reasons that are obvious from the perspective of his role as defense lawyer in the present circumstances, does not ask Dean or raise as a basis for any of his questioning of this historian is Steinberg's recanting of the written statement he provided the court and his move away from the 6 June 1942 date in his oral testimony. David makes no mention of this matter or of Dean's Russian-language skills or his expertise in Soviet source evidence, nor does he go back to Steinberg's lack of real historical expertise in the ESC evidence upon which he based his written statement and the early part of his testimony in the committal hearing. Neither does he, again for obvious reasons, make anything of Steinberg's insistence under cross-examination that his opinion on the 6 June date was based in part on evidence he himself characterized as "unreliable," the ESC protocol, and in part on a secondary source document of places and dates drawn up for his use by the SIU.

This part of the cross-examination of Dean and the subsequent interactions between the defense lawyer and the historian simply highlight the fact that the role of the lawyer in such circumstances is to tell a story, within the permissible limits of a criminal proceeding and the rules of professional ethical responsibilities, that benefits his client and which is supported by the strongest favorable reading of evidence available to the court. The historian, on the other hand, operates within a professional narrative context that demands that he not provide a plausible account but that he settle, however tentatively, always remaining open to competing versions supported by evidence and to the possibility that subsequent evidence might emerge, on the *most* plausible account he can offer. Thus, while Dean acknowledges that Steinberg's statement setting the 6 June 1942 date is "a possible interpretation," he does not share it.[84] In this instance Dean's reading of the historical documentary record and the information that flowed from that record means that the more or most plausible and acceptable historical narrative can only situate the liquidation of the Jews of Gnivan within a broad four-month window.

An important issue on which the cross-examination would then turn became a legal inquiry into historical methodology. David pointed out again, as he had in his original objection to ESC evidence, that the person who had given the evidence was dead. The question then became one of establishing the basis on which Dean formed his historical opinion on the date question and more specifically on his interpretation of the ESC protocols. In response Dean testified that he had extensive experience in the historical investigation of various types of war crimes documentary evidence, both with the SIU and the Metropolitan Police in London. From this practical experience he argued that his exposure to Soviet protocols had taught him that while contemporaneous statements are more likely to be reliable than those made many years after the event, eyewitnesses are not particularly trustworthy on the issue of fixing a precise date. This is even more so the case when, as with Shnayder, the same witness gives three different statements in a short period of time.[85] Dean applied logic and professional experience in determining which historical documents were most likely to be reliable in coming to an informed opinion about which version of events, which date (or dates) was most likely to be a truthful reflection of the state of historical knowledge. In addition, he applied his broader, more general knowledge of the Shoah in Ukraine to read, understand, and interpret the documentary record on which his opinion was based.[86]

But the fact remained that insofar as both Steinberg and Dean were concerned, each had made what lawyers would consider to be inconsistent written statements that were tendered to the court as part of their expert evidence. Steinberg sought with some vigor to resile from the precise idea that 6 June 1942 was the probable date of the liquidation at Gnivan by pointing to the unreliability of the evidence on which his opinion had been based. Dean sought to expand the "May or June" 1942 period to include at least another month on either side. Each change of historical opinion had a potentially profound effect on Berezowsky's attempt to establish an alibi defense. In the case of each of the two historians who testified at the committal, the defense had to focus on the question of prior inconsistent statements in an attempt both to negate their change of opinion and to refocus on the written statements, each of which better served the alibi issue.

David asked Dean exactly when he had changed his mind about the view expressed in the written statement tendered to the court, To which Dean replied: "This is a process of reassessing the available evidence and looking at it very closely. Initially I may have put too much emphasis on the fragmentary German documentation which is very fragmentary, whereas if you see it in the full context of all the killings in the Zhitomir area you can see that the period of killings is rather wider, they're [*sic*] given the historical development and the contemporary."[87]

Dean's assertion that he had revised his opinion through a more careful study of the documents and a reevaluation of the regional context is perfectly in keeping with the norms and standards of his profession. Evidence is reexamined and reevaluated as part of the normal process of "doing history." But for lawyers and judges changing one's mind after having tendered an official statement that forms part of the judicial record of proceedings, in a criminal trial for murder, is something that raises the discomfort level. Lawyers distrust the very notion that someone can change his or her mind and that they can offer a revised version of events. The rules of evidence and centuries of legal pragmatic sense have evolved to develop an essential dislike and inherent distrust of such occurrences. Complex rules about prior inconsistent statements, about witness reliability and credibility, which are essential components of a criminal process and its search for a juridical version of the truth surrounding a particular set of events, have been created and put into practice because legal experience teaches that a consistent story is more likely to be true than an inconsistent story.

David targeted another date issue, the date at which Dean had revised his opinion. When Dean replied that he had been in the process of reviewing documents and rethinking the question of the timeframe for the Gnivan liquidation in the month preceding his appearance in court, David asked why, given that his written statement had been composed and submitted in the last two weeks, Dean had not included his new opinion on the date question in that statement.[88] The historian replied that he had been reviewing documents to prepare his statement and rethinking the issue at about the same time but that he had also been under some pressure to finish the written document to submit it in time for his appearance.[89] Some of the Ludwigsburg documents had only just come to light, and his review of that material was ongoing.

> A. Well, when preparing my report I didn't have time to incorporate that material fully into the report but I had it prepared in case someone would ask me if I knew any further information about it.
>
> Q. So when you prepared the report of May or June of 1942, you had that, didn't you.

A. Yes.

Q. And you now say that material is one of the reasons why you
expand the dates.

A. Yes.

Q. But you had that while you were preparing the report
whereby you put May or June of 1942 as the date.

A. Yes. As I was trying to explain it's a process here I've only
slowly realised that perhaps I was being a bit too strict with
May or June, and again if you look at it closely, the available
historical evidence, so as you reassess everything you may
change your opinion.[90]

Dean continued to explain that the process and method of arriving
at a historical opinion is subject to constant revision and reexamina-
tion. David, on the other hand, adopted the legal and evidentiary
approach of attempting, without ever explicitly saying so, to establish
that the change of opinion at such a late stage may raise some doubts
about the intention behind it. The discrepancies between the two
approaches and the goals of each profession in the circumstances of
the Berezowsky committal become even starker in the subsequent
exchange, in which Dean states that it was only recently that it had
become clear, following the interpretation of the Captaincy Orders
and the training course schedules, that the actual date of the Gnivan
liquidation had become crucial to the case.[91]

Q. So your evidence is that since that time, since the last two
weeks, despite all the work you have done on this case over a
number of years, it has just hit you that you were too precise
about the dates, is that right. Is that an accurate summary of
the position you found yourself in.

A. I think that I came to that conclusion from a very close
examination of a large number of documents.

Q. Yes, but you came to that conclusion in the last couple of
weeks.

A. About two-and-a-half weeks ago, yes.

Q. After you had signed and prepared this statement.

A. At about the same time.[92]

The tenor of the competing professional discourses is evident. Dean continued to insist that his revision of his earlier and written opinion about the dates of the Gnivan massacre was nothing more than the result of a renewed and careful focus on preparing a professionally competent and acceptable examination of the entire and fully contextualized historical record. He simply did good history. On the other hand, David's focus on the timing of the revision on the date question invoked and echoed several interrelated legal/factual concerns central to his case. In addition to the standard evidentiary and credibility issues relating to prior inconsistent statements and the impeachability of the witness on that basis, the focus on the timing of the issue arguably goes to another possible impeachment issue. If Dean had revised the date of the liquidation in the recent past, after by his own admission, it had become clear that the date issue was a key component to reading the Captaincy Orders as part of an alibi defense for Berezowsky and the effect of the revision was to weaken that defense, it would be in the interests of the defense to imply, to open for the court the possibility, through this line of questioning, that a motivation other than one inspired by good history was the source of the change of dates.

The defense cross-examination at this stage may be seen as treating Dean's evidence not as that of an expert historian but as something akin to that of an agent for the prosecution, a police officer who, for example, remembers a new fact after learning of the defense strategy or who returns to a crime scene and discovers a new piece of incriminating evidence. This new evidence is what David characterizes as "an enormous re-interpretation" of the historical record on the question of the date of the Gnivan liquidation.[93] The lawyer then sought to return to the original written statement proffered by Dean and asked where the May or June date fit into the "new" evidence. Dean again asserted that the evidence available to him as a historian only permitted a relative degree of certainty about a broad date range: "I would say that the period of May or June is in the centre of a period in which there was a large number of Jewish actions in that area, but there were also actions in April and some actions in July. It is up to the court to decide how they will interpret the available evidence."[94]

LAW AND HISTORY IN THE CASE OF
MIKOLAY BEREZOWSKY

The court took up Martin Dean's challenge. The magistrate concluded that the prosecution had not managed to meet its burden and that as a result Berezowsky had no case to answer. Berezowsky's solicitor, Ian Press, for one, concludes that any other decision, on the evidence presented, would have been unacceptable.[95] Because such cases and decisions on no case submissions do not require the magistrate to give reasons, we can never really know with any certainty what the essential flaws in the prosecution case were. A reading of the witness statements and the transcripts of the committal does reveal that the eyewitness identification of Berezowsky as the man in charge of the roundup of Gnivan's Jews was problematic, to say the least.

Mikhail Raykis's testimony, for one, was riddled with contradictions and corrections. Extensive cross-examination of this witness revealed that statements he had made to the Soviet procurator assisting Australian investigators in the case had both been mistranslated and, more seriously for his credibility and for any idea that his account of events relating to the arrest of the Jews of Gnivan was accurate, contained declarations that he claimed he had never made. He admitted that he had signed the statement given to him by the Soviet procurator, Podrutskiy, without having read it carefully. Raykis had assumed that the written version was an accurate rendering of his oral declarations. He trusted the Soviet lawyer. Yet an exchange that took place during cross-examination on the crucial question of his identification of Berezowsky at the Village Administrative Center on the night the Jews were gathered there raises serious questions:

Q. Can you give an explanation as to why you say in your
statement that you signed that you saw him at the Village
Administration centre.

A. I do not know what the aim of this was, what Podrutskiy
wrote I can't say. I do not what I said [*sic*], but as I did not see
what's the point in my saying that I did see.

Q. Did you correct Mr. Podrutskiy.

A. No, I didn't do any correcting.

Q. Did you say, "I'm not signing that, I didn't say it, it's not
true."

A. He read it unto me and that was not there. I don't know
how it is here, the first time.

Q. So when he read it out the first time it was not there.

A. It was not.[96]

The testimony of Raykis was perhaps fatally undermined. His
original story of hiding during the search of his house and then
watching events from the woods as his family was killed had been
powerful and moving, but this cross-examination managed to cast a
shadow on all evidence gathered from Soviet sources by USSR legal
officials, whether SIU investigators and lawyers were present or not.
Other eyewitness accounts further undermined the prosecution case
against Berezowsky.

One eyewitness picked out a member of the gallery and identified him as Berezowsky, the head of the Gnivan Schutzmannschaft.
Another could not identify the defendant despite walking right past
him on his way to and from the witness stand. The historical evidence
was problematic, incomplete, and on several key issues contradictory.
Some historical documentary and expert opinion support could be
found for Berezowsky's consistent and long-standing assertion that
he had been on a training course when the liquidation in Gnivan
took place. Other evidence of a similar type could be said to have
left a hole in the alibi timeline. We may never know when the Jews
of Gnivan were herded from their homes in the middle of the night,

kept under guard, and abused as they huddled together on their last
night on earth and were taken to their execution place early the next
day. Nor will we know why the magistrate decided that there was
not enough evidence to send Mikolay Berezowsky to stand trial as
a war criminal.

But that does not mean that either law or history, or indeed law
and history, did not benefit or gain from the Berezowsky case. At
the level of rule of law discourse and practice, the system worked.
Each side presented its best arguments. Lawyers used their professional forensic skills in the service of their clients, and the magistrate reached a decision that most observers familiar with the case
would agree was justifiable in the circumstances, even if one might
conclude from all the evidence that Berezowsky was indeed head of
the Schutzmannschaft in Gnivan and that he had been present at
the arrest, roundup, and march to the killing pit of the village's Jews.
Law, if not some understandings of justice, was served.

At the same time, historical knowledge about the implementation
of the Holocaust in the Vinnitsa region of occupied Ukraine benefited
directly and indirectly from the Berezowsky case and the efforts of
the SIU investigators, historians, and lawyers. New archival sources
were uncovered and opened up to Western historians. More insight
into the operation and conclusions of the ESC in this part of Ukraine
came to light as the direct consequence of the Berezowsky investigations. The two principal experts in the case published professional
journal articles based on documents and experience gleaned from
the case, translating evidence gathered for a limited legal purpose,
to a more diverse audience of professional historians.[97]

Jonathan Steinberg enjoyed a brief period of broader public celeb-
rity as the result of his role as an expert witness in Berezowsky. The
Australian newspaper carried a two-page story titled "The Witness
Who Knew Too Much" in its 21–22 September 1996 "Weekend
Review."[98] The story obviously brought the Berezowsky case back
into the public realm, however briefly, and also served to emphasize the underappreciated and understudied role played by history

and historians in the Australian Nazi war crimes trial process. But as with all journalistic accounts, and especially those with a strong tendency toward populist hagiography, the tale reproduced in the *Weekend Australian* must be read with a large grain of salt and itself be placed into a fuller and more complex context. According to the story, "Steinberg was so thorough that he found Berezowsky his alibi, uncovering a paper trail that suggested that he might not have been present at the massacre."

Those more familiar with the actual record of the Berezowsky case might see this as an inaccurate and incomplete, not to say misleading, summary of the litigation and of Steinberg's role. The documents were uncovered through the hard work and diligent research of the SIU team generally, from the creation of an investigative and prosecutorial protocol with Soviet authorities, negotiated by Robert Greenwood, to the hours and days spent in archives by historians such as Konrad Kwiet and Martin Dean. The SIU provided all of the relevant documents, and a specially prepared timeline, to Steinberg. While it is no doubt true that Steinberg's interpretation of the Captaincy Orders and the training course documentation, particularly the confirmation of Berezowsky as *Unteroffizier*, did place him at the training course in May and June 1942, the second part of the alibi defense depended on fixing the date of the liquidation on 6 June 1942, something Steinberg did in his written statement based solely on the ESC protocol and the table of mass killings of Jews in the Vinnitsa region, each of which originated again with the SIU.

In addition, a reading of Steinberg's testimony reveals not the white knight historian diligently riding to the rescue of the defendant against all odds but a reluctant historian ultimately keen to undermine the evidence supporting the 6 June 1942 date and equally anxious to confirm the eyewitnesses who identified Berezowsky as the chief of police. Finally, we should not forget that the defense lawyers were aware from a very early stage, based on information from their client, that he asserted an alibi that placed him at the training course when the massacre occurred. The idea of the lone academic historian discovering the crucial smoking gun documents that cleared Berezowsky by himself, a version of Indiana Steinberg and the Shoah at Gnivan, is belied by the legal historical record of the Berezowsky case itself.

Whatever the journalistic or autobiographical excesses that might arguably have arisen, the benefit to historical knowledge that flowed out the Berezowsky case—as with the SIU investigation of Nazi war crimes, collaboration, and war criminals in Australia more generally—is beyond dispute. Archives were opened up, new paths of inquiry were pursued, and a necessary historically corrective focus of the pit killing mechanism in Eastern Europe and away from "Auschwitz" as the paradigm for the Shoah emerged. Erich Haberer perhaps captures the situation best in his study of the German Ludwigsburg apparatus, in which he also pays tribute to and recognizes not just the work of SIU and other historians working for American, British, and Canadian war crimes investigation bodies but the essential link between legal and historical practices, without which none of these revelations would have occurred: "Benefitting from their first-hand knowledge of in-house documentary collections and other material located in Lithuania, Latvia, Estonia, Belarus, Ukraine and Russia, they have paid particular attention to the Nazis' use of collaborators in their mission of genocide. Combining their judicially honed research skills with their knowledge of Third Reich history and Nazi occupation policy, these historians have 'individualized' history in the spirit of 'Ludwigsburg historiography.'"[99]

To which we might now add "Adelaide historiography."

FIVE

The Story of Daviborshch's Cart

Law, History, Truth, and the Holocaust in Ukraine

Saul Friedlander has identified the anxieties that have come to characterize debates about the historical construction of events known as the Shoah, the killing of European Jews by the Nazis and their national collaborators in occupied Europe. He writes: "On the one hand, our traditional categories of conceptualization and representation may well be insufficient, our language itself problematic. On the other hand, in the face of these events we feel the need of some stable narration; a boundless field of possible discourse raises the issue of limits with particular stringency."[1]

These concerns about processes, rhetoric, and memory have an impact on law as well. The idea of a stable narration of events and of facts is central not just to those who seek a limit to Holocaust history and discourse, especially in a world in which the politically pernicious phenomenon of Holocaust denial seems to know no end. It is also a key concern in constructing an understanding of the criminal investigative and trial processes as they relate to the Shoah. War crimes trials complicate these issues while, ironically, offering the pretense of proclaiming a clear limit. Law, especially criminal law, and the processes of a trial, are grounded in a final judgment about guilt or innocence. On its own terms law offers closure on all matters in dispute.[2] But in the context of war crimes trials law itself is confronted with the same inherent insufficiency of its own rhetorical structures and the problematic, if not impossible, search for a stable narrative about the Shoah in a legal context that Friedlander identifies as characteristic of history.

> But even if we leave the original story behind, or place it alongside other stories, in search of the truth about the action in question, we have not departed from the *kind* of account we started with: a story that recounts the action by starting from its meaning to those involved; its initiation in a perceived set of circumstances, its execution according to plan and means, and its arrival at its conclusion. Even in the juridical, journalistic, and historical contexts, this kind of account is usually judged perfectly adequate . . . As a result of an investigation into discrepancies and inconsistencies, we may end with a story that is different from the one we started with, but it's still a story.[3]

Police and lawyers, through documents and witnesses, tell a story about events, with the hope of persuading the finder of fact, the magistrate, the judge, or the jury that the story embodies the truth about the accused's guilt. The defense team strives to undermine the narrative, to disrupt its flow, to highlight its weaknesses, its flaws, its contradictions, to emphasize one narrative element, identity for example, which subverts the prosecution's story about the accused's guilt. Sometimes the defense will try to tell another story altogether, to offer a different version of the facts for the interpretative judgment of the finder of fact. "Berezowsky was at a training camp at the time the Jews of Gnivan were killed." But in all these cases the basic structure and the core elements remain the same. One side or the other, or both, tells a story. Each offers a narration of events that, in the case of law, will be rendered stable through the final act of judgment, of guilt or innocence, of proceeding to trial or finding no case to answer. Especially in a criminal trial in which the rules of evidence and the burden of proof might mean that an acquittal is not attributable to a greater believability or stability attributed by the jury to the defense story but, rather, to a lingering doubt remaining over the prosecution's case, the very idea of establishing a stable narration through law is undermined. There is a result, but that result may not reflect the true or complete story.

In such cases we confront in the legalized narratives the inherent conflict identified by Hannah Arendt in her controversial but influential discussion of the trial of Adolf Eichmann before an Israeli court.[4] In her oft-cited epilogue Arendt argues that all Holocaust-related trials have an apparent and recognized duality at their core. One goal that characterizes these proceedings is pedagogical or didactic.[5] From this perspective legal processes, most commonly criminal trials, are deployed with the express intent by the governmental authorities charged with the creation of the special statute under which the trials usually occur, and with the identification and prosecution of a particular accused, to offer to the general public a "memory lesson" about the Holocaust. The central dilemma for Arendt and for many today is that such a didactic or pedagogical focus "can only detract from law's main business: to weigh the charges brought against the accused, to render judgment, and to mete out due punishment."[6]

Arendt uses this argument and her analysis of the weaknesses (and strengths, a part of her argument often overlooked) of the Eichmann trial and of the International Military Tribunal (IMT) at Nuremberg, to argue not that law has no role to play but, instead, to assert that crimes of the nature and scale of the Shoah, genocide, and crimes against humanity can only be judged legitimately by an international court exercising a universal jurisdiction based in our common humanity. National trials such as the Eichmann proceedings or the three Australian cases run the inevitable risk of distorting history, memory, and the internal legitimacy of law.

The problem for Arendt, and for her successors, is that such trials, or perhaps more precisely the ways these trials are narrated, are almost by definition illegitimate. They focus on history and memory, on collective responsibility and guilt, and ignore the internal requirements for a liberal rule of law system.[7] They run the risk of becoming not legal but political proceedings, in other words show trials. More recently, Gerry Simpson has dealt with this concern though a subtle analytic lens that accepts that such proceedings historically have been, are today, and will always be political. At the same time, he establishes, convincingly in my view, that this idea of the "political" nature of these trials, must itself be contextualized. The simple fact that political—that is, not explicitly legal—factors are inevitably and inextricably present in the conceptualization of war crimes and crimes against humanity and in legalized attempts to deal with their consequences does not inherently transform a war crimes trial from one in which some political elements are present into a Stalinist show trial.[8]

None of these objections and caveats means that war crimes trials cannot per se serve memorial or didactic purposes or that historians have not profited from these proceedings and the investigations that have given rise to the prosecutions as valuable sources of historical knowledge. Instead, it simply means that at some level we must return to the dual anxiety expressed by Saul Friedlander, that the enormity of the Shoah both quantitatively and qualitatively poses an essential challenge to our ability to tell stories about the Shoah in ways that are appropriate to the genre in which the narration occurs.

For law these anxieties are familiar. Simpson's taxonomy serves as a useful introductory emplotment of the issues. He identifies three classes of issues that arise in relation to law's didactic/pedagogical function—proportion, incompatibility, and legitimation. By these he means: can law develop a semiotics commensurate with the horror of atrocities? Second, can law serve two masters—justice and history? Finally, does the history established through law in war crimes trials "lend authority to the prosecuting authority or state?"[9] Law and history, as we have seen, enter into conflict over the goals of individual justice and the nature and role of the expert historical witness in criminal proceedings. A study arising from Australian attempts to prosecute Heinrich Wagner shifts the focus onto another basic and central issue raised in all debates about law, history, memory, and justice in war crimes trials. The Wagner case highlights the anxieties shared between law and history over the instabilities of discourses and about the elusive nature of facts themselves. The Wagner prosecution highlights the impact that these instabilities might have both for a legal and historical search for truth and some collective attempt as embodied in war crimes proceedings to achieve a state of justice.

LAW, HISTORY, TRUTH, AND THE SEMIOTICS
OF "WAR CRIMES" TRIALS

It is useful to return briefly to Arendt's critique of the Eichmann proceedings in order to develop an argument about, or at least a context for, the Australian proceedings against Heinrich Wagner. Arendt argued against the Israeli trial not because she discovered an inherently fatal flaw in the conflict between criminal law's search for individual guilt and the enormity of the facts, historical reality, and issues relating to the killing of European Jews by the Nazis and their allies. Rather, she identified a conceptual flaw in existing legal categories that formed the basis of the Israeli case. For Arendt what Eichmann did, the crimes of which he stood accused, were crimes of genocide, mass murder, crimes against humanity.

This interpretation had two immediate consequences for her analysis. First, because of the universal nature of the harm, mere national tribunals were inherently unsuited to sit in judgment. National courts could and can make no claim to universal jurisdiction. Instead, an international court, entrusted with universal jurisdiction, was the only possible venue for such proceedings. In this respect she echoed, to a large extent before the fact, ongoing debates over the jurisdictional question of prosecutions for crimes against humanity, genocide, and war crimes and the conceptual status of national claims to the exercise of universal jurisdiction.

But the second, substantive objection raised to the trial of Eichmann in Jerusalem is of more central concern in the context of the Australian prosecution of Heinrich Wagner for crimes committed against the so-called mixed-race, or *Mischlinge*, children of Israylovka. For Arendt "nothing is more pernicious to an understanding of these new crimes, or stands more in the way of the emergence of an international penal code that could take care of them, than the common illusion that the crime of murder and the crime of genocide are essentially the same, and that the latter therefore is 'no new crime properly speaking.' The point of the latter is that an altogether different order is broken and an altogether different community is violated."[10] She reasserted her position in a postscript, in which she condemned "the inadequacy of the prevailing legal system and of current juridical concepts to deal with the facts of administrative massacres organized by the state apparatus."[11]

For all its failures and weaknesses international criminal law has come a long way in dealing with the fundamental concerns raised by Arendt in the early 1960s. But this book deals not with international criminal law and the history of the struggle to create an international criminal jurisdiction but with one small country's attempts to confront the larger lacunae that may make themselves manifest through a national system of criminal justice that prosecutes Holocaust perpetrators by way of an assertion, however circumscribed, of universal jurisdiction.

The specific tale of this chapter about the shooting of the Jewish children of Israylovka is proof that Arendt's concerns about the ethical and legal failures of the international community to deal with crimes of genocide, war crimes, and crimes against humanity were specifically addressed by Australia. The War Crimes Act as amended by the Australian Parliament in the late 1980s recognized both the specificity of the Shoah as a historical and ethical phenomenon and the need to create a new category of criminal offense to deal with that specificity. Other facts, however, first problematize Arendt's position and then serve to confirm the inherent fragility of law that informs all interventions of the subject of criminalizing the Holocaust.

The first issue that must be underlined is that the three Australian cases involve, at some important level of characterization, understanding, and narration, a different type of offense than that of which Eichmann stood accused. Eichmann, despite the prosecution's futile attempt to attribute direct responsibility for one personal killing, stood accused of crimes of bureaucracy. He was the quintessential desk killer of the Holocaust, an administrative official who used his expertise and position in the governmental apparatus to exterminate hundreds of thousands, if not millions, of European Jews. His was a state crime par excellence. He was found guilty because of his personal and professional involvement in what Arendt called "administrative massacres organized by the state apparatus." His crimes were the literal and figurative crimes of "Auschwitz"—the bureaucratized, industrialized killing of Jews, the manifestation in concrete form of Zygmunt Bauman's argument that the processes and public and private structures of modernity are to be found at the core of the Shoah.[12]

Heinrich Wagner, Ivan Polyukhovich, and Mikolay Berezowsky, on the other hand, found themselves at the opposite end of the killing spectrum from Eichmann. They did not involve themselves with deportation assembly camps, train transport, ramp selection, or mass gassings. They were, if the allegations against them were true, lower-level functionaries in an associated killing apparatus. They belonged to and participated in the same project as Eichmann, the Final Solution, but they were hands-on, artisan killers. Wagner lived in the same area where the *Mischlinge* children of Israylovka were rounded up. According to the prosecution case, he was involved in the use of Nikolay Nikitovich Daviborshch's horse-drawn cart to transport the children to a pit in the woods, not to an industrialized gassing facility. He allegedly shot the children as they were tossed into the air to fall into the pit. This was murder more than it was administrative massacre. This was not the Shoah of mobile gas vans or Zyklon B but "the Holocaust by bullets."[13]

This distinction reveals one of the fissures at the core of intersections between and among law, history, memory, and justice in relation to the Shoah and Holocaust-related trials. The Holocaust itself was constituted through a complex and multifaceted matrix of ideologies, actions, and actors. Eichmann, the bureaucrat who traveled throughout Europe organizing the machinery of deportations and mass killings in extermination camps, was a Holocaust perpetrator. Heinrich Wagner, who never traveled beyond the narrow confines of a few neighboring towns and villages in Ukraine, where he had lived in close vicinity to his victims, and who was alleged to have participated in the shooting of the Jews and the *Mischlinge* children of Israylovka, was also a Holocaust perpetrator. While Arendt's argument about the necessity for a new criminal law paradigm is perhaps persuasive in relation to Eichmann, and state crime, there would appear to be little to distinguish, other than at the level of motive, Wagner from any other cold-blooded killer.

But of course, that cannot be the sole truth of Wagner's case. The Australian federal government could only lay claim constitutionally to jurisdiction over Wagner if his actions could be said to fall somehow outside the ordinary confines of traditional, territorially limited understandings of murder. This condition meant that the crimes for which Wagner was charged had to fall within the complex set of definitions and cascading requirements set out in the War Crimes Act. The offense with which he was charged in relation to the *Mischlinge* children had to be a serious crime, in this instance murder (sec. 6 [1] [a]). It had also to have been at the time it was committed a crime (murder) in South Australia (sec. 6 [3] [b]). Additionally, the serious crime of murder must have been a war crime as defined in section 7—that is, in this case committed during the course of an armed occupation and then "(a) committed: (i) in the course of political, racial or religious persecution; or (ii) with intent to destroy in whole or in part a national, ethnic, racial or religious group, as such; and (b) committed in the territory of a country when the country was involved in a war or when territory of the country was subject to an occupation."[14]

In other words, the crime committed by Wagner must have been at one and the same time ordinary murder and extraordinary killing committed in pursuit of the Nazi policy of the Final Solution of the Jewish question. The Australian statute necessarily takes the Wagner case outside the strict confines of Arendt's ill-defined crimes of genocide or crimes against humanity that are of universal concern. Its requirement of the commission of a specific identifiable, ordinary crime such as murder, as recognized in contemporaneous, domestic criminal law, legally "Australianizes" the Holocaust. The War Crimes Act then returns to a status closer to the Arendtian ideal by establishing a set of special elements of racial persecution and war/occupation that transform the offense into a war crime, a crime of universal interest and concern.

The Wagner case, like those of Polyukhovich and Berezowsky, sits somewhat uncomfortably among the various roles attributed to law, justice, history, and memory first by the very nature of the statutory regime under which it was brought. War, occupation, and the Final Solution as historical facts become essential elements of the offense with which Wagner is charged. Arendt gets her wish in the sense that law creates a new categorical offense to deal with the historical and ontological horror of the Shoah. But at the same time the trial by necessity becomes didactic or pedagogical almost against the will of liberal legality. World War II, Operation Barbarossa, the military and civilian administration established under the Nazis in Ukraine, the role of local Ukrainian forces, Schutzmannschaft, *Hilfspolizei*, the part played by Volksdeutsche, the construction and narration of all these major historical issues come to the fore as essential elements of the basic (and new) criminal offense of a "serious war crime." History and law become symbiotic elements within the trial process, but throughout they retain a separate rhetorical status.

DAVIBORSHCH'S CART: NARRATING
THE SHOAH IN UKRAINE

The local population of Volksdeutschen, imprecisely or incompletely rendered in many English-language texts as "ethnic Germans," played an important, if complex and often ambiguous, role in Nazi-occupied

Eastern Europe in general and in Ukraine in this case. The idea of "Lebensraum" was a key component of Nazi population policy and the basis for German claims of a right to many of the occupied territories. The protection of local German-speaking populations was a vital ideological and propaganda component of these Nazi expansion plans.[15] More centrally, as Doris Bergen writes, "in a fundamental way, the dichotomy in nazi racial policy between Jews and Volksdeutsche created incentives for open support of anti-semitic activity. Nazi regulations made ethnic Germans the prime beneficiaries of property stolen from Jews. When Germans and their helpers deported and murdered Jews, they often reassigned the homes left vacant to ethnic Germans who either came from the region or had been resettled there."[16]

The Volksdeutsche communities encountered by the Einsatzgruppen as they swept their way through Ukraine in June and July 1941 had suffered in the Nazi worldview from intermarriage with local ethnic Poles, Russians, and Ukrainians, but they had largely maintained a separate identity, mainly through their distinct (i.e., nonorthodox) religious adherence. According to the newly arrived occupation forces, they had to be carefully nurtured back to their Germanic heritage and exposed in incremental doses to National Socialism.

One way in which local ethnic Germans were more fully incorporated into the new occupation regime was through their involvement in the local police force.[17] Heinrich Wagner was from the Volksdeutsche village of Springfeld. The village had a population of 222 individuals at the time of occupation and was situated roughly fifteen kilometers from Israylovka, the key location for the events that would resurface in the Australian prosecution some fifty years later.[18] A young man at the time, barely out of his teens, Wagner joined the police and served, among other roles, as an interpreter for the Gendarmerie. He was accused of having been a lead actor in the killings of the Jewish population of Israylovka in the summer of 1942. More specifically for the stories that follow, the prosecution argued that Wagner participated actively in the shooting of the *Mischlinge* children of the village.

One year after the arrival of German forces, as workers on the collective farms toiled in the fields throughout the region, the second wave of mass killings of Ukraine's Jewish population began. The remaining Jews in the village of Israylovka, later renamed Berezovatka, were rounded up by local, Ukrainian police in the final mass *Aktion*. As the Russian and Ukrainian inhabitants looked on from the doorsteps and windows of their houses, their neighbors, the Jews, were marched two kilometers to a ravine, which served as a killing pit, near the neighboring village of Kovalevka. They were shot by Ukrainian and German forces.

The same day, local police were given a list of names of so-called mixed-race children in Israylovka. They were the progeny of Jewish fathers and Ukrainian mothers. Pursuant to decisions made at the Wannsee Conference, which established the framework for the Shoah, a much broader definition of the newly fatal legal category "Jew" was applied to those of "mixed race" in the occupied territories than that which operated in Germany itself: "Persons of mixed blood of the first degree will, as regards the final solution of the Jewish question, be treated as Jews."[19] The Ukrainian policemen instructed the mothers to bring their children to the local administration building for "registration."

On this bright, sunlit summer morning in 1942 a twenty-year-old Ukrainian man, Nikolay Nikitovich Daviborshch, was going about his usual business. Too frail to have been drafted into the local police, Daviborshch was employed on the local collective farm. He made deliveries of water on his cart, a two-wheeled gig pulled by a twin team of horses. The day started out much like any other for Daviborshch as he made his way to Israylovka with a cart filled with water barrels. Events would soon change his life. As he began his delivery in the village, he was accosted by two Ukrainian police officers, Zhilun and Gering, and told to bring his cart right away to the village administration building. After changing his team of horses, Daviborshch went in his cart to the town hall. There he was confronted by a scene of heartbreak and hardship that would haunt him for the rest of his life.

The mothers of the *Mischlinge* and their children were brought from the town officials' offices, where they had come for registration. Amid screams and cries of horror the children were torn by the police from their mothers' arms, grabbed, and thrown into the back of Daviborshch's cart. The women were beaten by the police as they resisted. Soon Daviborshch's cart, which measured three meters long by one meter wide, was filled with wailing children. They ranged in age from four months to eleven or twelve years old.

Once the children had been loaded into the cart by the police, Daviborshch, who had sat silently throughout the ordeal, accompanied by Schutzmann officer Zhilun, who sat behind him in the cart, and other police on horseback, ordered the horses to begin the journey to the ravine near the neighboring village of Kovalevka. Following directions from guards posted near the site, Daviborshch drove his cart off the road into the woods and stopped about five or six meters from the pit. Local police and some from nearby areas, who were awaiting their arrival, grabbed the children from the cart and dragged them to the edge of the pit. As they threw them in, they began shooting. Daviborshch was ordered to leave.

In 1964 the Soviet newspaper *Trud* (Labor) published an article titled "Wild Animals Disguised as Human Beings—'Traitors Shall Not Go Unpunished.'" The story identified Heinrich Wagner as a Jew killer. "The degenerate Heinrich Vagner was then eighteen years of age and this was only one of the bloody pages of this sadist's biography. Vagner escaped as did other criminals and was able to save himself from the wrath of the people. Now he is living peacefully, sheltering a safe 10,000 kilometres from the villages of Ustinovka and Berezovka. However, there they remember him; there they believe that justice will finally be done."[20]

Wagner was identified as living at an address in Adelaide. The Australian Embassy in Moscow translated the article and sent it to authorities in Canberra. On 7 August 1964 the Department of Immigration forwarded the results of its investigations to the head of the Australian Security Intelligence Organisation (ASIO), informing the intelligence service that while no trace of "Wagner" could be found, it was probable that he was in fact living under the name of Andrej Woijtenko.

> Enquiries made by the Commonwealth Migration Office, Adelaide disclosed that a Heinrich Wagner, born 9/1/22, and his wife, Erna, born 11/5/21, left 54 Gladstone Avenue, Kilburn about four years ago, and they are now living at 23 Clearview Crescent, Clearview, South Australia. It will be observed that the dates of birth of the person known as Wagner, and his wife, correspond with the dates of birth of Wijtenko and his wife, and that they, at one stage [*sic*] resided at the address given in the article. Whilst it is not possible to positively identify Heinrich Wagner as Andrej Woijtenko, there is every indication that they are one and the same person.[21]

As early as 1964, the Australian government was aware of the probable presence of a Nazi war criminal who had entered the country under an assumed identity. They also knew that "Woijtenko" had changed his name and was now known under his original identity, Heinrich Wagner. The file then fell into the bureaucratic oblivion of Cold War diplomacy until the Menzies Review received allegations once again referring to the *Trud* article, and SIU investigations commenced.[22] In 1991 Heinrich Wagner, of Hindmarsh Island, South Australia, was arrested by Australian police and charged in Adelaide with killing the children of Israylovka. The information read in part, "He did murder approximately nineteen children aged between about 4 months and 11 years of age, including both boys and girls, whose fathers were Jewish and mothers Russian/Ukrainian, many of whose names cannot be ascertained."[23]

Daviborshch and Zhilun were key witnesses against Wagner. They were the two surviving individuals who had been present at the pit where the *Mischlinge* of Israylovka had been delivered to their fate as part of the massacres of Ukrainian Jewry during the German occupation. What follows is a recounting of the two stories of what happened at the pit, in the forest, just off the road to Kovalevka. What emerges

5. Heinrich Wagner and wife outside Adelaide court. © Newspix.

from this retelling of one concrete set of events relating to the Shoah in Ukraine is the encounter between and among testimony, law, cross-examination, and advocacy, history, and the frailties of the human mind and spirit. Narrative stability, however desirable, collapses in the confrontation between law's need for individual culpability and history's and humanity's fragile complexity.

Daviborshch Recounts

The Berezowsky and Polyukhovich cases, each in its own way, demonstrated the complementary and contradictory narrative demands and structures of law and history. In the case against Wagner a primary concern was again this tension between two discursive practices each searching for a form of narrative stability and truth. Much of the evidence available against Wagner was to be found in the proof gathered by the Extraordinary State Commission (ESC) and its local subsidiary agencies in the immediate aftermath of the retreat of German forces and subsequently in Soviet criminal proceedings against Ukrainian police officials. When Special Investigations Unit historian Martin Dean tendered his written evidence in the case, Wagner's defense lawyers objected to many passages of his opinion evidence on the grounds that those parts of the document were grounded in inadmissible hearsay. They argued that any evidence based in ESC or Soviet proceedings was inadmissible because they could not possibly cross-examine those who had compiled the evidence about the circumstances surrounding the investigation.

In this respect they reiterated the original argument about Soviet protocol and ESC evidence as hearsay that had been proclaimed in the opening stages of historical expert evidence in the case against Berezowsky. If that Soviet evidence was hearsay, Dean's opinion, as historical double hearsay, could have no admissible basis in law.[24] The prosecution sought to argue that established practice in war crimes or Holocaust-related cases in other jurisdictions had permitted such expert opinion testimony when that opinion was grounded in historical documents. For the prosecution Dean's opinion evidence was precisely that, opinion evidence based on the careful study of documents using the witness's professional expertise.

The issue was therefore what historical and what consequent legal authority could be said to inhere in the ESC and related evidence. The court found that there were good grounds to exclude such evidence. It noted that part of Dean's own evidence concerning appropriate historical methodology asserted that historians had to interpret historical documents in relation to all relevant circumstances, including careful scrutiny of the source of the statement or document. Dean himself indicated that Soviet investigative and trial materials had to be subjected to special levels of scrutiny.[25] In addition, the laws of evidence generally require judicial skepticism toward any document prepared "in contemplation of litigation" because such documents will necessarily or probably carry the biases inherent in the position of the party wishing to invoke them.[26] Because ESC protocols formed part of a complex set of documentary and other evidence created by Soviet authorities with the aim of identifying war criminals for prosecution in the aftermath of Nazi occupation, they had clearly, as far as the magistrate at Wagner's committal was concerned, been prepared "in contemplation of litigation."

The court also pointed out that circumstances in the Soviet Union, both at the time of the ESC and in subsequent criminal proceedings, cast further doubt on the reliability of these historical sources. Stalinist repression, of which the court took judicial notice, was ever-present. This set of state practices was combined perhaps with personal animosity and the desire for retribution by witnesses against local collaborators who had worked with and for the Nazis. The joinder of these historical, political, and human factors meant that the evidence itself had to be treated as suspect.[27] Finally, the magistrate indicated that ESC and other proceedings were not in the same category of historical and valid legal processes, and therefore of reliability, as the IMT at Nuremberg and documents produced there. These were trials conducted not by untrustworthy Soviets but by the international community. Judges from the United States and United Kingdom, whose standards and safeguards would make evidence derived from and through the trial reliable, sat on the tribunal.[28] This legal assessment of the IMT trial and the verdict by the Adelaide magistrate is arguably problematic. A different conclusion about the absolute historical reliability of the IMT at Nuremberg on several points such as the Katyn massacre, itself based on fraudulent ESC material, is clearly possible. But the fact remains that the magistrate struck out large portions of Dean's statement.[29] As a matter of Australian law in the case against Wagner, the historical, and as a consequence the legal, value of ESC and Soviet trial material was apparently neutered.

Again, this decision by the presiding magistrate simply indicates that the application of standards of admissibility in the laws of evidence in a criminal trial is different from the application of rules of historical methodology in assessing the reliability of the same documents. It is not a conclusion that can be said in any meaningful sense to affect the epistemological status of the information to be found in these Soviet materials. Indeed, Dean's own statement made it clear that ESC and related evidence was reliable only following a deeper historiographical analysis of other facts and documents and after a careful professional reading and interpretation of all the evidence. On the other hand, the exclusion of such evidence as a basis for historical expert opinion does perhaps have a direct impact on any claim that committal hearings in these circumstances might have a broad and deep general pedagogic function about the Shoah. But the story of the story of the Shoah in *Wagner* and of the ESC and Soviet evidence does not end here.

The exclusion of the evidence proffered by Dean did in fact not mean that all ESC and Soviet investigative or trial protocol material was totally excluded. The main basis for the exclusion of Dean's evidence was the hearsay rule and the necessary corollary that the defense could not cross-examine on the statements, therefore depriving the accused of a fair trial if such evidence were admitted. In the circumstances of the Wagner case, however, two witnesses, Zhilun and Daviborshch, who had participated in the Soviet proceedings, were alive and available to be examined. This meant that important Soviet material would in fact be presented to the court and that the reliability and veracity of statements made in these proceedings would go to the heart of the most important substantive questions of the case against Heinrich Wagner.

In 1947 Ivan Konstantinovich Zhilun was arrested, interrogated, and tried for crimes of collaboration committed during his tenure as member of the local police during the occupation. Among the witnesses against him at his trial on 5 June 1947 was Nikolay Niki-tovich Daviborshch.[30] In this first judicial recounting of the events on the day the *Mischlinge* infants and children of Israylovka were killed, Daviborshch stated, "In summer 1942, in June or July, I don't remember the date, two policemen, ZHILUN and VAGNER, came to my place and ordered me to harness the cart and drive to the village Administration office."[31]

This statement contains a discrepancy on a minor element of the story that would be told by others that Daviborshch was already in the process of delivering the water when he was approached and instructed to drive to the administration office. In this version he was approached at home. But more significantly for subsequent Australian judicial proceedings, he identified both Wagner and Zhilun as having been present at the village. He went on to identify Zhilun as the policeman who had arrested the children and brought them to the village office. Zhilun, on the other hand, consistently asserted that the mothers of the children were simply instructed to bring their children for registration to the village administration office and that his active role was limited to helping to put the *Mischlinge* into Daviborshch's cart and riding along to the pit. Daviborshch added that Zhilun had played an active and physically aggressive role in the process of loading the children into the cart: "When the women—the children's mothers—dashed towards the cart which was taking their children away, policeman ZHILUN did not let them get near and beat them with the butt of his rifle."[32]

After describing taking the children, under Zhilun's instructions, along the road, Daviborshch offered the key piece of evidence about Zhilun's presence at the killing pit: "ZHILUN took the children off the cart, but I did not see who shot them because I had left . . . I was about 10 metres from the pit, but while they were taking the children off the cart they weren't throwing them into the pit and shooting them. I heard the shots when I'd already driven away."[33]

Daviborshch in this first version of his story places himself and his cart very close to the edge of the pit. Zhilun plays an active role in loading the children into the cart in the village, in beating off the mothers in their desperate attempts to save or even to say farewell to their children. Finally, Daviborshch states categorically that he did not see the shooting of the children. He drove away after they were unloaded and only heard the gunshots after he had left. Wagner is not present or identified in this version of the pit killing. Given that the focus of this Soviet proceeding was to establish Zhilun's liability, the last point is perhaps hardly surprising and not necessarily definitive in establishing that Wagner was or was not present. Zhilun was found guilty of, among other things, having participated in the delivery of the *Mischlinge* children to the execution site and was sentenced to twenty-five years in a "corrective labor camp."[34]

Daviborshch next testified about the massacre of the "children of mixed-race" from Israylovka in the 1957–58 proceedings against the former local police chief Marchik. During this case the Daviborshch version of events again changed subtly yet crucially. While confirming Zhilun's presence during the cart ride to the pit, Daviborshch this time stated that he was approached on the road as he was riding in his cart, a change from the original version, and identified "Vagner" only as the policeman who ordered him to the village administration building. He was able to identify Marchik only through hearsay.[35]

The next set of narratives from Daviborshch came as a direct result of the Australian investigations of Heinrich Wagner. The passage of forty-three years between the trial of Zhilun and the first Australian questioning gave rise to some important and significant changes in the narrative of the killing of the *Mischlinge* children of Israylovka. The interview that took place in the Ukrainian Socialist Republic in November 1990 is remarkable first for the simple fact that it occurred at all. The interrogation of a Soviet witness, in the presence of an Australian police investigator, was the result of many years of careful and delicate negotiations between Australian and Soviet and Ukrainian authorities. It, along with the other investigations carried out by the SIU, also embodies a significant victory for the rule of law in Australian war crimes proceedings.

Concern had been consistently voiced in Australia during debates over the introduction of the amendments to the War Crimes Act on the issue of the reliability of Soviet source documentary evidence. In addition to worries, unwarranted as it turned out in practice, about KGB forgeries, many in Australia had expressed doubts about the free and voluntary nature of witness statements emanating from the Soviet Union. From the very beginning of the investigative process Australian police and prosecution lawyers were careful to ensure that Australian rules of evidence and investigative practices and techniques would always inform the way they conducted themselves. While Ukrainian law demanded that certain procedures also be followed for any and all interrogations of witnesses on Ukrainian soil, all such encounters in the case against Wagner always occurred in the presence of, and were in fact led by, Australian officials.

When Daviborshch was interviewed on 12 November 1990 in Kirovograd in the Procurator's Office, police officer John Ralston of the SIU led the questioning. The senior assistant procurator present, Mr. Komendyak, warned both Daviborshch and the interpreter that they were bound to tell the truth and to give a true and faithful rendering of the questions and answers under articles 178, 179, and 128 of the Ukrainian SSR Criminal Code.[36] Daviborshch then answered Ralston's questions about events in Israylovka on a sunny summer day in 1942.

Daviborshch recounted how Zhilun and other policemen had approached him at the stables where he was loading water barrels and ordered him to go to the village administration building. The discrepancies are again minor and relate to the issue of exactly where he was approached by the police. In the various accounts Daviborshch was confronted on the road, at his house, and now at the stables. At another level the inconsistency becomes somewhat more significant because in this retelling of events Wagner is no longer present in Israylovka. But the next change in detail about what happened on the road to Ustinovka is central to the legal story of Wagner's participation in events at the forest killing pit. In recounting the scene at the village administration building, Daviborshch identified some of the mothers present because they were his neighbors in Israylovka: "I can't say how many children there were, I was very much upset and touched and moved. I knew all of them. I knew all of them. I knew all women."[37] Then he added, "They were mothers and of course they tried to take them away, they were yelping, crying screaming."[38]

He left the village with a cart full of crying Jewish children. In this telling, however, according to Daviborshch, he came nowhere near the pit. Instead of having driven the cart with the children to within ten meters of the killing site and having witnessed the unloading of the children by Zhilun and other unidentified police, here Daviborshch removes himself from the killing site altogether: "Then I was ordered to leave the cart, it happened on the main road and the cart with the children was taken further deep into the forest. I couldn't see any longer where they were taken."[39]

He reasserted his distance from the events by adding, "I didn't drop them off, I only left, I only brought them to the edge of the forest and they were taken further to the forest on this horse cart and then I was given empty horse cart."[40] He also stated, "There was a field, small field and after that for some 400 or 500 metres they were taken deep into the forest, I think."[41]

Far from being within ten meters of the killing pit, as he was in his 1947 version, Daviborshch in this telling finds himself more than a half-kilometer from the shooting area. He gave up his cart and saw nothing further. As for Wagner's role that day, Daviborshch recalls, "The policemen called, mentioned his name, but with what connection, I don't know why they mentioned his name."[42]

This version of events adds some important and moving color about the pandemonium at the village administration building as the women saw their children being loaded into Daviborshch's cart. It also gives voice to his own sadness, despair, and fear that day. Legally speaking, it is largely exculpatory of Wagner. Daviborshch admits that he only knew of Wagner by hearsay, by stories that circulated about an ethnic German from Springfeld, named Wagner, who held some high post in the police but whom Daviborshch did not know personally.[43] Furthermore, in this narrative Daviborshch was not present at the pit and could offer no information about the shooting of the *Mischlinge* children because he was on the road, more than a half-kilometer away, with any view blocked by distance and the forest.

Members of the Wagner defense team also interviewed Daviborshch in September 1992 in Berezovatka, formerly Israylovka.[44] Once again, the inherent problems of eyewitness narration were manifest. On the key question of Wagner's identity and his presence at the pit during the killing of the children, Daviborshch remained unmoved from his 1990 statement in response to John Ralston's questions: "The only thing I know about him is that I have heard Wagner, the name Wagner mentioned. That is what I have been saying before."[45]

He was consistent. "In all the statements they have been asking me I have heard the name but I have never seen him, never met him and I don't know him."[46] Daviborshch then confirmed the events at the village administration building, including his previous, but not original, assertion that Zhilun had instructed him to bring his cart and that Zhilun took part in loading the children.[47]

We now come to one of the most significant statements by Daviborshch, which finds an echo in the central conflict between law and history, testimony and documentary evidence, truth and justice, which came to characterize the Wagner case. The junior defense lawyer David Edwardson put Daviborshch's statement before the Kirovograd Military Tribunal in the 1947 trial of Zhilun to him. That statement differed in significant details about his presence at the pit from his responses to Australian questioning. Daviborshch offered his own rule of law critique. "Look, those people they will try to get you to say anything. It is different with you. But those trials, they were writing whatever they wanted to write. Listen to me. At that trial there was a sheet of paper, everything was prepared, there was only a photograph missing. They would put your photograph on it or somebody else's, and that's finished, the case is finished and it goes to trial and no matter what happens, that is the way we are being dealt with."[48]

Daviborshch's assertion about the artificial nature of proof and evidence at Soviet collaborator trials raises basic issues for our understanding of truth, justice, and law in Holocaust trials in both the USSR and in jurisdictions such as Australia and about their proper place in historical study. It is necessary to underline a simple difficulty that arises here for historical discourse, practice, and knowledge, in this case about one incident in the Holocaust in Ukraine. Christopher Browning in his work on perpetrator testimony as a source of reliable historical evidence has underlined the care with which such sources, with their inherent tendency to exculpation and minimization of involvement, must be approached.[49] Patricia Heberer and Jürgen Matthäus have more recently issued a warning about the importance of context and corroboration when using trial records and perpetrator testimony:

> The judicial record is extremely difficult to use for historical purposes, as are all postwar statements coming from the perpetrators themselves. Generally, the rule applies that the reliability of perpetrator testimony is greatest the further it is removed from the issue of personal guilt and the more it can be scrutinized against the background of other sources, such as witness testimonies, diaries, letters, or other wartime writings, rare as they usually are. Consequently, affidavits of the accused, created in the course of judicial investigations, should only be used with caution; they are a problematic source to gauge personal motivation of perpetrators at the time of the crimes.[50]

This particular caveat is perhaps more directly applicable to the considerations and analyses of Zhilun's statements, given that Zhilun is a convicted participant in atrocities. Daviborshch is at best a reluctant actor. Nonetheless, the concerns raised about the reliability of trial records and witness statements may perhaps take on a greater cogency when applied in the context of Soviet war crimes proceedings. Recent historiographical scholarship has identified the potential benefits to be derived from the increasingly more accessible records of Soviet war crimes investigations and trials.[51] Again, the positive aspects can be found at several different levels. Soviet war crimes investigations and trials may well be emerging as a new subgenre of historical research. These recently available materials offer new insights into and knowledge of specific events and local contexts of collaboration and the Shoah in the occupied Soviet Union, especially given the focused and local nature of most Soviet legal investigations. Such evidence might lead to important new analyses of such important historical questions as perpetrator motivations, or the evolving place of crimes against Jews in Soviet ideology and politics as revealed in the investigative and evidentiary focus of different proceedings at different times and in different places. In addition, from a socio-legal perspective the records of the Soviet war crimes program have the potential to fill in important historical gaps in our understandings of a key, yet largely forgotten or ignored, aspect of the evolution of the law and legal process relating to war crimes and genocide.

But while the study of Soviet investigations may have much to offer both law and history, the realities of the context of the Soviet Union and the various Socialist republics in the immediate post-occupation and postwar periods also call for the exercise of the hermeneutic caution underlined by Browning, Heberer, and Matthäus. Marina Sorokina offers a sobering assessment: "The documentary materials it [the ChGK, Special Commission in the USSR to Investigate Nazi Crimes] created and collected, however, have turned out to be the latest Russian mass grave. In the process of excavating it, historians will for a long time to come be faced with the sometimes fruitless task of distinguishing 'ours' from 'others,' and executioners from victims."[52] If the issue is so fraught and problematic insofar as the creation of a stable historical discourse about the Shoah in Ukraine is concerned, the idea that Soviet trial testimony is invariably, or even individually, tainted as Daviborshch asserted to the defense team in Berezovatka in September 1992, for a trial process aimed at establishing guilt beyond a reasonable doubt, the problematic nature of this type of evidence must be almost insurmountable.

For the moment I return to Daviborshch's far from stable account. "I was frightened, I was, but I was afraid that I would get shot here as well. As long as I was driving and following Zhilun I wasn't afraid, but the moment I saw what was going to happen, I was afraid that I will be finished off as the others."[53] At the same time, confronted with his 1947 statement, Daviborshch asserts, among other things, that the cart was already harnessed and had simply to be taken to the village administration building. He added that Zhilun did not participate in putting the children in the cart. Again, what he remembers with precision at this point is his own fear: "I was afraid of everybody. I was sitting on the cart and I thought I would be shot with the others."[54]

While in previous versions of the story Zhilun rode in the cart with Daviborshch and the children, in the 1992 narration Zhilun rode on horseback and Daviborshch followed with the children. Nevertheless, his presence reassured Daviborshch because he knew Zhilun as a neighbor from Israylovka. Along the road to Ustinovka the cart was stopped by police. Daviborshch finds himself even further from the killing pit than he had in his answer to Ralston's inquiry in November 1990: "When my cart was taken away I stopped it about, I was ordered to stop about 500–600 metres before the pit. Then I have got out. When I moved away, then I heard shots and then I guessed what has happened. Then I was standing there and I was afraid that the next one to be shot will be myself."[55]

Fundamentally, Daviborshch's story has changed little in this regard—he is a bit farther away from the pit. At each telling he is physically more distant. Psychologically, he always appears to be more proximate to the shooting. But in one key legal aspect his story has changed significantly. When asked where Zhilun was when all this, including the shooting, was taking place, Daviborshch now distanced the former policeman from the pit as well. Zhilun was on horseback, not on the cart. "He was patrolling the road."[56] In response to further detailed questioning by David Edwardson, Daviborshch was adamant about Zhilun's physical location and his role: "What happened after I left I don't know, he could have gone then, but whilst I was standing there, Zhilun and three other policemen were patrolling the road."

In this version of the story the events as recounted at Zhilun's 1947 trial are now completely refuted. Instead of driving in the cart to within ten meters of the pit, both Daviborshch and Zhilun are on the road, one standing awaiting the return of his cart, the other patrolling on horseback. Neither witnessed the pit shootings. If we take this version as the truth as experienced by Daviborshch, neither he nor Zhilun could possibly place Wagner at the ravine, let alone identify him as a shooter. While Daviborshch only knew Wagner through hearsay, Zhilun the policeman was in a different situation. He knew Wagner. The effect of the latest version offered by Daviborshch now went to the issue of whether Zhilun could reliably identify Wagner as having been present at the pit. According to Daviborshch, Zhilun himself was guarding the road, at least a half-kilometer away from the killing area, which was not visible from that position.

Daviborshch was too frail to travel to Australia to appear before the court in Adelaide during Wagner's committal. Exceptionally, he gave evidence on commission in Kirovograd, on videotape, before Justice Edward "Ted" Mullighan of South Australia, John Ralston of the SIU, Greg James QC and Grant Niemann for the prosecution, and Michael David QC and Lindy Powell, lawyers for the accused.[57] Many of the elements of the previous stories reasserted themselves. Daviborshch was approached by Zhilun during the delivery of water to the stables and told to come with his cart to the village administration building.[58] Zhilun in this narrative recasting was returned to the cart with Daviborshch on their journey to the edge of the forest two kilometers outside Israylovka.[59] But consistent with his most recent recollections of events, Daviborshch insisted that he was stopped on the main road and the cart was taken from him.[60] What happened to Zhilun as far as Daviborshch was concerned was lost in the mists of time, the vagueness of his memory, and his own unresolved psychological traumas.

> Q. Are you telling us that you can't say whether Mr. Zhilun remained at the road or not.
> A. Do you think I can remember that many things, that many details since 50 years passed.
> Q. So because 50 years have passed are you telling us you cannot remember whether Mr. Zhilun stayed at the road or went with the cart.

A. I cannot, I cannot, what can I remember. To explain it in
plain words, I was scared to death myself especially when I
heard those shots.[61]

*Zhilun Narrates the Shootings of the
Jewish Children of Israylovka*

Ivan Konstantinovich Zhilun served in the local Ukrainian police
force during the period of Nazi occupation. He had previously been
in the Red Army. Taken prisoner by the Germans, he escaped and
returned on foot to Israylovka, where he worked on a local collective farm until called to police duties. He was tried, convicted, and
sentenced to a twenty-five-year term at corrective labor in 1947 but
was released following an amnesty after serving eight years in the
Soviet Gulag. He returned to live in Israylovka/Berezovatka. It goes
without saying that the caveats and suspicions about his testimony as
a convicted perpetrator must be applied to any reading of the texts
that make up this part of the discussion.

Nonetheless, insofar as events concerning Heinrich Wagner's role
in the killing of the Jews of Israylovka are concerned, Zhilun's testimony can arguably, at least on its face, be characterized as reliable.
Zhilun's guilt is itself established, whatever concerns might remain
about the Soviet processes. He had been sentenced and served his
time in conditions that we cannot begin to imagine. He was a policeman, serving the Germans. There is no doubt he rounded up Jews
and led them to a killing site. What he says about Wagner and indeed
about the killing of the *Mischlinge* children more generally, insofar
as others are concerned, is largely unproblematic and is supported
by other testimony and evidence.

He would, however, in his later accounts of events at the killing pit,
insist on the fabricated nature of many of the statements that formed
part of the Ukrainian Soviet case against him. A careful study of his
various testimonies about the rounding up and killing of the *Mischlinge*
children of Israylovka is warranted for at least three reasons. First,
when examined in the light of other available evidence, what Zhilun

has to say about the killings in the summer of 1942 of the Jews of this small Ukrainian village does offer in microcosm an important study of "the Holocaust by bullets." Second, Zhilun's statements in their entirety constitute the strongest evidence against Heinrich Wagner. Zhilun had dealings with Wagner as a fellow policeman during the occupation and before the killings of Israylovka's remaining Jews. He knew him and could identify him. His testimony consistently placed Wagner at the pit and portrayed him as a shooter of Jewish children. Thus, on the limited question of narrowly focused proof of guilt beyond a reasonable doubt, Zhilun's testimony is central to this case in the history of Australian war crimes prosecutions. Third, as a consequence of his centrality in Wagner's prosecution, as a witness who placed Wagner at the killing site with a gun in his hand, the ambiguities of Zhilun's evidence throughout the years and his eventual rejection of the validity of significant parts of the version of events offered in the Soviet trial protocols both call into question the nature and reliability of those proceedings as historical evidence and raise fundamental issues about the ability of the Australian criminal justice system to deal with the frailties, concerns, and doubts that arose fifty or more years after the fact about the reliability of key evidence. Zhilun, perhaps even more than Daviborshch, is situated as a source of uncertainty in the history of Australia's war crimes program, at the crossroads of truth, justice, and law.

The first set of interrogations or interviews of Zhilun took place while he was being held by the military tribunal in Kirovograd in March 1947. He adopted a position then to which he held consistently throughout the more than half-century between his arrest and his testimony in the Wagner case. He was willing to admit to having played an active role in the rounding up of the adult Jews early in the day and that he had accompanied the *Mischlinge* children of Israylovka in the summer of 1942 to the forest pit. Nonetheless, he insisted that he "personally did not take part in shooting any of these persons."[62]

Whatever he said about his own active involvement in the killings, statements that we must always view with a grain of interpretive salt, his identification of those he placed among the actual shooters did remain consistent. He stated that among those who actively participated in the killing of Israylovka's Jewish population were Marchik, the police chief in Ustinovka; his assistant, Kozhan; gendarmes from Ustinovka and Bobrinets; and local Volksdeutsche police, including "Vagner."[63] Historically, an account that asserts the presence of both German police forces, the Gendarmerie and indigenous police units, at pit killings is uncontroversial. The existence of such mixed units in the second wave of killings in Ukraine during the spring, summer, and fall of 1942 was commonplace, even if the ethnic composition of killing units varied to some extent from place to place.[64]

At a subsequent interrogation Soviet investigators put the question of his active participation as a shooter directly to Zhilun. He again held firm and offered the following account, one that places him at the pit along with Daviborshch and his cart:

> No, I don't admit that, since I and GERING brought those children to the place of shooting on a cart; an inhabitant of the village of Berezovatka, the driver DAVIBORSHCH was with us. The German gendarmes and policemen took them from the cart and threw them into the pits. In the pit the children were then finished off by these same policemen and gendarmes. I knew that the arrested children were to be shot later, but I could not fail to arrest them since it had been ordered by MARCHIK, the head of Ustinovka District Police, who actually sent me to carry out the arrests. Having brought the children to be shot, I did not watch them shoot the children as I was very squeamish about that.[65]

Gering, or Ernst Hering, was convicted in 1997 by a German juvenile court (because of his age at the time of the offense) in Cologne of aiding and abetting the killing of the *Mischlinge* children and was sentenced to twenty months (suspended).[66]

On 21 May 1947, pursuant to standard Soviet criminal procedure, Zhilun was confronted with the statement of a witness against him, Tat'yana Kirsanovna Shul'kina, his neighbor in Israylovka, and the mother of Volodya and Tolya, two of the children who traveled to their fate in Daviborshch's cart. Zhilun again recognized the basic facts—that he had participated in the arrests of the adult Jews of Israylovka/Berezovatka earlier in the day and that together with his fellow policeman Gering, and Daviborshch, he had subsequently taken the children to be shot. Again, he insisted that he had not participated in the shootings. He once again identified Marchik and "Vagner" as having been among the shooters.[67] At his trial he repeated the story, without identifying any of the shooters but admitting that he had acted out of fear: "In arresting and sending citizens to the place of shooting I realised that I was committing a very great crime against humanity but I could do nothing, I was afraid of the Germans."[68]

On the same day Zhilun received his twenty-five-year sentence together with a suspension of rights of five years.[69] The military tribunal accepted Zhilun's account of events at the pit. He was found guilty of participating in the arrests of the Jewish population of Israylovka/ Berezovatka and for having transported the *Mischlinge* children to the shooting pit. The tribunal stated that the children "were also executed (by shooting) by the gendarmerie and the police force."

At the end of the first set of Soviet criminal proceedings, the stories of Daviborshch and Zhilun, on all important points, are virtually identical. Zhilun rode to the ravine in the forest off the road to Ustinovka in Daviborshch's cart. The cart had been filled with the *Mischlinge* children of Israylovka at the village administration office, where they had been brought for registration by their Ukrainian mothers. Zhilun and Daviborshch then drove the cart close to the pit, five to six or no more than ten meters away, and watched as the police and gendarmes unloaded the children and shot them. Daviborshch was overwhelmed with fear; Zhilun was obedient, perhaps fearful of retribution for disobeying a superior's orders and admittedly too squeamish to watch the execution itself. None of these emotions, of course, was enough to prevent both Daviborshch and Zhilun from taking their neighbors' children to their deaths, for no reason other than their absent fathers had been identified as Jews. These two concordant eyewitness accounts of the pit shooting of the *Mischlinge* children of Israylovka that emerged during the investigation and trial of Zhilun in 1947 are consistent with everything we know historically and anecdotally about this phase of the Holocaust. In addition, as far as the law goes, on these accounts both Daviborshch and Zhilun were present at the killing pit, and Wagner was identified by someone who knew him and had professional interactions with him before the events at the pit took place, in a relatively contemporaneous judicial hearing. The testimony identified Wagner as having been among those shooting the children.

Ten years after his trial, in January 1957, Zhilun repeated the general outlines of his story during the trial of Marchik, the Ustinovka police chief, first during an interrogation conducted by Lieutenant Goncharenko, of the Second Department, Kirovograd, KGB.[70] In this version of events Zhilun identifies "the interpreter Vagner" as an individual who met Daviborshch's cart on the road to Ustinovka.[71] Like Daviborshch, Zhilun moved some distance from the actual shooting pit in this next version of events. In addition, and ironically perhaps, he gave himself a somewhat more active role in events, albeit as a guard on the outside of the killing circle:

> Having traveled 3–4 kilometres, in a field near a plantation we saw a group of policemen and gendarmes who ordered me, Ernst GERING and Viktor IVASHCHENKO to take up guard about 50 metres in circumference in the form or [*sic*] an encirclement and, at that time, the gendarmes (I don't remember who exactly) began to take the children off the cart and throw them into the pit, while the other policemen were shooting at these children as they flew through the air.
>
> Since I was at a distance of about 50 metres from the place of shooting, I personally saw that the children were shot by the Head of Police MARCHIK, his assistant KOZHAN, the interpreter of the Gendarmerie VAGNER, Aleksandr GIBNER (I don't remember his patronymic) and others whom I don't know by surname.[72]

In this version of the Zhilun narrative he again places himself at the pit during the killings but at the somewhat greater distance of fifty meters and in a role as a perimeter guard. We do not know in this narration if the shootings made him squeamish. Again, however, the story is historically consistent and convincing in its broad general content. The participants belong to groups of police who took an active part in the Holocaust in Ukraine. Members of the Volksdeutsche did serve in such units and as locals often acted as interpreters for their native-born German comrades. Pit killings did take place in the manner described, including in some instances the presence of Schutzmänner as perimeter guards. They were brutal and gruesome affairs. Mass shootings of children were no different.[73] As a legal document, if we put aside for the time being issues about the authenticity of what was said, this statement again places Wagner at the pit in the forest outside Ustinovka. Zhilun puts a gun in Wagner's hand and killing in his heart.

At his confrontation with Marchik on 1 February 1958, Zhilun repeated the same details, including his placement at the perimeter, some "50–60 metres from the place of execution."[74] Significantly, he added, "The children were shot from ten-round rifles of the Russian type (TN: the self-loading Tokarev rifle, SVT) which had been specially brought there."[75]

Thirty years later, as investigations began into Wagner's wartime activity, the Procurator's Office in Kirovograd reexamined the files from the Zhilun and Marchik cases "on the instructions of the Procurator's Office of the USSR in relation to the documenting of the criminal activity of Andrej Wojtenko (Heinrich Friedrikovich Wagner) during the Great Patriotic War 1941–1945."[76] Zhilun was then interrogated for two and one half hours at the Procurator's Office. He reiterated his previous version of events, in which he admitted having participated in the arrest of the adult Jews of Israylovka and in the transportation of the *Mischlinge* children in Daviborshch's cart later that same day. He again identified "Vagner" as having been among the shooters at the pit "from their rifles."[77] The detail of the

Australian transcript is perhaps more telling. Here Zhilun declares: "I saw Vagner personally shot them. It all happened very quickly. That's all I know about him."[78]

Later, in response to more specific questioning, he elaborated on Wagner's role: "[TN: He threw them into the pit straight away and shot them in the air they had rifles, they were armed, semiautomatic rifles with 10 loadings]. No the cart stopped. The cart just stopped right near the pit and they were just taken off and shot immediately, so it all took a second."[79]

More detail followed, consistent in part with Zhilun's previous statements but this time returning to the original version from his own trial, placing himself not as a perimeter guard fifty meters away but much closer to the cart, to Daviborshch, and to the pit.

Q. Did you see Vagner shoot any child?
A. Definitely I did.
Q. Okay. Do you know how many Vagner shot?
A. I don't know. I couldn't count them it so quick. It was all very quick.
Q. Okay were they shot at the top of the pit, and then thrown in, or were they put in the pit and the shot?
A. Nobody put them anywhere. They were just thrown in and shot. As they flew they were shot in the air as they were dropped in, thrown in.
Q. And what type of weapon was Vagner using do you recall?
A. He had a pistol but they also had, especially for this purpose only they had semi-automatic rifles.
Q. Okay and did you see him using the automatic rifle?
A. Vagner?
Q. Yes.
A. Yes, I did of course.

Q. Okay and how far were you from Vagner, when this was taking place?
A. Right next to him, five meters, six meters.[80]

Zhilun was again interviewed by Australian SIU representatives in December 1989 at the Rovno Procurator's office. On that occasion Zhilun was confronted with a photo board but was unable to identify Wagner among the pictures.[81] In 1991 Australian investigators returned to Ukraine and interviewed Zhilun as he walked them through the village of Berezovatka indicating the places where the Jewish children had been gathered into the cart and led to their deaths.[82]

ZHILUN: CROSS-EXAMINATIONS OF HISTORY AND LAW

Zhilun, the only remaining eyewitness who continued to place himself and Wagner at the pit when the *Mischlinge* children of Israylovka/ Berezovatka were shot, was a key witness at Wagner's committal hearing in Adelaide in the late Australian winter and early antipodean summer of 1992. Daviborshch was too ill to make the journey from Ukraine, and in any event in the most recent version of his story he had placed himself so far away from the pit, more than a half-kilometer, that he had nothing to say about Wagner's presence. In addition, Daviborshch's knowledge of Wagner's identity had consistently been limited by his own account to local hearsay about a police official from Springfeld with the same surname as the accused. His utility as a prosecution identification witness was minimal. He did, however, remain potentially valuable as a defense witness. If his later versions could be established, he placed Zhilun not at the pit but patrolling the road, 500 to 600 meters from the killing spot, on horseback.

If Daviborshch's last story were believable, or more believable than other versions, then Zhilun's account that he had seen and witnessed Wagner shooting at the ravine could not be true, at least in the sense recognizable within the rules and principles of the Australian criminal justice system. Of course, if he were patrolling on the road a half-kilometer from the pit, Zhilun would have raised this fact much earlier, more particularly at his own trial. Instead, while the details of his distance from the shooting pit and his actual function at the execution site did vary somewhat, Zhilun consistently placed himself near where the children were killed. As a matter of legal evidence

and trial practice, these consistent statements against interest arguably made his version of events more credible than Daviborshch's
ever-changing accounts.

Under examination by the prosecution Zhilun reasserted his
claim that he had known Wagner as a leader in the local police in
the period before the *Aktion* and that he had seen him in Ustinovka
on a regular basis.[83] He then described in detail his return to the village and the loading of the *Mischlinge* children onto Daviborshch's
cart.[84] His testimony about events at the pit remained unchanged at
this stage. He rode with Daviborshch to within five or six meters of
the pit, whereupon the cart was stopped and the waiting police and
gendarmes descended upon the children "like hawks."[85] Then he
added: "Wagner took the youngest one and threw it into the pit and
shot in flight. It was very little."[86]

The youngest child on that day was probably no more than four
months old. Wagner threw the infant into the air and shot it, like
a clay pigeon, as it fell. Or at least the sole remaining eyewitness
described him as having done so, an eyewitness who had on a previous
occasion stated that while he could see Wagner among the shooters,
he was standing guard, not five to six meters away, but some fifty
meters from the pit. Now, however, we return to a primary element
of what would come to be constructed by the defense at least as the
legal truth about what happened at the pit, the means of killing. In
his earlier statements in the 1958 Marchik hearings and in his 1988
statement to Australian authorities, Zhilun was clear that the killings
had been done with Soviet 10 shot Tokarev semiautomatic rifles,
specially issued for the occasion, because Ukrainian Schutzmänner
would not normally have had access to such advanced weaponry or
to the necessary quantities of ammunition. He had also indicated on
another occasion that Wagner was equipped both with a rifle and a
pistol.[87] Once again, he stated that while the shooters were equipped
with rifles, Wagner shot with "a revolver."[88]

Zhilun, who had spent eight years in a Soviet punishment and reed-
ucation through labor camp, now faced a forensic cross-examination

by the lead defense lawyer, Michael David QC. This confrontation embodies in microcosm most if not all of the issues, concerns, and questions about the inherent instability of legal and historical discourses as they manifested themselves in the Australian war crimes proceedings. Truth and, as understood by the witness and by the judicial, criminal law system, fact, confronted the fluctuations that characterized the differing accounts that Zhilun (and Daviborshch) had given at various times in their narrative journeys through the Soviet and Australian criminal justice processes. The competing judicial structures of the Soviet Union and Ukraine and Australia were to be placed in strong juxtaposition, along with the frailties of human memory after fifty years. For Zhilun the perhaps understandable desire to place himself in as positive a light as possible while admitting active participation in escorting twenty young children to the killing pit would also come face to face with Australian concepts of the rule of law and evidentiary fairness in criminal trials.

David confronted Zhilun with Daviborshch's recent statement that the cart had in fact been stopped on the road some distance from the site of the shooting and that Zhilun had also stayed on the road patrolling on horseback. Zhilun flatly rejected this version of events.[89] Given the opportunity by David to address his previous statement that he had been a perimeter guard or that he had done something else at the pit that day, Zhilun insisted that he had done nothing more than watch.[90] David then laid the groundwork for a deeper exploration of Zhilun's narration of the pit killings:

> Q. You have given evidence and you still say the person you say is Wagner kill [*sic*] one small child with a pistol, is that the situation.
> A. Yes
> Q. You are absolutely sure he killed that child with a pistol.
> A. Yes.[91]

Zhilun was then confronted with his interrogation by the Soviet investigator in Kirovograd, his first narrative about the killing of the

Mischlinge children. Zhilun admitted signing the first interrogation protocol but then denied having read it.[92] When confronted with his other statements concerning the shootings and his role in escorting the children on Daviborshch's cart, Zhilun asserted that he had no memory of having been interrogated on any of the specifics or of having signed any of the protocols that David showed him:[93]

> A. The documents I have signed all, but I did not want to read the protocols generally. I did not read them at all.
>
> Q. Whoever wrote that document has lied when they have written what I have read out.
>
> A. Correct, naturally.
>
> Q. Because you say in this court none of that ever happened.
>
> A. Yes. Soviet court or the Soviet investigator used to say "We need the person but the charge we will find." That is how it was with us.
>
> Q. Are you saying they made this up.
>
> A. They fabricated so as it suited them.[94]

We return to the same issue as that raised by Daviborshch with Australian investigators and which had from the very beginning characterized parliamentary debates and public opposition to the introduction of war crimes legislation in Australia. Soviet interrogation and trial records are simply unreliable. They are fakes in the sense not that they are counterfeit documents but in the equally pernicious sense, according to Western, liberal jurisprudential sensibilities, that the statements contained therein and attested to by way of the contemporaneous signature of the witness or the accused, that the facts contained in accounts of witness statements, cannot be attributed to what the witness actually stated. If this is a true account of the falsity of Soviet legal statements, then the narrative found therein becomes not just unstable but entirely untrustworthy, whatever tools or how much contextual subtlety the interpreter, historian, or lawyer brings to them.

But even this instability becomes foundationally unstable as Zhilun

is put to further cross-examination. David put another statement
from a protocol to Zhilun, this time from the 2 April 1947 interrogation in which Zhilun claimed to have been too squeamish to watch
the shooting:

   Q. Is that the truth.
   A. Well, truth naturally.

David then proceeded:

   Q. What is the truth, that you did see them shoot the children
      or you did not see them shoot the children.
   A. Well, how — I saw and I didn't see.

   Q. If you said, "Having brought the children to be shot, I did
      not watch them shoot the children as I was very squeamish
      about it" that would be wrong would it.
   A. Naturally untruth.
   Q. That's an untruth.
   A. Naturally because I had indeed seen, why not?[95]

This re-narration of events at the pit continued along similar
lines.

   A. I did not come close to the pit. How they were, how it was
      there, I do not know.
   Q. You say you saw them shoot before they were thrown in the
      pit.
   A. Well, I don't know how it was.
   Q. Haven't you told —
   A. One couldn't see there. There were many of them standing
      there.
   Q. Haven't you told this court they were shot as soon as they
      were taken off the cart.
   A. Well, yes.
   Q. You didn't see the children in the pit, did you.
   A. No.

Zhilun persisted throughout cross-examination in his unchanging claim that he had seen Wagner and that the accused had been the one at the pit to pick up the youngest infant, throw it in the air, and shoot it as it fell. He also reaffirmed that he had seen Wagner shoot the baby with "either a revolver or a pistol."[96] When confronted with his statement from 1989 that the shooters had specially issued semiautomatic rifles, he prevaricated under close questioning by Michael David:

Q. What was he shooting with.
A. I don't remember very well, as it is said correctly, maybe I made a mistake. Maybe I didn't remember. He did have a pistol.

Q. You now don't know what he fired with.
A. Out of a rifle.
Q. Out of a rifle, is that right.
A. Yes.
Q. So it is a rifle now.
A. Yes, 10 loader.
Q. A 10 loader.
A. Yes.
Q. Are you sure of that.
A. Yes.
Q. Are you sure it was a 10 loader rifle he shot the child with.
A. Yes.
Q. And there are no problems with that, you are certain of that.
A. Yes.

At first glance the change in Zhilun's story may appear to be a minor inconsistency and one of little historical or forensic consequence. First, he still insists that Wagner always had a pistol and did not resile from that. More significantly perhaps, he still places Wagner at the pit, and he still identifies him as the individual who killed the youngest victim.

But the story of the revolver/pistol versus the Russian military rifle may have had more significant consequences, both as a matter of law and as matter of historical knowledge about who carried out the killings at the pit. One might, for example, after a review of each of the weapons in the versions of Zhilun's stories, come to the following analysis. For a young, fit, motivated Volksdeutsche policeman such as Heinrich Wagner, it would no doubt have been quite easy physically to have picked up a four-month-old infant with one hand, then to have hurled the child in the air and fired as it fell with the pistol held in the other hand and at the ready. Conversely, if Wagner had a Tokarev 10 loader, the task of picking up the child and throwing it may have been the same, but to shoulder a rifle and fire it with the two hands necessary to aim, even at close range, at a falling body would have been significantly more difficult. If the jury were convinced of this argument on the issue of which weapon he was armed with and which weapon he used to shoot the youngest child, the case against Wagner is significantly weakened. Zhilun saw him shoot the youngest child—that had always been his story. If it were not possible, or there were a reasonable doubt about how Wagner could have done what Zhilun now says, then Wagner, as a matter of law, was probably not guilty.

Intriguingly, the second war crime charge against Wagner, the unlawful killing of a Ukrainian railway worker, Ivan Vasilyevich Rudik, introduced evidence that might be seen to corroborate part of Zhilun's recollection about the pistol.[97] In that case the testimony of Nikolay Danilovich Velikiy was introduced to identify Wagner as the policeman who shot and killed Rudik. In his evidence-in-chief Velikiy identified Wagner as the man he had seen twice, once in a greenish gray *Gendarme*'s uniform and once in a blue Ukrainian Schutzmannschaft uniform.[98] Although the defense cross-examination attacked this identification and Velikiy's credibility, important information about the weapon used by Wagner was introduced. Velikiy was a professional artist, and the magistrate allowed the prosecution to admit into evidence, over defense objections, sketches drawn by

6. Drawing by witness Velikiy depicting Wagner as policeman. Crown copyright. Used by permission of the Attorney-General, South Australia.

the witness. In one rendering the policeman identified as Wagner is clearly, unambiguously, and graphically depicted wearing a pistol and holster.[99] In response to a direct question from the prosecution, Velikiy testified that "Wagner had a pistol on his belt in his holster on the left side."[100]

Moreover, in the protocol of his interrogation in the Procurator's Office during the 1958 investigation, Velikiy not only identified Marchik and Wagner but also stated clearly that he had witnessed Wagner kill the worker by three shots from his pistol.[101] The idea of Wagner armed with a pistol as part of his official function had been confirmed by another witness at the committal and had been on the judicial record since 1958.

The questions of identity and of the weapon used at the pit were crucial to the case against Wagner. But it is important again to underline the difference between a judicial verdict, of the finding of a case to answer at committal, and other, competing versions of the truth. If he were found not guilty, of course, that does not mean that he did not do what Zhilun said he did, nor does it mean that historians must or should or can ever accept such a verdict as the final word on what happened at the pit. But it does mean that historians would need to look very carefully at what Zhilun said at the various stages of his narrative journey from the pit outside Ustinovka in order to determine, with any degree of accuracy, or with some narrative stability at least, what happened. Historians, even those who study Holocaust perpetrators, quite naturally do not focus primarily or necessarily on individual guilt. That is not their primary task. Nonetheless, if we were to move the narrative analysis to another level, to an area that might be of historical import, a problem similar to that faced by jurists might arise.

Historians may not focus on the legal questions of individual guilt but they do ask other related questions. Who was at the pit killing? What units were involved? Were Ukrainian police, Schutzmannschaft, units among the perpetrators? What about the German Gendarmerie? *Volksdeutsche Hilfspolizei*? How much faith can we now put in Zhilun's account? Unlike Daviborshch, Zhilun was a policeman.

He knew some of the killers and recognized the uniforms and some of the members of the other units he saw at the pit. But if he did not see Wagner as a matter of law, what does history make of that? The story has changed, on this version of events, and if Zhilun were no longer to be believed, law, legal rules of evidence, the art of cross-examination, the rule of law as applied in the courts of South Australia at a committal hearing, would have played a key role in subverting a historical narrative. Other sources would be needed to determine with any accuracy in the historical sense that units of local and German forces participated in the mass shootings of the Jews of Israylovka. Indeed, other legal sources might be employed because Zhilun's fellow policeman, Gering, who was with him and the *Mischlinge* children on that sunny summer day in Ukraine in 1942, was convicted in Germany for participating in the same events.

Several stories unfold here, or perhaps a single story with multiple layers. One clear narrative is the art of a careful, closely read cross-examination by a top Australian criminal lawyer, competing with the story carefully constructed by SIU investigators and the prosecution lawyers. Added to this legal process story is the phenomenon of cross-examination through Ukrainian-English interpretation/translation and the cultural dissonance between the lawyer, the magistrate, and the witness. The next story is embodied in Zhilun's "I saw and I didn't see." This apparent logical impossibility perhaps contains an existential truth, one that might be recognized by a jury applying common sense rather than rules of precise grammar or logic to their interpretation of this testimony. The children were grabbed from the cart as Zhilun stood out of the way; they were dragged the five or six remaining meters to the edge of the pit and shot in a flurry of bullets, gun smoke, noise, the children's screams filling the air as the massacre was all over in a matter of a few seconds. Zhilun saw the firing, he heard the bullets and the screams, but from his vantage point he could not see over the edge and into the pit itself. There remains experiential logic to "I saw and I didn't see" to which we can relate as matter of ordinary experience.

Behind us a gunshot rings out, someone falls over, and as we turn around, we see blood spewing from the victim's chest and another individual holding a smoking pistol standing near the body. Did we see the shooting? No—but we saw enough of the surrounding circumstances, of the immediate situation and the aftermath, to convince a jury of the truthfulness of our account, in the absence of other evidence that might be found and which might either add credibility to our version or, conversely, might bring an entirely different narrative structure to the event. The uncertainty about what Zhilun saw on that day may remain because of his own words and the cross-examiner's skill, but that he "saw and he didn't see" somehow also remains a true story about the pit killing. But like all true stories, especially stories told in court about events from more than fifty years previously, there may be a competing, or least complimentary, story that sheds new light on, or casts a shadow over, the original version.

Zhilun's cross-examination certainly put the legal cat among the historical pigeons, especially insofar as the accuracy of Soviet investigations and trial proceedings were concerned. Zhilun rejected the accuracy of some, but not all, of the statements attributed to him in his 1947 prosecution. When David put more statements from Soviet files to him, Zhilun insisted over and over again that the documents that carried his signature could not be used because he had not, in fact, signed them. "Neither this nor this. This way I did not sign. I do not sign this way. That is not my signature. And it is the same here. And it is the same here."[102]

He went on: "I did not sign this; this is what I am telling you again. In the first instance, one had to sign here, here, here (REFERENCING THE BODY OF DOCUMENT) and that sort of thing is not here at all . . . The surname is mine, but the signature is not mine. In accordance with the law, I ought to sign here, here, here, here, here, but none of that is here (REFERRING TO VARIOUS POINTS IN BODY OF DOCUMENT)."[103]

Over and over again during the Adelaide committal hearing, Zhilun refuted his prior statements and asserted that he had not signed the documents produced by the Soviet procurators. At the same time, he affirmed the simple narrative that placed Wagner as a killer. The defense found itself in the midst of a difficult legal and historical issue. Zhilun remained the strongest witness against Wagner. He had consistently maintained that he had seen Wagner at the pit, shooting the children. There were some inconsistencies in his statements about the type of firearm used by Wagner and about some of the events surrounding the *Aktion* in Israylovka, but essential elements remained reasonably consistent after fifty years. Zhilun was a hardened former Red Army soldier and policeman who had served his own war crimes sentence in the Soviet Gulag. He was tough and unflinching. Both prosecutors and defense lawyers believed that he might well impress an Australian jury, a jury whose members would have heard other evidence linking Wagner to the mass shooting of young children.[104]

The defense wished to attack Zhilun's credibility, relying on prior inconsistent statements.[105] But many of those inconsistent statements appeared in the court records, the protocols provided by the Soviet and Ukrainian authorities. Zhilun asserted that the documents were fakes, forgeries (but he did maintain that some of the statements found therein were true). If the documents were fakes either in the sense that Zhilun did not sign them and his signature was therefore forged or in the sense that they did not convey accurately what had been said, then the status of the statements themselves became problematic. Of course, it is still logically possible that even in the case that Zhilun's signature had been placed on the protocol by someone else, the facts as set out are nonetheless an accurate rendering of events. The addition of his signature by a third party raises doubts about the veracity of the content of the protocols, but it does not in and of itself establish the falsity of the statements, especially because Zhilun himself recognized the accuracy of what was recorded. If the prior statements were not in fact, or in law, statements at all, they could not be invoked to attack Zhilun's credibility or could be invoked only after a lengthy preliminary process of establishing (or not) their authenticity.

Both Zhilun and Daviborshch disputed parts of the Soviet judicial record relating to events in Israylovka. Many of the statements found in the Zhilun and Marchik dossiers constitute the best evidence about events relating to the second-wave killings of the remaining Jewish adults and the *Mischlinge* children. They are detailed accounts from various actors—the mother of some of the children; an avowed accessory to the massacres, Zhilun; and the participant bystander, Daviborshch. Especially in the Zhilun case, the statements are reasonably contemporaneous, having been made in 1947. By that fact alone that evidence might be given more credit than differing subsequent versions, both in law and in historical analyses. Other narrations of the events, according to which Daviborshch gets farther and farther away from the pit with each telling, are more distant in time from the day at the pit, by a ravine, in the forest, off the road to Ustinovka, and are perhaps, in comparison with more temporally proximate versions, less reliable.

Psychological explanations of Daviborshch's growing and unresolved traumatization and increasing guilt as the years passed might offer an equally compelling narrative frame for placing and understanding his ever-growing physical and mental distance from events on that day. Certainly, it is plausible to make this argument based on his demeanor during the taped evidence on commission. But if the records are faked, historians find themselves in a similar position to that of the defense lawyers. While the stakes are different and the modes of analysis to be applied by historians and by the defense legal team are both influenced by the nature of their disciplines and the ways they can read texts, they both nonetheless face a text, or a series of texts, some or all of which might not be a text in any useful forensic or historical sense at all. Michael David sought to bring a temporary halt to Zhilun's cross-examination until the facts of and about the texts could be established to his satisfaction: "A lot of these documents which this witness says are fakes, are the basis for historical opinion. I won't raise that at this stage. I say the Crown tell us one way or the other whether these documents are genuine or not.

If the Crown can't tell us, then we have to find out. We have to find out whether these are Mr. Zhilun's signatures or someone else was writing for Mr. Zhilun. We have to find out whether those statements are taken or not taken, otherwise I cannot cross-examine this witness about those vital matters."[106]

The court was ultimately unimpressed. While recognizing the practical dilemma facing the defense team, the magistrate decided that the cross-examination of Zhilun should continue: "It seems the defence, in some way, will have to ultimately try and prove one way or the other that's his signature on the documents. It would be good with the resources and prosecution if something could be established that way. I can't order that to occur and I accept it is a problem."[107]

One possible solution did present itself. The parties sought to find out about the authenticity and veracity of the Soviet criminal investigation and trial process from the horse's mouth. Andrey Filipovich Bardas was deposed on commission in Ukraine the day after Daviborshch, in August 1993.[108] Bardas, a Red Army counterintelligence officer in the Great Patriotic War, had worked from 1946 to 1952 first as a senior investigator in the Kirovograd region and then as head of the investigations division. Bardas described in detail how the investigation of alleged war criminals had proceeded. On the interrogation process he stated that "the protocol as soon as it was ready, finished for a certain day, was read by the, person arrested [TN: or to him], and by the investigator and signed by both."[109] In addition, Bardas affirmed that all documents, protocols of confrontations, interrogations, and other documents were read, as required by law, to or by the accused.[110] Forgery of the accused's signature "is excluded. It is out of the question."[111]

Interrogations could last for as long as five days.[112] But beatings did not occur because, according to Bardas, there was simply no need to resort to such techniques: "No. There was never any physical assault and as matter of fact there was no need of it, because we had enough witnesses, enough eyewitnesses, to make the picture, the whole picture quite clear. People from the village where the accused lived and whose activity was known, where his activity was known, usually provided all set of evidence that was sufficient to come to the conclusions about it."[113]

Whether one believes Bardas's blanket assertion about the absence of physical coercion in KGB interrogations of persons identified as traitors to the motherland, the points he makes about the process and the nature of the evidence, and about the identity of accused and witnesses, are important and to some extent convincing in the context of both law and history. At the level of historical knowledge about the Holocaust in Ukraine, Bardas is right. Many local inhabitants knew who the killers were. The Soviet system of investigating and prosecuting war criminals was local in its application and its focus. The perpetrators with whom it dealt in the vast majority of cases such as Zhilun's were local inhabitants. The SIU had identified the proximity of the killing environment as a main advantage in such prosecutions by increasing the reliability and availability of eyewitnesses.[114] The crimes of the perpetrators were committed against their neighbors.[115] Zhilun lived in Berezovatka. He knew the Ukrainian women who had married Jewish men. He knew Daviborshch and his cart. And he knew his fellow policeman Wagner. The killings that took place in Ukraine, especially in the second wave, usually had a local contingent among the killers. The key evidence against Zhilun concerning the *Mischlinge* children came historically from Daviborshch and from Tat'yana Kirsanovna Shul'kina, the mother of Volodya and Tolya. Tat'yana saw her children being loaded into Daviborshch's cart after leaving the village administration office. She knew Daviborshch and Zhilun because they were her neighbors. The killings were carried out locally; the killings were close-up and personal at the edge of shooting pits, in nearby forests. Finally, we also know that in at least one case "in the town of Radomyshl on September 6, 1941, Sonderkommando 4a of Einsatzgruppe C shot the adult Jews but ordered the Ukrainian policemen to shoot the children."[116]

In any event, as far as the law is concerned, we will never know what happened. The case against Wagner did not proceed because of his ill health.[117] Ironically perhaps, Wagner's heart condition was diagnosed and confirmed by the leading cardiologist in Adelaide, nominated by the prosecution team, who happened to be Jewish.[118] We do not know if Zhilun would have returned to give evidence at trial or if his prior inconsistent statements could have been used against him. One thing we do know, however, is that one side or the other in Australia, if Bardas were to be believed, would have granted the imprimatur of Australian judicial approval to the proceedings and to the documents produced in the course of Soviet war crimes investigations.

The stories about Daviborshch's cart and the *Mischlinge* children of Israylovka must remain unstable and incomplete. This also means that historical knowledge about the same events will always be informed by these very narrative instabilities insofar as court records are concerned because the court records, both Soviet and Australian, constitute the best sources of knowledge about the killings of the Jews of Israylovka. History has other evidence in this case, beyond the instabilities, uncertainties, contradictions, and denials that surround the testimony of Daviborshch and Zhilun. Nikolay Stepanovich Kokhanov, for example, was a fourteen-year-old farmworker at the time of the pit killing. He was plowing a field with his workmates and saw and heard the first shooting of the adult Jews from a position in the nearby woods. Later in the day he saw a cart loaded with people leaving Israylovka. Two days later he visited the pit and saw cartridge cases from rifles and pistols on the ground.[119] Nikolay Grigoryevich Ivaschenko, then seventeen, was also working in the fields that day. After the shooting had finished, he went to the pit and saw the ground covered in blood, brains, and bullet holes.[120]

Australian investigators and forensic scientists gathered other evidence. The pit in the forest off what used to be the road to Usti-novka was excavated by these Australian police and other experts. The testimony of anthropologist Professor Emeritus Richard Wright indicates that the children's remains were found in a layer on top of the remains of the adults in the pit and that the children's skeletons were discovered in a random and scattered pattern, unlike the adult bodies below.[121] Professor Wright described what was uncovered during the pit excavation, including "the disorganized arrangement of the children, They are lying in all directions."[122]

In other words, archaeological findings from the pit excavation produced evidence consistent with stories that the children were killed after the adults had been shot and buried. Wright's findings also confirmed the account by Zhilun that the shooting of the *Mischlinge* children was a brutal, quick, and disorganized affair. We also know from the forensic dental and other medical evidence that the children ranged in age from a very young infant to early adolescents, and most, if not all, died of gunshot wounds.[123] Dr. Godfrey Oettle, an Australian forensic pathologist present at the excavation of the pit, was examined in relation to his findings and was shown a series of photographs of skeletal remains. One particular photograph shows in focus a shattered skull. On examination of it outside of that area, it was shown to have a bullet wound to the skull.

Q. Can you express the age of the child in those remains.

A. Yes, the age was thought from teeth to be approximately one year old.[124]

In other words, the story of science confirms the eyewitness accounts of the pit shootings, the ages of the children, the order of the *Aktion*, the adult Jews first, followed by the children, and the fact, from the disposition of the bodies, that the children were likely shot in a wilder, less disciplined or organized fashion than the adults. None of these findings puts Wagner at the pit, with a pistol or with a rifle, but a careful reading of this additional scientific text, and the evidence of the young eyewitnesses, might lead us to a version of events not much different from that first told by Daviborshch and Zhilun in 1947.

SIX

Translating Law, Translating History, in Australian War Crimes Trials

Eyewitnesses in the three Australian war crimes cases, both those who were Jewish survivors of the atrocities and non-Jewish Ukrainians, bystanders and perpetrators, had suffered psychologically from the trauma of the events. For some this means that their testimony might be considered to be more reliable than accounts in ordinary criminal cases because events would be fixed more firmly, more definitely, and, so the argument goes, more accurately, in their minds. On the other hand, trauma can adversely affect cognition. Memories can be fixed that do not necessarily coincide with physical reality. This does not mean that eyewitnesses are acting in bad faith when they recount that they saw "Ivanechko" at the *Aktion* in Serniki or the manager of the police, Mikolay Berezowsky, screaming at the huddled Jews of Gnivan, but it can in some circumstances call into question the truth or the verifiable accuracy of what they say. In their work arguing for a sociological account of the institutional frame in which testimony, particularly Holocaust survivor testimony, occurs, Aaron Beim and Gary Alan Fine argue, for example, that "a jury is more likely to find a testimony trustworthy if they are familiar with its narrative structure. If testimonies are consistent with what jurors expect of testimony in a courtroom (based on jurors' expectations about the law derived from the media and other encounters with representations of the law), then they are more likely to trust it than if the testimony deviates from these expectations."[1]

Other actors in the criminal justice system—police, lawyers, magistrates, and judges—operate from a similar standpoint, albeit one informed by a different set of expectations formed through experience and immersion in the system. When cultural, historical, and linguistic factors upset these narrative expectations, witness testimony can be perceived to be unreliable. In such instances the witness is recounting something in a way with which the Australian participants may be unfamiliar or to which they may bring a foreign interpretation that does not intersect with the intention of the witness in recounting or with that witness's lived experiences. Conversely, as was the case in Adelaide, the witness may be compelled to alter his or her own understanding of the way in which the story and its inherent truth are to be articulated by the imposition of an overriding legal set of rules and procedures. For Ukrainian witnesses this meant that they could no longer retell the story of what they saw or knew as a largely uninterrupted narrative, as they would in daily life or as they often had to Special Investigations Unit (SIU) agents. Instead, their tale was submerged in the to and fro of examination and cross-examination by Australian lawyers. Australian law requires that particular words be repeated back to the witness midway through a story. The word *gun*, for example, is not sufficiently precise. The lawyer wants to get a single piece of information—was it a machine gun? a revolver? a rifle? a shotgun?—while the witness only wants to finish the story, a story in which the type of weapon is unimportant to the underlying truth.

Translation makes it even more difficult to follow the flow and the cut and thrust of the examination and cross-examination of eyewitnesses. The narrative account of what happened in the forest outside Serniki, Israylovka, or Gnivan is weakened in the process. A jury may not hear what it expects to hear because the very practice of translation physically and temporally disrupts the flow of the story or because translation is poor or inaccurate. When the story of what happened on a summer day in 1942 in a forest in Ukraine appears in a context in which rules of evidence exclude or limit certain elements of what can be said and by whom, about what subject, the narrative flow of the legal process that seeks its truth in relation to limits imposed by evidentiary rules again interrupts, disrupts, and ultimately corrupts the competing narrative accounts of eyewitnesses.[2] As was the case with the evidence of expert historians, the Australian war crimes trials offer important insights into the ways in which law and legal processes interact with other conceptions of testimony, narrative, and the search for truth in relation to the Shoah.

War crimes trials from the International Military Tribunal (IMT) at Nuremberg to the Australian proceedings in Adelaide have narrated not just law and history but the story of narration itself. At Nuremberg the defendants and their lawyers were German; the judges came from the United States, the United Kingdom, France, and the USSR. Prosecution lawyers came from these and other victorious Allied powers. All of the issues of law and justice, history and interpretation, had to occur in a multilingual environment. At Nuremberg the innovation of simultaneous translation in major trials is one of the little recognized, but vital, historical legal precedents established for the prosecution of war crimes.[3]

Since Nuremberg the issue of simultaneous and other forms of translation and interpretation has featured prominently in the most well-known instances of international criminal law and the prosecution of alleged criminals for war crimes and crimes against humanity. The Adolf Eichmann trial in Jerusalem was characterized by translation into German, Hebrew, English, and other languages, with greater or lesser success. The later Israeli trial of John Demjanjuk faced similar translation difficulties in a number of other languages, including Ukrainian.[4] Of course, issues of interpretation and translation are posed in many contexts other than war crimes trials. Non-English-speaking defendants in Anglo-American countries are confronted with the dominant, if not official, English-language system from the time of arrest to trial and in their encounters with defense counsel.[5] In every circumstance in which linguistic issues arise for the defendant, basic concerns about the fundamental fairness of the proceedings, whether at the level of constitutional guarantees of equality or common law fair trial and abuse of process principles, are raised.[6]

Issues of translation and interpretation were central to the operation of the SIU. Most of the documents in all their investigations, and in the three prosecutions that went before the South Australian courts, were in languages other than English. The eyewitnesses in the trials spoke Ukrainian, Russian, Polish, or Hebrew. In addition to the hurdles that confronted the investigators in compiling evidence in such linguistic circumstances, the prosecution had to meet its fair trial, discovery burdens by providing accurate and reliable translations of documents and witness statements to the defense so that a proper case could be prepared. In each of the three cases the defense team had available to them translators and interpreters who could and did assist in reviewing documents and witness statements, checking SIU translations of key German documents introduced by the prosecution. They could be present in court to provide interpretation to the three defendants, none of whom was particularly fluent in English, as well as to the defense team concerning the translation being given to the court by the official interpreter.[7] These language issues raised important concerns for the defense lawyers about obtaining correct and complete instructions from their clients, thereby allowing the accused to fully participate in his defense. In addition, translation and interpretation issues would arise in the context of each of the three proceedings in more substantive areas of trial practice going directly to the evidence presented against Berezowsky, Polyukhovich, and Wagner.

Finally, and most crucially perhaps, translation and interpretation had to be provided for the court in all three cases and be presented to the jury in Polyukhovich's case. Grant Niemann, who acted for the prosecution, concluded that the translation/interpretation before the magistrates, court, and jury in the three Adelaide cases was "a dog's breakfast."[8]

Niemann's assessment was based not just in his experience in the Adelaide prosecutions but in his subsequent role as a prosecutor at the International Criminal Tribunal for Yugoslavia (ICTY) in The Hague. In those proceedings similar linguistic issues arose as witnesses testified in Serbo-Croatian dialects before lawyers and judges who did not speak these languages. Translation at the ICTY, while marred occasionally by the arguably incorrect admixture of dialects and accents—when, for example, a Croatian translator spoke for a Serbian defendant or vice versa—was far superior in Niemann's experience because it was simultaneous, rather than sequential, in nature. While the IMT process at Nuremberg had demonstrated the strengths and possibilities of simultaneous translation in war crimes trials, Australian practice in the Adelaide war crimes cases was sequential translation. The lawyer would ask a question of the witness in English, the query would be translated into Ukrainian for that witness, who would respond in that language, and that answer would be rendered from Ukrainian into English for the court, jury, and lawyers.

Participants in the process agreed that this solution was less than optimal. It was incredibly difficult for Australian lawyers, skilled in forensic questioning of witnesses, to establish a rhythm for their examination or cross-examination as they waited for the question and answer to be translated into and then from Ukrainian before proceeding to the next query.[9] One can only imagine what a jury of twelve ordinary residents of Adelaide made of the lengthy to-and-fro in Ukrainian as they adjudicated on whether the prosecution had established beyond a reasonable doubt that Ivan Polyukhovich was the Ivanechko present at the killing pit outside Serniki when eight hundred Jews were shot.

The issue of translation/interpretation in the Australian war crimes cases also posed serious and perhaps more interesting questions at two other interconnected levels. The first and most obvious for those who would wish to construct a socio-legal history of events that might approximate the touch and feel of the war crimes trials in Adelaide is that Australia follows the standardized practice of other countries where translation and interpretation form part of the criminal justice process. That practice consists of constructing the court record solely in English. The translation by the interpreter, to and from the witness, does not figure in the official transcript. Language differences and difficulties are thereby written out of the record.[10] While it is possible in many cases to consult and compare original language documents and their translation, this facility does not exist in relation to witnesses. As both a legal and a historical source, the transcripts of the Adelaide proceedings necessarily suffer from what might be important linguistic lacunae because we can never know what a witness really said.

The next area of interest in the Australian Nazi war crimes trial experience goes to the question of the exact role of the interpreter. The traditional legal construction of interpretation, which is in fact embodied in the absence of the translated dialog in the official transcript, is that the translator/interpreter is engaged in a simple machinelike process of rendering one language into another. While interpreters obviously speak at trials or committal hearings, they are figuratively meant to be neither seen nor heard. They record the lawyers' or the judge's questions and the witnesses' responses without intervention or autonomy on their part. They are simple lingual transmission lines. Of course, it is also common knowledge, and not just among translator/interpreters, that this can never truly be the case. If lawyers are intimately aware as part of their professional practices that language is a serious and subtle business, translators are also aware that literal translation along the transmission line is simply not possible. First of all, it cannot happen because no two languages share such literal commonalities in any way that would make sense, particularly in a process meant to establish, in however limited and restricted a fashion, the truth or at least permit a reconstruction of what happened.

More significantly in the Australian cases of Berezowsky, Polyukhovich, and Wagner, the language of the witnesses is and was constructed in a specific cultural and historical context.[11] The Ukrainian
spoken and understood by the inhabitants of Gnivan or Serniki or
Berezovatka is not a literary or highly educated version of the language. It is the Ukrainian spoken by peasants, many of whom had
never left their native village or district before coming to Adelaide
to testify. Their language was mixed in many cases with Russian but,
again, with a Russian that was spoken or understood by Ukrainian
peasants. In the case of Serniki witnesses in Polyukhovich, the situation was further complicated by the history of the region, which
had been part of Poland from the end of the Polish-Russian conflict
until the Soviet conquest subsequent to the Ribbentrop-Molotov
Pact. When he was arrested, for example, Ivan Polyukhovich was
interviewed in the presence not of a Ukrainian-language translator
but of a Polish-English interpreter.[12]

In addition to the precise issues relating to the kind of Ukrainian spoken by witnesses in the three cases, which include the ability
to find translators and interpreters with the adequate professional
expertise and competence in the cultural and linguistic contexts of
the witnesses, the proper nature of the interpreter's role would also
raise important cultural issues. Beyond the basic conflict between
law's restricted view of the practice of translation/interpretation
and a more flexible understanding of the process brought to bear by
interpreters and translators, a serious concern that in fact underlined
all of the Australian proceedings, and indeed many of the debates that
preceded the cases themselves, went to the issue of the translation,
in both a narrow and a broader social sense, of the cultural milieu
of the witnesses and of the court, the lawyers, and the members of
the jury. Intimately connected with this cultural question is the oft-
voiced anxiety about the pedagogical use of war crimes trials to convey
lessons about and of history. How can events in occupied Ukraine,
themselves constructed in a frame of ethnic, cultural, and religious
cohabitation, accommodation, and conflict throughout hundreds of

years, be understood by magistrates and jurors in Adelaide in the 1990s? How can facts and arguments raised within the limits of legal practice and discourse be retranslated into terms understandable by the Australian polity about these events of the Shoah in Ukraine?

In addition to these questions, within the strict confines of the legal process itself, is the issue of translating and interpreting culture and the conflict of cultural understandings of the parties involved. How can one, for example, within the rules of evidentiary admissibility and relevance, explain to the jury that Ukrainian peasants in 1942 were not in the habit of carrying watches or consulting calendars? They told time, hours, and months by the position of the sun in the sky and the agricultural process they were involved in—planting, harvest, feeding the cows in the fields—or in relation to religious festivals and holy days. September and July are and were not relevant or readily cognizable concepts for many of these witnesses. Yet for the lawyers on both sides the exact time of events was often crucial. In Berezowsky's case fixing the date of the Gnivan killings with precision would be key to the prosecution's ability to establish essential elements of the offense, the *actus reus*, and for both sides to refute or establish the defendant's alibi.

Historians can and did testify in the three cases about historical methodology, about the written record and gaps and lacunae therein. They can explain how documents were destroyed by acts of war or by the deliberate actions of the retreating Germans. They can give detailed explanations of the documents they have consulted and the reasoning processes recognized and practiced in the professional discourses of history and historians, all of which they have used to arrive at their conclusions. Who, if anyone, can testify to a jury that evidence and eyewitness recollection about the time of day depended on the sun and milking the cows? How can an Adelaide jury know that for Ukrainian peasants dark and light were the only meaningful colors for clothing, including uniforms? For prosecution and defense lawyers and for historians, the differences between and among black, green, and blue uniforms were absolutely essential to identifying perpetrators. The exact nature of the role of the interpreter in these and other contexts would arise throughout the Australian cases. Two examples illustrate the extent and importance of the concerns and issues that came to the fore in the prosecution of alleged Nazi collaborationist war criminals in Adelaide in the 1990s.

TRANSLATION, INTERPRETATION, AND LAW

The eyewitness testimony of Mikhail Raykis was central to the prosecution's case against Mikhail Berezowsky. As a young boy, Raykis had escaped the roundup of the Jews of Gnivan by hiding behind a door as the rest of this family was arrested. From his vantage points in the woods he had seen Berezowsky leading his family and neighbors to the killing pit, viewed the execution, and witnessed Berezowsky participating in mopping-up operations. At least that is the story of the *Aktion* in Gnivan with which Raykis began. That testimony was challenged and undermined by defense cross-examination on the facts, including the issue of the accuracy of Soviet protocols of his original statements and in particular by Berezowsky's lawyers' focus on important issues relating to the accuracy of the interpretation and translation of his testimony. According to some of his testimony, Raykis's original statement about witnessing the pit killings from a certain distance in the woods had been translated, "I heard the shooting but I saw the people naked."

Another version translated Raykis's testimony as having seen people's "heads," not "naked." The subtle distinction put Raykis in a different position in physical terms to the killing. This would then be relevant to the accuracy of his recounting what he had seen and heard. One version arguably placed him at some spot relatively close to the killing pit. He was an "ear witness" to the gunshots and eyewitness to the victims as they stood awaiting their inevitable fate. He was close enough to see them just before they were shot. They were naked. This aspect of the testimony of the eyewitness was consistent with the broad historical evidence, uncontested by the defense that Jewish victims were almost always made to undress before they were killed. Their clothes and other belongings, such as money and jewelry, were then expropriated. In this version of Raykis's testimony that he saw his family and the other Jews of Gnivan "naked," history and eyewitness testimony became mutually reinforcing as they constructed consistent narrative accounts of the pit killings. But after scrutiny of the translation/interpretation of this part of Raykis's account, it became clear that a crucial mistranslation had occurred. The Russian and Ukrainian words for *naked* and *head* are apparently similar.[13] The difference in the circumstances was very important.

If Raykis had used the word *naked*, then this placed him, by necessary implication, closer to the pit and confirmed the historical record of the pit killings. On the other hand, if he said that he had seen the "heads" of the Jews, this would tend to place him farther away from the actual killing site. In addition, it would be an arguably less forceful or less direct confirmation of the historical narration of Ukrainian pit killings. If all he saw was the heads, this made his testimony about these events somehow less forceful or compelling. More specifically, it undermined his direct identification evidence as it related to Berezowsky. Perhaps of equal importance, if this error in translation were established, it would raise doubts about the reliability and/or accuracy of other interpreted evidence and perhaps about the interpretation of the evidence as a whole. Eyewitnesses' narratives of events in Gnivan, and about Berezowsky, would be damaged because the English-language renderings of their statements would be destabilized.

At this point in the proceedings the interpreter went from being a mere cipher or neutral transmission line to playing the role of a witness in the case. The interpreter's explanation of the confusion between the terms points to the contextual nature of all translation practice and to the way in which context can sometimes be the source of confusion.

I have been approached about the matter. It is quite true that in view of the fact that there was testimony given about naked bodies and the rest of it prior, and the word that came out was in between one or the other, and just in gesticulating the word, "the head" the expression was clearly do you mean the head or do you mean naked, a bit like the English word "holey" or "wholly" and consequently it tended to hear words "naked" and naked was left and I had the opportunity of checking with the witness later on. It does appear that the word "heads" or "head" had been used rather than "naked."[14]

This statement offers clear evidence of the inherent problems of interpretation in criminal trials and in war crimes trials in particular. The interpreter was clearly confused by the language spoken by Raykis, by the witness's gesticulations that accompanied his emotional oral evidence, and by the broader contextual surrounding narrative about pit killings and naked Jews in Ukraine in 1942, only a small part of which emerges from reading transcripts of Raykis's testimony. The narrative constructed through the choice of *naked* was consistent with the surrounding context of the testimony and of other evidence at the trial and with history, but it was not, in fact, a correct or accurate version of what the witness had actually said. In addition, the interpreter, realizing that there was perhaps some ambiguity, consulted with the witness after the fact, an act of individual initiative that raised serious issues about the essential function of the interpreter in the criminal justice process.[15]

Additionally, this example highlights a potentially grave danger in all trials or committals in which translation/interpretation is central. The correctness of the translation can only be verified by another translator/interpreter or perhaps by a native speaker present in court. In other words, a court-sanctioned system of translation/interpretation, whether it be simultaneous or consecutive, will always be open to basic errors such as the similarity between *head* and *naked* in Ukrainian and Russian, errors that might well effect elements of the process that are essential to the outcome. Only the expensive and potentially cumbersome option of translators to check the translators would appear to offer some form of adequate safeguard to the defendant (and to the prosecution) in these cases.

But the real issue that remains as a matter of the jurisprudence of criminal procedure, evidence, and proof is that the testimony of the interpreter is itself a form of unreliable hearsay. The account of the error and the circumstances that led to its commission and its correction circulates centrally around what the interpreter states the witness said about what he meant outside the courtroom and outside the witness stand. At this stage of the proceedings, however, the magistrate was reluctant to go into further detail. It was sufficient that the official record of the transcript would record that there was a disagreement or some degree of confusion about what the witness, Raykis, had said, based on conflicting translations from the Ukrainian. Any further clarification could be achieved by the process of cross-examination. This approach takes us back to the problems that arise as a result of the fact that Australian (and most other) practice stipulates that the transcript records the translated version only. Everything appears in English. For the defense to establish the issue of what was said, both in terms of going to the statement itself and potentially to examine the consistency of what was said on this occasion with other statements, the actual terminology of the Ukrainian language testimony is essential.

With the agreement of the prosecution, the interpreter explained that the culprits were *holi* and *holiv*, the former meaning "naked" in the plural and the latter meaning "of heads" or "of the heads." He again asserted that the mistake was perfectly logical in the circumstances of testimony about killing pits and naked bodies.[16] "This is the instance to the best of my recollection. I'm talking about. The speech as it came out, it was emotional. The sentences were not complete. Syntax was somewhat shaky in places in any case and, therefore the word 'holi' came, the misacryonym [*sic*] and mishearing is quite within the realms of possibility and, therefore, I had to make a very split second choice and I chose 'naked' instead of having in retrospect been better off by saying 'heads' and that would have been absolutely acceptable."[17]

The interpreter then stated that another interpreter present in court had signaled his error to him and that he had subsequently sought a clarification from Raykis.[18] Defense attorney Michael David sympathized with the interpreter's position but made clear his displeasure at extrajudicial conversations with a witness while his cross-examination was still in progress.[19]

This brief interlude in the Berezowsky committal embodies many of the problems that can and did arise in such circumstances. Context is required to allow for a correct and accurate interpretation and rendition for the official record of what the witness said. But that context can and did itself lead to confusion about whether Raykis saw "naked" bodies or "heads" in the distance. The interpreter's testimony indicates that Raykis's evidence about the killing of his family was emotional, accompanied by grammatical and syntactical infelicity. The question that remains is how or if this emotional carriage of the witness can be successfully interpreted and translated in a context of a criminal trial with consecutive translation, in which the accuracy and reliability of the testimony are assessed by magistrates, judges, and jurors who can access the witness only through the prism of a less than complete account rendered through translation.

TRANSLATING CULTURE, TRANSLATING LAW

It would appear that after their failures to obtain convictions in the Polyukhovich and Berezowsky cases, the SIU and the office of the Director of Public Prosecutions (DPP) became acutely aware of the fundamental cultural and historical issues that operated as effective roadblocks to the successful pursuit of Nazi collaborationist war criminals in Australia. The horror of the Shoah was difficult enough for ordinary Australians to comprehend amid the peace, tranquility, and prosperity of Adelaide in the mid-1990s. The identification of the old men in the dock with the vigorous, virile, and evil mass killers of 1942 created an even greater sense of dissonance among Australians. When the narration of the specific events of the killing of the Jewish populations of Serniki and Gnivan had to be rendered by Ukrainian peasants or by traumatized survivors fifty years after the events, from

Ukrainian into English and into the English of a criminal law process, with burden of proof requirements and demands imposed by rules of evidence governing hearsay, for example, the potential for comprehension became ever more elusive.

As a result, the prosecution sought to lead evidence in Wagner's case from Ludmilla Stern, an SIU translator, concerning the cultural nature of translation and the difficulties and complexities of translation/interpretation in a cross-cultural context.[20] The prosecution argued that such evidence was the equivalent of anthropological expert evidence in Aboriginal land claims cases. There such testimony could be adduced to establish traditional cultural practices, oral traditions of storytelling that proved a particular group's history from time immemorial of a deep connection to the land. For the defense, on the other hand, permitting such testimony and allowing the documents produced by Stern to explain and elucidate the issues with concrete examples were completely and utterly prejudicial and inadmissible.

Stern identified a number of issues that had, in her opinion, resulted in serious breakdowns in communication during the legal process in Polyukhovich's and Berezowsky's trials. Ukrainian witnesses were unfamiliar with the adversarial common law criminal proceedings of Australia. Their experience with Soviet prosecutors and with Australian investigators before their arrival in Adelaide for the formal proceedings had always been that they could tell their own stories and simply narrate events as they understood them.[21] In addition, being exposed to new technology, such as video cameras, might have had an upsetting or at least unsettling effect on the witnesses and might have influenced their demeanors and their ability to present their testimony effectively.[22] In relation to more specific evidentiary matters, Stern explained how the identification of colors in the Ukrainian language spoken by the witnesses and in their cultural experience simply lacked the precision of English and of the questions posed by the lawyers in the cases.

Dark and light were familiar concepts, but the distinction between green and blue or brown or black was of little relevance to them.[23]

The question of color was central to the issues of identification and identity that formed the core of the prosecution and defense cases in each of the Australian trials. A Schutzmannschaft uniform was of a particular type and color. Incontrovertible historical expert evidence established the nature of the uniforms of indigenous Ukrainian forces. The historians had also given evidence about German demands for consistency and the problems posed by the shortage of appropriate supplies. This expert evidence had also described in great detail the overall German security apparatus in occupied Ukraine, the police hierarchy, the differences between the Order Police and the rural Gendarmerie, and the distinct uniforms worn by various elements of the German apparatus and by Ukrainian auxiliaries. Evidence from an eyewitness that might identify Berezowsky as wearing a dark green German uniform would not be consistent with the historical record. Evidence of Berezowsky in a dark uniform would be unproblematic, if unenlightening. Color was therefore essential to the legal process and to the questions of guilt or innocence but not necessarily to the Ukrainian witnesses.

Stern also sought to explain that the Ukrainian peasants who testified in the proceedings in Adelaide came from a cultural situation in which the source of knowledge was not subjected to strict Australian legal understandings of evidence and proof. People who lived in a small village knew of the forester "Ivanechko" or the "police chief" Berezowsky or the Volksdeutsche policeman/translator Wagner because other people in the village knew them. It was common knowledge. There was no distinction in that cultural circumstance between knowing someone called "Ivanechko" because he was your neighbor whom you saw every day or because people at the market spoke of "Ivanechko the forester" and perhaps pointed in the direction of a distant figure.

In criminal law, of course, the distinction between direct knowledge and experience, on the one hand, and inadmissible hearsay, on the other, is a core concept and one that lawyers attempt to identify and exploit at every turn.[24] In the three Adelaide war crimes cases it became evident that the reliability and/or admissibility of much of the eyewitness testimony so painstakingly gathered by SIU investigators as the result of truly remarkable police work came under direct and effective attack from the defense team, who did nothing more than invoke the standards agreed upon as the sine qua non of the Australian war crimes program, that all legal proceedings would occur under the rules, practices, and norms of the Australian domestic criminal justice system. Hearsay may not have been a familiar or relevant concept in Serniki or Gnivan, but it was in an Adelaide courtroom.

In addition to examining differences in grammar and syntax that made translation and interpreting from Ukrainian into English problematic, Stern also explained that linguistic differences existed in the three Australian cases because of the particular histories of the locales where the events occurred. The historical presence of Polish and/or Russian governmental apparatuses affected the language spoken by local inhabitants.[25] Indeed, their very understanding of what language they spoke was confusing. Various protocols of interrogations in Ukraine contained exchanges in which the witnesses were asked if they understood Russian or Ukrainian and in which language they wished to respond or be questioned. In several cases they replied that as far as they were concerned, there was no real difference and that they spoke and understood both. Their answers, according to Stern, revealed that they spoke local dialects in which the predominant Ukrainian language contained many Russian words. At the same time, the local language as spoken by the witnesses also retained other words and phrases that sounded the same but had different meanings in Ukrainian and Russian.[26]

If the witnesses did not know what language they spoke, how could a lawyer, magistrate, judge, or juror in Adelaide in the 1990s grasp the linguistic difficulties and issues that the prosecution now claimed were central to a complete and accurate presentation of their case? Again, we should note that linguistic analysis and the desire for deeper cultural context arise in their own particular legal context. Because the defense had approached the three cases on the basis that they were at their core criminal law cases, in which issues of identity and identification, alibi, witness credibility, and reliability were central to their line of attack, the prosecution was to a large extent inevitably hoisted on its own legislative petard. The cases were being treated by the defense as murder trials, not as war crimes trials, which meant that the eyewitness testimony was not just of greater importance, but it was important for a different reason than in other, better-known war crimes cases. This was not an instance, like in the cases of Adolf Eichmann or John Demjanjuk or even Imre Finta or Anthony Sawoniuk, in which witness experience and narrative were crucial to the creation either of the prosecution's case or the establishment of the human face of the victims and therefore of the humanity at the heart of the pedagogy of the Shoah as articulated in a war crimes trial. By focusing on the detail of the alleged substantive crime, murder, or being knowingly concerned in or aiding and abetting murder and largely ignoring the underlying elements of the offense under the Australian legislation—war, occupation, Nazi extermination policy—the defense effectively pulled the rug of the rhetorical, storytelling aspect of eyewitness testimony out from under the prosecution. The focus was shifted and defined by the defense—what did this witness see? When did they see it? Is their claim believable? Is it reliable? There was never a grand narrative of Holocaust suffering in the Adelaide cases.

At a relatively early stage of the Wagner committal the prosecution sought to introduce the detailed written submission on translation/ interpretation and intercultural misunderstanding prepared by Ludmilla Stern as part of its case on which she would, like the historians, be questioned by each side.[27] There can be no doubt that Stern's evidence offers a complex and intriguing analysis of the situation that obtained not just in Wagner but in Berezowsky and Polyukhovich as well. It is not really possible to grasp the core understandings in conflict during the examination of Ukrainian witnesses in particular without bringing to the analysis the elements that inform and underpin Stern's study.

No socio-legal portrayal of the Adelaide cases would be complete without highlighting the cultural and linguistic conflicts and misunderstandings that are evident in all three trials. But there is another element, law, that must be considered and which quite naturally dominated the debates when the prosecution sought to tender the document. Law is not interested in the middle of a committal on charges of war crimes and murder relating to the killings of the Jews and *Mischlinge* children of Israylovka in 1942 at a pit, in the forest, in investigating the complete, culturally sensitive narrative of lived Ukrainian peasant experience. It is concerned with and can only operate within the rules of evidence that inform all criminal justice proceedings. What happened on a particular day in 1942? Who saw what? Was Daviborshch at the pit, five to ten meters from where the children were thrown and shot as they fell, or was he stopped on the road, at least five hundred meters away? Was Zhilun patrolling the road on horseback, guarding the perimeter some fifty meters from the pit, or standing next to Daviborshch's cart, five meters from the killings? Did Wagner have a rifle or a pistol? What weapon did he use to shoot the four-month-old baby? Was Wagner even there that day?

The prosecution sought to make a direct parallel with Aboriginal cultural and land claims cases to convince the court that Stern's testimony was indeed relevant and admissible. For the defense the legal frame was completely different. They characterized Stern's evidence as an attempt to allow opinion evidence about the particular testimony of particular witnesses. Michael David objected for the defense: "This witness has no right to give an opinion as to what the witness meant to say, even if this witness was sitting in court watching that witness and even if that witness actually heard the interpreter interpret the language which she didn't hear. Her opinion as to what the witness meant to say has nothing to do with this matter before the court, and in my submission, really has nothing to do with those two cases if she was present hearing the evidence."[28]

The issue of what the witness meant to say is one to be elucidated, clarified, or clouded over and deliberately confused if necessary on examination-in-chief and on cross-examination of the witness him- or herself. It then becomes, as admissible evidence, part of the sovereign domain of the magistrate as finder of fact. These are the only legal rules that apply. The prosecution sought to argue that the introduction of such expert evidence, presented to a magistrate or the jury as ultimate finder of fact at a trial, did not remove from the jury the final right of determining what a particular witness meant to say. Instead, it was proffered to help the members of the jury apply their common sense by providing background information that would make them better able to assess what they had seen and heard. While the magistrate was apparently willing to allow specific evidence to be adduced in order to explain linguistic confusion as it arose, he was distinctly uneasy about the idea of presenting Stern's written submission as a background briefing for a jury or to raise the awareness of counsel or the court.

The magistrate insisted that scrutiny of the fairness and accuracy of the process of interpretation/translation was important but doubted that the method of using Stern's expert testimony, written or oral, was the best way.[29] He asserted that there were probably any number of cases being heard in the city at that time in which interpreters were being used but none in which expert evidence about the cultural context of interpretation was placed before the court. The prosecution reverted to an argument that highlights the ways in which the permissible narrative structure and content of the Australian war crimes trials reflected the overarching justice concerns voiced at the origins of the legislation and embodied in the War Crimes Act itself. These cases were always treated as ordinary criminal law events. This approach was then reinforced by the defense team's strategic decision to proceed as if they were defending someone charged with murder. In this instance Grant Niemann, speaking for the prosecution, attempted to redefine the circumstances of the Wagner committal as a situation involving extraordinary issues:

But in Adelaide today, this is the only case that's being presented
where the entirety of the evidence on the question of primary fact
is being led from witnesses who are from very different significantly
[*sic*] cultural backgrounds to Anglo-Australians and very significant linguistic backgrounds and, in my submission, it makes these
proceedings quite separate and distinct from the case where you
may have one witness, for example, who doesn't speak English and
is assisted by an interpreter, where the balance of the evidence or
the vast bulk of the evidence going to questions on primary fact
are called from Anglo-English speaking witnesses.[30]

Niemann's argument does not directly go the question of whether
the substantive criminal charges make the proceedings special. His
argument is couched in terms of the nature and quality of the evidence in this particular case as a matter of general rules of evidence.
Nonetheless, it is obvious that the reason that all of the evidence on
primary fact comes from Ukrainian witnesses is that the offense of
which the accused stands charged occurred in Ukraine in 1942. This
is the essential factual frame of all of the Australian war crimes prosecutions. The question put indirectly by the issue of the admissibility
of Stern's written statement about translation/interpretation in an
intercultural context is really a question about how these extraordinary
circumstances presented by the prosecution can or should be made
to fit within the basic rules of evidence.

The magistrate was not convinced by the prosecution's arguments
and refused to allow Stern's written statement to be entered. The
experience in the Berezowsky and Polyukhovich cases had been that
each side was assisted by an interpreter who followed the questions
and answers as interpreted and informed the lawyers if and when any
issue of accuracy arose. Any questions about the translation were dealt
with immediately through the process of questioning the witness.[31]
Not everyone was happy. Stern would recount how "the above cases
illustrate how evidence can become distorted in court in the process
of translation and as a result of cross-cultural difference, and how an

uninformed approach to such problems can lead to a communication breakdown. It is hoped that the lessons of this experience will assist in overcoming similar problems in the future."[32]

To the end Stern appears unwilling or unable to recognize the basic premise upon which all her statements are based and the central logical and jurisprudential flaw of her position. She chooses to privilege one context, Ukrainian peasant life and language, over another context, Australian criminal courts. There can never be a situation of perfect translation, nor can there ever be perfect communication. There was no communication breakdown in any relevant legal sense because relevant legal information, judicially recognized facts, were presented to the Australian courts. Like Konrad Kwiet, who holds firm to his belief that lawyers are not concerned with truth, Ludmilla Stern may be certain that evidence was "distorted." One person's truth is another person's inadmissible and prejudicial evidence. One person's distortion is another person's application of the hearsay rule.

Tradurre è tradire—to translate is to betray.

SEVEN

Telling Stories about the Shoah

Perpetrators, Victims, and the Politics of Australian
Identity in *The Hand That Signed the Paper*

FICTION, THE SHOAH, AND UKRAINE

Paul Ricoeur has identified the three principal genres that have been
used in our collective search for a form of narrative truth about the
Holocaust, or as Ricoeur puts it, a form of judgment about the Shoah.[1]
The three forms of judgment are the judicial, the historical, and the
literary. The focus here is primarily on the last two, the historical and
the literary, although it will be clear throughout this discussion that
the specter of the law haunts the readings that follow.

For Ricoeur each genre suffers from its own inherent limits when
confronted with the enormity of the Final Solution of the "Jewish
Question." For history the enormity of the processes of destruction
of European Jewry, the horror of the Holocaust's facticity, challenge
the genre's capacity to render the events in an intelligible form. Additionally, the discipline must also be wary of the demands for a moral
or ethical condemnation that are almost inherent in any study of
the extremes of human violence.[2] The challenge to the academic
discipline lies in the murky ground between simple and pure narration (assuming that this is possible), the facts and nothing but the
facts, and the social environment in which history is being written,

an environment in which the evils of the Nazi regime and its various killing apparatuses (and those who would deny their existence) must be confronted.[3]

A literary narrative of the Shoah will confront the same issues if we accept that an ethical reading and writing duty is imposed within and on literature. At the same time, a fictional account of the Shoah will also have to cope with the unwriting of history that is inherent in the literary genre. History is by definition fictionalized within a literary frame. By emphasizing the rhetorical element of historical events, literature by its very presence might undermine history's claim to epistemological status. But a literary rendering, in which category Ricoeur includes witness testimony, must also confront the basic question of its reception.[4] For Ricoeur the intersection, at the level of judgment of fact and fiction, confronts the citizen historian and the citizen writer, each of whom plays a role in the construction of an ethically informed collective memory.[5] At this moment of engagement with memory, history, and forgetting, Ricoeur argues that all those who encounter these texts must confront the question of judgment, the question of whether and how a particular text can, as it must, be subjected to a criterion of acceptability.[6] At this preliminary level all texts appear to be prima facie acceptable—in the context of the Holocaust, the account of a Nazi, a Jew, or a Ukrainian are to be confronted equally. The same assumptions are at work in a different but sometimes comparable interpretive situation, that of a criminal trial. The accused is presumed innocent, and the prosecution bears a burden of proof beyond a reasonable doubt. The purpose of the trial itself is to reach a judgment, and the tools of the legal process, rules of evidence, the function of the trier of fact, the credibility of the witnesses, are all deployed with that goal in mind.

Literary renderings are likewise bound by rules of social, political, and ethical judgment. They do not exist in isolation from the multiplicity of contexts into which they are thrown, and their merit is always a matter subjected to judgment. For Ricoeur we are dealing in literary accounts of the Holocaust with events that are supremely traumatic. The reader and writer are engaged in an effort to construct an ethical judgment about texts, as social artifacts, in order to place them somewhere as constituent elements of our collective identity and memory. Ricoeur proposes a psychoanalytic frame such as that adopted by Dominick LaCapra as offering an interpretive referent that is most appropriate to this social, political, and ethical task of judgment.[7] The question to be asked, in order for the judgment to be made, is always whether the text and its narration are likely to assist in the working through of the trauma at the core of collective understanding, identity, forgetting, and memory. Some have gone so far as to argue that a working through of the trauma can only be truly achieved through a literary genre, the only means of offering a transcendent truth through the laws of the genre itself. The freedom of the literary imagination allows us to confront and calm the demons that haunt our understandings of the Shoah.[8]

The Hand That Signed the Paper (1994) by Helen Demidenko articulates and narrates the trauma of the Shoah.[9] The novel tells its story from the authorial perspective of the Holocaust perpetrator and situates the Holocaust within a frame in which war is deployed as a kind of meta-narrative of explanation and/or excuse. The text is also situated both historically and intellectually around the events and public debates related to the Adelaide legal proceedings against Mikolay Berezowsky, Ivan Polyukhovich, and Heinrich Wagner. At the time of its publication and subsequently, it caused a significant and vociferous public debate about history, truth, and memory and engaged multiple issues surrounding the politics of authorial intent and Australian identity in relation to the Holocaust. Indeed, it is not an exaggeration to assert that perhaps more than the trials themselves, this novel about the trials, the Shoah, and its Ukrainian perpetrators focused public debate in Australia around issues relating to the appropriate place for the Shoah in present-day understandings about a pluralist or multicultural Australian society. The debate was often heated, as assertions about a Jewish conspiracy were never far from the surface. As a point of departure, therefore, adopting Ricoeur's and LaCapra's psychoanalytic frame appears appropriate.

NARRATING THE SHOAH IN UKRAINE: WAR, "RACE," AND MEMORY

Tony Judt has recently argued that both European and American identity have been largely constructed around a politics of forgetting.[10] In the case of the United States public consciousness is informed by a lack, a missing trauma, the absence of a brutal and deadly war on its territory. U.S. knowledge of, and identification with, the horrors of World War II, and the Shoah, have been constructed at one step removed from the harsh realities of death on one's doorstep. Literally, American memories of war are deterritorialized in a dramatic sense.[11] Even if one refers to the mass destruction of Native American populations or to slavery and the Civil War, for the vast majority of the population any sense of memory or identification through trauma is significantly displaced through the sublimating effects of time.

In a similar vein war is both literally and figuratively distant from Australian experience. World War I gave rise to a collective identity that figures and is refigured each year on 25 April through a day of remembrance for the war dead, the departed "diggers," and a reiteration of the ANZAC (Australian and New Zealand Army Corps) spirit. The realities of the conflict, of death and destruction, are now matters of historical memory. War in the Pacific during the 1940s is a real memory only for a few veterans, although it was invoked as an ideological trope in arguments against the introduction of war crimes legislation. Memories of an Aboriginal genocide, and the present-day politics of apology, figure prominently in collective attempts to remember and to construct a posttraumatic, postcolonial national identity, but again they remain at a distance, psychologically and physically, for most non–Aboriginal Australians. The European conflict that embodied and enabled the Shoah took place long ago and far away for the vast majority of Australian citizens. Like Americans, Australians construct war and the Shoah as memory and as history, and in each case the reality of death and destruction remains at an important remove.

In Europe, on the other hand, the social and collective experiences of war have created national and transnational memories that continue to traumatize individuals and nations. As Judt asserts: "War, in short, prompted behavior that would have been unthinkable as well as dysfunctional in peacetime. It is war, not racism or ethnic antagonism or religious fervor that leads to atrocity. War—total war—has been the crucial antecedent condition for mass criminality in the modern era."[12]

The Hand That Signed the Paper exemplifies and embodies Judt's condition precedent argument about war, race, memory, identity, and past and present—the Holocaust in Ukraine. Centuries of anti-semitism informed relations between the dominant Polish, Russian, and Ukrainian populations of Volhynia and Galicia and their Jewish neighbors. Periodic outbreaks of violence in the form of pogroms characterized the worst moments of these historical interactions. But it was only in the context of Blitzkrieg, the invasion of the Soviet Union in late June 1941 in Operation Barbarossa, and the context of German anti-Jewish ideology and total war, that pogromic violence and ethnic/religious antagonism could be transformed into the Shoah. "The Holocaust took place in a context of total war and could be continued and expanded only as long as the war went on. Moreover, it assumed many of the attributes of a military operation and was legitimized and understood by its perpetrators as an essentially military task that had a direct bearing on the security, or even the existence, of the nation."[13]

An important interpretive question is raised by these analyses. They posit war as a key factor giving rise to the Holocaust. We know from the historical and eyewitness evidence adduced in the three Australian war crimes prosecutions that Holocaust perpetrators in Ukraine were located within the German security apparatus and its Ukrainian auxiliary services. But there is a clear distinction, both historically and ethically, between asserting the key importance of war and wartime conditions in giving rise to the mass killing of Ukraine's Jews, on the one hand, and arguing that war, and the brutal realities of occupation and armed conflict, can be invoked as a form of excuse for the actions of the perpetrators, on the other. Thus, while the War Crimes Act itself places war and occupation as a condition precedent to its operation, it does not allow a defense of superior orders as an embodiment of "the war made me do it."

The idea of placing fifty-year-old events in a Ukrainian forest, beside a killing pit outside a village, before an Australian court was difficult, if not impossible. To add to that challenge some idea of narrating the reality of wartime conditions, occupation, and the facts of local collaboration in the mass killings of the Jewish population, as the informing background, was apparently beyond the capacities of both historical and legal discourse to explain in a way that might have been comprehensible to 1990s Australians. Perhaps literature could fill in the gap between fact and imagination and present the Shoah in Ukraine to an Australian public for whom war and mass death were but distant and vaguely defined collective memories. If the chapter of Holocaust perpetrators in Australia was to be reopened and rewritten so many years after Garfield Barwick's categorical closure, literature was possibly best placed to reinscribe the Shoah as a living memory and part of present-day Australian cultural, political, legal, and historical identity. It is in the context of the apparent pedagogic failure of the three Adelaide proceedings that Demidenko's novel emerged.

LITERARY PRIZES AND DEBATES ABOUT LITERARY ANTISEMITISM IN AUSTRALIA

Demidenko's *The Hand That Signed the Paper* is a multiple award–winning novel about the Shoah. In the book Demidenko deploys a first-person narration to recount events relating to the Holocaust in Ukraine and Poland.[14] The book tells the story of Vitaly and Evheny Kovalenko, the narrator Fiona's uncle and father and that of Kateryna, her aunt. Vitaly was a guard/executioner at the extermination camp at Treblinka, while Evheny participated in anti-Jewish *Aktionen* as a Ukrainian member of the ss. Kateryna married a German ss member of the Einsatzkommando responsible for the massacre of Jews at Babi Yar. As the novel opens, Vitaly has been charged under Australia's recent war crimes legislation targeting those, like Vitaly and Evheny, who had perpetrated crimes against humanity during World War II and had found safe haven in Australia in the postwar DP period.

The editors of a collection of materials on the controversies that swirled around the book from the time it was published in 1994 summarized the issue when they wrote: "That *The Hand That Signed the Paper* is a novel about evil, all protagonists and antagonists agree. Whether the novel itself is an evil work is a question of primary importance in the debate, and creates an important ethical precedent in Australia's short cultural history."[15]

Demidenko chooses a first-person narrator, Fiona, the niece/daughter, who sets about telling the story of her family's migrant experience in Australia and then delves into the darker aspects of family history through the nexus of Vitaly's pending prosecution and her father's possible implication in similar proceedings. The narrative structure of the novel is an account of events from the perspective of the accused perpetrators. Very quickly, Fiona gives way to her family members, mostly Vitaly and Kateryna, who tell their stories to her by way of taped statements sent to Fiona as the family's chronicler. Through this rather trite device she gives voice to the Kovalenko family's own perpetrators. Given that the actual war crimes proceedings in Adelaide were characterized by a perfectly understandable legal strategy of having the accused remain silent throughout, the idea of telling the story from this perspective could have opened up intriguing possibilities for public debate and for the process of constructing an ethical and pedagogical narrative of the Shoah in Ukraine and about war crimes trials and national identity in the Australian public sphere.

The reader soon realizes, however, that this is not the aim of *The Hand That Signed the Paper*. The questions of authorial voice and intent, and of reader reaction, to a text written from the perspective of largely unrepentant antisemites and Jew killers are writ large in the text itself and in the debates in the Australian media that soon surrounded the book's publication. In this instance the complex issues of intention and reception are further complicated by the question of authorial autobiography. The original manuscript of the book was written not in the voice of Fiona Kovalenko but in that of Fiona Demidenko. The surname of the family of Jew killers was that of the author herself. Throughout the events that surrounded the appearance of the book, from the praise of various competition juries and the support of those who saw great merit in the work,[16] to subsequent attacks on both the work and its author, Helen Demidenko consistently insisted that the work was one of "faction," a fictionalized account of her real family's story.[17] Demidenko the author always portrayed a persona who confirmed the genre-mixing nature of the novel.

In addition to presenting herself in public dressed in a Ukrainian peasant blouse, Demidenko reveled in recounting tales of her illiterate taxi driver father and the family's Ukrainian peasant background, complete with folk dancing demonstrations and stories of vodka fueled excess. The young English major Fiona who narrates the novel is mirrored in the young English major Helen.[18] At the same time, Helen offers a minor note of caution as she introduces the novel: "What follows is a work of fiction. The Kovalenko family depicted in this novel has no counterpart in reality. Nonetheless, it would be ridiculous to pretend that this book is unhistorical."[19]

The Kovalenko siblings who narrate their roles in the killing of Europe's Jews do not really exist; they are useful tools to tell a story. But given the public presentation of Demidenko as the daughter of poor, semiliterate Ukrainian migrants to Australia—migrants who had, like so many alleged war criminals, come to the country under false identities—and the obvious and self-proclaimed autobiographical parallels between Helen and Fiona, it was clearly left open to the reader to assume, as almost everyone who first read the novel in Australia did, that the fiction here is simply a semiotic one, accomplished in part through the editor's erasure of Demidenko and her reinscription as Kovalenko from the original manuscript to the published book.[20]

Indeed, the authorial warning that the book is at once fictional and historical—that is, that it is faction—is both contradicted and confirmed by the rest of the author's note. Demidenko writes: "For the names of all places in Ukraine, I have used the more familiar Russian and Polish spellings. Below is an alphabetical list of key names found in this book, and their correct Ukrainian spellings. For the names of people, I have used Ukrainian spellings. In Ukrainian, the letter 'g' is usually pronounced softly, as an 'h.'"[21]

The coding by Demidenko is transparent. She speaks Ukrainian and has an intimate knowledge of the complex history of the region that variously fell under Polish and Russian (Soviet) sovereignty. For the readers she has offered a more familiar usage than that available to Ukrainians such as herself. While the book is fiction, it is written by a Ukrainian Australian and is based in history. And that Ukrainian-Australian author shares significant biographical details with Fiona, the narrator.

The Hand That Signed the Paper was a literary sensation. It won the Vogel/*Australian* prize for best unpublished manuscript, the Australian Literary Society Gold Medal, and finally, the most prestigious prize available for Australian fiction, the Miles Franklin Award. For an author still in her twenties, the success of her family's story was remarkable. The Vogel/*Australian* award carried with it a guarantee of publication with the leading Australian publishing house, Allen & Unwin. The prize was awarded by a jury composed of leading Australian writers Jennifer Rowe and Roger McDonald and the Australian Broadcasting Corporation (ABC) journalist Jill Kitson. While McDonald expressed some reservations about certain antisemitic overtones in parts of the manuscript, Kitson carried the day. She became an ardent and very public supporter of the novel.

From the earliest stages of its publication, *The Hand That Signed the Paper* was positioned as offering an important new element in the construction of Australian cultural memory and identity. Because war and the Holocaust were so distant from the direct experience of most Australians, the narration of these events, as part of the lived history of migrants to the country, allowed voice to be given to those known as "new Australians." This signal in turn permitted the construction of an emerging multicultural national identity in which these distant events would be incorporated through the contemporary migrant narrative. Jill Kitson explained that the literary judges who awarded the accolades to the work were self-consciously playing a key role in this narrative construction of the new Australian identity: "They're incorporating into cultural memory, firsthand experience of the major historical events of the century. Events from which Australia has been largely insulated, but which are a growing component of contemporary Australian life."[22]

The first real signs of trouble emerged at Allen & Unwin. Stephanie Dowrick, a well-established writer and publisher in her own right, was also a part-time fiction editor at the publishing house. She expressed the view that the work was extremely problematic and that had the manuscript come to the publishing house via a normal submission route, she would have rejected it out of hand.[23] Leading Australian author Brian Castro also refused to have anything to do with the manuscript, as did the scholar and author Lynne Segal. Segal "was shocked by what she read. She was the first reader of *The Hand* who responded to it with a force of visceral disgust."[24]

After obtaining an opinion from a historical expert who confirmed on narrow and probably overly technical grounds that the manuscript was generally historically justifiable, Allen & Unwin went ahead with publication. The cover contains a blurb from Jill Kitson, one of the Vogel judges, who declared that the book offered "a searingly truthful account of terrible wartime deeds that is also an imaginative work of extraordinary redemptive power."

The novel was originally met with almost universal praise for daring to tell an unpalatable truth about one of history's darkest hours.[25] The members of the academic panel from the University of Western Sydney who sat on the Association for the Study of Australian Literature's Australian Literature Society's Gold Medal jury praised Demidenko's historical insight and her literary rendering of issues of great moral ambiguity.[26] Finally, the eminent members of Australia's most prestigious literary award panel, the Miles Franklin, saw Demidenko's narrative as one that gave voice to a new Australia, an Australia of migrant experience, one in which events of great historical moment had to be internalized as part of the nation's cultural mosaic. The citation read in part, "They [recent immigrants] are incorporating into the cultural memory first-hand experience of the major historical events of the century, events from which Australia has been largely insulated, but which are a growing component of contemporary Australian life—even to the extent of requiring of us intricate moral judgments, as the recent debate over the war crimes legislation highlighted."[27]

There can be little doubt that for the members of the Miles Franklin jury the novel fell into a set of social, political, historical, and legal narratives about and around the War Crimes Act and the Adelaide proceedings. Nor can there be any remaining doubt that the strength of the novel, in the eyes of its proponents, was that it offered what can only be seen, in light of what had happened in Adelaide, as a counter-narrative about the Shoah in Ukraine. The perpetrators are given voice so that "intricate moral judgments" can be made. In the context of debates over an emerging Australian identity, the novel was seen and constructed as offering a new frame for such judgments. An innovative, previously unheard perspective enters the difficult moral and ethical calculus within public discourse.

Dame Professor Leonie Kramer, a leading figure in academe and in cultural circles and a jury member, in what appears to have been her only public statement about the award and about Demidenko's novel, said of the book, "It's an account of human tragedy and of people who were willy-nilly during the war, involved in incidents over which they had no control, which caused great suffering and subsequently feelings of enormous guilt about the part they had been forced to play."[28]

It is obvious from the citation from the Miles Franklin jury, leading lights of the Australian academy and literary establishment—Kramer, Professor Harry Heseltine, Associate Professor Adrian Mitchell, and broadcaster Jill Kitson—that *The Hand That Signed the Paper* was being placed at the forefront of ongoing debates about Australian culture and national identity and that the Holocaust and the Adelaide war crimes trials were important framing elements in what was seen as a much broader cultural debate. The content of the literary jury's decision was determined, in important aspects of public discourse, by history and law, by the Shoah and the Adelaide trials. Again, following Ricoeur, each genre demands an ethical judgment from its participants. The Miles Franklin jury is quite explicit in its recognition, in its formal and informal pronouncements, that *The Hand That Signed the Paper* had to play a significant role in the formation of such judgments about the Shoah, war, collaboration, and the place of all these phenomena in the construction of an emerging Australian national memory and collective identity.

Indeed, the jury had to forge new ground about Australian identity in making the decision to recognize the book. The terms of the Miles Franklin award limited the prize to works of "Australian" fiction. In the years preceding the Demidenko book, a level of controversy had surrounded the correct meaning to be attached to this term. Previous juries had refused to give the award to significant Australian novels, or more precisely novels by major Australian authors, specifically because the subject matter of the books was deemed to have been insufficiently Australian.[29] In the case of *The Hand That Signed the Paper* a new line of cultural identity was drawn by the Miles Franklin jury as the understanding of what constituted an Australian work was rewritten to include a novel set for the most part in Nazi-occupied Eastern Europe.

At the same time, the novel was also being situated as a stalking horse for opponents of the war crimes legislation and the three cases in Adelaide. In addition to the judges' comments about the moral complexity of the issues raised by the novel, the book itself leaves

readers to encounter a distinct counter-narrative in relation to moral
and legal responsibility in relation to Holocaust perpetrators, their
motivation and their moral status. Notwithstanding Kramer's statement, the moral core of *The Hand That Signed the Paper* is empty. It is
characterized by the absence of feelings of guilt or moral culpability
by the perpetrators. The factor that structures blame or responsibility
is truly and accurately situated in relation to the events recounted in
the novel—that is, Babi Yar and Treblinka. It is a strangely abstract
and foreign one, war. War becomes not one, or even the principal,
historically relevant explanatory factor but the most morally weighty
element in reaching the complex ethical determination posed by
debates over the war crimes legislation.

Kramer, reflecting and reproducing the narrative constructed by
Demidenko, removes any notion of agency—and therefore any notion
of real moral, let alone legal, responsibility—from the Kovalenko
brothers. Their actions were "willy-nilly," involving "incidents over
which they had no control." Machine-gunning thousands of naked
terrified Jewish men, women, and children in the ravine at Babi Yar
is apparently for Kramer and her fellow judges something over which
Evheny, the "factional" character, had no control. Beating Jews as
they walked toward "heaven" at Treblinka, stealing their property
as they were led to the gas chambers, for Vasily, the other factional
brother, was also something for which he could not possibly be held
accountable.

Supporters of the book argue that Vasily and Evheny are fictional
characters, players in a novel that is simply a creation of the author's
imagination. This claim was clearly part of the defense of the book
and of Demidenko as controversy broke out soon after the award of
the Miles Franklin prize.[30] But two counterarguments must also be
raised. First, we need to return to the question of the problematic
authorial identity and authorial intent surrounding the novel. Demidenko clearly portrayed both Vasily and Evheny as something more
than mere products of her imagination. They were part of her autobiography and as a consequence more clearly moral agents, both in

their own right but more important, in the way in which she chose to use them. As Gerard Henderson, a critic of the book from its earliest days, wrote, "Helen Demidenko's *The Hand That Signed the Paper* is a loathsome book—all the more so because the author insists that her first novel is not just a work of fiction."[31]

Second, members of the juries that awarded the Vogel and Miles Franklin prizes in particular situated the book itself in a discourse of morality, ethical responsibility, judgment, and indeed of law and the politics of national identity and collective memory. Kitson wrote of the "extraordinary redemptive power" of the work, and Kramer placed it in the context of moral debates about responsibility and legal liability for war crimes in the real-life circumstances of then current Australian national debates about prosecutions in Adelaide. Indeed, it was precisely because Demidenko deliberately and self-consciously situated that particular and specific migrant experience of having war criminals in one's family as the main plot and narrative device of the novel that it was recognized and rewarded. It is and was at the time impossible to imagine that the novel would have received the praise and support it did were it not for the facts that Demidenko asserted and her ethnic Ukrainian identity as her public persona emphasized her autobiographical links with the book's characters. It is precisely this autobiography that lent the novel its aura of authenticity and which then meant that the judges could recognize and laud the emergence of a new and vital voice of the real-life migrant experience in Australia.[32]

The moral complexity of events that together constitute the Shoah, the reality of the perpetrator experience and perspective, heretofore silenced by a morally smug identification with the suffering of victims of Nazi atrocities, and the experiential reality of migrant life in Australia are factors identified specifically by those who chose to reward and recognize the merit of Demidenko's novel.[33] *The Hand That Signed the Paper* is important for its supporters in large part because it tells the story of the Holocaust from the particular perspective of the perpetrators and their families. It incorporates the lives of displaced persons, or "reffos," into the mainstream of Australian cultural memory and identity. This narrative of the war and the fate of European Jewry is also specifically invoked by both Demidenko and her supporters as a counter-narrative to what was clearly seen as an unjust set of legal proceedings against already sufficiently traumatized and suffering migrants.

This narrative version was the discourse of the Shoah, war crimes, war crimes trials, and Australian identity, which was met with resounding early critical approval. But it would soon change. One of the most vociferous and effective critics of the book, Robert Manne, succinctly summarized the case against *The Hand That Signed the Paper* when he wrote: "I found the book laughably inadequate to its subject and unmistakably antisemitic, in a way I had long since assumed no Australian literature could be. I found it morally and historically shallow, coarse and cold, even technically quite incompetent."[34]

HELEN DEMIDENKO AND THE SHOAH

A brief examination of the text itself reveals enough about Demidenko's agenda and perhaps that of many of her supporters to satisfy any burden of proof that one might wish to impose in reaching a judgment about the novel. Even taking into account the political and cultural climate in Australia at the time around the issue of war crimes trials and the discourses used by some members of Australian immigrant and ethnic groups, it is still difficult to understand how, after rereading the book today, the novel managed to escape a real critical evaluation upon (or before) its publication. It is perhaps even more difficult for the reader today to comprehend how supporters remain convinced that the book has any redeeming features whatsoever. Of course, support for the novel becomes clearer, or more easily understood, in part at least, when one takes into account the actual social, political, and legal environment into which the book emerged.

From the very beginning Demidenko sounds the by now well-known themes of opponents of war crimes trials in Australia. First, we encounter Fiona and her Australian roommate, Cathe, in a discussion about the developments in Fiona's uncle's case. Fiona tells her friend how hard the whole thing has been on her family. "When uncle Vitaly first heard about the trials, he hid under the kitchen table. Staciya came home from the shops and found him hugging the table leg and yelling: 'the Israelis are coming to get me!'"[35]

For Frank Devine this passage from Demidenko's novel "commands attention as dramatically as her later descriptions of bloody horror. The two-sentence depiction of fear and guilt, combining the comic with the pathetic and the terrifying, assures you are in the hands of a writer of superior moral and intellectual acuity."[36] Intriguingly, Devine discerns some expression or description of "guilt" where none appears evident in the text itself. There is certainly evidence of fear and pathos perhaps, but guilt does not emerge anywhere in this passage or elsewhere in the book. But more worrying still is Devine's assertion that the passage somehow reveals Demidenko's moral grasp.

The scene offers a stark introduction to the family saga and to the ideology of the entire novel. Poor Uncle Vitaly is a pitiful and frightened old man, hiding under the kitchen table. More significantly, he is hiding from "the Israelis." Not the Australian police, not even "the Jews," who would figure prominently in subsequent sections of the book, but the Israelis.[37] From the very outset of the Kovalenko family saga we are confronted with the idea that the war crimes trials are not really an Australian undertaking at all. Instead, an international conspiracy led by the Israelis is behind Australia's efforts to bring Holocaust perpetrators to justice. This idea reflects a prominent aspect of the parliamentary discourse employed by opposition members in their attempts to defeat the war crimes legislation. Allegations that Bob Hawke was the pawn of a Jewish and/or Israeli lobby and that the proposed law was not authentically representative of Australian interests or values appear consistently in the pages of Parliament's official record, *Hansard*. That this passage of the novel might have been read as a display of moral acuity by a prominent Australian journalist and commentator indicates the level of misunderstanding and what might less generously be identified as crass stupidity that appeared in Australian public discourse at the time.

The discussion between Fiona and Cathe also permits Demidenko to reinforce the theme of the basic and foundational injustice behind the trials in Adelaide. At the same time, she is also able to raise the key issue, underlined by Dame Leonie Kramer, the role of war and its supposed power to erase any notion of agency or moral responsibility. The invocation of the war narrative is strengthened here because it is one of the rare instances in the entire novel in which the speaker is not Fiona the narrator or any of her family. Instead, it is a normal "Anglo-Celtic" Australian voice that expresses the mainstream view of the war crimes trials. It is Fiona's roommate Cathe who articulates both her disgust at the trials and at war when she states: "I want you to understand . . . that . . . that I think it's wrong to try them. That trying people for what they did in a war legitimises other wartime activities that are left untried. War is a crime, of itself."[38]

Demidenko lays out her colors early. The argument is a simple one in which war trumps everything. By singling out the Holocaust, other war crimes are ignored, including the biggest crime of all, war itself. Moreover, she places the Holocaust clearly in the context of war, not as most scholars do, in order to contextualize the horror and to allow us to understand and identify some of the operative factors that led to mass killings but, instead, to relativize and to excuse. This narrative strategy has the same impact as that invoked by Kramer and her comments about the willy-nilly nature of the "events" portrayed in the novel, Babi Yar and Treblinka. It is also the same rhetorical device employed in parliamentary debates in which the British bombing of Dresden, the atrocities committed by Communist regimes such as those of Pol Pot and Afghanistan, were invoked as examples of equally iniquitous events being ignored by proponents of the war crimes legislation. This narrative strategy is fundamentally ahistorical, but it nonetheless underlines the politics and ideological positioning behind much of the debate surrounding the book.

War and war crimes, atrocities, and the Holocaust are but distant memories for most Australians. By arguing that Australians cannot really understand war and the events portrayed in *The Hand That Signed the Paper* and then asserting as a result that this incomprehensible reality "war" was what caused the perpetrators to act as they did, the pedagogical narrative set out by the novel and its supporters removes the Shoah and the killers from our comprehension and from our judgment. Of equal pedagogical, cultural, and ethical importance is the correlative counter-narrative that attributes authenticity to the version of events as presented by Demidenko and her family of characters. They have direct firsthand, lived experience. They possess direct personal knowledge of the willy-nilly, a knowledge that we can never possess. By removing events and actors from our ability to understand what we have not lived, this way of telling a story about the Shoah in Ukraine negates our capacity for critical ethical judgment and instead seeks to impose a single truth. The desired outcome seems to be the creation of a historical counter-narrative of the Shoah to displace the heretofore predominant version as given by "the Jews," or as Vitaly would have it, "the Israelis."[39] As a matter of basic logic and jurisprudence, Cathe's Australian position on the war crimes trials is easily falsifiable. It is simply not true or logically consistent to assert that punishing some offenses and not pursuing others leads to the legitimation of those other crimes.

What is at stake is a moral and jurisprudential elision that Demidenko uses, deliberately I believe, in order to relativize the Shoah and to reduce any notion of perpetrator responsibility that might have informed Australian attempts to prosecute alleged war criminals. The real question should be, and is, first of all: is what is punished or pursued a crime itself? This is the question that Demidenko, in the voice of Cathe, chooses to ignore and which she then completely forgets in the rest of the book. She engages in morally suspect category confusion by going directly to the second question in the logical chain. Again, this subsequent issue was raised in political debates around the original war crimes legislation and in political and legal critiques of the Australian situation. By narrowly focusing on an oxymoronic limited universal jurisdiction, the Hawke government and its successors have allowed perpetrators of crimes against humanity, atrocities, and war crimes in other conflicts to fall into the vacuum of Australian law that targeted only the Shoah.

The real question for judgment at all relevant levels is whether the other acts that are not pursued can also be classified as "criminal." If they are classified and conceived as such, the acts themselves are not legitimized by non-punishment. It is perhaps the system of justice, depending on the gravity of the offense, that is delegitimized for failing to pursue and punish serious offences or to make those offenses against international law punishable in the domestic legal system. But in the absence of other factors the offense that is punished is not made illegitimate because other heinous acts escape sanction.

But Demidenko does not want an informed or subtle debate about the nature of punishment, legality, and legitimacy. She does not want a multifactorial discussion or analysis. Instead, she wants to repeat the canard of selective prosecution, of show trials. Her protagonist's uncle is being pursued by the Israelis, while others escape the net of justice. Moreover, and perhaps more significantly, as Cathe says, war itself is a crime. Whatever Vasily and Evheny did was done in war, and war is the biggest crime of all. Cathe and Fiona seem incapable of asking why war or what definition of war could cause, let alone excuse, the shooting of Jews at pits throughout Ukraine or the gassing of hundreds of thousands of Jews—men, women, and children—at Treblinka.

The author's main frame of reference and one that is foisted upon the reader relentlessly is that of Ukrainian suffering. More particularly, Ukrainian suffering during the period of Soviet rule is invoked over and over again as an explanation of and a justification for atrocities and mass murder committed by Ukrainians against Jews following the German invasion. The story of the Shoah in Ukraine and in the death camps of Poland is told not just from the perspective of Ukrainian collaborators and perpetrators but from the perspective of Ukrainian collaborators and perpetrators who were justified in what they did. For Fiona and her family the perpetrators are first and foremost victims. The stories told by Vitaly, Kateryna, and Evheny are tales of childhood deprivation under the Stalinist regime. Homes and farms are taken away as the process of collectivization is imposed on the Ukrainian peasantry. Ukrainian children are forced to leave their families to attend Communist school, where Russian is taught and the Ukrainian language is forbidden. The churches are closed, believers persecuted. The greatest tragedy of all is the famine, the *Holomodor*, in which Ukrainians starved to death in one of the richest farmlands in Europe. The culprits behind all this suffering of innocent Ukrainians were the Communists.

But Demidenko/Vitaly/Evheny/Kateryna's recounting does not stop there. Instead, the entire narrative of the book that won the Vogel and Miles Franklin prizes, the book of great "redemptive power," is constructed on a blatant repetition of the standard canard of modern antisemitism, that the Bolshevists were Jews. Jews controlled Stalin, and more specifically they controlled the Narodnyi komissariat vnutrennikh del (NKVD), the Soviet intelligence agency, which arrested, deported, and killed Ukrainians. As Soviet forces retreated in the face of the German military onslaught of late June and early July 1941, the NKVD executed hundreds of its enemies. Of this, there is no historical doubt. But for Demidenko & Company it was not the NKVD that committed atrocities; it was Jews, because Jews and Bolshevists are synonymous, and for some reason known only to antisemites, it is their quality as "Jew" that always predominates. Demidenko writes: "Some of the oldest students were taken to a communist prison in Kiev. People heard from these students that the guards and kommissars were Jewish and Russian, and that the prisoners were all Ukrainian."[40]

The Hand That Signed the Paper is full of examples of the deliberate joinder of the terms *Jews/Bolshevists*, *Jews/Communists*. There can be no doubt that for Vitaly/Evheny/Kateryna there was simply no distinction. When Kateryna first speaks in the early pages of the book, her narration focuses on the suffering imposed on Ukraine by the Soviets and on the famine in particular. She speaks of "the communists and Jews" and of her deepest desire to kill "every communist and Jew in the Ukraine." The local commissar is Ukrainian, but his wife, the real power in the household, is not; she is "a Jewish doctor" and "a Jewess from Leningrad." She is "Doctor Judit."[41] On page 29 we find the description three times—"the Jewess from Leningrad." Demidenko is relentless and unsubtle. The discourse is crudely antisemitic. The Jews are the source of Ukrainians' suffering, and the revenge that was imposed in the Shoah was not only understandable, it was justified.

Some supporters of Demidenko, in response to claims that the book was antisemitic, asserted that those who made such suggestions suffered from a fundamental interpretive error. Her characters were antisemitic, but the author was not. The breach in the wall separating author from character was one that could lead to such dangerous and hurtful assertions. Of course, it was Demidenko herself who deconstructed the traditional barrier of the genre by deliberately offering an autobiography and a public persona that openly asserted the factional character of the work. Moreover, in private conversation she did not hesitate to utter antisemitic remarks.[42] She reiterated this sentiment in public as well. When Gerard Henderson pointed out during a head-to-head interview on one of ABC Television's leading current affairs programs, *The 7:30 Report*, that the work was historically flawed and that, for example, Stalin was in charge of the Soviet Union during the *Holomodor* and he certainly was neither Jewish nor a "pro-semite," Demidenko retorted that Henderson's comments indicated that he was "speaking on behalf of Jews."[43] The idea that Ukrainian antisemitism was limited to the fictionalized members of the Kovalenko family simply does not stand up either to textual or extratextual, autobiographical scrutiny.

The one time in the entire book when the voice in which an account is written does not belong to Fiona or one of her relatives is found on two pages in which we are given privileged access to a letter written by Dr. Judit to her mother.[44] Beyond asking the obvious question about how this incongruous discourse made it through the publisher's editing process, one might also inquire about the purpose of this brief interlude. The answer is obvious. In her letter Judit characterizes the Ukrainian population as drunkards, as people who propagate like good Catholics, and whose own backwardness and sloth had brought about the famine. This is Demidenko's sole attempt to flesh out a real Jewish character in the book. Like her Ukrainian protagonists, however, Judit the Jewess from Leningrad is a one-dimensional caricature, a Communist fanatic who hates Ukrainians. All her actions, abusing local peasants, spitting on them, destroying religious artifacts, are then made explicable by this brief passage. More important, when the villagers abuse and kill her, they are simply exacting their rightful revenge.

More fundamental to the critique of the work and to the significant questions about Australian public discourse about the book, about the Holocaust and about the cultural place of the Adelaide war crimes trials in Australian public memory and national identity in a multiethnic country, two facts indicate that neither Demidenko nor her supporters paid much attention to the accuracy of this work of faction. The rhetorical construction of a particular and pernicious history/memory was much more central to the project. On several occasions in discussions about her Uncle Vitaly's situation and possible proceedings against her father, Fiona and her family members refer to her uncle having to go to Adelaide to stand trial. The historical fact referred to here, the reference that Australian readers at the time would have picked up and recognized as part of the public meaning being interrogated and constructed, is the three proceedings against Polyukhovich, Berezowsky, and Wagner, all of which took place in the South Australian capital. The synonymous relationship between Adelaide and war crimes trials for Nazi collaborators was and is factually accurate.

But the fuller and more complete rendering of the legal fact would indicate that the proceedings took place in Adelaide only because the three accused were residents of the city and its suburbs. Adelaide was not Nuremberg, chosen by the prosecution in large part for its symbolic significance in the Nazi imaginary, although the equivalence might have been Demidenko's underlying semiotic strategy. To assert that the government wished to bring poor, sick, frightened Vitaly, who was driven to a stroke by the pressure of the threatened prosecution, from his home in Queensland a thousand miles away to Adelaide to stand trial is simply another way for Demidenko to attack the basis and foundational fairness of the proceedings themselves. Yet the War Crimes Act, notable for its attempt to ensure the fairest of fair trials, contains a specific provision (sec. 13) mandating that the trial of an accused under the act should take place in his or her home state. Adelaide/Nuremberg is a figment, like so much else, of Demidenko's limited, but politically powerful, imagination.

The more significant historical fact that was drawn to the attention of the publishers from the very beginning of the process is the one that is missing from *The Hand That Signed the Paper*.[45] This is the historical experience of antisemitism and antisemitic violence in Ukraine, an experience and a historical truth that puts to rest the entire premise of the novel. In other words, Demidenko ignores centuries of endemic Ukrainian antisemitism and pogromic violence against Jews. To have paid attention to this real history as a plot or narrative device would have diminished if not fatally wounded the operative thesis and explanatory scheme of the book. If antisemitism existed in Ukraine as part of the embedded and deeply felt national, social, and cultural practice, and if that antisemitism informed Vitaly, Evheny, and Kateryna's hatred of Jews and participation by the brothers in the Shoah, the narrative offered by Demidenko becomes fatally flawed.

The idea that Jewish Bolshevists conspired to make the Ukrainian people suffer and that it was a reaction to this phenomenon that was the sole and/or dominant informing factor in the brothers' participation in the Nazi killing machine would then be radically undermined, and Demidenko would be left without a book. Ukrainian antisemitism must have been caused by the Jews for the stories told by the Kovalenko family about the Shoah in Ukraine to make any sense and to be truthful in a believable sense within the narrative structure of the novel. This is the point at which fact and fiction meld together and *The Hand That Signed the Paper* becomes little more than an antisemitic rant.

Other historical inaccuracies, fables, and fabulations seem to confirm this basic point about the novel. Both Kateryna and Vitaly are portrayed as fair-haired and blue-eyed—in other words, Aryan in appearance. One might ask a series of important questions here about Demidenko's decision to portray her family as being at one and the same time typical suffering Ukrainian peasants and perfect Aryan specimens. Surely she could not fail to know that as Slavs, Ukrainians were never going to be part of the "Master Race" that would rule the "Thousand Year Reich." Moreover, one need only regard the multiple self-images of Demidenko as the blonde-haired, blue-eyed Ukrainian ice maiden to begin asking some serious questions about just where she and the book stand on issues of race, ethnicity, and antisemitism.

Examples of racial, eugenic, ideological confusion in the narrative abound. Kateryna's love interest, ss Captain Wilhelm Hasse, enters into a full sexual relationship with Kateryna after having just met her. But we also know that at university Hasse's favorite reading was Friedrich Nietzsche and Arthur De Gobineau. Surely someone as self-aware of the role of the heroic superman in the Nazi Volksgemeinschaft as an ss captain, and an ss captain who was familiar with the "racial science" of De Gobineau, would not have simply set about having sex with a Ukrainian woman. Everything we know about ss racial policy and practice would indicate that the absence of a careful and documented family tree showing that Kateryna was a racially pure Aryan would have prevented sexual relations between the two, let alone marriage. But Demidenko appears more interested in propagating a family tree of racially pure blood in the latest generation to let a bit of history stand in her way.

The positive critical response that greeted the novel upon its publication would appear to have justified all of Demidenko's aesthetic, political, and ideological choices. The Australian public and the Australian literary establishment welcomed the new ethnic voice with open arms. Her antisemitism, her relativization of the Holocaust, and her justificatory explanations of her family and their roles as Jew killers all appear to have fit into a set of Australian cultural understandings that were commonly shared. As Robert Manne put it: "Helen Demidenko had self-consciously embarked upon a campaign of what one might call moral revisionism with regard to the Holocaust. What was truly astonishing—I imagine even to her—was how little Australian critical resistance she encountered."[46]

But things were about to change.

DEMIDENKO AND THE POLITICS OF IDENTITY IN AUSTRALIAN LITERARY DISCOURSE

Helen Demidenko was a fraud. The blonde-haired, blue-eyed Aryan child of semiliterate Ukrainian immigrants, garbed in a peasant blouse from her ancestral homeland, adept at the vodka-fueled celebratory folk dances of rural Ukraine, was, it turned out, Helen Darville, the daughter of solidly middle-class English migrants to Australia, now living the dreamed-of good life in a Brisbane suburb.[47] After original vociferous denials, the "Demidenko" identity shifted again and again, until at last any pretense that the author of *The Hand That Signed the Paper* had any connection—direct, indirect, or otherwise—to the Ukrainian community or the Holocaust was publicly destroyed.

Darville had performed an act of self-transformation, of self-mythification. She had performed in public as the daughter of Ukrainian immigrants.[48] Her persona had troubled members of two leading ethnic groups, the Australian Jewish and Ukrainian communities already suffering strained relations as a result of the political and cultural struggles surrounding the passage and implementation of Australia's war crimes legislation.[49] She had played the ethnic card to perfection in the minds of the Anglo-Celtic literary and cultural establishment. The controversy that followed raised at its core the question about whether the book would have been published, let alone won any awards or have been lauded by the great and the good of the literary world in Australia, had it been written by Helen Darville, the daughter of English migrants. Indeed, we might also begin to inquire how and why Darville/Demidenko's portrayal of her Ukrainian immigrant family as semiliterate drunkards and Jew haters was a vision that was so readily accepted as both factual and as an accurate and acceptable vision of an authentic Australian migrant experience as read through the eyes of literary judging panels and Australian journalists.

Of course, Darville is not the first author to pull off a literary hoax by placing a false autobiography as an identifying feature at the heart of a work of fiction. Nor was she the last. More recently, James Frey, Margaret Seltzer/Jones, and Laura Albert/JT LeRoy have all been revealed as authors who fictionalized an autobiographical link to their work of fiction in order to increase its authenticity and thence its marketability.[50] Demidenko was not even the first author to fake an autobiographical link to the Holocaust. Binjamin Wilkomirski played out his role as Holocaust survivor in spite of clear indications that his story was a lie.[51] Most recently, Misha Defonseca's autobiographical account of her escape from the Nazis and her survival among wild wolves was revealed to have been a work of fiction.[52]

Each of these instances raises interesting and important questions about, and provides insights into, the Demidenko/Darville case in Australia. Others have been found, like Darville, to have created an authorial persona with the clear intention of asserting and publicly proclaiming that even though their work was fiction, it could be more accurately and authentically characterized as a fictionalized account of the author's life experience. Defonseca's and Wilkomirski's accounts fell across genre lines in the other direction, from autobiography to fiction, from fact to falsification. Questions of the laws and practices of the applicable genre(s), and the transgressive effect of faction, all need to be considered in any full account of the phenomenon of falsified authorial identity and its different manifestations. What is particularly important in the context of this story is that the Demidenko/Darville issue raises serious questions in the context of Australian culture at the time. What do we now make of Dame Leonie Kramer's analysis of the willy-nilly and the difficult social and political questions arising out of the Adelaide war crimes cases? Once Darville's identity was revealed, the debates focused almost exclusively on one key elemental question: is the book antisemitic?

Supporters of Demidenko again argued forcefully that such accusations misunderstood the nature and laws of the fiction genre. These charges of antisemitism confused the narrative voice(s) within the novel and the author as an individual outside the work. At some perhaps ironic level the supporters' position appears at first blush to be bolstered and strengthened by the unmasking of Helen Darville. The author's autobiographical posing had lent weight to an argument that it was impossible and naive to separate author and text in the circumstances surrounding the author's own declarations. Once the posing is revealed as a fiction, one might argue, any attempt to identify the author with the textual manifestations falls by the wayside. Because she is no longer Ukrainian-Australian, Darville's book can become more authentically a Ukrainian-Australian story.

But the argument in favor of the separation of the book from its author is not as clear as its supporters might wish. Darville/Demidenko made a specific and free choice, absent a diagnosed mental illness, to become Helen Demidenko.[53] Her statements as Demidenko, both in the book and in her persona's interactions, can then be brought into question, interrogated and interpreted according to Ricoeur's ethical frame. Is the choice to make public antisemitic statements after having published a historically falsifiable and arguably antisemitic novel within some conception of freedom and artistic endeavor that we must accept?

Alone among the well-known cases of artistic impersonation, of taking on an autobiographical role to give the character, protagonist, narrator, of one's novel or work of faction some deeper authenticity in the mind of the reader, the Demidenko/Darville choice was to give authentic voice to antisemitic Jew killers, to Holocaust perpetrators. She does not portray herself or her family falsely as victims of the

Nazis. She portrays them as mass killers. How, if at all, can this narrative of the Shoah be seen to have helped in any way to work through the trauma of the Holocaust? What ethical hermeneutic frame can be imposed on the unrelenting synonymous relationship between Jews and Communists that characterizes the novel? The entire structure of *The Hand That Signed the Paper*, its form and its content, are designed to obscure responsibility, to deny culpability, and to attack those who seek another form of healing through justice and memory. There is no ethical complexity or moral difficulty exposed in the narrative of the novel, nor is any to be found in the arguments of many of its supporters. Jill Kitson and Dame Leonie Kramer were mistaken or deluded when they found moral, historical, cultural, and ethical complexity in the novel. War for them was willy-nilly; the characters of Vitaly and Evheny had no control over events or indeed over their actions. The novel gives authentic, autobiographical voice to this reality in the opinion of the Australian cultural elite who celebrated the emergence of a new voice and a new Australian experience, killing thousands of Jews.

Helen Demidenko/Darville may be free in some general sense to write what she wants and to adopt a public persona that is clearly falsifiable. None of this artistic freedom removes her ethical responsibility or the freedom of readers to impose an ethically informed and historically sensitive and politically aware reading on the entire Darville/Demidenko text. Robert Manne seeks to name the stakes involved in the novel's representation and reception: "No one among the early reviewers even discussed the question of the responsibility a novel such as this might bear towards historical truth. No one saw how dangerous was the absence, in a novel dealing with issues as large as the Ukrainian Famine and the Holocaust, of a clearly identified and morally unambiguous authorial voice."[54]

Manne does not, in my view, put the case strongly enough. The problem in/with *The Hand That Signed the Paper* is not the absence of a "morally unambiguous authorial voice"; the problem is precisely that such a voice is present. Demidenko/Darville has a moral vision, one of relativism in which the *Holomodor* and the Holocaust are factually, historically, and morally equivalent. She presents a vision in which the killing of Jews is always the killing of Bolshevists and in which the author identifies herself by a conscious narrative of history and a choice of narrating voices that are, with one minor exception, always the voices of the killers, the unpunished killers, the killers and their accomplices, in the cases of Vitaly and Evheny and Kateryna.

The authorial and authoritative impersonation perpetrated by Demidenko/Darville outside the text of the novel, but clearly and unambiguously within the broader cultural text of the social and literary phenomenon of *The Hand That Signed the Paper*, was and is a moral choice about the Holocaust. Helen Darville became Helen Demidenko. "Demidenko" is named in accounts of the Shoah as being a Ukrainian auxiliary at the Babi Yar killing pit. The name features in Martin Gilbert's seminal historical account *The Holocaust: A History of the Jews of Europe during the Second World War*.[55] In D. M. Thomas's *The White Hotel* (problematic for other reasons relating to truth) Demidenko is identified as the man who rapes the central character with his bayonet.[56] Demidenko/Darville chose for her fictional autobiography, in both its form and its narrative substance, among the worst Holocaust perpetrators. She made a moral choice and gave voice to the characters. This may be depicted by some as simple postmodern playfulness, but that does mean we need to accept the rules of that game or that we have to play at all.

The voice she gave is one of moral relativism, of a lack of affect at the time of the killing, of justifiable fear of and feelings of revenge toward the Jewish Bolshevists. The voice she chose is one that argues that because war is the worst crime, there can be no moral or legally justifiable basis for putting Holocaust perpetrators on trial. The narrators of *The Hand That Signed the Paper* become not perpetrators but victims, victims of the *Holomodor*, victims of the Bolshevists, victims of the Jews, victims of the Israelis who pursue an old man hiding under his kitchen table. Helen Demidenko/Darville becomes the victim of the politically correct brigade whose members cannot tell fact from fiction and who push their ideology into fields of literary endeavor that are immune from such considerations.

Demidenko/Darville herself becomes a victim of her own actions. Attempts were made to medicalize and pathologize her, thereby removing her and her characters from our moral judgment. In this version fictional characters from the novel and the fictional character of Helen Demidenko all can invoke identifiable medical excuses. Vitaly and Evheny obviously suffer from what we today might call post-traumatic stress disorder. But in the reality of the narrative of *The Hand That Signed the Paper* the only one of the characters in the whole saga who seems to suffer such a problem is Demidenko/Darville herself. Neither Vitaly nor Evheny is truly bothered by what they have done. There is no moral vision in the novel except the one asserted throughout the book that Holocaust perpetrators do not regret their actions because they have, as victims of the Jews, nothing to regret. They have kept their photos of themselves in ss uniforms beneath the Ukrainian flag. Vitaly continues to wear the gold-framed glasses he so admired when he took them from an executed Jew. Only Darville herself appears as a "self-traumatized perpetrator." Subsequent self-justifications for her actions relate consecutively to stories of an abusive and unhappy home life with a philandering father, dyslexia, and undiagnosed Asperger's syndrome. We must pity her, not judge her.[57]

In the end we are left with a coda to the novel in which Fiona spends her time continuing to engage in vaguely left, green politics. As part of that persona, she writes letters to the newspapers protesting against the ongoing war crimes trials. In another key but overlooked passage in the novel, Fiona and her sister meet while on their way to the lawyer's office to discuss Vitaly's case. Her sister proclaims: "This is all because of the silver budgie Zionist, bloody Hawkie. Bob Hawke. Shit."[58]

Once again, the Kovalenko family makes its views clear. Those factionalized opinions reflect a significant part of the political and ideological debate that swirled around the war crimes issue in real-life

Australian social and legal discussions. According to this narrative that circulated politically and culturally in Australia when the war crimes legislation was introduced and to which Fiona now gives voice, the whole war crimes trials process was a plot carried out by the Jews and the Zionist lobby that controlled Bob Hawke, the Australian prime minister at the time.

There can be no doubt that without Hawke's support the legislation would not have been introduced or passed, nor is there any doubt about Hawke's long-standing connections to and friendships with the Jewish community and with the Israeli trade union movement. But here one must ask how this type of comment about the "Zionist" Bob Hawke and Fiona's anti–war crimes trials efforts fit into a careful moral consideration of the issues raised by the War Crimes Act, contrary to claims made by Dame Leonie Kramer. This is not a considered, thoughtful debate about the morality of trying war criminals fifty years after the event in a land far away from the locus of the killings. Instead, what we find reflected by Demidenko/Darville is once again an antisemitic, anti-Zionist prejudice that informed the crudest parts of the political debate in Australia at the time.

Indeed, it may not stretch the imagination to suggest, as has Mark Aarons, that a large part of the success of *The Hand That Signed the Paper* and the support it received can be attributed to an anti-Zionist, pro-Palestinian politics that was then taking root on the left of Australian politics[59]—a happy, for some at least, combination of these left-wing forces and more conservative elements among the literary elite that saw Demidenko as a new, non-left answer to debates about ethnic diversity as part of Australian cultural identity, into which the Demidenko persona played well. The child of drunken antisemites, of ignorant, folk-dancing, vodka-swilling Ukrainians, as an exemplar of the migrant experience, goes some way to explaining the remarkable success of the book and its early uncritical reception among many who should have known better.

At the end of the book Fiona finally travels to Treblinka. There she meets a young German man. Their conversation turns to the purpose of their respective visits. He informs her that his aunt died there, and she tells him her uncle was a guard. Is this the time for reconciliation, for a working through the traumas of the past? Hardly—the young man's aunt was a Quaker who was killed for helping Jews. It is too late to ask her uncle how he felt. There is no truth for the perpetrator, no moral reckoning with the past by the Ukrainian killer. Nor are the victims of the Holocaust even present anymore. Treblinka is a place where a Quaker was killed. All we learn from the final lines of the book is that if you help the Jews, you will be treated like a Jew.

This is the moral vision of *The Hand That Signed the Paper*. There is no complex treatment of the social and political debates that surrounded the introduction of the war crimes legislation in the late 1980s in Australia. There is no subtle or nuanced inquiry into the issues of justice, memory, and law that must inform any real debate about the history of Australian efforts to prosecute Holocaust perpetrators fifty years after events in Europe, a history that was still current as the book was rewarded and lauded. There is no investigation of the difficult questions of the integration of racial, religious, or ethnic minority groups into a multicultural Australian nation or of how concepts of humanity, justice, and criminal responsibility might inform these issues. There is no attempt to consider the text of *The Hand That Signed the Paper* in light of what Peter Christoff described as "an expanded range of critical yardsticks and tools" that are required to judge the complexities of the new, multicultural Australian polis.[60]

The book and the majority critical response simply closed their eyes to the historical tragedy of the Shoah. Through a deceitful authorial strategy combining the worst of ethnic political identity and stereotypes, on the one hand, and elite literary reaction, which found a deeper resonance in the political world, on the other, *The Hand That Signed the Paper*, the novel and the cultural, social, and political phenomenon, painted a morally relativistic vision in which "poor and hungry Ukrainians shot Jews for bread and sausage and vodka."[61]

Jill Kitson, the undying and original supporter of the merit and innovation, the new, pluralist Australian vision, of *The Hand That Signed the Paper*, insisted on the book's "extraordinary redemptive power." There is no redemption for the Jews killed by Vitaly and Evheny and Wilhelm Hasse. Instead, they were Bolshevists who brought their fate upon themselves. There is no redemption for the Zionist Bob Hawke who introduced the war crimes legislation. There is no redemption for the early critics of the book who were simply classified as politically correct censors or representatives of the Jews. As Pamela Bone put it: "Redemptive for whom? Redemptive for men who bayoneted Jewish babies and machine-gunned hundreds of innocent people?"[62]

Unfortunately, the narrative of *The Hand That Signed the Paper* does not offer redemption even for them. They do not seek it. They do not desire it. Vitaly and Evheny want to be left alone in their old age to live out their lives in Australia. They want to live in a Garfield Barwick dreamland of peace and quiet, of a chapter closed forever. They never, in the 157 pages of the Demidenko/Darville opus, ask for forgiveness or redemption. They ask only to be left alone. Nor is there any redemption for the writer or the reader. *The Hand That Signed the Paper* is a dirty, grubby piece of work. The sad reality of the book itself and of its critical acceptance, and the elite support for it, leaves a distinctly distasteful impression of a political and social world in which it was clear that as far as the Shoah was concerned, it happened far away and long ago. It was much too messy and complex for us to grasp properly. Everything was willy-nilly. The book removes morality and ethics from our role as readers and citizens and relativizes the Holocaust. It places the proceedings in Adelaide firmly outside any understanding of history and memory graspable by ordinary Australians. Immigrant Australians have the ability to seize and understand these events, but what they know is not the version we have been taught.

Nor is there redemption for Helen Demidenko/Darville, or as she still later became, Helen Dale. Greg James QC, the lead lawyer for the prosecution in the Polyukhovich case, relates how his examination of an Israeli witness was disrupted by muttered comments from the public gallery. As the questioning continued, so did the muttering. After some time the words from the audience became clearer, and it was evident to James that the member of the public was engaged in antisemitic derision of the "Jews" as they testified. James turned to discover the source of the hateful slurs, a strapping young man. Next to him sat a striking blonde woman. Only later, as a result of the publicity around *The Hand That Signed the Paper*, did James recognize the woman accompanying the antisemite at the trial in Adelaide as Helen Demidenko.[63]

EIGHT

Law, Memory, and Justice

The Australian Experience

The three trials of alleged Nazi criminals that took place under the Australian war crimes legislation are exemplary studies in the art of police investigation and the benefits that can be derived from international legal cooperation in the pursuit of those accused of the commission of atrocities and violations of international criminal law norms. Special Investigations Unit (SIU) investigators, historians, and lawyers tracked down witnesses to events in Ukraine during the Nazi occupation fifty years after the fact. These witnesses were identified through the combined expertise of historians and police officers. Their evidence was gathered by police and lawyers in often very difficult conditions in Ukraine, the United States, Canada, and Israel. The many positive elements that can be gleaned from the Australian experience must be compared, however, with the negative aspects of the three cases. Many of the practical and principled juridical problems that arose in the Adelaide trials persist in international criminal law.[1] In particular, questions and difficulties surrounding eyewitness accounts, testimonies, and identification came to the fore in each of the three cases. Eyewitness identification evidence is always inherently fragile.[2] These problems were exacerbated in the Adelaide proceedings as a result of a number of factors, not least the passage of so much time.[3]

During the debates surrounding government plans to introduce the War Crimes Act, several members of the social and legal elite, as well as representative bodies of the legal profession, expressed their opposition to the proposed prosecution of war criminals. Justice Michael Kirby, then president of the New South Wales Court of Appeal and later a member of the country's High Court, argued at a conference held at McGill University that basic principles of fairness and respect for the human rights of the accused would bar any prosecution after the passage of so much time, "lest our temples of justice in the courts become debased."[4] The Law Council of Australia expressed grave concerns over the question about whether a fair trial could ever occur in circumstances in which serious doubts on the availability and reliability of key evidence persisted.[5] David Pennington, Anglican archbishop of Melbourne, insisted that "forgiveness was better than trying to avenge crimes long after they had been committed."[6] The New South Bar Association condemned the government's proposals as fundamentally unfair. Moreover, the president of the Bar Association, Ken Handley QC, asserted that the bill was "an expensive propaganda exercise" and added that should the bill become law, it would do a great disservice to Australia's commitment to multiculturalism. He added in familiar tones, "We should leave these ancient crimes behind us and not rekindle all the hatred that led to these crimes and which these crimes have in turn created within the surviving victims."[7]

These interventions by leading legal and religious figures appeared to lend support to the positions being articulated by the formal Liberal/National political opposition and by the various non-Jewish groups that had long advocated for a decision once again, or once and for all, to close the chapter. Captive Nations rhetoric about Soviet perfidy, Australia as a haven of justice, and the values of domestic fair trial concepts were articulated by lawyers and Christian clergy alike.

These advocates of the status quo wanted a return to the Menzies/
Barwick era, in which all ethnic communities could live under a
domestic vision of the rule of law that included both amnesia of the
Shoah and amnesty for its perpetrators. The politics of war crimes
prosecutions as articulated by these opponents also set out a dangerous moral equivalency between the position of communities among
which alleged perpetrators could be found and the Australian Jewish communities that were motivated in this version of the story by
hatred. The perpetrators and the victims were placed by law and
religion, or by the leaders of law and the majority religion, on an
equal and equivalent moral plane. Kirby's rhetorical flourish united
the sacred and the profane as law was presented as embodying an
immanent Australian morality.

But once again, only one story of law's possibilities was articulated
by the judge. Ironically perhaps, the possibility set forth by Kirby was
based in an undeclared weakness in law itself. For Kirby war crimes
trials would be impossible because courts could not deliver justice
to defendants after such a passage of time. Implicit in this critique is
the idea that Australian prosecutions of alleged war criminals would
result in convictions and that those convictions would be grounded
in a system that ignored fundamental norms of fairness on which
the criminal justice system normally rests. Of course, the Adelaide
war crimes trial experience brought the lie to Kirby's intervention.
The legal system of Australia did bring justice and fairness to the
proceedings in Adelaide. The prosecution authorities in particular
were scrupulous in their case preparation and trial strategy. Outside
advice was sought from independent legal experts to ensure that
the proposed prosecutions conformed to the standards of normal
criminal cases. The defense was granted unlimited access and significant support and resources to finance their own investigations and
examinations of potential witnesses. In many respects there was more
fundamental fairness in the Adelaide war crimes trials than might be
encountered in the day-to-day operation of criminal law in South
Australia. Whether the results in a broader sense—or with reference

to other ideals, other evidence, other narrative possibilities—offered justice is another story.

Upon the facade of forgive and forget, or more precisely forget, a set of concomitant legal/justice arguments was erected in opposition to war crimes trials. The passage of time would result in fundamental procedural unfairness for anyone accused; Soviet source evidence that would necessarily inform most prosecutions were they to eventuate would be invariably, incontrovertibly, and inevitably forged, be counterfeit, or be unreliable on some other basis informed by Cold War values. Australian criminal justice would be indelibly tainted if the bill were enacted. Yet what was always elided, most often by a cursory nod of the head to the horrors of the Nazi regime, was the fact that it was impossible, historically, politically, and even morally and ethically to close the chapter because the book of Nazi collaborationist war criminals in Australia had been irrevocably opened. As events in Adelaide also demonstrated, difficulties with Soviet source evidence and those caused by the passage of time actually weighed more heavily against the prosecution than the accused.

Mark Aarons's unremitting and painstaking journalism had presented the Australian public and its politicians with the true history of the disgraceful background of state complicity in allowing Nazi war criminals into the country. Revelations in the United States, Canada, and the United Kingdom of similar histories had altered the international political and moral environment in which all debates and decisions about the fate of these escapees from justice could occur. The *Menzies Report* added official confirmation to the narrative. SIU investigations had already begun to amass the proof in the details of many individual cases. It would only have been possible to forget this history by turning a blind eye to a situation that raised fundamental questions about Australia's dark legacy in relation to Nazi war criminals, about the nation's self-identity as a liberal rule of law jurisdiction, and about the country's place in the international arena of civilized nations that had since the Moscow Declaration condemned war crimes and the Shoah in uncertain juridical and moral terms. In addition, real and important issues about the nature of Australian society, about the fate and place of multiculturalism and equality, were brought to the fore.

The invocation of justice arguments as a per se bar to pursuing Nazi war criminals, Holocaust perpetrators, not only indicated a decontextualized and ahistorical understanding of the rule of law but also allowed collective amnesia, willful obscurantism, and not too subtle antisemitism among some elements of some immigrant communities, and some more long-established groups, to find support behind apparently neutral and Australian norms of justice. In Australia the entire Helen Demidenko/Darville episode would reveal in stark terms just how much Australian debates about national identity, multiculturalism, and war crimes trials were infused with an often blatant and public anti-Jewish discourse.

The "discovery" of this discourse among cultural elites found its echoes in interventions around the rhetorics of religion and law. There can be little doubt, at least in retrospect, that this juridical and religious (Christian) one-dimensional and ahistorical version of a rule of law discourse served, perhaps unintentionally, to buttress overt antisemitism. In this respect Australia was not alone. Similar arguments were put forward in relation to attempts to change the legislative regime in Canada.[8] Respected members of the legal elite of that country advocated visions of history and law that reflected long-standing biases among and between ethnic communities.[9] In the United Kingdom antisemitism figured prominently in parliamentary debates in which Christian forgiveness was contrasted with an Old Testament desire for bloody revenge.[10] The leaders of public opinion and public life in Australia who intervened on the question offered no alternative vision about the place of the Shoah in Australian life and culture. They offered no detailed critique of the historical reality of the presence with government permission and acquiescence of mass murderers in Australia. There was no call for curricular reform, or social education, about the Holocaust and perpetrators in the country. There was nothing more than a mealy-mouthed and weak invocation of fairness for killers of Jewish men, women, and children.

Despite protests from these legal and religious elites, with their narrow view of liberal legality and the Holocaust, the bill did become law, and three cases made their way into the Australian criminal justice system. None of their apocalyptic mutterings was ever justified in reality. The stories of Ivan Timofeyevich Polyukhovich, Mikolay Berezowsky, and Heinrich Wagner, only part of which have been recounted here, when conceived as pure rule of law narratives, demonstrate that Australian courts and Australian criminal law were perfectly capable of dealing with these complex matters, relating to events that occurred long ago—in the spring, summer, and fall of 1942—and far away in Ukraine, then occupied by the Germans, and in a fashion that was consistent with rule of law and justice principles. There was no distortion of liberal legality; no defendant was adversely affected by the passage of time or by the use, however limited, of Soviet source evidence.

Indeed, in the cases of Polyukhovich and Berezowsky all of these elements and the basic principles of Australian criminal law and procedure worked most clearly to the advantage of the accused. The passage of time meant that the prosecution case became weaker and weaker as witnesses died or became too ill to travel and to testify. In all of the cases more than adequate provision through special legal aid terms was made for necessary defense expenses.[11] In Wagner the most fundamental principles of fairness embodied in the discretion of the prosecutor to desist from further proceedings because the physical well-being of the defendant would be jeopardized if the case continued were invoked. The Australian government persisted in this understanding "in the interests of justice" even in the face of subsequent adverse publicity from American TV investigative journalists, who claimed that Heinrich Wagner appeared to be in the finest health and to be enjoying a tranquil existence.[12]

In other self-referentially legal terms the experience in the Adelaide war crimes trials was equally positive and certainly innovative. Relatively untried and untested mechanisms for the taking of overseas evidence on commission in criminal proceedings were implemented

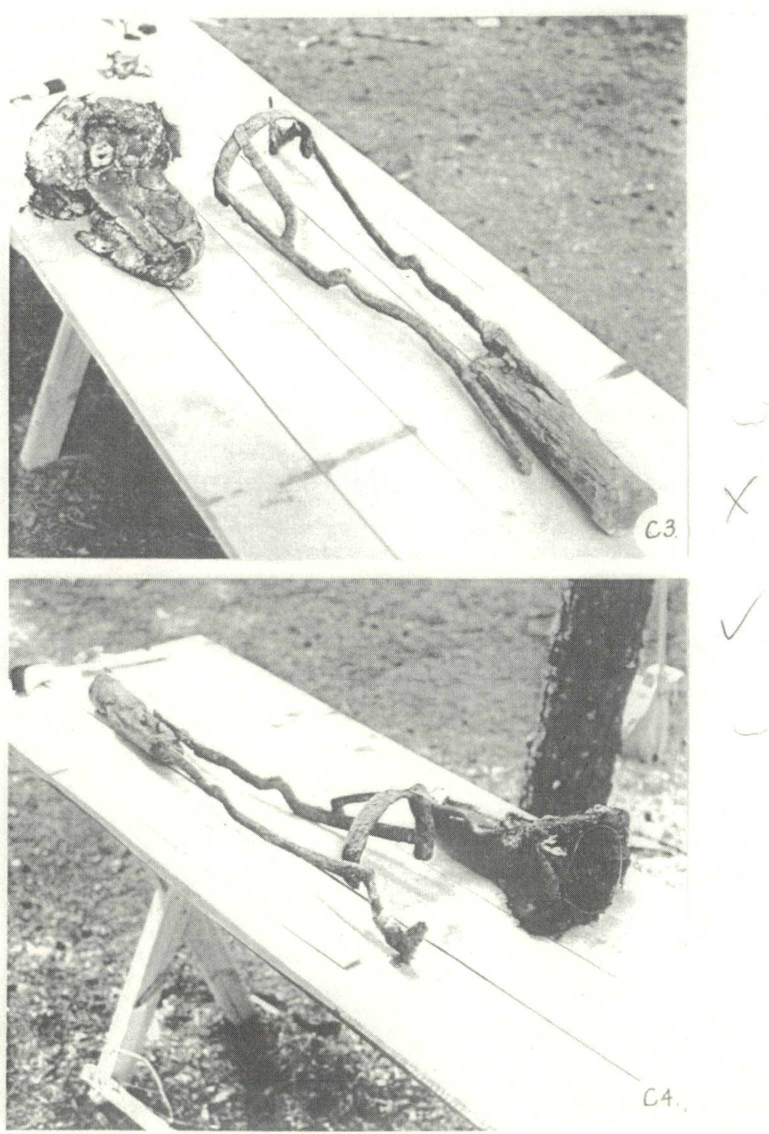

7. Artificial leg from the Serniki pit excavation. The victims of the second wave of killings were predominantly the elderly, women, and children. Crown copyright. Used by permission of the Attorney-General, South Australia.

as the teams for the prosecution and the defense together traveled to Serniki to take the testimony of locals too ill to make the trip to Adelaide for the trial.[13] Likewise, in Wagner's case commission evidence from Andrey Bardas and Nikolay Daviborshch was also obtained on the ground in Ukraine.[14]

After the three cases were finished and the SIU had completed its work, Australian expertise in many aspects of the complex investigation and pursuit of mass atrocities was recognized internationally. Questions of archaeology and forensic dentistry, the use of advanced carbon dating techniques, combined with careful police work, were central to Australian practice. These techniques were internationally recognized as Australians from police officers to archaeologists became part of the teams investigating war crimes and crimes against humanity in the former Yugoslavia. Graham Blewitt and Grant Niemann used the skills and experience gained in the cases of the three Adelaide war crimes suspects to become prosecutors at the International Criminal Tribunal in The Hague.

The failure of the Adelaide prosecutions was simply a failure of results. But again, this characterization is accurate only if one believes that the accused were in fact guilty. In writing of his involvement in, and study of, the prosecution of John Demjanjuk in Israel, Dutch psychologist Willem Wagenaar wrote: "If all parties involved present the best available information, the court's verdict will represent the best approximation of truth. It will always be a subjective judgment, and therefore fallible. But it is not for expert witnesses to criticize the verdict when the verdict seems to be in contradiction with their testimony . . . If the reader wants an answer to the question whether John Demjanjuk is Ivan, I can only refer to the court's verdict. It is the best answer we have."[15]

What is perhaps left un- or under-articulated in Wagenaar's account is that the best answer is perhaps neither best nor an answer in many other senses. Serious and important questions remain about Justice Cox's decision to strike out most of the charges in *Polyukhovich* or about the DPP's continuing refusal to revisit the issue of Heinrich

Wagner's health purely within a legal and jurisprudential understanding of the issues at stake. History and the historical evidence may well lead someone who reads the cases to conclude that law did a disservice to truth. This does not mean that law failed or the Australian cases came to the wrong conclusions in any absolute sense. The best answer is neither the final nor the right answer to a metaphysical certainty. As Wagenaar admits, the result of the legal process is an approximation. It would certainly be open to argument that the best evidence was not submitted by all parties in all three cases. Konrad Kwiet's experience at trial in *Polyukhovich* has left him convinced that the law is little concerned with truth.[16] Ludmilla Stern was unhappy with the failure properly to, in her view at least, cope with and grasp issues of intercultural and inter-lingual complexity.

The Australian cases were run according to the rules of evidence and proof in a criminal trial prosecuted according to the Anglo-American common-law tradition. It is arguable, and indeed probable, that much of the best historical evidence was excluded by decisions of the judge and magistrates involved applying the rules of evidence. The key to placing Wagenaar's and similar arguments in a proper and more nuanced context is to put the real emphasis on his use of the term *available*. Availability is determined, naturally and beyond dispute, both by physical reality and by legal rules. In the Adelaide cases witnesses died or became too ill to participate. Cultural dissonance meant that some evidence was not presented in a full context. Translation errors played a significant role in some instances. Outside legal rules of hearsay and admissibility, in another narrative of events set out by the best available evidence in the application of historical methodology, a different conclusion might well have been reached.

In *Polyukhovich*, for example, some of the best legally available evidence was surprisingly excluded. The count in relation to the events at and near Khokum's shed when Polyukhovich was alleged to have shot the two escaping fifteen-year-olds — as the column of Jews from the Serniki ghetto was being led to the killing pit — was struck out by the judge. The Crown sought to introduce evidence, largely

8. The Stubla—Serniki, Ukraine, November 1991. Photo courtesy of the Hon. Michael David QC and Lindy Powell QC.

obtained by Milton Turk, a Jewish survivor from Serniki to have the count reinstated. Turk, skilled in the use of surveying tools, returned to Serniki with SIU representatives. Equipped with a theodolite, he demonstrated scientifically that the sightlines from the location of Khokum's shed to the banks of the Stubla were sufficiently clear and close enough to have allowed the witness to have seen events as they were described.[17] Had the trial judge during his visit to Serniki to take commission evidence viewed the site, he might well have allowed the prosecution to pursue the count in relation to the two boys. The mighty Stubla over which the bridge near where the boys were shot passed is a pitiful stream, not a wide and powerful body of water, which the use of the term *river* and the description of a bridge crossing it might have left in the mind of an Australian judge.

The lesson of Khokum's shed is the lesson that emerges from

a careful examination of each of the Australian cases. Events in all three instances were subjected to differing, often competing, narrative constructions. The stories were sometimes told in the difficult to understand and translate testimony of Ukrainian peasants subject to Australian rules of evidence and procedure and the unwritten psychological factors of cross-cultural misunderstandings and the misinterpretation of demeanor. Sometimes historical methodology confronted the restrictions of legal rules. In other instances law itself was confronted internally with competing versions of events and differing interpretations of facts and of legal rules. In all of this, sorting out the best evidence available is perhaps, if not impossible, better left for ethical judgment and all that is entailed by that process. Neither law nor history can fully, completely, or finally answer that ethical demand. This is a key lesson that the Australian experience with Nazi trials in relation to the Shoah can teach us.

BEYOND LAW? LESSONS FROM ADELAIDE

In 1990 the federal cabinet, taking into account the shifting political climate, the slow advance of the investigation process, and the ever-increasing cost of running the SIU and prosecuting war crimes, decided to set a final date for the process. In the absence of any new and important developments, the SIU would not be funded beyond the end of June 1992, although a temporary support structure was created to allow the remaining legal proceedings to take place after that date.[18] Under section 21 of the act the attorney general had to report on an annual basis on the operation of the statute. Reports were filed for the years ending in June 1990, 1991, 1992, and 1993 and provide a good introduction to the history of the SIU and Australian war crimes investigations and trials. A global report was presented to the attorney general by Robert Greenwood QC in September 1993. The total expense associated with the operation of the SIU was a little over fifteen million dollars (AUD), of which six million went to salary costs and nine million to all associated administrative expenses.[19]

The prosecution of Heinrich Wagner was the last to be brought by the DPP following the SIU investigations. This did not mean that no evidence was available against any other individuals or that there were no longer any Nazi war criminals living in Australia. The case of Konrad Kalejs, who was pursued by authorities in Canada and the United States and excluded from those countries, refused entry to the United Kingdom, and sent back to the land whose passport he carried, Australia, is the most well-known example of a case not pursued by Australian authorities.[20] Despite continuing pressure from the Australian Jewish community, the government refused to back down on its decision.[21] The Kalejs fiasco ended when the war criminal died before the Australian government could agree to an extradition request by Latvian authorities in the historical absence of a bilateral treaty arrangement. The federal government then established a war crimes task force within the Immigration Department to deal with the issue. Canada, after the failure to prosecute Imre Finta successfully, decided to pursue alleged war criminals actively along a route of denaturalization and deportation pioneered by the United States. The Australian system, on the other hand, was reactive, awaiting foreign requests in relation to alleged war criminals. Even that formalized structure was ended in 2007.[22]

Nonetheless, revelations about Nazi war criminals still emerge, as a few dedicated journalists continue to cover a story that appears to interest neither the government nor the general public.[23] Some of the tales that have been made public since the dissolution of the SIU and of Australian moral resolve in relation to the rule of law, national memory, and the Shoah echo in a familiar fashion with the past. These new tales repeat themes similar to those that have circulated since the early postwar period, through Aarons's first broadcasts and the debates surrounding them. They include ASIO links, mysteriously missing immigration files, and intimate connections, in the case of Lajos Polgar, a former member of the Arrow Cross in Hungary, with prominent figures in the Australian Liberal Party hierarchy, including former prime minister Malcolm Fraser.[24] More recently, the Australian court system has been faced with attempts to extradite another

Hungarian immigrant accused of shooting a Jew on a Budapest street while a member of the country's army during World War II. Charles Zentai mounted a High Court challenge to proceedings against him, waging both a legal and public relations campaign against his extradition in what could be Australia's last "Nazi" case.[25]

Mark Aarons has highlighted the dangers of Australia's collective failure to engage legally, socially, and politically with the ethical dimension of the presence of war criminals in the country.[26] The War Crimes Act was amended to deal exclusively with war crimes and crimes against humanity committed in Europe during World War II. As a result, other atrocities, from other times and places, were not covered by Australian legislation. Aarons has documented the presence of war criminals from Afghanistan, Cambodia, and the former Yugoslavia, none of whom was subject to the provisions of the War Crimes Act. Since then, other Australian journalists have detected potential war criminals from these countries as well as Iraq, Sri Lanka, Turkey, India, Lebanon, Nepal, and Sierra Leone.[27] The presence of large diasporic communities from the former Yugoslavia figured strongly in the original ABC revelations about the presence of Nazi collaborators in Australia and in the uncovering of their connections within the ruling hierarchy of the Liberal Party in New South Wales. In addition to a newer influx of refugees from the conflict, the more recent civil wars in the former Yugoslavia have also meant that some people living in Australia but identifying with their ethnic origins returned to participate in the fighting there, sometimes allegedly taking part in the war crimes and crimes against humanity that characterized those wars.[28] The most well-known case involved Dragan Vasiljkovic, a former Australian army reservist who was alleged to be Captain Dragan, leader of a Serb militia unit that committed massacres against Croats.[29]

An examination of the history of the politics and law of Australian war crimes trials and other developments demonstrates how the limited focus of the amendments introduced by the Hawke government and pursued by the SIU led to a situation in which war crimes and crimes against humanity more broadly considered were placed largely outside any domestic Australian narrative. The trials in Adelaide were long and laborious processes, and the press and general public soon lost interest.[30] The formal opposition in Parliament led by the Liberal/National coalition was soon reinforced by a loss of initiative because of the nature of the crimes involved in the lengthy siu investigations, committal, and trial processes. This was further exacerbated because of a changing power dynamic in the federal Labor Party as Bob Hawke gave way to Paul Keating, who refused to pursue the war crimes prosecution policy of his predecessor.

Perhaps the biggest failure of politics in relation to the war crimes trials was that neither the introduction and passage of the amendments that led to the arrests of Polyukhovich, Berezowsky, and Wagner, nor subsequent revelations about other war criminals still calling Australia home, had any broad or deep purchase among the Australian public generally. This is partly attributable to the political and propaganda efforts of the various immigrant communities that managed to portray themselves as victims in much of the public debate. They constructed collective and convincing narratives around the war crimes issue. The Demidenko affair, and the way in which *The Hand That Signed the Paper* and the author's fictionalized immigrant persona were received by elites on both the left and right of Australian culture and society, revealed the depth to which this victimization narrative had penetrated and the extent of an acceptable and patent antisemitism as part of the social and political discourse about war crimes, crimes of the Shoah, and subsequent atrocities. The pedagogic function of war crimes legislation and the prosecution of perpetrators is meant to inform the public and capture a level of ethical concern that can and should become an integral part of public discourse around these issues. Social and political debate about how these ethical concerns need to be integrated into a cultural dynamic of national identity and Australian values was, sadly, never part of the Australian Nazi war crimes trials experience.

The idea that the Shoah and the presence of unpunished perpetrators were Australian concerns never became an integrated part of the cultural and political dynamic of the country. Australians may well consider themselves to be part of the Western democratic tradition of civilized nations governed by the rule of law; their government may accede to extradition requests from other jurisdictions; and the nation may have signed on to the International Criminal Court regime. But the question of atrocity and genocide is not part of the country's core identity. Perhaps one layer of explanation resides in the internal dynamic of Australian conquest, colonization, settlement, and "genocide" of its native Aboriginal populations. This is still a story that is narrated in collectively hushed tones after decades of collective amnesia. Only with the election of a Labor government under Kevin Rudd in 2007 has the political discourse of apology entered the official national lexicon. In these circumstances, in a country where the Holocaust has been removed from the high school curriculum in the most populous state, New South Wales, it is perhaps not surprising that Australia and Australians did not embrace the pedagogical possibilities that might have been opened up by the introduction of the War Crimes Act and the active pursuit of Nazi collaborationist war criminals in the cases of Polyukhovich, Berezowsky, and Wagner.[31]

David Hirsh has argued with insight and passion that prosecutions of the perpetrators of genocide and crimes against humanity can and do embody and embed overarching concepts and social understandings of cosmopolitan justice. This comprehension, he claims, is narrated as a central aspect in the process of forming a new transcendent discursive matrix in which law and ethics are core parts of international and national self-conceptions. He explores the invocation of notions of cosmopolitan justice in the context of national efforts to prosecute perpetrators by focusing on the successful UK prosecution of Anthony Sawoniuk, a former policeman in German-occupied Belarus.[32] At the practical and conceptual levels the UK trial of Sawoniuk faced many of the same issues confronted in the Australian proceedings. The War Crimes Act 1991 followed the Australian path of rendering and combining a complex mix of international law norms relating to war and war crimes and domestic criminal offences such as murder. The UK law also limited itself temporally and geographically to locales in Germany or under German occupation from 1 September 1939 to 5 June 1945.[33] As with the Australian War Crimes Act, the UK statute combined international legal norms with existing and long-established principles and practices of the ordinary criminal justice system, amid controversy among legal commentators who raised many of the same justice concerns as had their Australian counterparts.[34]

The ideological or narrative challenges faced in the Sawoniuk prosecution mirrored those that arose in the three Australian cases. The trial qua trial had to be situated alongside the phenomenon of the trial as the embodiment of the ideals of a transcendent and ethically informed instance of cosmopolitan justice. These legal discursive structures and practices then had to be located somewhere in the historiographical emplotment of Nazi war crimes trials as part of a profound narrative about identity, law, justice, and history. As was the case in Australia, an important structural hurdle to the pursuit of these other extralegal goals was to be found in the nature of the case itself, a limited tale of *mens rea*, *actus reus*, identity, and so forth, in which the Shoah as an extraordinary, or a limit, case is displaced somewhere near or beyond the boundary of legal practice. Comparing the Eichmann and Sawoniuk cases, Matthew Weinert argues that the analyses offered by Hannah Arendt and David Hirsh share a common problem: "The failures of the Jerusalem court in *Eichmann* and the British court in *Sawoniuk* rested with judges and lawyers who refused to . . . acknowledge the unparalleled nature of the crimes under consideration. Each placed the crimes in a conventional dialogue of murder. Thus it becomes the work of the sociologist and the scholar, among others, to interpret court proceedings and expose their pearls their wisdom, and make them available to future law creation and legal proceedings."[35]

This description conveys the multilayered problematic of the Australian war crimes trials experience in a nutshell. Trials could only take place in the national context of Australia if the ordinary processes and norms of criminal justice and criminal law were adhered to. The rule of law as the antithesis of Nazi collaborationist brutality in occupied Ukraine could only manifest its power and justify in an ideologically and legally coherent fashion a quest for justice by establishing a domestic legally recognizable framework. Law then diminishes and reduces competing ideas of truth and justice through this very self-defining process. The enormity of the Shoah, the mass killings of Jews in pits and ravines, in forests and fields, had to be translated into debates about uniform color and the type of weapon allegedly carried.

The universality of the ethical and moral condemnation of perpetrators of the Shoah and the deontological basis for prosecuting them fifty or more years after the events in question, which serve as the foundational norms for the statutory regime that domesticates and nationalizes international law and an implicit ideal of universal jurisdiction—or as Hirsh would have it, cosmopolitan justice—are made to disappear, as they must, if local rule of law ideals are to be applied in such cases. The translation of the universal to the local context must, almost by definition, betray the ethical imperative behind the pursuit of Nazi killers. In a real sense the difficulties of intercultural confusion and misunderstanding that characterized the Polyukhovich, Berezowsky, and Wagner proceedings in Adelaide pale in comparison with the internal failures of law itself in these cases. Law did not fail because the accused were not convicted; it failed because it could never transcend its own narrative limits, limits that were and are essential if we are to have law at all.

As Weinert intimates, the translation of the translation, the rendering of the legal proceedings in Adelaide into another narrative form, is the job of sociologists, journalists, and historians. The story of the three Australian war crimes trials is a story about trials and about law. It is a narrow story with wide implications. Did Ivanechko ride a horse? Did he carry a rifle, a pistol, or a submachine gun? Did Berezowsky wear a green, a blue, or simply a dark uniform? Did Wagner shoot the *Mischlinge* children at the pit with a rifle or a pistol?

Was he at the killing pit at all? The story of the trials is also a story of circumstances before, after, and beyond the trials. It is about cultural difference, between Ukrainians and Jews and between Australian jurors and Ukrainian peasants and Israeli Holocaust survivors. It is about history, the role of the Schutzmannschaft in ghetto clearances and antipartisan activities, about Nazi occupation policy and the economic role of the forestry administration in occupied Ukraine. It is also about the ways in which *heger* helped protect the forests and killed Jews at the same time. More important perhaps, it is the story of how we can or cannot tell these stories at the same time and in the same place.

Shoshana Felman has returned to Hannah Arendt's analysis to argue that juridical events such as the Eichmann trial must be placed alongside other cultural phenomenon if they are to be decoded in a meaningful way.[36] For Felman the Eichmann trial and its pedagogical, historical functions are completed by an analysis of the Claude Lanzmann film *Shoah* (1985), in which testimony is resituated after the legalized framing in the trial has established a public limit, just as Australian reactions to and interpretations of the Adelaide war crimes trials can be more fully contextualized and understood if we take into account the Demidenko/Darville literary affair. Felman argues that the Eichmann trial's true meaning and function lie in law's ability to act as a limit. The Eichmann trial allowed for the creation of a limiting interpretive framework in which the previously silenced enormity of the Shoah could be articulated and situated.

For Felman the existence of law and rules of evidence and procedure ensured that the Shoah could no longer be portrayed as something so enormous and complex in its scope, scale, and application that it was beyond our grasp and our imagination. Law, the search for a verdict, imposed a limit on any idea that the Holocaust could not be grasped because it had to be seized in the context of determining the culpability of the accused. Moreover, *Eichmann* fits precisely in an already established Nuremberg precedent, to which it acts as a necessary supplement. "The Eichmann trial follows the tradition set up by the Nuremberg tribunal, but with a crucial difference of perspective. Whereas the Nuremberg trials view murderous political regimes and their aggressive warfare as the center of the trial and as the center of what constitutes a 'monumental history,' the Eichmann trial views the victims as the center of what gives history its monumental dimensions and what endows the trial with its monumental significance as an act of historic justice."[37]

The Eichmann trial, however, was not without its tensions at this level. As Lawrence Douglas argues, the narratives offered by the witnesses/survivors did not always easily fit into the understandings of the legal actors about the nature and purpose of a criminal trial. Nonetheless, a form of narrative synergy was found. "For it was the narratives of the survivor witnesses that came to exercise the gravest threat to the court's control over the trial; and it was the court's response to this testimony that most powerfully revealed its strategies for recuperating its understanding of legitimate judicial function."[38]

For Felman this symbiotic relationship between and among witness and historical narrative and judicial professional discursive autonomy is to be found not in Arendt's critique of the Eichmann court but in a different understanding of the nature of the juridical function in war crimes trials. Law acts as a mode of transmission of narrative experience. More significantly, this narration of experience in Holocaust trials is achieved through law's power to translate and to reorganize knowledge and history from the private experience of the victim into the realm of public, official legal knowledge because "the trial is, primarily and centrally, a *legal process of translation* of thousands of private, secret traumas into one collective, public and communally acknowledged one."[39]

According to this interpretation of law and history, the criminal trial in relation to the Shoah concretizes this transformation/translation of private suffering into public, collective, national (perhaps cosmopolitan?) knowledge because law effectively writes history in these proceedings.[40] While this is an arguable position in light of the particular context of the Eichmann case in Israel in the early 1960s, Felman's argument about monumental history, like Arendt's claim about the legal specificity of jurisdictional capacity over Holocaust crimes, would seem to misapprehend the Australian case entirely.

While proponents of the trials no doubt had in mind a series of prosecutions in which the testimony of survivors would combine with the professional narrative reconstruction of the Third Reich and the Final Solution proffered by historians to create not just a case beyond reasonable doubt against the individual accused but also a concrete history lesson for the public of Australia and the world, this was clearly not what happened in Adelaide. The world has largely ignored the Australian Nazi war crimes trial experience. The broad Australian public reacted in a similar manner. More important, the application of common-law rules and practices in relation to evidence precluded the introduction of narrative accounts by witnesses, either in the guise of professional historical accounts or as the stories of eyewitnesses. The difficulties of intercultural communication and consecutive translation further lessened the narrative flow and coherence of almost every eyewitness in all three cases.

Finally, the defense strategy of litigating the three cases not as Holocaust or even really as war crimes cases but, instead, as simple murders meant that the narrative focus was always limited to issues of identity and the reliability of witnesses on questions of detail. Gerry Simpson has argued extensively about the positioning of history and ideology in war crimes trials. He concludes that many see Holocaust-related trials as an opportunity to establish in the judicial forum an officialized version of historical truth, an argument reiterated by historians such as Henry Rousso and Donald Bloxham who oppose or criticize, to a greater or lesser degree, the law/history nexus in such trials. Conversely for Simpson, such cases can give rise to the presentation of competing or dissident historical accounts.[41] The Adelaide trials offered none of these possibilities. The Holocaust was not contested. The mechanics of the Shoah in Ukraine, the operation of the Schutzmannschaft in localized killing operations, all remained unchallenged as a matter of law and of history. Expert testimony from internationally recognized historians such as Raul Hilberg and Christopher Browning on the origins and implementation of the Final Solution entered the official record of the Adelaide cases virtually without question. When historical testimony was contested, such as was the case of Martin Dean's use of ESC and Soviet trial material in *Wagner* or Konrad Kwiet's detailed work on the Forestry Administration in Ukraine in *Polyukhovich*, or Jonathan Steinberg's and Martin Dean's evidence about the date of the Gnivan killings in *Berezowsky*, objections were formulated and cross-examinations conducted on the basis of ordinary rules of evidence in criminal proceedings. There was no dissident history.

The rest of the contest in the Adelaide trials took place in a more isolated, more restricted legal context. Could the prosecution establish beyond a reasonable doubt that a particular Schuma unit was deployed at a particular ghetto liquidation on a given day and that the accused was present and participating? The pedagogic function of war crimes trials in the sense about which debate has raised so much interdisciplinary ire was virtually absent from the Australian Nazi war crimes trials. History was not absent from the trials. The materials produced; the archival sources identified, explored, and exploited; and the scholarship that has flowed from the Polyukhovich, Berezowsky, and Wagner cases have added immeasurably to our knowledge of the fate of the Jews of Ukraine.

Significant historical controversy was absent from the trials. There were no competing or dissident historical accounts produced, as there were in Canada in the case of Imre Finta or even in the UK trial of Anthony Sawoniuk. Following the will of the Australian Parliament, the Adelaide trials proceeded on the only basis on which they could have been and were permitted to proceed, as ordinary criminal law prosecutions. The cosmopolitan nature of the offenses and of the import of moral and ethical principles in relation to the Shoah, war crimes, and crimes against humanity, in the Australian context, were to be found only in the discursive practices of journalism and politics that preceded and informed the introduction and passage of the War Crimes Act by the Bob Hawke–led Labor government. Beyond those gains law dominated the proceedings themselves.

In his searching analysis of cosmopolitan justice in the face of mass atrocity, David Hirsh writes: "There are many ways of producing truth: law, fiction, journalism, art, memoir, historiography, religion, science, astrology. All have their own rules, methods and norms but also their own claims and purposes. If we understand these different approaches to truth-finding as social processes, then we do not have to judge that one is authentic and the others fake; but nor do we have to judge that they are all equally valid. While they overlap, they all have distinct objectives and ways of operating."[42]

The Australian experience—from revelations in the immediate postwar period that among recently arrived immigrants seeking a new and better life in Australia were Holocaust perpetrators, through the Cold War politics and rhetoric of Garfield Barwick's closed chapter, to Mark Aarons's efforts to bring the story of Nazi collaborators back into the limelight, to the political debates around the introduction and passage into law of the War Crimes Act, to the activities of the SIU, the Demidenko affair, through to the conclusion of the Polyukhovich, Berezowsky, and Wagner prosecutions, and the dissolution of the SIU and the war crimes program—embodies many of these competing visions of truth, articulated from many perspectives. The plea put forward by Paul Ricoeur that judgment is the act that unites all the perspectives and disciplines that have been invoked in the legal history of the Australian Nazi war crimes experience has a particular resonance here. That judgment, which commands our ethical intervention, can and must be invoked in any assessment of the Australian proceedings and of the evidence—legal, historical, testimonial, and indeed fictional—proffered in this context.[43]

In researching and writing this book, I have been granted privileged access to the transcripts, witness statements and other key documents that formed the heart of the law and the history of the Polyukhovich, Berezowsky, and Wagner cases. I have been able to view hours and hours of witness interviews that took place in Krinichevatka, Serniki, and Svetlovodsk, Ukraine. Much of this book is based on these previously unexamined materials. SIU documentation for the most part remains locked away and is at present inaccessible to lawyers and historians. While there may be understandable reasons grounded in concerns about privacy and even legal privilege that might have justified this situation, enough time has passed for a serious reconsideration of this practice. Most, if not all, of those investigated are now dead. The Shoah, in terms of the Australian investigations and the materials uncovered by SIU historians and lawyers is quite literally now history. It is time to open up the judicial and historical archives so that historians and others might have access to this important material. We need to allow the process of historical, legal, political, and social narration and judgment to take place. The Australian experience (along with the American, Canadian, and English war crimes processes) may indeed be properly characterized by Erich Haberer in terms of the interactions between law and history: "Both observed the rules and discourse of their respective professions and neither blurred the distinction between justice legally applied and truth historically defined."[44]

Unless and until the documentary bases of the Australian cases, from transcripts to archival material, are made more readily available, debates about the legacy and import of the Australian cases that took place in Adelaide and the war crimes investigation process more generally, will occur in a context of far from satisfactory and imperfect information. If we believe that the proper understanding of law, history, the Shoah, genocide, and crimes against humanity must form part of our civilized quest for a world in which justice is a primary value, the ethical imperative of judgment can be achieved only through publicly, democratically available sources. This book is but a first, incomplete, and tentative step in that direction.

Notes

A NOTE ON LANGUAGE

1. Mendelsohn, *Lost*, 42–43.

2. Hrytsenko, "Imagining the Community," 197–222.

3. Bartov, *Erased*.

INTRODUCTION

1. Statement of Offense, *DPP v. Wagner*, January Sessions, Supreme Court of South Australia.

2. Morgan, "New Evidence," 163–77.

3. Information for an Indictable Offense, pursuant to the *Justices Act 1921*, 26 January 1989, Robert William Reid, informant.

4. Information for an Indictable Offense, pursuant to the *Justices Act 1921*, 21 August 1991, Paul Gregory Malone, informant.

5. *R. v. Anthony Sawoniuk*, Court of Appeal, Criminal Division, 10 February 2000; *R. v. Imre Finta* 1 (1994): SCR 701.

6. *War Crimes Act 1945* (as amended).

7. Landsman, *Crimes of the Holocaust*; Hasian, *Rhetorical Vectors of Memory*; Heberer and Matthäus, *Atrocities on Trial*.

8. Browning, "German Memory, Judicial Interrogation, Historical Reconstruction," 34.

9. Interview with Konrad Kwiet, Sydney, 28 April 2008.

10. Demidenko, *Hand That Signed the Paper*.

11. Ricoeur, "Devant l'inacceptable," 3–18.

12. Marrus, "History and the Holocaust in the Courtroom," 215–39.

13. Blanchot, *Writing of the Disaster*, 3.

14. Ricoeur, *Memory, History, Forgetting*, esp. 315–33.

15. Ricoeur, "Devant l'inacceptable," 7–11.

16. Bartov, *Murder in Our Midst*, 133.

17. LaCapra, *Representing the Holocaust*; LaCapra, *History and Memory after Auschwitz*.

18. Dintenfass, "Truth's Other," 1–20.

1. HISTORY, WAR CRIMES, AND LAW IN UKRAINE

1. Hrytsenko, "Imagining the Community," 197–222.

2. Boshyk, *Ukraine during World War II*.

3. Spector, *Holocaust of Volhynian Jews*; Brandon and Lower, *Shoah in Ukraine*.

4. Snyder, *Reconstruction of Nations*.

5. See, generally, Bartal and Polonsky, *Galicia*; Polonsky, *Jews in the Polish Borderlands*; Potichnyj and Aster, *Ukrainian-Jewish Relations in Historical Perspective*.

6. Mazower, *Dark Continent*, 40.

7. Prusin, *Nationalizing a Borderland*.

8. Gross, *Revolution from Abroad*; Borzęcki, *Soviet-Polish Peace of 1921*.

9. "Secret Additional Protocol," 78.

10. Megargee, *Barbarossa, 1941*. This is the British version of *War of Annihilation*.

11. Bartov, *Hitler's Army*.

12. Hamburg Institute for Social Research, *German Army and Genocide*; Heer et al., *Discursive Construction of History*.

13. Arad, Krakowski, and Spector, *Einsatzgruppen Reports*; Prusin, "Community of Violence."

14. Browning, *Ordinary Men*; Goldhagen, *Hitler's Willing Executioners*.

15. Matthäus, "What About the 'Ordinary Men'?" 136.

16. Naimark, *Fires of Hatred*.

17. Snyder, *Reconstruction of Nations*, 159–60.

18. Ruding, "Historical Representation of the Wartime Accounts of the Activities of the OUN-UPA."

19. Shekhovtsov, "By Cross and Sword."

20. Öhman, "From Famine to Forgotten Holocaust."

21. Frankel, *Dark Times, Dire Decisions*.

22. Gross, "Jewish Community in the Soviet-Annexed Territories."

23. Melamed, "Organized and Unsolicited Collaboration in the Holocaust," 237–38.

24. Lower, "'Anticipatory Obedience' and the Nazi Implementation of the Holocaust in the Ukraine."

25. Lower, *Nazi Empire-Building and the Holocaust in Ukraine*; Berkhoff, *Harvest of Despair*.

26. Kruglov, "Jewish Losses in Ukraine," 283–84.

27. Kruglov, "Jewish Losses in Ukraine," 283.

28. Pohl, "Murder of Ukraine's Jews under German Military Administration," 55.

29. Dean, "German *Gendarmerie*," 171.

30. Dean, *Collaboration in the Holocaust*.

31. Fredj, *Mass Shooting of Jews in Ukraine*; Desbois, *Holocaust by Bullets*.

32. Pohl, "Murder of Ukraine's Jews under German Military Administration," 58.

33. Pohl, "Murder of Ukraine's Jews under German Military Administration," 75n237.

34. Gitelman, "History, Memory and Politics"; Jones, "'Every Family Has Its Freak.'"

35. Fraser, *Law after Auschwitz*, chaps. 7–10.

36. Ginsburgs, *Moscow's Road to Nuremberg*; Kochavi, *Prelude to Nuremberg*.

37. *People's Verdict*.

38. Ginsburgs, "Laws of War and War Crimes on the Russian Front during World War II"; Hirsch, "Soviets at Nuremberg."

39. "Franklin D. Roosevelt on the Execution of Hostages by the Nazis," 25 October 1941, Department of State, *Bulletin*.

40. Reproduced in *Punishment for War Crimes*, 15.

41. *Punishment for War Crimes*.

42. Matthäus, "Lessons of Leipzig," 3–23.

43. "Declaration Concerning Atrocities Made at the Moscow Conference."

44. "Declaration Concerning Atrocities Made at the Moscow Conference."

45. "Declaration Concerning Atrocities Made at the Moscow Conference."

46. *History of the United Nations War Crimes Commission*.

47. *History of the United Nations War Crimes Commission*, 113, 158–60.

48. Ginsburgs, "Moscow and International Legal Cooperation."

49. *Soviet Government Statements on Nazi Atrocities*, 7–10; Berkhoff, "'Russian' Prisoners of War."

50. *Soviet Government Statements on Nazi Atrocities*, 19.

51. *Soviet Government Statements on Nazi Atrocities*, 22.

52. Molotov, *Note Concerning the Monstrous Atrocities and Acts of Violence.*

53. Molotov, *Note Concerning the Monstrous Atrocities and Acts of Violence*, 3.

54. Molotov, *Note Concerning the Monstrous Atrocities and Acts of Violence*, 3–4.

55. Molotov, *Note Concerning the Monstrous Atrocities and Acts of Violence*, 29.

56. Molotov, *Note Concerning the Monstrous Atrocities and Acts of Violence*, 30.

57. *Soviet Government Statements on Nazi Atrocities*, 57–62.

58. *Soviet Government Statements on Nazi Atrocities*, 61.

59. See, for example, *New Soviet Documents on Nazi Atrocities*, 49, 70, 93.

60. Jones, "'Every Family Has Its Freak.'"

61. *Soviet Government Statements on Nazi Atrocities*, 55.

62. Feferman, "Soviet Investigation of Nazi Crimes in the USSR," 588–89.

63. Feferman, "Soviet Investigation of Nazi Crimes in the USSR," 588–89.

64. Ginsburgs, *Moscow's Road to Nuremburg*, 38.

65. Ginsburgs, *Moscow's Road to Nuremburg*, 38–39.

66. Sorokina, "People and Procedures," 801.

67. Sorokina, "People and Procedures," 39.

68. Feferman, "Soviet Investigation of Nazi Crimes," 591.

69. Feferman, "Soviet Investigation of Nazi Crimes," 598.

70. Ehrenburg and Grossman, *Complete Black Book of Russian Jewry*; Rubenstein and Altman, *Unknown Black Book*; *Black Book.*

71. Sorokina, "People and Procedures," 802.

72. *Soviet Government Statements on Nazi Atrocities*, 107–36.

73. Cryer and Boyster, *Tokyo International Military Tribunal.*

74. Ginsburgs, *Moscow's Road to Nuremberg*, 41.

75. Pohl, "Murder of Ukraine's Jews," 75n237.

76. Penter, "Collaboration on Trial," 783.

77. Dean, "Where Did All the Collaborators Go?" 791.

78. Ginsburgs places the death penalty rate at 8.9 percent of 2.5 million convicted, or over 220,000 executions. *Moscow's Road to Nuremberg*, 41.

79. *People's Verdict*; Bourtman, "'Blood for Blood, Death for Death.'"

80. Feldbrugge, "War Crimes in Soviet Criminal Law," 292–95.

81. Ginsburgs, "Laws of War and War Crimes," 263.

82. "Trial of the Case of the Atrocities Committed," 7–44.

83. "Verdict," 44.

84. Feldbrugge, "War Crimes in Soviet Criminal Law," 293.

85. "Trial of the Case of the Atrocities Committed," 45.

86. "Trial of the Case of the Atrocities Committed," 113.

87. "Trial of the Case of the Atrocities Committed," 124.

88. Penter, "Collaboration on Trial," 787.

89. Prusin, "'Fascist Criminals to the Gallows,'" 8.

90. Feldbrugge, "War Crimes in Soviet Criminal Law," 298.

91. Prusin, "'Fascist Criminals to the Gallows.'"

92. Penter, "Collaboration on Trial," 786.

93. Douglas, *Memory of Judgment*.

94. Penter, "Collaboration on Trial," 786.

95. Penter, "Collaboration on Trial," 783–84.

96. Dean, "Where Did All the Collaborators Go?" 798.

97. See Feldbrugge, "War Crimes in Soviet Criminal Law," 295–98.

98. *Nazi Crimes in Ukraine*, 278.

99. See, for example, Hanusiak, *Lest We Forget*; Luciuk, "Unintended Consequences in Refugee Resettlement."

100. Molchanov, *There Shall Be Retribution*, 5–6.

101. *Le crime méthodique*, 176–78.

102. Feldbrugge, "War Crimes in Soviet Criminal Law," 295.

103. "From the Verdict of the Volyn Regional Court in the Case of Traitors of Homeland Dufanetz N. G., Bubela A. L. and Rybachuk F. Ye.," 348–49.

104. "From the Verdict of the Ternopol Regional Court in the Case of Traitors of Homeland Sotsky Ye. D. and Ostrovsky Ya. G.," 28 October 1982, 353–57.

105. Molchanov, *There Shall Be Retribution*; *History Teaches a Lesson*; *Ukrainian People Accuse*.

106. Rückerl, *Investigation of Nazi Crimes*, 61–62.

2. A BRIEF POLITICAL AND LEGAL HISTORY

1. *History of the United Nations War Crimes Commission*.

2. Letter from Ben Chifley, prime minister, to the UK secretary of state for commonwealth relations, 1 October 1947, box 5, Ll.03 G5, folder UNWCC, Ex Oz Archives, Aug 88, Aarons Collection, State Library of New South Wales (hereafter cited as AC).

3. House of Representatives, *Hansard*, 22 March 1961, 451–52.

4. Aarons, *Sanctuary*; Aarons, *War Criminals Welcome*. For an official account of the screening process and the entry of war criminals into Australia, see Menzies, *Review of Material*.

5. Rutland, *Edge of the Diaspora*, 245–47.

6. Rutland, *Edge of the Diaspora*, 245–51.

7. "Migrants Tell Startling Stories to Police of Ex-Nazis Here," *Sunday Herald*, 18 December 1949; "Twelve Alleged Nazi War Collaborators in Security Quiz," *Truth*, 24 December 1949; "Two of Hitler's Men Found Here," *Argus*, 9 June 1950.

8. *Genocide Convention Act No. 27, 1949.*

9. "Volks' Spread the Goebbels Plan," *Argus*, 12 September 1950.

10. *Statement by the Minister for Immigration: The Hon. Harold Holt*, Australian Archives CRS A 445 item 194/2/3 P 3, in "War Criminals Program Documents," folder "Miscellaneous," ML/03 G1, box 1, AC; Tampke, *Germans in Australia*, 134–56.

11. Whitlam and Stubbs, *Nest of Traitors*; Manne, *Petrov Affair*.

12. *Report of the Royal Commission on Espionage*, 241–50.

13. Williams, "Suppression of Communism by Force of Law."

14. *Australian Communist Party v. Commonwealth ("Communist Party Case")*, [1951] HCA 5; (1951) 83 CLR 1 (9 March 1951); Douglas, "Cold War Justice."

15. Murray, *Split*; Henderson, *Mr. Santamaria and the Bishops*.

16. Rutland and Caplan, *With One Voice*, 53–59.

17. Rutland and Caplan, *With One Voice*, 50–52.

18. On the difficulties of Melbourne-Sydney relations, see Rutland, *Jews in Australia*, 75–78.

19. House of Representatives, *Hansard*, 7 November 1951.

20. "Twelve Alleged Nazi War Collaborators in Security Quiz," *Truth*, 24 December 1949.

21. Internal report, 12 January 1950, "Various correspondence about identity, etc., AG's Department, Jewish complainant, etc.," Australian Archives A 445 item 271.2.4, in folder "Alleged Nazi Collaborators in 'Melbourne Truth' 1950," ML/03 G1, box 1, AC.

22. "Secret Surveillance/Intelligence Files, Australian Archives A6122XR ITEM Voh 169 re: Communist Influence," in folder "Jewish Council to Combat Fascism and Anti-Semitism," box 1, AC.

23. "Note for Minister," 18 January 1950, in folder "Alleged Nazi Collaborators in 'Melbourne Truth' 1950," AC.

24. Rutland, *Edge of the Diaspora*, esp. chap. 10, 225–56; Rutland, *Jews in Australia*, 59–65.

25. Folder "Miscellaneous," box 1, AC.

26. Folder "Jewish Council to Combat Fascism and Anti-Semitism," box 1, AC.

27. House of Representatives, *Hansard*, 22 March 1961, 451–52.

28. House of Representatives, *Hansard*, 22 March 1961, 452.

29. Aarons, *War Criminals Welcome*, chap. 21, 444–53.

30. Aarons, *War Criminals Welcome*, 454.

31. Marrus, *Holocaust in History*, 4.

32. Interview with Mark Aarons, Sydney, June 2008; Aarons, *Sanctuary*.

33. Interview with Mark Aarons, Sydney, June 2008; Aarons, *War Criminals Welcome*, 383–89.

34. Aarons, *Sanctuary*, xxix.

35. Deschênes, *Commission of Inquiry on War Criminals*; Matas and Charendoff, *Justice Delayed*.

36. Hetherington and Chalmers, *Report of the War Crimes Inquiry*.

37. Caplan, "Road to the Menzies Inquiry"; Jeremy Jones, "Australia and Nazi War Criminals—An Interim Report," 6 May 1986, box 15, AC.

38. Aarons, *Sanctuary*, 279.

39. Interview with Mark Aarons, Sydney, June 2008.

40. Interview with Mark Aarons, Sydney, June 2008.

41. Jones, "Australia and Nazi War Criminals—An Interim Report," 6.

42. Koscharsky, *First Wave Emigrants*; Luciuk, *Searching for Place*.

43. Caplan, "Road to the Menzies Inquiry," 66.

44. Caplan, "Road to the Menzies Inquiry," 68–69.

45. Douglas, *Memory of Judgment*. Cf. Hasian, *Rhetorical Vectors of Memory*.

46. Caplan, "Road to the Menzies Inquiry," 69.

47. Rutland and Caplan, *With One Voice*, 288–89; Troper and Weinfeld, *Old Wounds*.

48. Senate, *Hansard*, 1644; House of Representatives, *Hansard*, 2394.

49. House of Representatives, *Hansard*, 30 April 1986, 2733.

50. Senate, *Hansard*, 29 April 1986, 1940; Senate, *Hansard*, 27 May 1986, 2719.

51. House of Representatives, *Hansard*, 1 May 1986, 2881.

52. House of Representatives, *Hansard*, 5 May 1986, 916, 3045.

53. House of Representatives, *Hansard*, 5 May 1986, 3045ff.; House of Representatives, *Hansard*, 5 May 1986, 3052ff.

54. House of Representatives, *Hansard*, 5 May 1986, 3049ff.

55. House of Representatives, *Hansard*, 5 May 1986, 3054.

56. Senate, *Hansard*, 29 May 1986, 2963.

57. Menzies, *Review of Material*, 3.

58. Menzies, *Review of Material*, para. 2.12, 12.

59. Menzies, *Review of Material*, para. 2.13, 12–13.

60. Menzies, *Review of Material*, para. 3.29, 25.

61. Menzies, *Review of Material*, para. 10.18 (1), 121.

62. Menzies, *Review of Material*, recommendations, 180–83.

63. Menzies, *Review of Material*, 180.

64. House of Representatives, *Hansard*, 24 February 1987, 593–95.

65. House of Representatives, *Hansard*, 24 February 1987, 596.

66. House of Representatives, *Hansard*, 28 October 1987, 1612.

67. House of Representatives, *Hansard*, 24 February 1987, 595.

68. House of Representatives, *Hansard*, 28 October 1987.

69. See Menzies, *Review of Material*, para. 16.1ff., 149ff.

70. House of Representatives, *Hansard*, 26 November 1987, 2733.

71. House of Representatives, *Hansard*, 26 November 1987, 2732.

72. House of Representatives, *Hansard*, 26 November 1987, 2733.

73. House of Representatives, *Hansard*, 26 November 1987, 2735.

74. House of Representatives, *Hansard*, 26 November 1987, 2734ff.

75. House of Representatives, *Hansard*, 26 November 1987, 2745–46.

76. House of Representatives, *Hansard*, 26 November 1987, 2790.

77. House of Representatives, *Hansard*, 26 November 1987, 2793–99.

78. House of Representatives, *Hansard*, 26 November 1987, 2799ff.

79. House of Representatives, *Hansard*, 26 November 1987, 2803–7.

80. Senate, *Hansard*, 26 November 1987, 2531.

81. Senate, *Hansard*, 15 December 1987, 3063.

82. Senate, *Hansard*, 15 December 1987, 3063.

83. Senate, Standing Committee on Legal and Constitutional Affairs, 1 and 2 February 1989, Official *Hansard* Report.

84. Zumbakis, *Soviet Evidence*.

85. Senate, Standing Committee on Legal and Constitutional Affairs, 1 February 1989, 3–51.

86. Senate, Standing Committee on Legal and Constitutional Affairs, 1 February 1989, 97–120.

87. Senate, Standing Committee on Legal and Constitutional Affairs, 1 February 1989, 52–96.

88. Senate, Standing Committee on Legal and Constitutional Affairs, 1 February 1989, 155, submission, 8.

89. Dackiw, "Denaturalization of Suspected Nazi Nar Criminals."

90. Senate, Standing Committee on Legal and Constitutional Affairs, 1 February 1989, 168, submission, 21.

91. Senate, Standing Committee on Legal and Constitutional Affairs, 1 February 1989, 176.

92. Senate, Standing Committee on Legal and Constitutional Affairs, 2 February 1989.

93. Senate, Standing Committee on Legal and Constitutional Affairs, 2 February 1989, 335, submission, 2.

94. Zumbakis, *Soviet Evidence*.

95. Sopinka and Ukrainian Canadian Committee, *"The Taking of Soviet Evidence."*

96. Senate, Standing Committee on Legal and Constitutional Affairs, 2 February 1989, Australian Federation of Ukrainian Organisations, 5 April 1986, "Statement of Concern about the Existence of Alleged War Criminals in Australia," 360.

97. Senate, Standing Committee on Legal and Constitutional Affairs, 1 February 1989, 128, submission, 4.

98. *Report: Commission of Inquiry on War Criminals*, app. 1-M, *Decision Concerning Foreign Evidence*, 890.

99. *Report: Commission of Inquiry on War Criminals*, 890–91.

100. Hetherington and Chalmers, *Report of the War Crimes Inquiry*, 94, para. 9.18.

101. "Matters Relating to the War Crimes Amendment Bill 1987," *Report*, ix.

102. Senate, *Hansard*, 15 December 1988, 4246.

103. See Cesarani, *Justice Delayed*, 190ff.

104. Senate, *Hansard*, 15 December 1988, 4305ff.

105. Senate, *Hansard*, 15 December 1988, 4246.

106. Tom Burton and Glenn Milne, "Aussie War Crimes? Impossible, Say RSL, Opposition," *Sydney Morning Herald*, 15 November 1988.

107. Senate, *Hansard*, 4310.

108. Senate, *Hansard*, 4310ff.

109. Senate, *Hansard*, Senator Panizza, Liberal, Western Australia.

110. Senate, *Hansard*, 4354.

111. Senate, *Hansard*, 16 February 1988, 4373.

112. Senate, *Hansard*, 4375.

113. Senate, *Hansard*, 4376.

114. Mike Seccombe, "War Crimes Bill Passes Emergency Session," *Sydney Morning Herald*, 22 December 1988.

115. See Australia, Attorney-General's Department, *Report on the Operation of the War Crimes Act 1945 to June 1990*; and subsequent reports, 1991–94; *Report of the Investigations of War Criminals in Australia*.

116. Interview with Grant Niemann, Adelaide, April 2008.

3. AUSTRALIAN WAR CRIMES TRIALS

1. Interview with the Hon. Greg James QC, Sydney, April 2008.

2. Peter Hughes, "850 War Murders: Man Charged," *Sydney Morning Herald*, 27 January 1990.

3. Bevan, *Case to Answer*; interview with Grant Niemann, Adelaide, April 2008.

4. *Polyukhovich v. Commonwealth*, [1991] HCA 32; (1991) 172 CLR 501; Triggs, "Australia's War Crimes Trials."

5. Spector, *Holocaust of the Volhynian Jews*, app., table A, 363.

6. Spector, *Holocaust of the Volhynian Jews*, table 7, 66, 71–72.

7. Spector, *Holocaust of the Volhynian Jews*, 199–200.

8. Employment card, March 1943 for Johann Poljuchowitsch/Jan Polucho-wicz, Pass no. 1745, documents p/6/kc and p/11/kc, seized by Australian Federal Police pursuant to a search warrant issued in Adelaide, 25 January 1990, Polyukhovich Materials. The complete history of the Deutsche Forstverwaltung Ukraine remains to be written. For neighboring Poland, see *Documents Relating to the Administration of Occupied Countries*.

9. Documents p/1/jj; p/2/jj; p/7/kc; p/9/kc; p/14/kc; p/15/kc—documents relating to work in Germany.

10. Documents p/4/kc, I.R.O. Processing Cards; p/21/kc, letter from Department of Immigration, 7 February 1952.

11. Testimony of Marriage, 11 May 1949, document p/19/kc, seized pursuant to warrant issued on 25 January 1990.

12. Reproduced in *Ukrainian People Accuse*, 48.

13. Document M, p/31/pm, "Description of Documents Seized under Search Warrant," Polyukhovich Materials.

14. "sa Ukrainians to Probe 'Nazi in Seaton' Claim," *Adelaide Advertiser*, 27 December 1986; "I'm That Man, but I'm No War Criminal, Says Pensioner," *Adelaide Advertiser*, 30 December 1986.

15. Interview with Mark Aarons, Sydney, June 2008.

16. Aarons, *War Criminals Welcome*, 475; folder "Ivan Polyukhovich," ml 776/03, m3, box 28, ac; testimony of Mark Aarons, Polyukhovich Committal Hearing, 4 May 1992, 461–71.

17. Heberer and Matthäus, "Introduction," xx.

18. Rousso, *Haunting Past*, 48–83.

19. Wildt, "Des vérités qui diffèrent."

20. Bloxham, *Genocide on Trial*, 221.

21. Hasian, *Rhetorical Vectors of Memory*, 135–43; *R. v Anthony Sawoniuk*, Court of Appeal, 10 February 2000, 2000 wl 473.

22. Douglas, *Memory of Judgment*.

23. *Trial of Adolf Eichmann*; Landau, *Demjanjuk Trial*.

24. Douglas, *Memory of Judgment*, 257.

25. Landsman, *Crimes of the Holocaust*; *R. v. Finta*, [1994] S.C.R. 701.

26. Information for an Indictable Offense, *Justices Act 1921*, Adelaide Magistrates' Court, Polyukhovich Materials.

27. Information for an Indictable Offense, *Justices Act 1921*, 7 August 1990.

28. Statement of Offense, *dpp v. Polyukhovich*, Supreme Court of South Australia.

29. "Where there is direct evidence of the *actus reus* and that evidence is capable of supporting an inference of *mens rea*, there is a case to answer except in the extreme case, as perhaps of testimony which is manifestly self-contradictory or

the product of a disorderly mind, envisaged by the Privy Council, in which the direct 'evidence' is so incredible as to amount to no evidence." *R. v. Bilick and Starke*, [1984] 36 S.A.S.R. 321, 337 (per King, cj).

30. I owe this insight to my colleague Lawrence McNamara.

31. Record of interview with Jan Poluchowicz, 25 January 1990, Polyukhovich Materials.

32. Interviews with the Hon. Michael David qc and Lindy Powell qc, Adelaide, April 2008; and interviews with the Hon. Greg James qc and Konrad Kwiet, Sydney, April 2008.

33. Letter from Graham Blewitt, siu to Superintendent V. G. Sontag, rcmp War Crimes Unit, Ottawa; similar letters to Mike Wolf (U.S.); Chief Superintendent Gad Watermann, National Criminal Investigation Unit, Nazi Crimes, Jaffa; Detective Chief Superintendent E. Bathgate, War Crimes Unit, Metropolitan Police, ml 776/03, m3, box 28, ac.

34. *Robert William Reid v. Ivan Timofeyevich Polyukhovich*, Committal Proceedings, 1446–86 (hereafter cited as Polyukhovich Committal).

35. Public Hearings, Canberra, 1 and 2 February 1988; "Matters Relating to the War Crimes Amendment Bill 1987," *Report*.

36. Public Hearings, 1 February 1988, 52–96; Public Hearings, 2 February 1988, 427–77; "Matters Relating to the War Crimes Amendment Bill 1987," *Report*, app. 5–7, Correspondence with senior prosecutor for War Crimes, Attorney-General's Department of the USSR; chief state prosecutor, Hungary; assistant federal secretary, Justice and Organisation of the Administration, Yugoslavia, 119–24.

37. Memorandum of Understanding, para 2, 1 November 1990, agreed 1 November 1991, box 28, ac.

38. Interviews with the Hon. Michael David qc, Lindy Powell qc, and Grant Niemann, Adelaide, April 2008; and the Hon. Greg James qc and Konrad Kwiet, Sydney, April 2008.

39. Polyukhovich Committal, 1487, copy of Statement of Raul Hilberg, phii.

40. *War Crimes Act 1945*, sec. 5, 6, 7.

41. Gruner, *Jewish Forced Labor under the Nazis*.

42. "Field Verdict," Polyukhovich Committal, ppr3a, 6.

43. Polyukhovich Committal, 1496.

44. Polyukhovich Committal, 1526–27.

45. Polyukhovich Committal, 1527.

46. Polyukhovich Committal, 1523ff.; 1548ff.

47. Polyukhovich Committal, 1496.

48. Polyukhovich Committal, 1497.

49. Polyukhovich Committal, 1519.

50. Polyukhovich Committal, 1503–5.

51. Polyukhovich Committal, 1494.

52. Polyukhovich Committal, 1506.

53. Polyukhovich Committal, 1530.

54. Rückerl, *Investigation of Nazi Crimes*.

55. Polyukhovich Committal, 1508–9.

56. Polyukhovich Committal, 1517, 1529.

57. Polyukhovich Committal, 1518.

58. Heberer and Matthäus, "Introduction," xxii.

59. Polyukhovich Committal, 1529ff.

60. Referring to table 5 in "Ghetto Liquidations around Serniki in Autumn 1942," created by Kwiet and introduced by the prosecution.

61. Polyukhovich Committal, 1530–31.

62. Polyukhovich Committal, 1531–32.

63. Polyukhovich Committal, 1532.

64. Polyukhovich Committal, 1532.

65. *Director of Public Prosecutions v. Ivan Timofeyevich Polyukhovich*, Supreme Court of South Australia, 1993, 475/92, 1087 (hereafter cited as Polyukhovich Trial).

66. Polyukhovich Trial, 56–131; Hilberg, "Statement of Witness," December 1992.

67. Hilberg, "Statement of Witness," December 1992; Fredj, *Mass Shooting of Jews in Ukraine*.

68. Hilberg, "Statement of Witness," 7.

69. Polyukhovich Trial, 1032ff.

70. Polyukhovich Trial, 1061ff.

71. Polyukhovich Trial, esp. 1068–81.

72. Polyukhovich Trial, 1062.

73. *Evidence Act 1929*, sec. 34.

74. Polyukhovich Trial Materials, "Facts to Be Admitted by the Accused," para. 4.

75. Polyukhovich Trial Materials, "Facts to Be Admitted by the Accused," para. 8.

76. Polyukhovich Trial Materials, 1068.

77. Polyukhovich Trial Materials, 1078–79.

78. Polyukhovich Trial Materials, 1079–82.

79. Polyukhovich Trial Materials, "Facts to Be Admitted by the Accused," para. 8.

80. *Ukrainian People Accuse*, 47–48.

81. Polyukovich Trial Materials, 1190ff.

82. Polyukhovich Trial Materials, 1202.

83. Polyukhovich Trial Materials, 110; and argument on voir dire, 1230–31.

84. Polyukhovich Trial Materials, 1217.

85. Polyukhovich Trial Materials, 1240.

86. Polyukhovich Trial Materials, 1240–55.

87. Interview with Konrad Kwiet, Sydney, April 2008.

88. See Konrad Kwiet, "Table V, Ghetto Liquidations around Serniki, Autumn 1942," Polyukhovich Trial Materials.

89. Polyukhovich Trial Materials, 1227.

90. Polyukhovich Trial Materials, 1249.

91. Polyukhovich Trial Materials, 1250.

92. Polyukhovich Trial Materials, 1258.

93. Polyukhovich Trial Materials, 1259.

94. Polyukhovich Trial Materials.

95. Polyukhovich Trial Materials, 1263.

96. Polyukhovich Trial Materials, 1273ff.

97. Polyukhovich Trial Materials, 1283.

98. Interview with Konrad Kwiet, Sydney, April 2008.

99. Polyukhovich Trial Materials, 1286.

100. Polyukhovich Trial Materials, 1287.

101. Polyukhovich Trial Materials, 1287–88.

102. Polyukhovich Trial Materials, 1294ff.

103. Polyukhovich Trial Materials, 1298–99.

104. Polyukhovich Trial Materials, 1306.

4. MIKOLAY BEREZOWSKY

1. Information for an Indictable Offense, *Paul Gregory Malone v. Mikolay Berezowsky*, Adelaide Magistrate's Court, Committal Proceedings (hereafter cited as Berezowsky Committal).

2. Information for an Indictable Offense, Berezowsky Committal.

3. Haberer, "History and Justice."

4. Haberer, "History and Justice," 488.

5. Haberer, "History and Justice," 497ff.; *War Crimes Act 1945*, sec. 16, "The fact that, in doing an act alleged to be an offense against this Act, a person acted under orders of his or her government or of a superior is not a defence in a proceeding for the offense, but may, if the person is convicted of the offense, be taken into account in determining the proper sentence."

6. Haberer, "History and Justice," 497, 502–3; De Mildt, *In the Name of the People*.

7. Haberer, "History and Justice," 501–2.

8. Littman, *Pure Soldiers or Sinister Legion*; Cesarani, *Justice Delayed*, esp. chap. 6, 102–33.

9. Haberer, "History and Justice," 490.

10. Berezowsky Committal Materials, Protocol, 26 September 1948.

11. Berezowsky Committal Materials, Protocol, 10 December 1948, 2.

12. Berezowsky Committal Materials, Protocol, 18 February 1950, 2, 5.

13. Berezowsky Committal Materials, Protocol.

14. Berezowsky Committal Materials, Protocol, 17 May 1950, 2.

15. *Paul Gregory Malone v. Mikolay Berezowsky*, Adelaide Magistrates Court, 25241/1991, Transcript of Proceedings, 53 (hereafter cited as Berezowsky Transcript).

16. Berezowsky Transcript, 193.

17. Berezowsky Transcript, 194.

18. Berezowsky Transcript, 196, 199.

19. Berezowsky Transcript, 201.

20. Berezowsky Transcript, 194.

21. Christopher Browning, "Report on the Historical Evidence Concerning the Prosecution of Heinrich Wagner," 15ff., *John Hunter Ralston v. Heinrich Wagner*, Magistrates Court, South Australia, 91-25252; *DPP v. Heinrich Wagner*, Supreme Court of South Australia, January 1993 (Wagner Materials); Jonathan Steinberg, "Communication for the Purposes of Litigation: Historical Evidence in the War Crimes Act Prosecution of Mikolay Ivanovich Berezowsky," Berezowsky Committal Materials, esp. 52ff.; Berezowsky Transcript, 592; Testimony of Martin Dean, 662.

22. Berezowsky Transcript, 206–7.

23. Berezowsky Transcript, 208.

24. Berezowsky Transcript, 217–19.

25. Berezowsky Transcript, 209–10.

26. Berezowsky Transcript, 214–15.

27. Berezowsky Transcript, 285.

28. Berezowsky Transcript, 284.

29. Berezowsky Transcript, 288.

30. Berezowsky Transcript, 293.

31. Bevan, *Case to Answer*, 189.

32. Bevan, *Case to Answer*, 101.

33. Bevan, *Case to Answer*, 240.

34. Protocol, 12 April 1945.

35. "Statement of the Commission to Establish and Investigate Crimes by the German-Fascist Invaders and Their Accomplices in the Tyvrov District, 11 October 1944," Berezowsky Committal Materials, 7.

36. Berezowsky Transcript, 515–16.

37. Steinberg, "Communication for the Purposes of Litigation."

38. Berezowsky Transcript, 520, 587.

39. Berezowsky Transcript, 525–26.

40. Berezowsky Transcript, 528, 603.

41. Berezowsky Transcript, 533ff.

42. Steinberg, "Communication for the Purposes of Litigation," 42ff.

43. Berezowsky Transcript, 576–78.

44. Berezowsky Committal Materials.

45. Berezowsky Transcript, 582.

46. Berezowsky Transcript.

47. Berezowsky Transcript, 583, 612–16.

48. Berezowsky Transcript.

49. Berezowsky Transcript, 605.

50. Berezowsky Transcript, 601.

51. Berezowsky Transcript, 602.

52. Steinberg, "Communication for Purposes of Litigation," 53–54.

53. Berezowsky Transcript, 586.

54. Berezowsky Transcript, 609.

55. Berezowsky Transcript, 601ff.

56. Berezowsky Transcript, 604.

57. Berezowsky Transcript.

58. Berezowsky Transcript, 605.

59. Berezowsky Transcript, 607.

60. Berezowsky Transcript, 606.

61. Berezowsky Transcript, 606–7.

62. Berezowsky Transcript, 610.

63. Berezowsky Transcript, 608.

64. Berezowsky Transcript.

65. Berezowsky Transcript, 615.

66. Berezowsky Transcript, 616.

67. Berezowsky Transcript, 617.

68. Berezowsky Transcript, 618.

69. Berezowsky Transcript.

70. Berezowsky Transcript, 619.

71. Berezowsky Transcript, 619–21.

72. Berezowsky Transcript, 649.

73. Berezowsky Transcript, 665–66.

74. Haberer, "History and Justice," 510.

75. *Nazi Crimes in Ukraine.*

76. Berezowsky Transcript, 655ff.

77. Berezowsky Transcript, 657.

78. Berezowsky Transcript, 658.

79. Berezowsky Transcript, 663.

80. "Statement of Witness, Dr. Martin Christopher Dean," Berezowsky Materials, 22.

81. Berezowsky Transcript, 663ff.

82. Berezowsky Transcript, 663.

83. Berezowsky Transcript, 664.

84. Berezowsky Transcript, 664.

85. Berezowsky Transcript, 666.

86. Berezowsky Transcript, 667.

87. Berezowsky Transcript, 669.

88. Berezowsky Transcript, 669.

89. Berezowsky Transcript, 670.

90. Berezowsky Transcript, 672.

91. Berezowsky Transcript.

92. Berezowsky Transcript, 673.

93. Berezowsky Transcript.

94. Berezowsky Transcript, 674.

95. Interview with the Hon. Michael David QC, Adelaide, April 2008.

96. Berezowsky Committal Transcript, 135.

97. Steinberg, "Third Reich Reflected"; Dean, "German *Gendarmerie*."

98. Jamie Walker, "The Witness Who Knew Too Much," *Weekend Australian*, 21–22 September 1996.

99. Haberer, "History and Justice," 508.

5. THE STORY OF DAVIBORSHCH'S CART

1. Friedlander, *Probing the Limits of Representation*, 5.

2. Ricoeur, *Memory, History, Forgetting*.

3. Carr, "Narrative Explanation and Its Malcontents," 21.

4. Arendt, *Eichmann in Jerusalem*.

5. Douglas, *Memory of Judgment*.

6. Arendt, *Eichmann in Jerusalem*, 253.

7. Hasian, *Rhetorical Vectors of Memory*.

8. Simpson, *Law, War and Crime*.

9. Simpson, *Law, War and Crime*, 79.

10. Arendt, *Eichmann in Jerusalem*, 272.

11. Arendt, *Eichmann in Jerusalem*, 294.

12. Bauman, *Modernity and the Holocaust*.

13. Fredj, *Mass Shooting of Jews in Ukraine*.

14. Sec. 7 (3).

15. Lumans, *Himmler's Auxiliaries*; Lumans, "Reassessment of *Volksdeutsche* and Jews."

16. Bergen, "Nazi Concept of 'Volksdeutsche,'" 571 (original note reference omitted from quotation).

17. Dean, "Soviet Ethnic Germans and the Holocaust in the Reich Commissariat Ukraine," 248–71.

18. Affidavit of Konrad Kwiet, Wagner Historical Documents, 1993, 3.

19. Noakes, "Development of Nazi Policy towards the German-Jewish 'Mischlinge,'" 291–354.

20. Translation from Australian Embassy Moscow to Secretary Department of External Affairs, 29 April 1964, in Wagner Materials, ML/776/03 M6, box 31, AC.

21. Translation from Australian Embassy Moscow to Secretary Department of External Affairs, 29 April 1964.

22. Australia, Attorney-General's Department, *Report of the Investigations of War Criminals in Australia*.

23. Information of an Indictable Offense, *Ralston v. Wagner*, 5 September 1991.

24. Wagner Committal Transcript, 947ff.

25. Wagner Committal Transcript, 955–56.

26. Wagner Committal Transcript, 956.

27. Wagner Committal Transcript, 956–65.

28. Wagner Committal Transcript, 959.

29. Wagner Committal Transcript, 958–59.

30. "Protocol of a Court Hearing, Military Tribunal of the Kirovograd Garrison of the Kiev Military District," Wagner Committal Documents.

31. "Protocol of a Court Hearing, Military Tribunal of the Kirovograd Garrison," 7.

32. "Protocol of a Court Hearing, Military Tribunal of the Kirovograd Garrison."

33. "Protocol of a Court Hearing, Military Tribunal of the Kirovograd Garrison," 8.

34. Verdict, Sentence No 30, Kirovograd City Garrison Military Tribunal, 5 June 1947, Wagner Committal Materials.

35. Protocol, 20 February 1958, Wagner Committal Materials.

36. Transcript of interview with Nikolay Nikitovich Daviborshch, 12 November 1990, at Kirovograd, Wagner Committal Materials.

37. Transcript of interview with Daviborshch, 12 November 1990, 6.

38. Transcript of interview with Daviborshch, 12 November 1990, 16.

39. Transcript of interview with Daviborshch, 12 November 1990, 4.

40. Transcript of interview with Daviborshch, 12 November 1990, 9.

41. Transcript of interview with Daviborshch, 12 November 1990, 5.

42. Transcript of interview with Daviborshch, 12 November 1990.

43. Transcript of interview with Daviborshch, 12 November 1990, 11.

44. Interview with Nikolay Nikitovich Daviborshch and Gabby Brown, by David Edwardson and interpreter John Strokowsky, Wagner Committal Materials, also filed as exhibit GAB 6, in the Supreme Court of South Australia as part of the defense motion for a stay of proceedings, *DPP v. Heinrich Wagner*, SCCRM-92-780, 8 January 1993.

45. Interview with Daviborshch and Brown, by Edwardson and interpreter Strokowsky, 1.

46. Interview with Daviborshch and Brown, by Edwardson and interpreter Strokowsky, 5.

47. Interview with Daviborshch and Brown, by Edwardson and interpreter Strokowsky, 9.

48. Interview with Daviborshch and Brown, by Edwardson and interpreter Strokowsky, 10–11.

49. Browning, "German Memory, Judicial Interrogation, and Historical Reconstruction."

50. Heberer and Matthäus, "Introduction," xxii.

51. Feferman, "Soviet Investigation of Nazi Crimes in the USSR," 587–602; Sorokina, "People and Procedures."

52. Sorokina, "People and Procedures," 831.

53. Interview with Nikolay Nikitovich Daviborshch, 6 September 1992, 10.

54. Interview with Nikolay Nikitovich Daviborshch, 6 September 1992, 12.

55. Interview with Nikolay Nikitovich Daviborshch, 6 September 1992, 14.

56. Interview with Nikolay Nikitovich Daviborshch, 6 September 1992, 15.

57. Videotaped evidence on commission, 9 August 1993, Kirovograd, Ukraine, and transcript.

58. Videotaped evidence on commission, 9 August 1993, and transcript, 2.

59. Videotaped evidence on commission, 9 August 1993, and transcript, 6, 7.

60. Videotaped evidence on commission, 9 August 1993, and transcript, 4.

61. Videotaped evidence on commission, 9 August 1993, and transcript, 8–9.

62. Protocol of an Interrogation of the Accused Ivan Konstantinovich ZHILUN, 29 March 1947, Wagner Committal Documents, 1.

63. Wagner Committal Documents, 2.

64. Penter, "Collaboration in the Holocaust," 789–90; Browning, "Report on the Historical Evidence Concerning the Prosecution of Heinrich Wagner," esp. at sec. 7, "The Schutzmannschaft and Volksdeutsche Hilfspolizei," 15ff.

65. Protocol of Interrogation of the Accused, 2 April 1947, 3.

66. Dean, "Soviet Ethnic Germans and the Holocaust in the Reich Commissariat Ukraine," 249.

67. Protocol of Confrontation, 21 May 1947.

68. Protocol of a Court Hearing, Military Tribunal of the Kirovograd Garrison of the Kiev Military District, 5 June 1947, 6.

69. Verdict, sentence no. 90.

70. Protocol of Interrogation, Kirovograd, 15 January 1957, Wagner Committal Materials.

71. Protocol of Interrogation, 3.

72. Protocol of Interrogation, 4.

73. Klee, Dressen, and Riess, *Good Old Days,* 137–54.

74. Protocol of Confrontation, 1 February 1958, Kirovograd, 2.

75. Protocol of Confrontation.

76. Protocol of an Archival Criminal Matter, 15 June 1988.

77. Protocol of an Archival Criminal Matter, 3.

78. Transcript of interview with Ivan Konstantinovich Zhilun, 23 December 1989, Rovno Procurator's Office, Wagner Committal Materials, 4.

79. Wagner Committal Materials, 28.

80. Wagner Committal Materials, 29–30.

81. Statement of Robert William Reid, 12 August 1992, Wagner Committal Documents.

82. Transcript of Scene Interview with Ivan Konstantinovich Zhilun Taken on 19 March 1991 in the Village of Berezovatka, Wagner Committal Documents.

83. Wagner Committal, Transcript, 453–55.

84. Wagner Committal, Transcript, 462–65.

85. Wagner Committal, Transcript, 465.

86. Wagner Committal, Transcript.

87. Transcript of Interview with Ivan Konstantinovich Zhilun on 23 December 1989 at Rovno Procurator's Office, Wagner Committal Materials, 29–30.

88. Wagner Committal, Transcript, 466.

89. Wagner Committal, Transcript, 646.

90. Wagner Committal, Transcript, 648.

91. Wagner Committal, Transcript, 649.

92. Wagner Committal, Transcript, 652.

93. Wagner Committal, Transcript, 653ff.

94. Wagner Committal, Transcript, 656.

95. Wagner Committal, Transcript, 661.

96. Wagner Committal, Transcript, 683.

97. Information, *John Hunter Ralston v. Heinrich Wagner, Justices' Act*, 5 September 1991.

98. Wagner Committal, 730ff., 739–68.

99. Wagner Committal, 742.

100. Wagner Committal.

101. Transcript of the Protocol of Interrogation of Velikiy, 10 January 1958, 1–2.

102. Transcript of the Protocol of Interrogation of Velikiy, 663.

103. Transcript of the Protocol of Interrogation of Velikiy, 665–66.

104. Interview with the Hon. Greg James QC, Sydney, April 2008; interview with the Hon. Michael David QC, Adelaide, April 2008.

105. "Caught in a Web of Lies," 277–302.

106. Closing Argument by the Hon. Michael David QC, 671.

107. Committal transcript, 675.

108. Transcript of Evidence Taken from Andrey Filipovich Bardas, 10 August 1993, Svetlovodsk, Wagner Materials.

109. Transcript of Evidence Taken from Bardas, 5.

110. Transcript of Evidence Taken from Bardas, 7.

111. Transcript of Evidence Taken from Bardas, 12.

112. Transcript of Evidence Taken from Bardas, 22.

113. Transcript of Evidence Taken from Bardas, 12–13.

114. See SIU document 3995, "First Draft Historical Review of Gendarmerie/Ukr. Police Cases," 11 February 1991, 4, in Wagner Materials, ML/776/03 M6, box 31, AC.

115. The complexities of the proximity of the perpetrators and victims is explored in another context in the debates surrounding Jan T. Gross's study of antisemitism in *Neighbors*; Polonsky and Michlic, *Neighbors Respond*.

116. Berkhoff, *Harvest of Despair*, 64.

117. Australia, Attorney-General's Department, *Report on the Operation of the War Crimes Act 1945 to June 1994*.

118. Interviews with Lindy Powell QC and Grant Niemann, Adelaide, April 2008.

119. Committal Proceedings, Testimony, 529ff.

120. Committal Proceedings, Testimony, 343ff.

121. Testimony, Committal Transcript, 119–39. See also Wright, "Investigating War Crimes."

122. Testimony, Committal Transcript, 130.

123. Testimony of Thomas Howard Oettle, 915–31.

124. Testimony of Thomas Howard Oettle, 919.

6. TRANSLATING LAW, TRANSLATING HISTORY

1. Beim and Fine, "Trust in Testimony," 73.

2. Dembour and Haslam, "Silencing Hearings," 151–77; McNamee, "Writing the Rwandan Genocide," 309–30.

3. Gaiba, *Origins of Simultaneous Interpretation*.

4. Morris, "Justice in Jerusalem," 1–10.

5. Berk-Seligson, *Bilingual Courtroom*.

6. Braverman, "Place of Translation in Jerusalem's Criminal Trial Court," 239–77.

7. Interview with the Hon. Michael David QC, Adelaide, April 2008.

8. Interview with Grant Niemann, Adelaide, April 2008.

9. Interviews with the Hon. Michael David QC and Grant Niemann, Adelaide, April 2008.

10. Morris, "Justice in Jerusalem," 4.

11. Morris, "Interlingual Interpreter," 271–91.

12. Polyukhovich Committal, Examination of Rosa Leventhal, 454ff.

13. Berezowsky Committal Transcript, 110–11.

14. Berezowsky Committal Transcript, 112.

15. Berezowsky Committal Transcript, 113.

16. Berezowsky Committal Transcript, 114–15.

17. Berezowsky Committal Transcript, 115.

18. Berezowsky Committal Transcript, 115–16.

19. Berezowsky Committal Transcript, 116–17.

20. Stern, "Investigating War Crimes," 45–49; affidavit, 22 October 1992, produced in the case of *The Queen v. Ivan Timofeyevich Polyukhovich*, Supreme Court of South Australia, SCRRM-92-475, Polyukhovich Materials; *John Hunter Ralston v. Heinrich Wagner*, Magistrates Court, South Australia, 17 August 1992, Wagner Committal Materials, 148ff.

21. Stern, "Investigating War Crimes," 46.

22. Stern, "Investigating War Crimes," 48.

23. Stern, "Investigating War Crimes," 48–49.

24. Stern, "Investigating War Crimes," 49; affidavit, 20–21.

25. Affidavit, Polyukhovich Materials, 12–18.

26. Affidavit, Polyukhovich Materials, 16–18.

27. Wagner Committal Proceedings, 148ff.

28. Wagner Committal Proceedings, 148.

29. Wagner Committal Proceedings, 151–52.

30. Wagner Committal Proceedings, 154.

31. Wagner Committal Proceedings, 158.

32. Stern, "Investigating War Crimes," 49.

7. TELLING STORIES ABOUT THE SHOAH

1. Ricoeur, "Devant l'inacceptable," 3–18.

2. Ricoeur, "Devant l'inacceptable," 7.

3. Evans, *Telling Lies about Hitler*.

4. Evans, *Telling Lies about Hitler*, 16; Voldman, "Le témoinage et l'écriture de l'histoire."

5. Wald, "Foreword," 901–22.

6. Ricoeur, "Devant l'inacceptable," 17; Ricoeur, *Memory, History, Forgetting*.

7. LaCapra, *Representing the Holocaust*; LaCapra, *History and Memory after Auschwitz*.

8. Wolfzettel, "La littérarisation de l'horreur."

9. Demidenko, *Hand That Signed the Paper*.

10. Judt, "What Have We Learned, if Anything?" 16–20.

11. Deleuze and Guattari, *Anti-Oedipus*.

12. Judt, "What Have We Learned, if Anything?" 18.

13. Bartov, Grossmann, and Nolan, *Crimes of War*, xv.

14. Demidenko, *Hand That Signed the Paper*.

15. Jost, Totaro, and Tyshing, *Demidenko File*, vii.

16. Riemer, *Demidenko Debate*.

17. David Myers, "Faction a Minefield for Novelists and Historians," *Courier Mail*, 23 August 1995.

18. Prior, *Demidenko Diary*.

19. Demidenko, *Hand That Signed the Paper*, vi.

20. Prior, *Demidenko Diary*, 117.

21. Demidenko, *Hand That Signed the Paper*, vi.

22. *Sunday*, Channel 9 Television Australia, transcript, "Helen Darville Breaks Her Silence," 8 June 1997, 2.

23. Manne, *Culture of Forgetting*, 34–43.

24. Manne, *Culture of Forgetting*, 38.

25. Jost, Totaro, and Tyshing, *Demidenko File*.

26. Manne, *Culture of Forgetting*, 62–63.

27. Jost, Totaro, and Tyshing, *Demidenko File*, 26.

28. Jost, Totaro, and Tyshing, *Demidenko File*, 36.

29. Christoff, "Forum on the Demidenko Controversy."

30. Riemer, *Demidenko Debate*.

31. "Playing Loose with the Truth in This Work of 'Fiction,'" *Sydney Morning Herald*, 27 June 1995.

32. Richard Glover, "Fantasy Starts in Suburban Cringe," *Sydney Morning Herald*, 22 August 1995.

33. Frank Devine, "Agenda-Setters Brought to Book," *Australian*, 24 July 1995.

34. Manne, *Culture of Forgetting*, 1.

35. Demidenko, *Hand That Signed the Paper*, 2.

36. Devine, "Agenda-Setters Brought to Book."

37. Michael Gawenda, "Criticism Need Not Signify a Conspiracy," *Age*, 9 October 1995.

38. Demidenko, *Hand That Signed the Paper*, 4.

39. Gawenda, "Criticism Need Not Signify a Conspiracy."

40. Demidenko, *Hand That Signed the Paper*, 78.

41. Demidenko, *Hand That Signed the Paper*, 8, 9, 15, 22.

42. Manne, *Culture of Forgetting*, 20–23.

43. Jost, Totaro, and Tyshing, *Demidenko File*, 70.

44. Demidenko, *Hand That Signed the Paper*, 22–25.

45. Manne, *Culture of Forgetting*, 40–43.

46. Manne, *Culture of Forgetting*, 51–52.

47. David Bentley, "Questions Posed on Author's Past," *Courier-Mail*, 19 August 1995.

48. Hatzimanolis, "Multiple Ethnicity Disorder"; Mycak, "Demidenko/Darville."

49. See Philip Mendes, "Jews, Ukrainians, Nazi War Crimes and Literary Hoaxes Down Under," www.join.org.au.

50. Motoko Rich, "A Family Tree of Literary Fakers," *New York Times*, 8 March 2008; Scott Timberg, "James Frey Rises from the Ashes," *Los Angeles Times*, 20 May 2008.

51. Eskin, *Life in Pieces*.

52. Lawrence Van Gelder, "Holocaust Memoir Turns Out to Be Fiction," *New York Times*, 3 March 2008.

53. Subsequent elaborations of the Demidenko/Darville narrative have attempted to attribute at least partial responsibility for the identity charade to her dyslexia and undiagnosed Asperger's syndrome. Jensen and Harvey, "Pain That May Explain Helen Darville," *Sydney Morning Herald*, 9 May 2008.

54. Manne, *Culture of Forgetting*, 52.

55. Gilbert, *Holocaust*.

56. Thomas, *White Hotel*.

57. Young, "Self-Traumatized Perpetrator"; ABC Radio National, "All in the Mind," 29 April 2006.

58. Demidenko, *Hand That Signed the Paper*, 81.

59. Interview with Mark Aarons, Sydney, June 2008.

60. Christoff, "Forum on the Demidenko Controversy," 16.

61. Demidenko, *Hand That Signed the Paper*.

62. "A Harsh Sting in the Tale," *Age*, 9 June 1995.

63. Interview with the Hon. Greg James QC, Sydney, April 2008.

8. LAW, MEMORY, AND JUSTICE

1. Cryer, "Witness Evidence before International Criminal Tribunals," 411–39.

2. Rattner, "Social Science v. the Judicial System," 97–106.

3. Nesselson and Lubet, "Eyewitness Identification in War Crimes Trials," 71–94.

4. Peter Benesh, "Trial Delays May Be Unfair to Nazis: Kirby," *Sydney Morning Herald*, 10 November 1987.

5. Glenn Milne, "Law Council Hits at War Crimes Bill," *Sydney Morning Herald*, 1 December 1988.

6. Helen Pitt, "Archbishop Urges Block on War Crimes Bill," *Sydney Morning Herald*, 5 December 1988.

7. Glenn Milne, "War Crimes Bill Damned as Propaganda," *Sydney Morning Herald*, 13 December 1988.

8. Himka, "War Criminality," 9–24; Troper and Weinfeld, *Old Wounds*.

9. Sopinka and Ukrainian Canadian Committee, *"The Taking of Soviet Evidence."*

10. Cesarani, *Justice Delayed*.

11. Interviews with the Hon. Michael David QC, Lindy Powell QC, and Ian Press, Adelaide, April 2008.

12. Max Uechtritz, "U.S. Report Says Australia a War Criminals' Haven," *The 7:30 Report*, ABC Television (Australia), broadcast 12 June 1999, www.abc.net.au/7.30/stories/s71308.htm.

13. Polyukhovich Trial Materials, Evidence Taken on Commission in Serniki, Ukraine, Pursuant to s. 7 (d) of the *Commonwealth Evidence Act*, no. 475/1992, 3 May 1993.

14. Transcript of Evidence on Commission Taken from Andrey Filipovich Bardas, 10 August 1993, Svetlovodsk, Ukraine; and Transcript of Evidence on Commission with Nikolay Nikitovich Davyborshch, 9 August 1993, Krinichevatka, Ukraine; interviews with the Hon. Michael David QC and Lindy Powell QC, Adelaide, April 2008.

15. Wagenaar, *Identifying Ivan*, 172.

16. Interview with Konrad Kwiet, Sydney, April 2008.

17. Affidavit of Robert William Reid, in DPP v. *Ivan Timofeyevich Polyukhovich*, Supreme Court of South Australia, 8 February 1993, Motion for Dissolution of Stay of Proceedings.

18. Australia, Attorney-General's Department, *Report on the Operation of the War Crimes Act 1945 to June 1994*.

19. Australia, Attorney-General's Department, *Report of the Investigations of War Criminals in Australia*.

20. Fraser, *Law after Auschwitz*, 404–18.

21. "Unfinished Business," editorial, *Review* (Australia/Israel & Jewish Affairs Council) (September 1999).

22. Tom Hyland, "Australia Kills Off War Crimes Unit," *Age*, 20 January 2007.

23. Interview with Mark Aarons, Sydney, June 2008.

24. Natasha Robinson, "Fraser Link to Nazi Backer," *Australian*, 25 August 2005; "Wartime Fascist Cleared by ASIO," *Australian*, 25 August 2005.

25. *O'Donoghue v. Ireland, Zentai v. Republic of Hungary, Williams v. United States of America*, [2008] HCA 14, (23 April 2008); Jane Cadzow, "Is This the Face of a Murderer?" *Good Weekend Supplement, Sydney Morning Herald*, 14 June 2008; Peter Kohn, "Extradition of Zentai to Hungary Stalls," *Australian Jewish News*, 30 November 2009; AAP, "Alleged War Criminal Zentai Granted Bail," *Sydney Morning Herald*, 16 December 2009.

26. Aarons, *War Criminals Welcome*.

27. Debra Jopson, "Danger of Being Seen as War Crimes Haven," *Sydney Morning Herald*, 5 December 2005.

28. Kate McClymont and Selma Milovanovic, "I'm a Prisoner of My Past, Says Dr. Z," *Sydney Morning Herald*, 2 February 2008.

29. *Vasiljkovic v. Commonwealth of Australia*, [2006] HCA 40 (3 August 2006); "War Crimes: Calling Australia Home," *Four Corners*, ABC Television, www.abc .net.au/4corners/stories/s104149.htm.

30. Interview with David Bevan, Adelaide, April 2008.

31. "Holocaust Should Be Taught: Gillard," *Australian*, 5 October 2008.

32. Hirsh, *Law against Genocide*; *R. v. Anthony Sawoniuk*, 2000 WL 473 (Court of Appeal–Criminal Division); *Anthony Sawoniuk v. United Kingdom (2001)* (European Court of Human Rights, 28 May 2001); "Nazi War Criminal Sawoniuk Dies in Jail," *Guardian*, 7 November 2005.

33. *War Crimes Act 1991*, chap. 13, sec. 1, (1).

34. Richardson, "War Crimes Act 1991," 73–87.

35. Weinert, "Cosmopolitan Law—and Cruelty—on Trial," 38–39.

36. Felman, "Theaters of Justice," 201–38.

37. Felman, "Theaters of Justice," 212.

38. Douglas, *Memory of Judgment*, 122.

39. Felman, "Theaters of Justice," 227.

40. Felman, "Theaters of Justice," 230.

41. Simpson, *Law, War and Crime*.

42. Hirsh, *Law against Genocide*, 146.

43. Ricoeur, *Memory, History, Forgetting*.

44. Haberer, "History and Justice," 510.

Bibliography

Aarons, Mark. *Sanctuary: Nazi Fugitives in Australia*. London: Mandarin, 1990.

————. *War Criminals Welcome: Australia, a Sanctuary for Fugitive War Criminals since 1945*. Melbourne: Black, 2001.

Aarons, Mark, and John Loftus. *Ratlines*. London: Mandarin, 1991.

Abella, Irving, and Harold Troper. *None Is Too Many: Canada and the Jews of Europe, 1933–1948*. Toronto: Lester & Orpen Dennys, 1982.

Arad, Yitzhak, Israel Gutman, and Abraham Margaliot. *Documents of the Holocaust: Selected Sources on the Destruction of the Jews of Germany, Austria, Poland and the Soviet Union*. Jerusalem: Yad Vashem, 1981.

Arad, Yitzhak, Shmuel Krakowski, and Shmuel Spector, eds. *The Einsatzgruppen Reports: Selections from the Dispatches of the Nazi Death Squads' Campaign against the Jews, July 1941–January 1943*. New York: Holocaust Library, 1989.

Arendt, Hannah. *Eichmann in Jerusalem: A Report on the Banality of Evil*. New York: Penguin, 1977.

Aster, Howard, and Peter J. Potichnyj. *Jewish-Ukrainian Relations: Two Solitudes*. Rev. ed. Oakville ON: Mosaic Press, 1987.

Ata, Abe (I.) Wade. *Religion and Ethnic Identity: An Australian Study*. Vol. 1. Richmond VIC: Spectrum Publications, 1988.

Australia, Attorney-General's Department. *Report of the Investigations of War Criminals in Australia*. Canberra: Australian Government Publishing Service, 1993.

———. *Report on the Operation of the War Crimes Act 1945*. Canberra: Australian Government Publishing Service, 1990, 1991, 1992, 1993, 1994.

———. *Report on the Operation of the War Crimes Act 1945 to June 1994*. Canberra: Australian Government Publishing Service, 1994.

Australia, Parliament, Senate. *Matters Relating to the War Crimes Amendment Bill*. Report by the Senate Standing Committee on Legal and Constitutional Affairs, February 1988.

———. *Reference War Crimes Amendment Bill 1987*. Senate Standing Committee on Legal and Constitutional Affairs, Public Hearings, 2 and 3 February 1988, vols. 1 and 2. Canberra: Commonwealth of Australia, 1988.

Baranova, Olga. "Nationalism, Anti-Bolshevism or the Will to Survive? Collaboration in Belarus under the Nazi Occupation of 1941–1944." *European Review of History* 15 (2008): 113–28.

Bartal, Israel, and Antony Polonsky. *Galicia: Jews, Poles and Ukrainians, 1772–1918*. Vol. 12 of *Polin: Studies in Polish Jewry*. Oxford: Littman Library of Jewish Civilization, 1999.

Bartov, Omer. *Erased: Vanishing Traces of Jewish Galicia in Present-Day Ukraine*. Princeton: Princeton University Press, 2007.

———. *Germany's War and the Holocaust: Disputed Histories*. Ithaca NY: Cornell University Press, 2003.

———. *Hitler's Army: Soldiers, Nazis, and War in the Third Reich*. New York: Oxford University Press, 1992.

———. *Mirrors of Destruction: War, Genocide, and Modern History*. Oxford: Oxford University Press, 2000.

———. *Murder in Our Midst: The Holocaust, Industrial Killing, and Representation*. New York: Oxford University Press, 1996.

Bartov, Omer, Atina Grossmann, and Mary Nolan, eds. *Crimes of War: Guilt and Denial in the Twentieth Century*. New York: New Press, 2002.

Bauman, Zygmunt. *Modernity and the Holocaust*. Ithaca NY: Cornell University Press, 1991.

Beevor, Antony, and Luba Vinogradova. *A Writer at War: Vasily Grossman and the Red Army, 1941–1945*. London: Pimlico, 2006.

Beim, Aaron, and Gary Alan Fine. "Trust in Testimony: The Institutional Embeddedness of Holocaust Survivor Testimonies." *European Journal of Sociology* 48 (2007): 55–75.

Berenbaum, Michael, ed. *A Mosaic of Victims: Non-Jews Persecuted and Murdered by the Nazis*. London: I. B. Tauris, 1990.

Bergen, Doris L. "The Nazi Concept of 'Volksdeutsche' and the Exacerbation of Anti-Semitism in Eastern Europe, 1939–45." *Journal of Contemporary History* 29 (1994): 569–82.

———. "The *Volksdeutsche* of Eastern Europe and the Collapse of the Nazi Empire, 1944–1945." In *The Impact of Nazism: New Perspectives on the Third Reich and Its Legacy*, ed. Alan E. Steinweis and Daniel E. Rogers, 101–28. Lincoln: University of Nebraska Press, 2003.

Berkhoff, Karel C. *Harvest of Despair: Life and Death in Ukraine under Nazi Rule.* Cambridge MA: Belknap/Harvard University Press, 2004.

———. "The 'Russian' Prisoners of War in Nazi-Ruled Ukraine as Victims of Genocidal Massacre." *Holocaust and Genocide Studies* 15 (2001): 1–32.

Berk-Seligson, Susan. *The Bilingual Courtroom: Court Interpretation in the Judicial Process.* Chicago: University of Chicago Press, 2002.

Bevan, David. *A Case to Answer: The Story of Australia's War Crimes Prosecution.* Kent Town SA: Wakefield Press, 1994.

The Black Book: The Nazi Crime against the Jewish People. New York: Jewish Black Book Committee, 1946.

Bloxham, Donald. *Genocide on Trial: War Crimes Trials and the Formation of Holocaust History and Memory.* New York: Oxford University Press, 2001.

Borzęcki, Jerzy. *The Soviet-Polish Peace of 1921 and the Creation of Interwar Europe.* New Haven: Yale University Press, 2008

Boshyk, Yury, ed. *Ukraine during World War II: History and Its Aftermath.* Edmonton: Canadian Institute of Ukrainian Studies, 1986.

Bourtman, Ilya. "'Blood for Blood, Death for Death': The Soviet Military Tribunal in Krasnodar, 1943." *Holocaust and Genocide Studies* 22 (2008): 246–65.

Brandon, Ray, and Wendy Lower, eds. *The Shoah in Ukraine: History, Testimony, Memorialization.* Bloomington: Indiana University Press, 2008.

Braverman, Irus. "The Place of Translation in Jerusalem's Criminal Trial Court." *New Criminal Law Review* 10 (2007): 239–77.

Brayard, Florent, ed. *Le génocide des Juifs entre procès et histoire 1943–2000.* Brussels: Complexe, 2000.

Browning, Christopher. "German Memory, Judicial Interrogation, and Historical Reconstruction: Writing Perpetrator History from Postwar Testimony." In *Probing the Limits of Representation: Nazism and the "Final Solution,"* ed. Saul Friedlander, 22–36. Cambridge MA: Harvard University Press, 1992.

———. *Ordinary Men: Reserve Police Battalion 101 and the Final Solution in Poland.* New York: HarperCollins, 1992.

Caplan, Leslie. "The Road to the Menzies Inquiry." BA (Honours) Thesis, School of Modern Languages, Macquarie University, Sydney, 1996.

Carr, David. "Narrative Explanation and Its Malcontents." *History & Theory* 47 (2008): 19–30.

"Caught in a Web of Lies: Use of Prior Inconsistent Statements to Impeach Witnesses before the ICTY." *Boston College International and Comparative Law Review* 31 (2008): 277–302.

Cesarani, David. *Justice Delayed: How Britain Became a Refuge for Nazi War Criminals*. London: William Heinemann, 1992.

Christoff, Peter. "Forum on the Demidenko Controversy." *Australia Book Review* 173 (August 1995): 14–20.

Cienciala, A. M. *Katyn: A Crime without Punishment*. New Haven: Yale University Press, 2008.

Le crime méthodique. Moscow: Éditions en Langues Étrangères, 1963.

Cryer, Robert. "Witness Evidence before International Criminal Tribunals." *Law and Practice of International Courts and Tribunals* 3 (2003): 411–39.

Cryer, Robert, and Neil Boyster. *The Tokyo International Military Tribunal: A Reappraisal*. New York: Oxford University Press, 2008.

Dackiw, Borys W. "Denaturalization of Suspected Nazi War Criminals: The Problem of Soviet-Source Evidence." *Columbia Journal of Transnational Law* 24 (1985–86): 365–96.

Deák, István, Jan T. Gross, and Tony Judt, eds. *The Politics of Retribution in Europe: World War II and Its Aftermath*. Princeton: Princeton University Press, 2000.

Dean, Martin. *Collaboration in the Holocaust: Crimes of the Local Police in Belorussia and Ukraine, 1941–1944*. Basingstoke UK: Macmillan, 2000.

———. "The German *Gendarmerie*, the Ukrainian *Schutzmannschaft* and the 'Second Wave' of Jewish Killings in Occupied Ukraine: German Policing at the Local Level in the Zhitomir Region, 1941–1944." *German History* 14 (1996): 168–92.

———. "Soviet Ethnic Germans and the Holocaust in the Reich Commissariat Ukraine, 1941–1944." In *The Shoah in Ukraine*, ed. Ray Brandon and Wendy Lower, 248–71. Bloomington: Indiana University Press, 2008.

———. "Where Did All the Collaborators Go?" *Slavic Review* 64 (2005): 791–98.

"Declaration Concerning Atrocities Made at the Moscow Conference, October, 1943." In *A Decade of American Foreign Policy: Basic Documents, 1941–49*. Comp. at the request of the Senate Committee on Foreign Relations by the Staff of the Committee and the Department of State. Washington DC: U.S. Government Printing Office, 1950.

Deleuze, Gilles, and Félix Guattari. *Anti-Oedipus: Capitalism and Schizophrenia*. Trans. from the French by Robert Hurley, Mark Seem, and Helen R. Lane. Minneapolis: University of Minnesota Press, 1983.

Dembour, Marie-Bénédicte, and Emily Haslam. "Silencing Hearings? Victim-Witnesses at War Crimes Trials?" *European Journal of International Law* 15 (2004): 151–77.

Demidenko, Helen. *The Hand That Signed the Paper*. Sydney: Allen & Unwin, 1994.

Desbois, Patrick. *The Holocaust by Bullets*. New York: Macmillan, 2008.

Deschênes, Hon. Jules. *Commission of Inquiry on War Criminals*, pt. 1: *Public*. Ottawa: Canadian Government Publishing Centre, 1986.

Diner, Dan. "Varieties of Narration: The Holocaust in Historical Memory." In *Beyond the Conceivable: Studies on Germany, Nazism and the Holocaust*, 177–86. Berkeley: University of California Press, 2000.

Dintenfass, Michael. "Truth's Other: Ethics, the History of the Holocaust, and Historiographical Theory after the Linguistic Turn." *History & Theory* 39 (2002): 1–20.

Dobroszycki, Lucjan, and Jeffrey S. Gurock, eds. *The Holocaust in the Soviet Union: Studies and Sources on the Destruction of the Jews in the Nazi-Occupied Territories of the USSR, 1941–1945*. Armonk NY: M. E. Sharpe, 1993.

Documents Relating to the Administration of Occupied Countries in Eastern Europe, no. 1: *The German Exploitation of Polish Forests*. New York: Polish Information Center, n.d.

Douglas, Lawrence. *The Memory of Judgment: Making Law and History in the Trials of the Holocaust*. New Haven: Yale University Press, 2001.

Ehrenburg, Ilya, and Vasily Grossman. *The Complete Black Book of Russian Jewry*. New Brunswick NJ: Transaction, 2007.

Eskin, Blake. *A Life in Pieces: The Making and Unmaking of Binjamin Wilkomirski*. New York: W. W. Norton, 2002.

Evans, Richard J. "History, Memory and the Law: The Historian as Expert Witness." *History & Theory* 41 (2002): 326–45.

———. *Telling Lies about Hitler: The Holocaust, History and the David Irving Trial*. London: Verso, 2002.

Feferman, Kiril. "Soviet Investigation of Nazi Crimes in the USSR: Documenting the Holocaust." *Journal of Genocide Research* 5 (2003): 587–602.

Feldbrugge, F. J. M. "War Crimes in Soviet Criminal Law: A Propos the Lukianoff Case." *Review of Socialist Law* 10 (1984): 291–301.

Felman, Shoshana. "Theaters of Justice: Arendt in Jerusalem, the Eichmann Trial, and the Redefinition of Legal Meaning in the Wake of the Holocaust." *Critical Inquiry* 27 (2001): 201–38.

Finder, Gabriel N., and Alexander V. Prusin. "Collaboration in Eastern Galicia: The Ukrainian Police and the Holocaust." *East European Jewish Affairs* 34 (2004): 95–118.

Frankel, Jonathan, ed. *The Fate of the European Jews, 1939–1945: Continuity or Contingency?* Studies in Contemporary Jewry 8. Oxford: Oxford University Press, 1997.

Fraser, David. *Law after Auschwitz: Towards a Jurisprudence of the Holocaust*. Durham NC: Carolina Academic Press, 2005.

Fredj, Jacques, ed. *The Mass Shooting of Jews in Ukraine 1941–1944: The Holocaust by Bullets.* Paris: Mémorial de la Shoah, 2007.

Friedlander, Saul. *Nazi Germany and the Jews, 1939–1945: The Years of Extermination.* New York: HarperCollins, 2007.

———, ed. *Probing the Limits of Representation: Nazism and the Final Solution.* Cambridge MA: Harvard University Press, 1992.

Gaiba, Francesca. *The Origins of Simultaneous Interpretation: The Nuremberg Trial.* Ottawa: University of Ottawa Press, 1998.

Gerhard, Gesine. "Food and Genocide: Agrarian Politics in the Occupied Territories of the Soviet Union." *Contemporary European History* 18 (2008): 45–65.

Gilbert, Martin. *The Holocaust: A History of the Jews of Europe during the Second World War.* New York: Henry Holt, 1986.

Gilroy, Paul. *Between Camps: Nations, Cultures and the Allure of Race.* London: Penguin, 2001.

Ginsburgs, George. "Laws of War and War Crimes on the Russian Front during World War II: The Soviet View." *Soviet Studies* 11 (1960): 253–85.

———. "Moscow and International Legal Cooperation in the Pursuit of War Criminals." *Review of Central and East European Law* 21 (1995): 1–40.

———. *Moscow's Road to Nuremberg: The Soviet Background to the Trial.* The Hague: Martinus Nijhoff, 1966.

Gitelman, Zvi, ed. *Bitter Legacy: Confronting the Holocaust in the USSR.* Bloomington: Indiana University Press, 1997.

———. "History, Memory, and Politics: The Holocaust in the Soviet Union." *Holocaust and Genocide Studies* 5 (1990): 23–37.

Golbert, Rebecca. "'Neighbors' and the Ukrainian Jewish Experience of the Holocaust." In *The Holocaust in International Perspective*, ed. Dagmar Herzog, 233–52. Vol. 7 of *Lessons and Legacies*. Evanston IL: Northwestern University Press, 2006.

Golczewski, Frank. "Shades of Grey: Reflections on Jewish-Ukrainian and German-Ukrainian Relations in Galicia." In *The Shoah in Ukraine*, ed. Ray Brandon and Wendy Lower, 114–55. Bloomington: Indiana University Press, 2008.

Goldhagen, Daniel Jonah. *Hitler's Willing Executioners: Ordinary Germans and the Holocaust.* New York: Alfred A. Knopf, 1996.

Griffiths, C. J., and T. M. Oettle. "Forensic Odontology in War Graves Exhumations in the Ukraine." *Journal of Forensic Odontostomatology* 11 (1993): 68–69.

Gross, Jan T. *Fear: Anti-Semitism in Poland after Auschwitz.* New York: Random House, 2006.

———. "The Jewish Community in the Soviet-Annexed Territories on the Eve of the Holocaust." In *The Holocaust in the Soviet Union: Studies and Sources on the Destruction of the Jews in the Nazi-Occupied Territories of the USSR, 1941–1945*, ed. Lucjan Dobroszycki and Jeffrey S. Gurock, 155–71. Armonk NY: M. E. Sharpe, 1993.

———. *Neighbors: The Destruction of the Jewish Community in Jedwabne, Poland.* London: Arrow, 2003.

———. *Revolution from Abroad: The Soviet Conquest of Poland's Western Ukraine and Western Belorussia.* Princeton: Princeton University Press, 1988.

Gruner, Wolf. *Jewish Forced Labor under the Nazis: Economic Needs and Racial Aims, 1938–1944.* Cambridge: Cambridge University Press, 2006.

Haberer, Erich. "History and Justice: Paradigms of the Prosecution of Nazi Crimes." *Holocaust and Genocide Studies* 19 (2005): 487–519.

Hamburg Institute for Social Research. *The German Army and Genocide: Crimes against War Prisoners, Jews, and Other Civilians, 1939–1944.* New York: New Press, 1999.

Hanusiak, Michael. *Lest We Forget.* Toronto: Progress, 1976.

Hasian, Marouf A., Jr. *Rhetorical Vectors of Memory in National and International Holocaust Trials.* East Lansing: Michigan State University Press, 2006.

Hatzimanolis, Efi. "Multiple Ethnicity Disorder: Demidenko and the Cult of Ethnicity." In *Women Writing: Views and Prospects, 1975–1995.* Canberra: National Library of Australia, 1995, www.nla.gov.au/events/ww.html.

Headland, Ronald. *Messages of Murder: A Study of the Reports of the Einsatzgruppen of the Security Police and the Security Service, 1941–1943.* London: Associated University Presses, 1992.

Heberer, Patricia, and Jürgen Matthäus, eds. *Atrocities on Trial: Historical Perspectives on the Politics of Prosecuting War Crimes.* Lincoln: University of Nebraska Press, 2008.

———. "Introduction: War Crimes Trials and the Historian." In *Atrocities on Trial: Historical Perspectives on the Politics of Prosecuting War Crimes*, ed. Patricia Heberer and Jürgen Matthäus. Lincoln: University of Nebraska Press, 2008.

Heer, Hannes, Walter Manoschek, Alexander Pollak, and Ruth Wodak, eds. *The Discursive Construction of History: Remembering the Wehrmacht's War of Annihilation.* New York: Palgrave Macmillan, 2008.

Henderson, Gerard. *Mr. Santamaria and the Bishops.* Sydney: Hale & Ironmonger, 1983.

Herbert, Ulrich. *National Socialist Extermination Policies: Contemporary German Perspectives and Controversies.* Oxford: Berghan Books, 2000.

Hetherington, Sir Thomas, and William Chalmers. *Report of the War Crimes Inquiry.* London: HMSO, 1989.

Hilberg, Raul. *The Destruction of the European Jews.* Rev. and definitive ed. 3 vols. New York: Holmes & Meier, 1985.

―――. *Perpetrators, Victims, Bystanders: The Jewish Catastrophe, 1933–1945.* New York: HarperPerennial, 1993.

Himka, John-Paul. "Ukrainian Collaboration in the Extermination of the Jews during the Second World War: Sorting Out the Long-Term and Conjunctural Factors." In *The Fate of the European Jews, 1939–1945: Continuity or Contingency?* ed. Jonathan Frankel, 170–89. Vol. 13 of *Studies in Contemporary Jewry*. Oxford: Oxford University Press and the Institute of Contemporary Jewry, 1997.

―――. "War Criminality: A Blank Spot in the Collective Memory of the Ukrainian Diaspora." *spacesofidentity* 5 (2005): 9–24.

Hirsch, Francine. "The Soviets at Nuremberg: International Law, Propaganda, and the Making of the Postwar Order." *American Historical Review* 113 (2008): 701–30.

Hirsh, David. *Law against Genocide: Cosmopolitan Trials.* London: Glasshouse, 2003.

―――. "The Trial of Andrei Sawoniuk: Holocaust Testimony under Cross-Examination." *Social & Legal Studies* 10 (2001): 529–45.

History of the United Nations War Crimes Commission and the Development of the Laws of War. 1948. Reprint, Buffalo: William S. Hein, 2006.

History Teaches a Lesson. Kiev: Politvidav Ukraini, 1986.

Hrytsenko, Oleksandr. "Imagining the Community: Perspectives on Ukraine's Ethno-cultural Diversity." *Nationalities Papers* 36 (2008): 197–222.

Hunczak, Taras. *On the Horns of a Dilemma: The Story of the Ukrainian Division Halychyna.* Lanham MD: University Press of America, 2000.

Hunczak, Taras, and Dmytro Shtohryn, eds. *Ukraine: The Challenges of World War II.* Lanham MD: University Press of America, 2003.

Jones, Jeffrey W. "'Every Family Has Its Freak': Perceptions of Collaboration in Occupied Soviet Russia, 1943–1948." *Slavic Review* 64 (2005): 747–70.

Jost, John, Gianna Totaro, and Christine Tyshing, eds. *The Demidenko File.* Ringwood VIC: Penguin, 1996.

Judt, Tony. "What Have We Learned, if Anything?" *New York Review of Books* 55, no. 7 (1 May 2008): 16–20.

Kamenetsky, Ihor. *Hitler's Occupation of Ukraine (1941–1944): A Study of Totalitarian Imperialism.* Milwaukee WI: Marquette University Press, 1956.

Karlsson, Klas-Göran, and Ulf Zander, eds. *Echoes of the Holocaust: Historical Cultures in Contemporary Europe.* Lund: Nordic Academic Press, 2003.

Klee, Ernst, Willi Dressen, and Volker Riess, eds. *"The Good Old Days": The Holocaust as Seen by Its Perpetrators and Bystanders.* New York: Free Press, 1991.

Kleinberg, Ethan. "Haunting History: Deconstruction and the Spirit of Revision." *History & Theory* 46 (2007): 113–43.

Kochavi, Arieh J. "The Moscow Declaration, the Kharkov Trial and the Question of a Policy on Major War Criminals in the Second World War." *History* 76 (1991): 401–17.

———. *Prelude to Nuremberg: Allied War Crimes Policy and the Question of Punishment.* Chapel Hill: University of North Carolina Press, 1998.

Kordan, Bohdan S. *Canada and the Ukrainian Question: 1935–1945.* Montreal: McGill-Queen's University Press, 2001.

Koscharsky, Halyna, ed. *First Wave Immigrants: The First Fifty Years of Ukrainian Settlement in Australia.* Huntington NY: Nova Science Publishers, 1998.

Kosyk, Wolodymyr. *L'Allemagne national-socialiste et l'Ukraine.* Paris: Publications de l'Est Européen, 1986.

Kruglov, Alexander. "Jewish Losses in Ukraine, 1941–1944." In *The Shoah in Ukraine*, ed. Ray Brandon and Wendy Lower, 272–90. Bloomington: Indiana University Press, 2008.

LaCapra, Dominick. *History and Memory after Auschwitz.* Ithaca NY: Cornell University Press, 1998.

———. *Representing the Holocaust: History, Theory, Trauma.* Ithaca NY: Cornell University Press, 1994.

Landau, Asher Felix, ed. *The Demjanjuk Trial.* Tel Aviv: Israel Bar Publishing House, 1991.

Landsman, Stephan. *Crimes of the Holocaust: The Law Confronts Hard Cases.* Philadelphia: University of Pennsylvania Press, 2005.

Langer, Lawrence L. *Admitting the Holocaust.* Oxford: Oxford University Press, 1995.

———. *Holocaust Testimonies: The Ruins of Memory.* New Haven: Yale University Press, 1991.

Langerbein, Helmut. *Hitler's Death Squads: The Logic of Mass Murder.* College Station: Texas A&M University Press, 2004.

Lawriwsky, Michael. "The Role of Ukrainian Churches in the Ukrainian Community in Australia." In *Religion and Ethnic Identity: An Australian Study*, ed. Abe Wade Ata, 1:72–89. Richmond VIC: Spectrum, 1988.

Lipstadt, Deborah E. *History on Trial: My Day in Court with a Holocaust Denier.* New York: Harper Perennial, 2005.

Littman, Sol. *Pure Soldiers or Sinister Legion: The Ukrainian 14th Waffen–SS Division.* Montreal: Black Rose, 2003.

Lower, Wendy. "'Anticipatory Obedience' and the Nazi Implementation of the Holocaust in the Ukraine: A Case Study of Central and Peripheral Forces in the Generalbezirk Zhytomyr, 1941–1944." *Holocaust and Genocide Studies* 16 (2002): 1–22.

———. *Nazi Empire-Building and the Holocaust in Ukraine.* Chapel Hill: University of North Carolina Press, 2005.

———. "'On Him Rests the Weight of the Administration': Nazi Civilian Rulers and the Holocaust in Zhytomyr." In *The Shoah in Ukraine*, ed. Ray Brandon and Wendy Lower, 224–47. Bloomington: Indiana University Press, 2008.

Luciuk, Lubomyr. *Searching for a Place: Ukrainian Displaced Persons, Canada and the Migration of Memory*. Toronto: University of Toronto Press, 2000.

———. "Unintended Consequences in Refugee Resettlement: Post-War Ukrainian Immigration to Canada." *International Migration Review* 20 (1986): 467–82.

Lumans, Valdis O. *Himmler's Auxiliaries: The Volksdeutsche Mittelstelle and the German National Minorities of Europe, 1933–1945*. Chapel Hill: University of North Carolina Press, 1993.

———. "A Reassessment of *Volksdeutsche* and Jews in the Volhynia-Galicia-Narew Resettlement." In *The Impact of Nazism: New Perspectives on the Third Reich and Its Legacy*, ed. Alan E. Steinweis and Daniel E. Rogers, 81–100. Lincoln: University of Nebraska Press, 2003.

Lupul, Manoly R. "Ukrainian-Jewish Relations in Canada." In *Ukrainian-Jewish Relations in Historical Perspective*, ed. Peter J. Potichnyj and Howard Aster, 461–68. Edmonton: Canadian Institute of Ukrainian Studies, 1988.

Manne, Robert. *The Culture of Forgetting: Helen Demidenko and the Holocaust*. Melbourne: Text, 1996.

———. *The Petrov Affair: Politics and Espionage*. Sydney: Pergamon, 1987.

Margolian, Howard. *Unauthorized Entry: The Truth about Nazi War Criminals in Canada, 1946–1956*. Toronto: University of Toronto Press, 2000.

Marrus, Michael R. "History and the Holocaust in the Courtroom." In *The Holocaust and Justice*, ed. Ronald Smelser, 215–39. Vol. 5 of *Lessons and Legacies*. Evanston IL: Northwestern University Press, 2002.

———. *The Holocaust in History*. 1987. Reprint, New York: Penguin, 1993.

Martin, Jean I. *Community and Identity: Refugee Groups in Adelaide*. Canberra: Australian National University Press, 1972.

Matas, David, with Susan Charendoff. *Justice Delayed: Nazi War Criminals in Canada*. Toronto: Summerhill Press, 1987.

Matthäus, Jürgen. "Controlled Escalation: Himmler's Men in the Summer of 1941 and the Holocaust in the Occupied Soviet Territories." *Holocaust and Genocide Studies* 21 (2007): 218–42.

———. "The Lessons of Leipzig: Punishing German War Criminals after the First World War." In *Atrocities on Trial: Historical Perspectives on the Politics of Prosecuting War Crimes*, ed. Patricia Heberer and Jürgen Matthäus, 3–23. Lincoln: University of Nebraska Press, 2008.

———. "What About the 'Ordinary Men'? The German Order Police and the Holocaust in the Occupied Soviet Union." *Holocaust and Genocide Studies* 10 (1996): 134–50.

Mazower, Mark. *Dark Continent: Europe's Twentieth Century*. New York: Penguin, 1999.

McCormack, Timothy L. H., and Gerry J. Simpson, eds. *The Law of War Crimes: National and International Approaches*. The Hague: Kluwer Law International, 1997.

McNamee, Eugene. "Writing the Rwandan Genocide: The Justice and Politics of Witnessing after the Event." *Law & Critique* 18 (2007): 309–30.

Megargee, Geoffrey. *Barbarossa, 1941: Hitler's War of Annihilation*. Stroud UK: Tempus, 2007.

Melamed, Vladimir. "Organized and Unsolicited Collaboration in the Holocaust: The Multifaceted Ukrainian Context." *East European Jewish Affairs* 37 (2007): 217–48.

Mendelsohn, Daniel. *The Lost: A Search for Six of Six Million*. New York: HarperCollins, 2006.

Menzies, Andrew. *Review of Material Relating to the Entry of Suspected War Criminals into Australia*. Attorney-General's Department. Canberra: Australian Government Publishing Service, 1987.

Mildt, Dirk Welmoed de. *In the Name of the People: Perpetrators of Genocide in the Reflection of Their Post-War Prosecution in West Germany — "Euthanasia" and "Aktion Reinhard" Trial Cases*. Leiden: Brill, 1996.

Molchanov, Vladimir. *There Shall Be Retribution: Nazi War Criminals and Their Protectors*. Moscow: Progress, 1984.

Molotov, Viacheslav. *Note Concerning the Monstrous Atrocities and Acts of Violence Perpetrated by the German Fascist Invaders in the Occupied Soviet Areas and the Responsibility of the German Government and Military Command for These Crimes*. Moscow: Foreign Language Publishing House, 1942.

Morgan, Ed. "New Evidence: The Aesthetics of International Law." *Leiden Journal of International Law* 18 (2005): 163–77.

Morris, Ruth. "The Interlingual Interpreter — Cypher or Intelligent Participant?" *International Journal for the Semiotics of Law* 6 (1993): 271–91.

———. "Justice in Jerusalem: Interpreting in Israeli Legal Proceedings." *Meta* 43 (1998): 1–12.

Murray, Robert. *The Split: Australian Labor in the Fifties*. Melbourne: Cheshire, 1972.

Mycak, Sonia. "Australian and Canadian Community Culture and Community Life: Can We Learn from Each Other's Mistakes?" In *First Wave Emigrants: The First Fifty Years of Ukrainian Settlement in Australia*, ed. Halyna Koscharsky, 31–48. Huntington NY: Nova Science Publishers, 2000.

———. "Demidenko/Darville: A Ukrainian-Australian Point of View." *Australian Literary Studies* 21 (2004): 111–33.

Naimark, Norman M. *Fires of Hatred: Ethnic Cleansing in Twentieth-Century Europe*. Cambridge MA: Harvard University Press, 2001.

Nazi Crimes in Ukraine, 1941–1944: Documents and Materials. Kiev: Naukova Dumka, 1987.

Nesselson, Debra, and Steven Lubet. "Eyewitness Identification in War Crimes Trials." *Cardozo Law Review* 2 (1980–81): 71–94.

New Soviet Documents on Nazi Atrocities. London: Hutchinson, 1943.

Noakes, Jeremy. "The Development of Nazi Policy towards the German-Jewish 'Mischlinge' 1933–1945." *Leo Baeck Institute Yearbook* 34 (1989): 291–354.

Öhman, Johan. "From Famine to Forgotten Holocaust." In *Echoes of the Holocaust: Historical Cultures in Contemporary Europe*, ed. Klas-Göran Karlsson and Ulf Zander, 223–49. Lund: Nordic Academic Press, 2003.

Penter, Tanja. "Collaboration on Trial: New Source Material on Soviet Postwar Trials against Collaborators." *Slavic Review* 64 (2005): 782–90.

The People's Verdict: A Full Report of the Proceedings at the Krasnodar and Kharkov German Atrocity Trials. London: Hutchinson, 1944.

Piotrowski, Tadeusz. *Poland's Holocaust: Ethnic Strife, Collaboration with Occupying Forces and Genocide in the Second Republic, 1918–1947*. Jefferson NC: McFarland, 2007.

Pohl, Dieter. "The Murder of Ukraine's Jews under German Military Administration and in the Reich Commissariat Ukraine." In *The Shoah in Ukraine*, ed. Ray Brandon and Wendy Lower, 23–76. Bloomington: Indiana University Press, 2008.

Polonsky, Antony. *Jews in the Polish Borderlands: Focusing on Jews in the Borderlands of Former Poland-Lithuania*. Vol. 14 of *Polin: Studies in Polish Jewry*. Oxford: Littman Library of Jewish Civilization, 2001.

Polonsky, Antony, and Joanna Michlic, eds. *The Neighbors Respond: The Controversy over the Jedwabne Massacre in Poland*. Princeton: Princeton University Press, 2004.

Potichnyj, Peter J., and Howard Aster, eds. *Ukrainian-Jewish Relations in Historical Perspective*. Edmonton: Canadian Institute of Ukrainian Studies, 1988.

Prior, Natalie Jane. *The Demidenko Diary: Who Is She Really?* Port Melbourne VIC: Mandarin, 1996.

Prusin, Alexander Victor. "A Community of Violence: The SiPo/SD and Its Role in the Nazi Terror System in Generalbezirk Kiew." *Holocaust and Genocide Studies* 21 (2007): 1–30.

———. "'Fascist Criminals to the Gallows!': The Holocaust and Soviet War Crimes Trials, December 1945–February 1946." *Holocaust and Genocide Studies* 17 (2003): 1–30.

———. *Nationalizing a Borderland: War, Ethnicity, and Anti-Jewish Violence in East Galicia, 1914–1920*. Tuscaloosa: University of Alabama Press, 2005.

Punishment for War Crimes: The Inter-Allied Declaration Signed at St. James' Palace, London, on 13th January, 1942 and Relative Documents. London: Inter-Allied Information Committee/HMSO, 1942.

Rattner, Arye. "Social Science v. the Judicial System: The Impact of Accumulated Knowledge of Eyewitness Identification on Criminal Procedures." *International Journal of the Sociology of Law* 23 (1995): 97–106.

Redlich, Shimon. *Together and Apart in Brezezany: Poles, Jews, and Ukrainians, 1919–1945.* Bloomington: Indiana University Press, 2002.

Report of the Investigations of War Criminals in Australia. Canberra: Australian Government Publishing Service, 1993.

Report of the Royal Commission on Espionage. Sydney: Government Printer of New South Wales, 1995.

Richardson, A. T. "War Crimes Act 1991." *Modern Law Review* 55 (1992): 73–87.

Ricoeur, Paul. "Devant l'inacceptable: Le juge, l'historien, l'écrivain." *Philosophie* 67 (2000): 3–18.

———. *Memory, History, Forgetting.* Trans. Kathleen Blamey and David Pellauer. Chicago: University of Chicago Press, 2004.

Rieber, Alfred J. "Civil Wars in the Soviet Union." *Kritika: Explorations in Russia and Eurasian History* 4 (2003): 129–62.

Riemer, Andrew. *The Demidenko Debate.* Sydney: Allen & Unwin, 1996.

Rousso, Henry. *The Haunting Past: History, Memory and Justice in Contemporary France.* Trans. Ralph Schoolcraft. Philadelphia: University of Pennsylvania Press, 2002.

Rubenstein, Joshua, and Ilya Altman, eds. *The Unknown Black Book: The Holocaust in the German-Occupied Soviet Union.* Bloomington: Indiana University Press, 2008.

Rückerl, Adalbert. *The Investigation of Nazi Crimes, 1945–1978: A Documentation.* Heidelberg: C. F. Müller, 1979.

Ruding, Anders. "Historical Representation of the Wartime Accounts of the Activities of the OUN-UPA (Organization of Ukrainian Nationalist-Ukrainian Insurgent Army)." *East European Jewish Affairs* 36 (2006): 163–89.

Rutland, Suzanne D. *Edge of the Diaspora: Two Centuries of Jewish Settlement in Australia.* Rev. ed. Sydney: Brandl & Schlesinger, 1997.

———. *The Jews in Australia.* Melbourne: Cambridge University Press, 2005.

Rutland, Suzanne D., and Sophie Caplan. *With One Voice: A History of the New South Wales Jewish Board of Deputies.* Sydney: Australian Jewish Historical Society, 1998.

Sabrin, B. F., ed. *Alliance for Murder: The Nazi-Ukrainian Nationalist Partnership in Genocide.* New York: SARPEDON, 1991.

Satzewich, Vic. *The Ukrainian Diaspora*. London: Taylor & Francis, 2002.

Schmortte, Jan. "Attitudes towards German Immigration in South Australia in the Post–Second World War Period, 1947–1960." *Australian Journal of Politics and History* 51 (2005): 530–44.

"Secret Additional Protocol." In *Nazi-Soviet Relations, 1939–41: Documents from the Archives of the German Foreign Office*, ed. Raymond James Sontag and James Stuart Beddie. Washington DC: Department of State, 1948.

Sharfman, Glenn. "The Jewish Community's Reactions to the John Demjanjuk Trials." *Historian* 63 (2000): 17–34.

———. "The Quest for Justice: The Reaction of the Ukrainian-American Community to the John Demjanjuk Trials." *Journal of Genocide Research* 2 (2000): 65–87.

Shekhovtsov, Anton. "By Cross and Sword: 'Clerical Fascism' in Interwar Western Ukraine." *Totalitarian Movements and Political Religions* 8 (2007): 271–85.

Shepherd, Ben. *War in the Wild East: The German Army and Soviet Partisans*. Cambridge MA: Harvard University Press, 2004.

Simpson, Gerry. *Law, War and Crime: War Crimes Trials and the Reinvention of International Law*. Cambridge: Polity, 2007.

Skinner, Mark, and Jon Sterenberg. "Turf Wars: Authority and Responsibility for the Investigation of Mass Graves." *Forensic Science International* 151 (2005): 221–32.

Smelser, Ronald, ed. *The Holocaust and Justice*. Vol. 5 of *Lessons and Legacies*. Evanston IL: Northwestern University Press, 2002.

Smelser, Ronald, and Edward J. Davies II. *The Myth of the Eastern Front: The Nazi-Soviet War in American Popular Culture*. Cambridge: Cambridge University Press, 2008.

Snyder, Timothy. *The Reconstruction of Nations: Poland, Ukraine, Lithuania, Belarus, 1569–1999*. New Haven: Yale University Press, 2003.

Solonari, Vladimir. "Patterns of Violence: The Local Population and the Mass Murder of Jews in Bessarabia and Northern Bukovina, July–August 1941." *Kritika: Explorations in Russian and Eurasian History* 8 (2007): 749–87.

Sopinka, John, QC, and Ukrainian Canadian Committee. *"The Taking of Soviet Evidence in the Course of Any Proceedings under Any Circumstances . . . Would Be in Violation of the Principles of Fundamental Justice."* Toronto: Justinian Press, 1986.

Sorokina, Marina. "People and Procedures: Toward a History of the Investigation of Nazi Crimes in the USSR." *Kritika: Explorations in Russian and Eurasian History* 6 (2005): 797–831.

Soviet Government Statements on Nazi Atrocities. London: Hutchinson, 1946.

Spector, Shmuel. "The Holocaust of Ukrainian Jews." In *Bitter Legacy: Confronting the Holocaust in the USSR*, ed. Zvi Gitelman, 43–50. Bloomington: Indiana University Press, 1997.

———. *The Holocaust of Volhynian Jews, 1941–1944*. Jerusalem: Yad Vashem, 1990.

Steinberg, Jonathan. "The Third Reich Reflected: German Civil Administration in the Occupied Soviet Union, 1941–4." *English Historical Review* 110 (1991): 620–51.

Steinweis, Alan, and Daniel L. Rogers, eds. *The Impact of Nazism: New Perspectives on the Third Reich and Its Legacy*. Lincoln: University of Nebraska Press, 2003.

Stern, Ludmilla. "Investigating War Crimes: A Language Problem." *Sydney Papers* 7 (1995): 45–49.

Thomas, D. M. *The White Hotel*. New York: Viking, 1981.

Tolstoy, Nikolai. *Trial and Error: Canada's Commission of Inquiry on War Criminals and the Soviets*. Toronto: Justinian Press, 1986.

The Trial of Adolf Eichmann: Record of Proceedings in the District Court of Jerusalem. 9 vols. Jerusalem: State of Israel, Ministry of Justice, 1992.

"The Trial of the Case of the Atrocities Committed by the German Fascist Invaders in Kharkov and the Kharkov Region." In *The People's Verdict: A Full Report of the Proceedings at the Krasnodar and Kharkov German Atrocity Trials*, 1–83. London: Hutchinson, 1944.

Trials of War Criminals before the Nuernberg Military Tribunals, vol. 4: *"The Einsatzgruppen Case"; "The RuSHA Case."* Washington DC: U.S. Government Printing Office, 1950.

Triggs, Gillian. "Australia's War Crimes Trials: All Pity Choked." In *The Law of War Crimes*, ed. Timothy L. H. McCormack and Gerry J. Simpson, 123–49. The Hague: Kluwer Law International, 1997.

Troper, Harold, and Morton Weinfeld. *Old Wounds: Jews, Ukrainians and the Hunt for Nazi War Criminals in Canada*. Markham ON: Viking, 1988.

Ukrainian People Accuse . . . Lviv: Kamenyar Publishers, 1987.

"Verdict." In *The People's Verdict: A Full Report of the Proceedings at the Krasnodar and Kharkov German Atrocity Trials*, 39–44. London: Hutchinson, 1944.

Voldman, Danièle. "Le témoinage et l'écriture de l'histoire." In *Passeports pour le vrai/le faux*, ed. Françoise Reumaux, 147–62. Paris: Kimé, 2005.

Wagenaar, Willem A. *Identifying Ivan: A Case Study in Legal Psychology*. Hemel-Hempstead: Harvester-Wheatsheaf, 1988.

Wald, Patricia. "Foreword: War Tales and War Trials." *Michigan Law Review* 106 (2008): 901–22.

Weinert, Matthew S. "Cosmopolitan Law—and Cruelty—on Trial." *Human Rights and Human Welfare* 4 (2004): 33–43.

Westermann, Edward. *Hitler's Police Battalions: Enforcing Racial War in the East.* Lawrence: University Press of Kansas, 2005.

Wette, Wolfram. *The Wehrmacht: History, Myth, Reality.* Cambridge MA: Harvard University Press, 2006.

Whitlam, Nicholas, and John Stubbs. *Nest of Traitors: The Petrov Affair.* 2nd ed. St Lucia: University of Queensland Press, 1985.

Wildt, Michael. "Des vérités qui diffèrent: Historiens et procureurs face aux crimes Nazis." In *Le Génocide des Juifs entre procès et histoire, 1943–2000,* ed. Florent Brayard, 245–60. Brussels: Éditions Complexe, 2000.

Williams, George. "The Suppression of Communism by Force of Law: Australia in the Early 1950s." *Australian Journal of Politics and History* 42 (2008): 220–40.

Wolczuk, Kataryna, and Galina Yemelianova. "When the West Meets the East: Exploring Ethnic Diversity in Eastern Europe." *Nationalities Papers* 36 (2008): 177–95.

Wolfzettel, Friedrich. "La littérarisation de l'horreur." In *Écrire après Auschwitz: Mémoires croisées France-Allemagne,* ed. Karsten Garscha, Bruno Gelas, and Jean-Pierre Martin, 73–94. Lyon: Presses Universitaires de Lyon, 2006.

Wright, Richard. "Investigating War Crimes: The Archaeological Evidence." *Sydney Papers* 7 (1995): 39–44.

Yekelchyk, Serhy. "The Civic Duty to Hate: Soviet Citizenship as Political Practice and Civic Emotion (Kiev, 1943–1953)." *Kritika: Explorations in Russian and Eurasian History* 7 (2006): 529–56.

Young, Allan. "The Self-Traumatized Perpetrator as a 'Transient Mental Illness.'" *L'Évolution Psychiatrique* 67 (2002): 630–50.

Zabarko, Boris. *Holocaust in the Ukraine.* Trans. Marina Guba. London: Vallentine Mitchell, 2005.

Zumbakis, S. Paul. *Soviet Evidence in North American Courts.* Chicago: Americans for Due Process, 1986.

Index

Page numbers in italics refer to
illustrations.

Aaron, Moishe, 3
Aarons, Mark, 58–61, 65, 66, 68, 78,
    99, 293, 300, 309, 318
Adelaide Advertiser, 99
Afghanistan, 76, 279, 309
Albert, Laura, 288
Arendt, Hannah, 194, 196, 197, 200,
    312, 314, 315, 316
Argus, 61
Auschwitz, 7
Australia: Aboriginal populations in,
    255, 259, 266, 311; anti-Semitism
    in, 54, 55, 56, 64–65, 67; ethnic
    politics of, 64–65; and historical
    understanding of Holocaust,
    94–145, 198, 199, 254–55, 266,
    268, 272, 280, 311, 318; postwar
    immigrant policies of, 51–58;
Soviet espionage ring in, 53;
    Ukrainian migrant communities
    in, 62, 63; war crimes trials in,
    102, 103–4, 108–9, 311, 317; and
    war criminals, 50–58, 71, 308. *See
    also* New South Wales
The Australian, 189
Australian and New Zealand Army
    Corps (ANZAC), 266
Australian Broadcasting Corporation
    (ABC), 59, 60, 65, 66, 76, 88, 99,
    271
Australian Federation of Ukrainian
    Organisations, 70, 81
Australian Literature Society, 271,
    273
Australian Security Intelligence
    Organisation (ASIO), 203, 308
Australian War Crimes Act:
    amendments to, 7–8, 10, 72–73,
    74, 94, 197, 210, 309; events and

Australian War Crimes Act (*cont.*) debates leading to, 63–89, 104–5, 298; and Japanese war criminals, 72; jurisdiction of, 73–74, 199–200; offenses included in, xv, 5, 90–93, 109, 199–200; passage of, 72–73, 302, 318; principles of, 90–93, 104, 267–68; provisions of, 89–93, 199, 260, 285; retrospectivity of, 73, 75; and Soviet extradition requests, 26, 56, 71, 74, 76–77, 79–80; Special Investigations Unit and, 75, 79, 86, 94, 99, 113, 114–15, 122, 131, 146, 148, 156, *157*, 165, 166, 170, 190, 206, 297, 307, 310, 318, 319; structure of, 15–16, 90–93

Background Briefing, 60
Baltic Council of Australia, 78, 79
Bardas, Andrey Filipovich, 238–39, 240, 304
Bartov, Omer, 12, 19
Barwick, Garfield, 56–58, 62, 67, 69, 70, 103, 268, 295, 299, 318
Bauman, Zygmunt, 198
Beim, Aaron, 242
Belarus, 7
Berezovatka. *See* Israylovka
Berezowsky, Mikolay, *147*, *157*; alibi for, 152–53, 154, 161–62, 167–68, 169, 173, 190, 193; arrest of, 6, 146; case of, xiii, xv, 6, 11, 89, 93, 146–91, 302; committal hearing of, 107, 108, 148, 151, 158, 250–54; escape of, to Australia, 29; as head of Schutzmannschaft unit, 20, 152–56, 158–61, 189, 256, 313; war crimes committed by, 6, 15, 16, 26, 111, 152–53, 242

Bergen, Doris, 201
Bevan, David, 94–95
Blewitt, Graham, 304
Bloxham, Donald, 102, 316
Bondarev, Viktor Nikolayevich, 113
Bone, Pamela, 295
Bowen, Lionel, 71, 72–73, 75
Brownhill, David, 89
Browning, Christopher, 19, 214, 215, 317
Bulanov (accomplice), 40

Cambodia, 76, 309
Canada: Criminal Code of, 7, 105; Royal Commission of Inquiry of, 60, 62, 68, 81, 83, 84; Supreme Court of, 7; Ukrainian immigrant populations in, 62; and war criminals, 7, 26, 61, 105, 308, 317
Caplan, Leslie, 61
Captive Nations, 88, 89, 103, 114, 298
Carrick, John, 67
Carswell, Robert, 160
Castro, Brian, 272
Chifley, Ben, 50, 51, 57, 66, 67
Chipp, Don, 65
Christie, Douglas, 105, 110, 112
Christoff, Peter, 294
Churchill, Winston, 29
Cold War, xiii–xiv, 26–27, 43–49, 51–52, 89, 318
Complete Black Book of Russian Jewry (Ehrenberg and Grossman), 37
concentration camps, 56
Cox, Brian, 9, 100, 134, 139, 141, 142, 144, 304
Crichton-Browne, Noel, 89
Croatia, 309

Czechoslovakia, 114

Dale, Helen, 295
Darville, Helen: agenda of, 272,
    273, 274–75, 277–87, 301, 310,
    314; counter-narrative of, 10, 82,
    263–96; fraudulent identity of,
    287–96; *The Hand That Signed
    the Paper*, 10, 265–96, 310
Daviborshch, Nikolay Nikitovich:
    deliveries by, 2, 3; and
    transportation of *Mischlinge*
    children, 198, 202–3, 205–18; as
    witness, 3, 198, 202, 204–18, 304
David, Michael: and Berezowsky
    case, 163, 164, 172, 173, 174,
    176, 177, 180, 181, 182, 184, 185;
    and Polyukhovich case, 110, 116,
    121, 125, 135, 136–37, 140; and
    Wagner case, 217, 227, 228, 230,
    235, 237, 254, 259
Dean, Martin, 23, 39, 44, 122,
    124, 148, 152, 161, 177–87, 190,
    206–8, 317
Defonseca, Misha, 288
De Gobineau, Arthur, 286
Demidenko, Helen. *See* Darville,
    Helen
Demjanjuk, John, 103, 104, 244,
    258, 304
Deschênes, Jules, 60, 62, 68, 81, 83
Devine, Frank, 278
Dorge, Captain (regional
    commander), 166, 167, 168, 175,
    177
Douglas, Lawrence, 102, 103, 104,
    315
Dowrick, Stephanie, 272

Edwardson, David, 110, 213, 216

Ehrenberg, Ilya: *Complete Black
    Book of Russian Jewry*, 37
Eichmann, Adolf, 54, 59, 103, 104,
    149, 194, 196–98, 244, 258, 312,
    314–16
Einsatzgruppen, 1, 19
Endrey, Anthony, 82
Executive Council of Australian
    Jewry (ECAJ), 53, 61, 62, 63, 66,
    78, 79, 89

Feferman, Kiril, 36, 37
Feldbrugge, F. J. M., 43
Felman, Shoshana, 314, 315, 316
Fel'shtayn, Yarina, 2
fiction, 10, 12–13
Fine, Gary Alan, 242
Finta, Imre, 7, 105, 149, 258, 308,
    317
Four Corners, 60
France, 101
Franz, Tatyana Nicolayevna, 113
Fraser, Malcolm, 308
Frey, James, 288
Friedlander, Saul, 192, 195

Geneva Convention, 41
Gering, Ernst, 2, 202, 220, 221, 234
German-Soviet Nonaggression Pact,
    18
Gibner, Aleksandr, 222
Gilbert, Martin: *The Holocaust*, 291
Ginsburgs, George, 35, 36, 39
Gnivan, 5–6, 14, 20, 111, 146–91, 317
Goldhagen, Daniel, 19
Goncharenko, Lieutenant (KGB), 222
Greenwood, Robert, 79, 114, 190,
    307
Grossman, Vasily: *Complete Black
    Book of Russian Jewry*, 37

Gurevich, Klavdiya, 2

Haberer, Erich, 149, 150, 151, 179, 191, 319
Hague Convention, 40–41
Hamer, David, 88
Handley, Ken, 298
The Hand That Signed the Paper (Demidenko), 10, 265–96, 310
Hansard, 278
Hasian, Marouf A., Jr., 102, 103, 105, 110, 111
Hawke, R. J. L., 61, 68, 71, 74, 75, 86, 87, 89, 278, 281, 292, 293, 295, 309, 310, 318
Heberer, Patricia, 101, 214, 215
Henderson, Gerard, 276, 283
Henke, Josek, 113
Hering, Ernst. *See* Gering, Ernst
Heseltine, Harry, 274
Hilberg, Raul, 59, 106, 115, 129, 130, 135, 138, 139, 140, 317
Hirsh, David, 311, 312, 313, 318
history, 9–10, 12, 101–2, 142, 151, 192–93
Hitler, Adolf, 29
Holocaust: as crime against humanity, 62; denial of, 192; enormity of narratives of, 13, 195–96, 263–96; historiography of, 131; international awareness of, 58, 59; judicial narratives of, 263; justice and, 85; literary narratives of, 263, 264, 265; perpetration of, 199
The Holocaust (Gilbert), 291
Holt, Harold, 52, 54
horses, 2, 125, 202
Hungarian Arrow Cross, 56, 308
Hungary, 7, 308, 309

India, 309
International Criminal Court, 311
international criminal law: on crimes against humanity, 102–3; emergence of, 7, 28, 30; Moscow Declaration and, 30, 31, 47, 71, 73, 74, 98, 300; on pedagogical function of trials, 109, 131, 311, 317; principles of, 30; St. James Palace Declaration and, 29–30, 48; strengths and weaknesses of, 197
International Criminal Tribunal, 304
International Criminal Tribunal for Yugoslavia (ICTY), 246
International Military Tribunal (IMT): multilingual environment of, 244, 246; at Nuremberg, 7, 10, 28, 31, 37, 38, 48, 61, 102–3, 104, 194, 207, 244, 246, 315; reliability of Soviet evidence in, 207
Iraq, 309
Israel, 61, 103, 194, 196, 244, 293
Israylovka, 1, 2, 14, 20, 111, 192–241, 259, 304
Ivaschenko, Nikolay Grigoryevich, 240
Ivashchenko, Viktor, 222

Jackson, Robert, 28
James, Greg, 94, 217, 295–96
Japan, 38
Jewish Anti-Fascist Committee (JAFC), 36–37
Jewish Council to Combat Fascism and Anti-Semitism, 54, 55, 56
Jewish populations: crimes of collaboration by, 11; mass murder of, 1–3, 16; *Mischlinge* children of, 1–2, 3, 111, 197,

199, 200–201, 202–3, 204, 210, 259, 313; in postwar Australia, 53, 54–56, 103; presence of, xiv; Soviet recognition of, 33, 34, 41, 42, 47, 215
Jones, Jeremy, 61
Judt, Tony, 266, 267

Kalejs, Konrad, 308
Keating, Paul, 310
Khokum's shed, 3–5, 107, 305. *See also* Serniki
Khuda, Ivan, 159
Kigel, Nina, 2
Kirby, Michael, 298, 299
Kitson, Jill, 271, 272, 274, 276, 290, 295
Kokhanov, Nikolay Stepanovich, 240
Komendyak (procurator), 211
Kostyukhovich, Dmitry Ivanovich, 3–4, 13
Kovalevka, 1, 3, 202, 203, 204
Kozhan (assistant to Marchik), 220
Kramer, Leonie, 273, 274, 275, 276, 279, 289, 290, 293
Krupko, Pyotr Stephanovich, 106
Kwiet, Konrad, 9, 97, 113, 115–25, *126–27*, 128–45, 178, 190, 262, 305, 317

LaCapra, Dominick, 265, 266
Landsman, Stephan, 105
Lanzmann, Claude, 314
Lebanon, 309
Lepsheyeva, Vanda Stanislavovna, 162
Linnas, Karl, 58
literature, practices of, 12–13
Lozhkina, Nadezhda, 2

MacGibbon, David, 89

Magill (SS), 123–24
Manne, Robert, 277, 287, 290
Marchik (police chief), 210, 220, 221, 222, 223, 233, 237
Marrus, Michael, 10
Matthäus, Jürgen, 19, 101, 214, 215
McDonald, Roger, 271
Megargee, Geoffrey, 18
Meisslein, Johann, 116, 119
Melamed, Vladimir, 22
Mel'nik, Pyotor Mefod'yevich, 160
memory, 9, 11, 194–95, 242–44, 266, 311, 317
Mendelsohn, Daniel, xiii
Menzies, Andrew, 68–69, 70
Menzies, Robert, 56, 299
Menzies Report, 60, 68, 69, 71, 74, 75, 204, 300
Mere, Ain, 58
Meyer, Bruen, 113
Mikhaylovskiy (police officer), 159
Mitchell, Adrian, 274
Molotov, Viacheslav, 31, 32
Moscow Declaration, 30, 31, 47, 71, 73, 74, 98, 300
Mulligan, Edward, 217
murder vans, 39–40

Naimark, Norman, 20
Narodnyi komissariat vnutrennikh del (NKVD), 21, 25, 26, 282
Nazi Crimes in Ukraine, 1941–1944, 179
Nazi Germany: Allied prosecution of war crimes by, 29–30; and collaborators, xv, 11, 22, 23–24, 25, 26, 38–39; German Order Police of, 19, 23; mass extermination plan of, 1, 4, 24, 125; National Socialist regime in,

Nazi Germany (*cont.*)
112; occupation of Ukraine by,
xiii, 1–10, 18–19, 82, 112; and
Operation Barbarossa, 18,
95, 112, 121, 200, 267;
Sicherheitspolizei und
Sicherheitsdienst security
units of, 23; SS units of, 1, 40;
Wehrmacht of, 19
Nepal, 309
New South Wales, 60, 66, 67
Niemann, Grant, 135, 138, 217,
245–46, 260, 261, 304
Nikolaychuck, Afanasiy Andreyvich,
159

Oettle, Godfrey, 241
Organization of Ukrainian
Nationalists (OUN), 44
Organization Todt (OT), 116

Papon, Maurice, 101
Pennington, David, 298
Penter, Tanya, 39, 41, 42, 43, 44, 45
Pivcova, Suzanah, 113
Podrutskiy (procurator), 187
Pohl, Dieter, 23, 25, 39
Poland, 18, 248, 257, 281
Polgar, Lajos, 308
Pol Pot, 76, 279
Polyukhovich, Anna, 98
Polyukhovich, Ivan Timofeyevich,
95, 96; arrest of, 4–5, 26, 94, 106,
310; case of, xiii, xv, 4–5, 9, 11,
89, 93, 95–145; committal hearing
of, 106, 113–25, *126–27*, 128–45;
escape of, to Australia, 29, 98,
138; as forest warden, *96, 97*; in
German police force, 20, 95, *96*,
97; investigations of, 99, 100,

106–7, 302; as Ivanechko, 97, 100,
111, 136, 137, 145, 242, 246, 256,
313; trial of, 48, 106, 107, 128–45;
war crimes committed by, 4, 9,
15, 16, 19, 98–99, 112, 132–33
Polyukhovich, Luba, 98
Polyukhovich, Maria Andreyevna, 98
Polyukhovich, Sidor, 4
Powell, Lindy, 110, 158, 217
Press, Ian, 187
Prusin, Alexander Victor, 42, 43, 45

Ralston, John, 211, 213, 216, 217
Raykis, Betya, 5, 6
Raykis, Filya Abramovich, 6
Raykis, Liza, 5, 6
Raykis, Manya, 5, 6
Raykis, Mikhail Abramovich, 5, 6,
13, 156, 161, 162, 176, 187–88,
250–54
Raykis, Sonya, 5, 6
Reith, Peter, 74, 75, 85
Returned Services League (RSL), 87
Ribbentrop-Molotov Pact, 18, 21,
77, 91, 95, 248
Ricoeur, Paul, 11–12, 263, 264, 266,
274, 318
Roma populations, 56, 58
Roosevelt, Franklin D., 29
Rousso, Henry, 101, 316
Rowe, Jennifer, 271
Rozenes, Michael, 107
Rudd, Kevin, 311
Ruddock, Phillip, 76, 79
Rudik, Ivan Vasilyevich, 231
Russia, 1, 2, 8. *See also* Soviet
Union; Ukraine
Rybkina, Kharitina, 2

Sawoniuk, Anthony, 7, 102, 105, 110,
149, 258, 311, 312, 317

Segal, Jacob, 55

Segal, Lynne, 272

Selemenev, Vyacheslav, 113

Seltzer, Margaret, 288

Serbia, 309

Serniki, 3–5, 14, 19, 20, 95, 111, 116,
121–23, *126–27*, 132, 206, *303*,
304–6, *306*

Shnayder, Moisey Srul'yevich, 162–
63, 169, 170, 176, 179, 182

Shoah (film), 314

Shul'kina, Tat'yana Kirsanovna, 2,
220–21, 239

Shul'kina, Tolya, 2, 221, 239

Shul'kina, Volodya, 2, 221, 239

Sierra Leone, 309

Simpson, Gerry, 195, 316

Slovak Hlinka Guard, 56

Slovenia, 60

Snyder, Timothy, 20

Sorokina, Marina, 37, 215

*Soviet Evidence in North American
Courts* (Zumbakis), 78–79

Soviet-Polish War, 18

Soviet Union: archival holdings
of, 9; Cold War ideology of,
59; Criminal Code of, 39–40,
41; establishment of, 17, 18;
Extraordinary State Commission
of, 34–38, 40, 41, 47, 49, 85, 156,
162, 163, 164, 169, 170, 171,
174, 178, 179, 182, 189, 205–6,
207, 208; government statements
on Nazi atrocities in, 31–33;
Great Patriotic War of, 33, 47,
223, 238; Jewish populations as
enemies of, 21–22, 269; Katyn
massacre by, 37, 207; Kharkov
war crimes trials in, 10, 28–29,
39–44; Krasnodar war crimes
trials in, 10, 28–29, 39–44; and
legal proceedings against war
criminals, 25–49, 57–59, 65, 74,
98–99, 156; Moscow Declaration
and, 30, 31, 47, 71, 98, 300;
occupation of Baltic states by,
77; People's Commissariat for
Foreign Affairs of, 33; reliability
of war crimes evidence of, 76, 79,
80, 81, 83–84, 85, 114–15, 206,
207–8, 210, 300. *See also* Russia;
Ukraine

Special Investigations Unit (SIU), 60,
75, 79, 86, 94, 99, 113–15, 122,
131, 146, 148, 156, *157*, 165, 166,
170, 190, 206, 297, 310, 318, 319

Spender, Syd, 72

Sri Lanka, 309

Stalin, Joseph, 21, 22, 88, 282, 283,
291

Standing Committee on Legal and
Constitutional Affairs, 78, 85, 114

Steinberg, Jonathan, 148, 152, 153,
161–78, 181–83, 189, 190, 317

Stern, Ludmilla, 255, 256, 257, 258,
260, 261, 262, 305

St. James Palace Declaration, 29–30,
48

Terebun, Anna Vasilyevna, 113

Thomas, D. M.: *The White Hotel*,
291

Treblinka, 269, 275, 279, 281, 293,
294

Trud, 203, 204

Truth, 55, 61

Turkey, 309

Ukraine: anti-Semitic attitudes in,
263–96; Babi Yar massacre in, 32,

Ukraine (*cont.*)
36, 275, 279, 291; collaborators
in, 22, 23–24, 25, 26; German
occupation of, xiii, 1–10, 6, 82,
112; interethnic issues in, 16,
17, 20; Kirovograd region of, 3;
nationalist ambitions of, 17, 18,
21, 22; Polish rule of, 18, 248,
257, 281; Rovno district of, 5;
Schutzmannschaft police in, 1,
5, 20, 23–24, 25, 26, 41–42, 110,
111, 112, 116, 123, 125, 136,
137, 141, 144, 146, 150, 158–61,
165–67, 175, 200, 256, 314; Soviet
occupation of, 21, 22, 25, 82,
267, 281; Stubla River in, 3, *306*;
Volksdeutsche communities in,
200–201
Ukraine, mass killing in:
Daviborshch's cart and, 1–3, 198,
202, 204–18, 304; first wave of, 1,
5, 19, 97; in Gnivan, 5–6, 14, 20,
111, 146–91, 317; in Israylovka,
1–3, 14, 20, 111, 192–241, 259,
304; Khokum's shed and, 3–5,
107, 305; of *Mischlinge* children,
1–2, 3, 111, 192–241, 259; second
wave of, 1, 19–20, 22–23, 24, 34,
139, 171, 202, 220; in Serniki,
3–5, 14, 19, 20, 95, 111, 116, 121,
122, 123, *126–27*, 132, *303*, 304,
305–6, *306*
United Kingdom, 7, 26, 61, 83, 301,
311–12
United Nations Genocide
Convention, 52
United Nations War Crimes
Commission (UNWCC), 31, 38,
50, 51
United States, 26, 27, 59–60, 70, 266

Urbancic, Ljenko, 60, 66

Vasiljkovic, Dragan, 309
Velikiy, Nikolay Danilovich, 231, 233
Viks, Ervin, 56, 58
Vorona, Nikolay Grigoryevich, 158,
159

Wagenaar, Willem, 304, 305
Wagner, Erna, 204
Wagner, Heinrich, *205, 232*; as
Andrej Woijtenko, 204, 223;
arrest of, 3, 204, 310; case of,
xiii, xv, 3, 11, 90, 93, 192–241;
committal hearing of, 107, 108,
207, 208, 225, 236, 255, 258, 260–
61; escape of, to Australia, 29,
204; in German police force, 20;
health of, 305; investigations of,
302, 304; trial of, 196, 197, 307–8;
as Volksdeutsche in Ukraine, 201,
231; war crimes committed by,
3, 15, 16, 111, 198, 199, 201–2,
203, 207, 208, 225, 236, 255, 258,
260–61
Wannsee Conference, 202
war crimes, Holocaust related:
amnesty related to, 11; Australian
experience with trials of, 112,
297–319; contexts in trials
of, 13–14, 242–54, 305, 315;
excavation of sites of, 240–41,
303; historical encounters in trials
of, 10–14, 108–11, 116, 125–26,
129–31, 149–52; investigations
related to, 240–41, 297–319;
narrations in trials of, 192–93;
Nazi collaborators of, xv, 38–39;
offenses included in, 9; reliability
of Soviet evidence on, 76, 79, 80,

81, 83–84, 85, 87, 114–15, 206,
300; rhetorical vectors and, 110,
111; third-party trials of, 11
Waten, Judah, 55
Weekend Australian, 190
Weinert, Matthew, 312, 313
West Germany, 10, 116, 149–150
The White Hotel (Thomas), 291
Whitlam, Gough, 59
Wilkomirski, Binjamin, 288
Woijtenko, Andrej. *See* Wagner,
Heinrich
World Jewish Congress, 61
World War I, 17, 30
World War II, 11

Wright, Richard, 240–41

Yugoslavia, 53, 304, 309

Zentai, Charles, 309
Zhilun, Ivan Konstantinovich: trial
and sentencing of, 213, 216, 218,
221, 226, 236; as Ukrainian police
officer, 2, 3, 13, 202, 203, 208,
209, 218–25; war crimes of, 209,
210, 211, 216, 218–31, 233–41; as
witness, 204, 208, 209, 218–31,
233–41
Zumbakis, S. Paul, 81; *Soviet
Evidence in North American
Courts*, 78–79